EXPLORING T

EXPLORING THE MUSICAL MIND

cognition, emotion, ability, function

John Sloboda

Professor of Psychology
Keele University
UK

OXFORD
UNIVERSITY PRESS

OXFORD
UNIVERSITY PRESS

Great Clarendon Street, Oxford OX2 6DP

Oxford University Press is a department of the University of Oxford.
It furthers the University's objective of excellence in research, scholarship,
and education by publishing worldwide in

Oxford New York

Auckland Cape Town Dar es Salaam Hong Kong Karachi
Kuala Lumpur Madrid Melbourne Mexico City Nairobi
New Delhi Shanghai Taipei Toronto

With offices in

Argentina Austria Brazil Chile Czech Republic France Greece
Guatemala Hungary Italy Japan South Korea Poland Portugal
Singapore Switzerland Thailand Turkey Ukraine Vietnam

Oxford is a registered trade mark of Oxford University Press
in the UK and in certain other countries

Published in the United States
by Oxford University Press Inc., New York

A catalogue record for this title is available from the British Library

Library of Congress Cataloging in Publication Data

(Data available)

ISBN 0 19 853012 9 (Hbk)
ISBN 0 19 853013 7 (Pbk)

10 9 8 7 6 5 4 3 2

Typeset by Cepha Imaging Private Ltd., Bangalore, India.
Printed in Great Britain
on acid-free paper by Biddles Ltd., King's Lynn, Norfolk

PREFACE

1 Why this book

I first proposed this book to Oxford University Press for two reasons, one positive, one negative. The positive reason was that I wanted to bring together in one place a number of chapter-length pieces I had written about music over the years. These pieces all shared some of the following characteristics:

- They went beyond reporting of specific research studies to reflect on wider issues, of theory, methodology, or practical application.
- They were originally published in sources which have become hard to access (for example in books now out of print)
- They complemented, or went beyond, the issues and preoccupations of my only other 'single-author' book—*The Musical Mind*, first published in 1985.
- I had been told, by colleagues or readers, that they contained material of current value, which merited their reprinting in more accessible form.

This is a 'solo' book, in that almost all the contributions have me as sole author. However, I do see this book as in a very real sense 'belonging' to all those who have shared and supported my intellectual journey. What I have achieved would be impossible without their help. I have felt it important to fully acknowledge all who have contributed to my work, and I do this both within the acknowledgments section on pages xvii–xxiii, and also by including a complete bibliography of my academic publications (pp. 421–429), which explicitly records the contributions of each of my co-authors in the proper way.

The negative reason for this book was that, at the time I first made the proposal to Oxford University Press in early 2003, I sincerely believed that this book might be among my last published contributions to the field of music psychology. I felt that there might be more pressing calls on my time and intellectual energies for the foreseeable future.

In thinking about how to frame and introduce this set of readings, I have felt compelled to attempt to articulate, and possibly achieve some reconciliation of, these positive and negative motivations. This is because the issues I have faced, as an individual scientist and writer, are issues which face many intellectual and professional people in one way or another. In exploring and debating these issues my goal is to assist anyone with an interest in music and the mind to situate their interest within the broadest possible context. These issues are, at root, about the responsibility of scientists, writers, and practitioners as citizens, and how we remain true to our wider responsibilities to society within our chosen specialist paths. Rather than have these broader concerns skew this preface out of shape, I have decided to include my reflections on these matters within a specially written chapter not published elsewhere, which appears as Chapter 23.

2 Structure, organization and context

The chapters are organized into four main Parts, which represent four distinct areas in which I have worked. Each of these areas would be generally accepted as core to an understanding of the musical mind.

Part A (Cognitive processes) starts with research on cognitive processes in music reading, and spreads out from reading to the activities with which reading normally interacts, namely, perception and memory of music, and music performance. The core concept binding together the contributions in this part is that of 'mental representations'—categorical and rule-based abstractions from the complex musical surface. The nature and functioning of these representations is the central concern of mainstream cognitive psychology. However, the last two contributions in this section demonstrate how concern with cognition (particularly semantics) leads inevitably to a consideration of the role of the emotions in music cognition.

Perception and cognition remains the core concern of English-language music psychology as evidenced by the preponderance of books and journal articles addressing this sub-area (see, for instance, Krumhansl, 1990, 1991; McAdams and Bigand, 1993; Deliège and Sloboda, 1997; Palmer, 1997; Deutsch, 1999). The chapters of this book are not intended to provide a comprehensive overview of the state of the field, rather they illustrate core concerns through issues (reading, memory recall, semantics) which have remained, by and large, rather under-studied, despite their intrinsic interest. Two current growth areas in music cognition are the study of brain mechanisms (e.g. Peretz and Zatorre, 2003) and modelling of music perception and cognition through computation and artificial intelligence (e.g. Tillman, Bharucha, and Bigand, 2000). Whilst acknowledging the vibrancy of these approaches, this book remains firmly within the core psychological tradition, where overt human behaviour is the central form of data, and explanatory frameworks are developed in primarily intentional and functional terms (Sloboda and Juslin, 2001).

Part B (Emotion and motivation) examines how emotion impacts at every stage of the musical chain, from composer, through performer, to listener. It also addresses the question of how emotional responses to music develop through childhood, and how differences in emotional musical biographies can lead to gross differences in motivation for musical activity across the lifespan. A key concept of this Part is that of the 'peak experience', a high-intensity psycho-physiological response to music which has both immediate and long-lasting effects, and the attaining of which is a prime reason why many people engage with music. The research on emotion reflects an increasing engagement of the research community in the 1990s (see Juslin and Sloboda, 2001). It is now generally accepted that only a joint consideration of the 'cold' processes of cognition and the 'hot' processes of emotion and motivation allows proper understanding of skill development and ways in which music is used in society. Motivation has become a particularly key concept in research on music education and processes of learning (O'Neill and McPherson, 2002).

Part C (Talent and skill development) focuses on the psychological processes underlying the acquisition of different levels of musical skill, with a specific emphasis on performance skills within the classical conservatoire tradition. The question of whether there are innate differences in 'talent' looms large in this work, and the approach taken by my collaborators and myself has been to see how many individual differences could be accounted for by differences in learning experiences, and the motivational and social contexts in which that learning takes place (Howe, Davidson and Sloboda, 1998). A central concept of this Part is 'practice', and what its characteristics and support demands are (Ericsson, 1996).

The research on skill development is a contribution to the 'expertise' research field, pioneered by Herbert Simon, William Chase and others in the 1960s and 1970s (e.g. Chase and Simon, 1973), who provided a very clear intellectual grounding for much good contemporary work. Where our work differs from the earlier work is in its extensive use of biographical and interview methods to supplement more traditional experimental techniques. This approach has been further developed by some of the most influential contemporary studies of musical learning (e.g. Green, 2002; Chaffin, Imreh, and Crawford, 2002).

Part D (Music in the real world) reflects the way in which contemporary thinking about music has more fully embraced social and cultural considerations (e.g. Hargreaves and North 1997; Cook, 1998;

Small, 1998; De Nora, 2000; McDonald, Hargreaves and Miell, 2002). Musical skills (of both performing and listening) are highly dependent on the cultural and individual functions and values which music adopts within particular social and historical contexts. This section contains a range of contributions, mainly preliminary and to some extent speculative, exploring how these broader cultural considerations may impact on, and relativize, much of our scientific knowledge about musical activity. Uses of music in the home, in the street, in church, and in the concert hall, may have rather little in common with one another. A key concept for this Part is 'functionality'—what the music is *for*, in the minds of both producers and consumers.

This area of interest represents a natural intellectual progression from the concerns of the previous two Parts. Motivational structures and skill development systems are much more open to cultural influences than basic cognitive processes. However, such issues cannot be addressed solely with the intellectual resources of psychology. They open music behaviour up to the full range of the social sciences, including sociology, anthropology, and the political sciences. This implies a larger, and potentially less achievable, challenge than the previous two discontinuities, at least in relation to the constraints of an individual career within an individual discipline. These are issues that psychologists individually, and psychology in its current state of development, may simply be as yet unprepared to grasp productively.

The Musical Mind was deliberately open-ended. It tried not to achieve closure on any of the issues raised there, but aimed to express confidence that psychology possessed the resources to make further progress on important (and answerable) questions. The subsequent decades have fully vindicated that confidence. If a book covering the topic areas of *The Musical Mind* were to be written today, there would be much newer, and better, results to report.

Exploring the Musical Mind is similarly open-ended. Its trajectory leads from the relatively safe and comfortable 'normal science' of the cognitive paradigm (one of the most successful and stable paradigms of 20th-century psychology) through the 'unsafe' area of emotion (one of the most problematic and 'unparadigmatic' areas of modern psychology), to questions which cannot be solved, even in principle, using the intellectual resources of psychology alone. Although I think that a reader will find, within these pages, some better answers to important questions than were available 20 years ago, my more fervent hope is that the reader will be encouraged to embrace better, and more far-reaching questions, than were typically being asked in the field at the time of the publication of *The Musical Mind*.

I do not retain the same certainty that answers to these questions will be easily obtained, but I do retain the hope that, in another 20 years, the field of music psychology will be at least as different by then as it has become in the last quarter century.

3 The individual chapters

The decision to include a particular chapter in this volume was influenced by a number of factors. Paramount among them was that each chapter should be complete in itself and, in some sense, a 'good read'. By this I mean that each chapter is trying to make a point, carry through an argument, and engage a reader in an implicit dialogue.

My primary selection criterion for each chapter was that it should contain some substantial and unique material, and that each chapter should contain some material not previously included within any book that I have written or edited. For instance, although Chapters 1 and 2 both report research on the psychology of music reading, Chapter 1 is unique in its discussion of educational implications, and Chapter 2 is unique in its coverage of the ability of expert sight-readers to add appropriate non-notated expression to their sight-reading. A few chapters are completely unique, in that they contain, or refer to, no significant material elsewhere within the set. However, uniqueness should not be confused with importance. Where I have considered an idea, or a set of data, to be of great importance, I have tended to refer to it repeatedly. Indeed, overlaps provide a natural way for a reader with a specific set of interests to select the subset which most interests him or her, and to navigate from one chapter to another in a way that reflects his or her priorities rather than the imposed structure of the book.

To assist the reader to navigate the book with some sense of main and recurrent themes, I have provided a table at the end of this introduction which lists the main topic areas of each chapter, and an indication of the key chapters with which it has some overlap. As good musical themes bear repetition within a coherent musical composition, I also hope that repeated themes within the book allow key ideas to be set in different contexts, where different aspects of their importance may be highlighted.

The variation in style between these chapters is less than in a multi-author volume, although writings spanning a 30-year period cannot be totally stylistically consistent. The most strikingly dated aspect of earlier chapters is the use of the masculine where non-sexist conventions would now prescribe gender-neutral terminology. After some debate, I decided that history should not be rewritten, and that the original text should stand, partly as a witness to the social changes that have taken place in my short professional career. I have, however, taken the opportunity to update references which were 'in press' at time of original citation, so that readers wishing to locate these sources could do so on the basis of accurate information.

References

Chaffin, R., Imreh, G., and Crawford, M. (2002) *Practicing Perfection: memory and piano performance*. Mahwah, NJ: Lawrence Erlbaum.

Chase, W. G. and Simon, H. A. (1973) The mind's eye in chess. In W. G. Chase (Ed.) *Visual Information Processing*. New York: Academic Press.

Cook, N. (1998) *Music: a very short introduction*. Oxford: Oxford University Press.

Deliège, I. and Sloboda, J. A. (Eds.) (1997) *Perception and Cognition of Music*. Hove: Psychology Press.

De Nora, T. (2000) *Music In Everyday Life*. Cambridge: Cambridge University Press.

Deutsch, D. (Ed.) (1999) *The Psychology of Music, 2nd edn. New York: Academic Press*.

Ericsson, K. A. (Ed.) (1996) *The Road to Excellence: the acquisition of expert performance in the arts and sciences, sports and games*. Mahwah, NJ: Lawrence Erlbaum.

Green, L. (2002) *How Popular Musicians Learn: a way ahead for music education*. Aldershot: Ashgate.

Hargreaves, D, J. and North, A. C. (Eds.) (1997) *The Social Psychology of Music*. Oxford: Oxford University Press.

Howe, M. J. A., Davidson, J. W., and Sloboda, J. A. (1998) Innate talent: reality or myth? *Behavioural and Brain Sciences*, **21.3**, 399–442.

Juslin, P. N. and Sloboda, J. A. (Eds.) (2001) *Music and Emotion: theory and research*. Oxford: Oxford University Press.

Krumhansl, C. L. (1990) *Cognitive Foundations of Musical Pitch*. New York: Oxford University Press.

Krumhansl, C. L. (1991) *Music psychology: tonal structures in perception and memory*. Annual Review of Psychology, 42, 277–303.

McAdams, S. and Bigand, E. (Eds.) (1993) *Thinking in Sound: the cognitive psychology of human audition*. Oxford: Oxford University Press.

McDonald, R., Hargreaves, D. J., and Miell, D. (Eds.) (2002) *Musical Identities*. Oxford: Oxford University Press.

O'Neill, S. A. and McPherson, G. E. (2002) In R. Parncutt and G. E. McPherson (Eds.) *The Science and Psychology of Music Performance: creative strategies for teaching and learning*. New York: Oxford University Press.

Palmer, C. (1997) Music performance. *Annual Review of Psychology,* **48**, 115–138.

Peretz, I. and Zatorre, R. (Eds.) (2003) *The Cognitive Neuroscience of Music.* New York: Oxford University Press.

Sloboda, J. A. (1985) *The Musical Mind: the cognitive psychology of music.* London: Oxford University Press.

Sloboda, J. A. and Juslin, P. N. (2001) Psychological perspectives on music and emotion. In P. N. Juslin and J. A. Sloboda (Eds.) *Music and Emotion: theory and research.* Oxford: Oxford University Press, pp. 71–104.

Small, C. (1998) *Musicking: The Meanings of Performing and Listening.* Hanover, NH: Wesleyan University Press.

Tillman, B., Bharucha, J. J., and Bigand, E. (2000) Implicit learning of tonality: a self-organising approach. *Psychological Review,* **107.4**, 885–913.

Chapter	Key topics	Chapters sharing significant concerns
PART A Cognitive processes		
1 The psychology of music reading	Structural cues within notation The role of musical knowledge in reading Teaching music reading	2
2 Experimental studies of music reading: a review	Review of early reading research Experiments varying skill level and structure in text Expressive sight-reading	1, 13, 15
3 The uses of space in music notation	Comparison of text and music notations Historical trends in notation development Conceptual issues in the design of notation Psychological issues in the design of notation	
4 Immediate recall of melodies	Problems of transcription from sung performance Analysis of errors in sung recall Memory representations for melodies	5
5 Cognition and real music: the psychology of music comes of age	Nature of scientific paradigms Is music psychology paradigmatic? The contribution of Lerdahl and Jackendoff	4, 8, 14
6 Psychological structures in music: core research 1980–1990	Citation as a means of assessing significance of research The contribution of Krumhansl Establishing a sense of tonal centre Hierarchies in tonal representation	
7 Book review of *Language, Music and Mind*	The relationship of philosophy of music to psychology of music Nuance and ineffability in music Different ways in which music might be said to have 'meaning'	8, 20
8 Does music mean anything?	Is parsing sufficient for understanding in music? Dynamic feelings as precursors of meaning 'Thrills' as proto-emotions	5, 7

Chapter	Key topics	Chapters sharing significant concerns
PART B Emotion and motivation		
9 Music as a language	Musical phonology, syntax, and semantics Peak musical experiences in childhood Motivation for long-term commitment to music	11, 14
10 Music psychology and the composer	Different models for composer-psychologist dialogue Relationship of composition to functions of music Music as an aid to cognitive restructuring	20, 21
11 Empirical studies of emotional response to music	Free verbal emotional responses to music Verbal responses within forced categories Extrinsic and intrinsic antecedents of musical emotion	9, 12, 13
12 Emotional responses to music: a review	Accounting for variation between and within people Methods for measuring emotional response How musical events elicit emotion	11
13 Musical performance and emotion: issues and developments	Different expressive roles of performers Connection between music structure and expressive devices Evidence for deliberate planning of expressive communication	2, 11

Continued

Chapter	Key topics	Chapters sharing significant concerns
PART C Talent and skill development		
14 Musical expertise	Social and cultural relativity of musical expertise Musical skill acquisition in non-instructional settings Precursors of musical expertise	5, 9, 17
15 Musical ability	Cultural exposure as a primary source of basic ability Expressive playing in sight-reading as a strong test of ability How to develop technical and expressive skill together	2, 16
16 The acquisition of music performance expertise	Is musical skill inherited? The role of practice Different learning mechanisms for technical and expressive skill	15, 17
17 Are some children more gifted for music than others?	The role of early learning in skill development Social support mechanisms for skill development Motivational factors predicting success or dropout	14, 16

Chapter	Key topics	Chapters sharing significant concerns
PART D Music in the real world		
18 Everyday uses of music	Importance of situation and volition in determining effects of music Free verbal descriptions of music's role in everyday life Music in public places	10, 19, 22
19 Music: where cognition and emotion meet	Mismatch between music's value to people and their level of musical skill Tracking everyday uses of music in real time Societal barriers to engagement with music	18
20 Music and worship: a psychologist's perspective	Can music have assumed common effects within a defined situation? Parallels between different ways of listening to music and different aspects of worship Ineffability as a core concept in both music and worship	7, 10
21 Emotion, functionality, and the everyday experience of music	Reasons why young adolescents give up instrumental engagement Cultural trends associated with disengagement from formal music Responses of the education system to cultural change	10
22 The sound of music versus the essence of music	Cultural trends which deindividuate the musical experience How science can be misused in the interests of cultural homogenization of the musical experience Research which demonstrates the strong contribution of the individual to the nature of the musical experience	18
23 Assessing music psychology research	The social benefits of music psychology research Differentiating the above from the social benefits of music Differing levels of engagement with social issues evident in research	

John A. Sloboda
Keele, April 2004

ACKNOWLEDGEMENTS

Anniversaries are no more than arbitrary round numbers, but powerful in human affairs nonetheless. The publication date for this book, 2004, marks exactly 30 years since my first academic publication in music psychology (Sloboda, 1974). It also marks 30 years of continuous membership of the faculty at Keele University, where, under the supportive championing of successive heads of Psychology (the late Ian Hunter 1974–1982, James Hartley 1982–1992, Angus Gellatly 1992–2000) music psychology has been encouraged and enabled to flourish and develop. This book is a tribute to them, and all those who have worked at Keele, or collaborated with members of the Keele music psychology group, to establish the knowledge and activity base on which the papers in this volume are built.

Research collaborators

My main debt is to my co-authors and co-editors: teachers, colleagues, and students. Everything in this book shows their influence. They are listed in chronological order of date of first co-publication (given), with current or most recent institutional affiliation where known. Although a few of these 25 have not collaborated directly on music projects, their influence on the way I think about many things, including music, has been palpable.

Andrew Gregory	(1980)	University of Manchester
Judy Edworthy	(1981)	University of Plymouth
Don Rogers	(1983)	Keele University
Beate Hermelin	(1985)	Goldsmiths College, University of London
Neil O'Connor	(1985)	Deceased
David Parker	(1985)	Liverpool John Moores University
Angus Gellatly	(1989)	Open University
Michael Howe	(1990)	Deceased
Jeff Hopkins	(1992)	Keele University
John McLeod	(1993)	Abertay University

Rita Aiello	(1994)	Julliard School of Music, New York
Warren Brodsky	(1994)	Ben Guiron University of the Negev, Be'er Sheva
Mitch Waterman	(1994)	University of Leeds
Jane Davidson	(1994)	University of Sheffield
Irene Deliège	(1995)	University of Liège
Derek Moore	(1995)	University of East London
Eric Clarke	(1997)	University of Sheffield
Richard Parncutt	(1997)	University of Graz
Matti Raekallio	(1997)	Sibelius Academy of Music, Helsinki
Susan O'Neill	(1997)	Keele University
Peter Desain	(1997)	University of Nijmegen
Stephen Newstead	(1997)	University of Plymouth
Patrik Juslin	(2001)	University of Uppsala
Andreas Lehmann	(2001)	University of Würzburg
Antonia Ivaldi	(2001)	Loughborough University

I would wish to draw special attention to the two deceased members of the above list. Neil O'Connor had a far greater influence on me the bare record might suggest, which shows only one co-authored publication. From 1971 to 1974 I was jointly supervised in my PhD studies by Neil O'Connor and Beate Hermelin, in the MRC Unit for Developmental Psychology at University College London. For being in the right intellectual shape to be taken on by them I must also acknowledge my debt to several members of the Psychology Department at Oxford University, where I did my first degree. Of these, my greatest debt by far is to Patrick Rabbitt, under whose apprenticeship I learned something of what it meant to be a cognitive psychologist in the mould of Pat's great 'master' and father of post-war British experimental psychology, Donald Broadbent. It was with gentle promptings from O'Connor and Hermelin that I undertook my first experiment on music cognition in 1972. My original planned research topic was the development of language reading in children, and I might still be a language specialist rather than a music specialist if they had not seen that my extracurricular musical interests and my academic research interests begged to be integrated. Their act of faith (there being almost no serious music psychology research being undertaken in British psychology departments in those days) consistently reinforced and encouraged me to take creative and integrative risks. O'Connor and Hermelin were not specialists in music, indeed, they self-confessedly professed this. They were, however, superb scientists, and inspired supervisors. In that sense, O'Connor and Hermelin are unacknowledged co-authors on almost everything I wrote, certainly in the first 15 years of my postdoctoral career. Their elegant and deceptively simple approach to the design and reporting of experiments (see, for instance O'Connor and Hermelin, 1978) influenced my own scientific practice enormously, and their commitment to charting and enabling the intellectual capacities of a marginalised and under-valued group, the learning disabled, was an inspiration which was to directly underpin the most important and productive research collaboration of my working life, that with the late Michael J. A. Howe.

The record shows 18 co-authored publications with Mike Howe over a ten-year period between 1990 and 2000. Many more of my publications (around another 20) refer to, and build on, the work I undertook with him and our principal collaborator Jane Davidson. Mike and I first met in 1988 and I was immediately swept up in his burning passion to understand and encourage excellence and its development across the range of human abilities. Like Hermelin and O'Connor, he wished to demystify both exceptional performance and the blocks which appear to limit people from achieving excellence. But unlike them, he was comfortable in ranging far beyond the confines of the factorial experiment to pursue his wide-ranging intellectual agendas, employing survey research, biographical and other text-based methods, which were marshalled into a range of outputs of which the academic journal article was only one (see, for instance, Howe, 1990). His willingness to paint on a very broad canvas, through books and book chapters, employing rhetoric and polemic (often motivated by strong and explicit liberal and humanitarian impulses), taught and encouraged me to be more bold, inclusive, and socially engaged, in my academic work.

Research support

My second debt goes to those people, both students and colleagues, whose efforts, although not resulting in joint publications, have been directly influential or enabling for my own work. Former students in this category include Graca Mota, Laura Neilly, Vicki De Las Heras, and Jane Ginsborg. As with many university teachers, my research progress has depended on the support of those who have provided time and resources to do research, particularly in environments away from the home base. Key research advances have been made with the help of Henry Shaffer (University of Exeter), Maria Manturszewska and colleagues at the Chopin Academy of Music, Warsaw; Anders Ericsson (Florida State University); Kari Kurkela

(Sibelius Academy, Finland); Daniel Levitin (McGill University, Montreal). Research reported in this book has been financially supported by several special research awards from Keele University, the Economic and Social Research Council of Great Britain, the Nuffield Foundation, and the Leverhulme Trust.

My work has been hugely helped by the increasingly numerous and increasingly focused outlets for music psychology. In 1974 there was only one, very young, specialist journal (*Psychology of Music*) attached to the one scholarly body that then existed: the Society for Research in Psychology of Music and Music Education, now renamed SEMPRE—Society for Education, Psychology, and Music Research (*www.sempre.org.uk*). This UK-based organization offered one of my earliest and most supportive conference platforms, and published my very first research paper. The foresight of Arnold Bentley, Desmond Sergeant, Anthony Kemp, Rosamund Shuter-Dyson, and others mainly working at Reading University and the Roehampton Institute, in seeing the need in the early 1970s for reviving music psychology research cannot be overestimated. Reviving is the correct word, because although there had been leaders of the field, working on both sides of the Atlantic, their work left little trace in the years immediately after the Second World War when behaviourism was at its height, and even laypeople knew that psychology was mainly about rats running mazes. Herbert Wing (UK) and Carl E. Seashore (USA) were arguably the last in a line of key figures beginning a century earlier with Helmholtz and Stumpf (Germany). At the time I started my researches these key figures had all but been forgotten by the 'mainstream' of contemporary British psychology.

If SEMPRE provided the organizational support for my early endeavours, then two key individuals provided the direct intellectual nourishment: the late Christopher Longuet-Higgins in the UK, and Diana Deutsch in the USA. At the time I began my research into music, the work of these two were oases in a relative intellectual desert. I avidly read every word they wrote on music (such as Deutsch, 1972, and Longuet-Higgins, 1972). Their writings proved that forward-looking scientific work of the highest order, both methodologically and theoretically, could be carried out, borrowing from and extending the tools of experimental psychology and artificial intelligence. Both people were extraordinarily generous in promoting my work. If Christopher Longuet-Higgins ever tired of writing the numerous references and testimonials I requested of him, he never showed it. Diana Deutsch was responsible for giving me my first big publishing 'break', an invitation to contribute a chapter on music performance to her seminal and hugely influential *The Psychology of Music* (Deutsch, 1982).

My second 'break', and the one which has undoubtedly created the longest working relationship of my professional career, came when a contemporary from Oxford, Adam Hodgkin, joined Oxford University Press as a junior editor, and was asked to scout among the people he knew for 'new talent' for the press. As early as 1978, he suggested to me that OUP might be interested in a book on the Psychology of Music. At the time I put the idea to one side, but it niggled at me, and around two years later I tentatively returned to the idea. The far-sighted Science and Medicine Editor of that time, Bruce Wilcock, not only accepted the idea, but signed me up as the fifth contributor to a new, prestigious, monograph series, the Oxford Psychology Series, whose series editors were Larry Weiskrantz, Endel Tulving and Donald Broadbent. *The Musical Mind* was the result, a book which is my single most widely cited publication, and which, to my great surprise, is still selling well today. Twenty-five years, three editors, and seven books later, I view my relationship to Oxford University Press as one of the most consistent and enabling ones of my publishing career. I wish to acknowledge fulsomely the tireless and consistently pro-active support of Bruce Wilcock's two successors in the Science and Medicine department at the Clarendon Press, Vanessa Whitting and Martin Baum. Under Martin's firm direction OUP has now built up an ever more impressive music psychology list, one which shows every sign of continual growth and renewal.

Diana Deutsch was to have further profound influences on my career path (as I am sure she has had on many others). In 1983 she founded the second English language journal devoted entirely to the psychology of music—*Music Perception*. I was invited to become a contributor and a consulting editor at a very early stage. *Music Perception* gave the discipline its first journal of fully international standing (to whose standards *Psychology of Music* and other more recent arrivals have needed to conform). These two journals, together with the more recent European *Musicae Scientiae*, have provided key outlets for the research community, and are all represented in the selection of items republished here. Each journal is also associated with a scholarly body. Diana Deutsch was the founding President of the North American Society for Music Perception and Cognition (SMPC). *Musicae Scientiae*, whose founding editor is Irene Deliège, is the journal of the European Society for the Cognitive Sciences of Music (ESCOM). ESCOM, and its journal, arose as a direct response to yet another initiative of Diana Deutsch. Together with Edward Carterette, Kengo Ohgushi, and others, in 1989 she founded the world conference series known as the

International Conference on Music Perception and Cognition (ICMPC). This was the first time that the music psychology confraternity was encouraged to organize in truly global fashion. Again, through Diana's good offices, I was invited to attend the First ICMPC in Kyoto, and discussions with co-attendees led to the realisation that (a) the conference needed to circulate around the globe in a planned way on successive occurrences, and (b) that each conference required strong local and regional organisation. ESCOM was formed initially to provide an organisational host for the Third ICMPC (Liège, Belgium, 1994), although its remit is now far wider. ICMPC, and its supporting organizations, have provided the means for researchers to interact and present their work informally, prior to publication. These conferences now routinely attract several hundred papers. Almost everything I and my colleagues and students have published in the last 15 years has first been shared with colleagues (and improved through the ensuing discussion) at a meeting sponsored by, or supported by, organizations such as ICMPC, ESCOM, or SEMPRE. The ICMPC web-site provides a convenient set of links to its supporting organisations and details of conferences, past and future (*www.icmpc.org*).

The life of a researcher does not proceed purely on academic support and resources. Support of family, teachers, and friends has been key. For encouraging me equally in both music and science, and expecting much of me, I am deeply indebted to my parents, Mary Sloboda and the late Mieczyslaw Sloboda. Equally important encouragement has also come from inspired teachers at all levels prior to university. In music, my experiences with my first piano teacher, the late Phyllis Leach, fitted everything that our later research discovered about successful first teachers of the musically able. The schools I attended, Pinner Park Primary School, and St Benedict's School Ealing, provided some outstanding teachers of science, culture, and music—with skills that I am only now coming to realize are rather rare. At many times, particularly times of discouragement and stress, friends and loved ones have been there to validate and re-invigorate. Now is not the time to list those still living—they know who they are. However, 2003 saw the death through illness of a particularly close friend and intellectual companion, Ruth Clayton. As a world-class academic in her own field of genetics, and as a passionate advocate of both the arts and radical social reform, she represented for me the best of what it means to be an intellectual. Her probing but validating engagement with my intellectual journey, and her constant attempts to help me clarify the personal and political meanings of that journey, have been a profound influence on the course of my life over the last 15 years.

I dedicate this book to the memory of Neil O'Connor (1917–1997), Ruth Clayton (1925–2003), and Mike Howe (1940–2002).

References

Deutsch, D. (1972) Effect of repetition of standard and comparison tones on recognition memory for pitch. *Journal of Experimental Psychology,* **93.1**, 156–162.

Deutsch, D. (Ed.) (1982) *The Psychology of Music.* New York: Academic Press.

Longuet-Higgins, H. C. (1972) Making sense of music. *Proceedings of the Royal Institute of Great Britain,* **45**, 87–105.

Howe, M. J. A. (1990) *The Origins of Exceptional Abilities.* Oxford: Blackwell.

O'Connor, N. and Hermelin, B. (1978) *Seeing and Hearing and Space and Time.* London: Academic Press.

Sloboda, J. A. (1974) The eye-hand span: an approach to the study of sight-reading. *Psychology of Music,* **2**, 4–10.

CONTENTS

Permissions xxvii

A Cognitive processes

1 The psychology of music reading 3
2 Experimental studies of music reading: a review 27
3 The uses of space in music notation 43
4 Immediate recall of melodies 71
5 Cognition and real music: the psychology of music comes of age 97
6 Psychological structures in music: core research 1980–1990 117
7 Review of *Language, Music, and Mind* by Diana Raffman 153
8 Does music mean anything? 163

B Emotion and motivation

9 Music as a language 175
10 Music psychology and the composer 191
11 Empirical studies of emotional response to music 203
12 Emotional response to music: a review 215
13 Musical performance and emotion: issues and developments 225

C Talent and skill development

14 Musical expertise 243
15 Musical ability 265
16 The acquisition of musical performance expertise: deconstructing the 'talent' account of individual differences in musical expressivity 275
17 Are some children more gifted for music than others? 297

D Music in the real world

18 Everyday uses of music listening: a preliminary study 319
19 Music: where cognition and emotion meet 333
20 Music and worship: a psychologist's perspective 345
21 Emotion, functionality, and the everyday experience of music: where does music education fit? 361
22 The 'sound of music' versus the 'essence of music': dilemmas for music–emotion researchers 375
23 Assessing music psychology research: values, priorities, and outcomes 395

Bibliography 421

Index 431

PERMISSIONS TO
REPRODUCE MATERIAL

Chapter	Acknowledgement requested by original publisher
1 The psychology of music reading	Reprinted by permission of Sage Publications Ltd from *Psychology of Music* (1978) Vol. 6, pp. 3–20.
2 Experimental studies of music reading: a review	© 1984 by The Regents of the University of California. Reprinted from *Music Perception*, Vol. 2.2, by permission of the University of California Press.
3 The uses of space in music notation	Reprinted from *Visible Language* (1981), Vol. 15, pp. 86–100 by permission of Prof. Sharon Poggenpohl, Editor/ Publisher, Institute of Design, Chicago, IL.
4 Immediate recall of melodies	Reprinted from P. Howell, I. Cross, and R. West (Eds.) *Musical Structure and Cognition*. London: Academic Press, pp. 143–167, copyright © 1985, with permission from Elsevier.
5 Cognition and real music: the psychology of music comes of age	Reprinted from *Psychologica Belgica*, Vol. 26(2), pp. 199–219, with permission from the Belgian Psychological Society.
6 Psychological structures in music: core research 1980–1990	Reprinted from J Paynter, R. Orton, T. Seymour, and T. Howell (Eds.) (1992) *A Compendium of Contemporary Musical Thought*, London: Routledge, pp. 803–839, by permission of Thomson Publishing Services.

7	Book review of *Language, Music and Mind*	Reprinted from *Mind and Language* (1993), Vol. 9.3, pp. 377–385, with permission from Blackwell Publishing Ltd.
8	Does music mean anything?	Reprinted from *Musicae Scientiae* (*http://musicweb.hmt-hannover.de/escom/english/MusicScE/MSstart.htm*) (1998), Vol. 2.1, pp. 21–32, by permission of the European Society for the Cognitive Sciences of Music.
9	Music as a language	Reprinted from F. Wilson and F. Roehmann (Eds.) *Music and Child Development: Proceedings of the 1987 Biology of Music Making Conference.* St. Louis, Missouri: MMB Music Inc. 1989, pp. 28–43. Permission sought.
10	Music psychology and the composer	Reprinted from S. Nielzen and O. Olsson (Eds.) *Structure and Perception of Electroacoustic Sound and Music.* Amsterdam: Elsevier. 1989, pp. 3–12.
11	Empirical studies of emotional response to music	Originally published in M. Riess-Jones and S. Holleran (Eds.) (1992) *Cognitive Bases of Musical Communication.* Washington: American Psychological Association, pp. 33–46. Copyright © 1992 by the American Psychological Association. Reprinted with permission.
12	Emotional responses to music: a review	K. Riederer and T. Lahti (Eds.) *Proceedings of the Nordic Acoustical Meeting (NAM96).* Helsinki: The Acoustical Society of Finland. 1996, pp. 385–392. Permission sought.
13	Musical performance and emotion: issues and developments	Reprinted from S.W. Yi (Ed.) *Music, Mind, and Science.* Seoul: Seoul National University Press. 1999, pp. 220–238. Permission sought.
14	Musical expertise	© Cambridge University Press. Reprinted with permission from K. A. Ericsson and J. Smith, Eds. (1991) *Towards a General Theory of Expertise: Prospects and Limits*, Cambridge University Press, pp. 153–171.

15 Musical ability   © John Wiley and Sons Ltd. Reprinted
                                            with permission from G. Bock, and
                                            K. Ackrill, (Eds.), (1993) *The Origins and
                                            Development of High Ability*, Chapter 7,
                                            pp. 106–113.

16 The acquisition of   Reprinted from K. A. Ericsson (Ed.)
   music performance   *The Road to Excellence: the Acquisition
   expertise   of Expert Performance in the Arts and
                                            Sciences, Sport and Games*. Mahwah, NJ;
                                            Lawrence Erlbaum Associates. 1996,
                                            pp. 107–126. Permission sought.

17 Are some children   First published in Italian as 'Dotu
   more gifted for music   musicali e innatismo?'. In J. J. Nattiez
   than others?   (Ed.) *Enciclopedia della Musica: Vol II
                                            Il sapere musicale*. Torina: Giulio Einaudi
                                            Editore. 2002, pp. 509–529. Not
                                            previously published in English.
                                            Permission sought.

18 Everyday uses of music   Reprinted from S.W. Yi (Ed.) *Music, Mind,
                                            and Science*. Seoul: Seoul National
                                            University Press. 1999, pp. 354–369.
                                            Permission sought.

19 Music: where cognition   Reprinted from *The Psychologist*. **12.4,**
   and emotion meet   450–455. Permission sought from the
                                            British Psychological Society.

20 Music and worship: Reprinted from T. Hone, M. Savage, and
   a psychologist's   J. Astley (Eds.) *Creative Chords: Studies
   perspective   in Music, Theology and Christian Formation*.
                                            Leominster: Gracewing. 2002, pp. 110–125.
                                            Permission sought.

21 Emotion, functionality,   Originally published in *Music Education
   and the everyday   Research* (2001), Vol. 3 no. 2, pp. 243–253
   experience of music   (*http://www.tandf.co.uk/journals/carfax/
                                            14613808.html*) and reproduced here by
                                            permission of Taylor and Francis Ltd.

22 The sound of music   Reprinted from *Musicae Scientiae*
   versus the essence   (*http://musicweb.hmt-hannover.de/escom/
   of music   english/MusicScE/MSstart.htm*) (2002),
                                            Vol. 6.3 (special issue on music and
                                            emotion), pp. 235–253, by permission
                                            of the European Society for the
                                            Cognitive Sciences of Music

COGNITIVE PROCESSES

CHAPTER 1

THE PSYCHOLOGY OF MUSIC READING

1.1 Introduction

The ability to read in one's native tongue is, in most cultures, an almost essential qualification for full membership of society. Accordingly, the attention devoted to the reading process by educationalists and psychologists has been immense. The ability to read music is, if not essential, an irreplaceable asset to anyone who indulges in musical activity. Yet the amount of attention devoted to music reading by teachers, educationalists and psychologists has, on the whole, been very small, It is not the intention here to provide an historical or sociological analysis of the neglect of this aspect of musical ability, nevertheless, before proceeding, two points need to be established: firstly that influential commentators on psychological aspects of music have, in fact, had very little to say about music reading; secondly that this neglect is unjustified in consideration of the importance of musical literacy for overall musical competence.

Seashore (1938) mentions sight-reading twice in his classic book *The Psychology of Music*. The first mention is in the context of 'Twelve rules for efficient learning in music' addressed to the aspiring pupil. He says:

> Build larger and larger units. At certain advanced stages we learn by wholes, but the best rule for learning in general is to learn one small specific thing at a time; then weave these larger units together, and so on, until the task is completed. In doing this you acquire the power to learn larger and larger units. Take the analogy of learning to read. The child first learns to see individual letters, to associate these with sounds, to weave the sounds into words, the words into phrases, the phrases into clauses. . . . As he learns to read, reading becomes easier because he reads in larger and larger units. This is exactly parallel to sight reading in music. . . .

This passage is misleading on at least two counts. Firstly it is not the case that the child learning to read prose always starts with letter–sound associations and builds upwards. In a language like English there arc so many irregular words that such a method would not suffice. It appears from the errors made by beginning readers that many of them operate at a higher level of abstraction, using the printed page as an aid to extracting the sense of the passage rather than individual letters (e.g. Weber, 1970). Secondly, the parallel to sight-reading in music cannot be 'exact' because there are no exact parallels to words, phrases, clauses, and sentences which make up the larger units of language. Until the aspiring reader knows what the larger units arc—chords, bars, beats, or whatever, Seashore's parallel could not be applied.

Seashore's second mention comes in a section containing advice to the teacher. He rightly stresses the intimate connection between reading and aural training, but is unhelpful on the specifics of training methods. The instruction to 'Pass by natural stages from the mechanics of sight-reading to the singing and playing for pleasure and the preparation of repertoire' rather evades the issue. If he is saying—concentrate on the music and the reading will look after itself—then we must assume that he is rejecting the possibility that reading can be taught, and suggesting that it is something that 'just happens'.

Buck (1944) does not believe that reading ability 'just happens'. On the contrary, he proposes that hard work and virtuous application is required:

> If you are a slow reader, remember that anyone can read a piece
> at a bar a minute, and there is no other excuse than laziness for
> not acquiring speed. If the child struggling with the cat sentence
> were to lament that she would never be able to read rapidly 'like
> a grown-up', you know that she is talking nonsense, and that
> the speed at which you and I can read English is not due to clev-
> erness or any special gift. And the same is true, with no qualifi-
> cation, about the reading of music. To confess that you are a bad
> reader is to confess laziness. . . .

Nonetheless, he might just as well have shared Seashore's view, for he really gives no concrete advice to the learner. Laziness can only be attributed to someone who knows what he should be doing but does not do it. Buck does not exactly say what one should do to acquire speed. It may be that poor readers work very industriously at their reading, but in an inappropriate way.

Shuter (1968), in a book specifically on musical ability, does not deal with reading as a substantive issue at all, although it is mentioned briefly in a couple of places as a component of musical skill. More recently, Critchley and Henson (1977) in the introduction to a collection of invited papers on

'Music and the Brain' explicitly acknowledge that a chapter on music reading is one of the major omissions of their collection. Finally, Davies (1978), in the first major text on psychology of music to be published since Shuter (1968), mentions reading only in passing. This is perhaps understandable, since the book is 'concerned almost wholly with music from the standpoint of the listener. . . . '. Experimental research into music reading has also been slight in quantity. Bean (1938), Weaver (1943), Van Neuys and Weaver (1943), Lannert and Ullman (1945), and Kwalwasser (1955) have studied various aspects of skilled sight-reading, mainly on the piano. Research carried out in an educational context has concentrated more on sight-singing, and ways of teaching it (e.g. Hillbrand, 1923; Hammer, 1963).

It is hardly necessary to state that a musician with sight-reading facility has an immense advantage over other musicians in nearly all walks of musical life. Many professional musicians could simply not perform their jobs without a high level of reading skill, and even among amateurs a good reader is more likely to be able to enter fully into the more rewarding and fulfilling aspects of musical life. It seems to be part of musical folk-lore that good sight-readers have poor musical memories, but the reason for this is probably that they do not need to develop efficient memorising strategies, rather than that they are incapable of so doing. Surely no one would wish to claim that musicians whose jobs demanded memorisation, such as opera singers, would be worse off for being good readers. After all, professional actors do not seem to suffer as a result of being able to read their scripts unaided. I wish to argue further, however, that reading facility is not simply a useful additional skill for a musician to have. It is, in a sense, necessary for full membership of the musical community.

There are basically two types of composer, the improviser and the writer. The improviser (or composer/performer) conceives a musical idea which he communicates to his listeners directly in performance. The writer communicates indirectly through a score which must be read, understood, and realised by a performer. It would not, I think, be unfair to say that the composer-writer predominates in our musical culture. Musical notation is, therefore the medium, or language, of his communication. It is not simply a set of instructions for performance (except, maybe for some forms of contemporary notation—see Karkoschka, 1972; Cole 1974)—it actually embodies aspects of the structure, or meaning, of the music which would not be present in a *physical* description of the sounds (i.e. details of frequency, duration, and amplitude of various notes).

Specifically, just knowing the pitch of a note does not tell one anything about its tonal significance; and just knowing the duration of a note does not tell one anything about its rhythmic significance. The score makes explicit a musical relationship between notes by the use of key signatures, accidentals, and rhythmic notation, etc. Longuet-Higgins (1972) cites the following example, which would not instantly be recognised by most readers as a musically illiterate transcription of the opening few measures of the British National Anthem.

Example 1.1

Nonetheless, if executed by a performer, the auditory effect would be correct. All that the performer would miss would be a sense of comprehension, until he recognised the 'tune' through hearing what he played. An analogous situation in language can be obtained by asking someone to read out the following nonsensical French sentence: 'Pas de lieu Rhone que nous'. It often takes the reader some time to realise that the sounds he is producing can be interpreted sensibly as the English sentence 'Paddle your own canoe'.

When the composer of the National Anthem chose to write it in the way we are now accustomed to seeing it, it was because he wished to convey that the melody made sense conceived as being in triple time and containing the tonal sequence tonic–tonic–supertonic–, etc. This vital information is plain for any reader to see, without his having to execute a single note. When he does come to perform the notes, therefore, he already *knows* what the music means and can perform it in such a way as to make that meaning explicit. The poor reader cannot do this. He is in precisely the position of the prose reader trying to make sense of 'Pas de lieu Rhone que nous'. The meaning is not apparent to him on inspection so he has to listen to what he plays or sings and try to make sense of that. Whether he succeeds will, in part, depend upon his musicality, that is, his ability to hear what makes musical sense. But it will also depend upon something less tangible and predictable—his ability to switch between ways of looking at (or in this case hearing) a musical message.

A famous demonstration of fixation is that devised by the cartoonist W. E. Hill in 1915, entitled 'My Wife and My Mother in Law' (Figure 1.1). Many people can see only the old woman or only the young woman, even after instruction. One's first schema for viewing the picture can make it almost impossible to switch to the alternative perception. If a musician

Figure 1.1 'My Wife and my Mother-in-law'. A reversal figure created by the cartoonist W. E. Hill; first published in *Puck* in 1915. The young woman's chin is the old woman's nose.

misperceives the musical meaning of a passage, he may therefore be unable to switch to the correct interpretation without difficulty.

There is, of course, an objection to this line of argument. Surely, one may argue, listeners in the concert hall experience no difficulty in perceiving the music as the composer intended. Why then, should a reader have any difficulty hearing the meaning once he has executed it? The answer to this objection lies, I believe, in a consideration of the difference of 'cognitive load' on a reader and a listener. Essentially, a listener has just one thing to do, that is, listen. A reader not only has to listen. He also has to decide what notes to play next with reference to the score, organising his motor behaviour, as well as trying to remember the aural impression created by the notes he has already played. He can often be in the worst position to appreciate the overall meaning behind what he is doing. Even so, listeners frequently do 'mis-hear' music. This is especially true, for instance, at the start of a piece, where misperceptions of rhythmic structure are quite common even among musically sophisticated listeners.

Longuet-Higgins (1972, 1976) and Steedman (1977) have studied this issue in the context of producing computer programmes which correctly transcribe melodies, the programmes thus acting as 'intelligent' musical listeners. Using the themes of J. S. Bach's '48' fugues from the 'Well Tempered Clavier' performed in a 'dead-pan' fashion on an organ keyboard, they find that it is often impossible to correctly interpret the tonal or rhythmic structure of the theme till several measures have passed. Steedman (1977) develops some ingenious ideas as to how a listener might attempt to work out rhythmic structure in an ambiguous passage, which involve, among other things, looking out for repetitions of tonal sequences. There is a sense, though, in which this is placing rather too much responsibility on the listener. Very few performers will, in fact, give an entirely dead-pan performance of a theme. Even on an organ keyboard it is possible to indicate accent by variations in durations of notes. On most other instruments variations in amplitude, pitch, and timbre for individual notes are also possible. Thus, in all cases except those where one has good reason to believe the composer intended ambiguity it is part of the performer's job to present music to the listener in a way that creates no ambiguity, by whatever means are available to him.

Consider, for instance, the following sequence of notes:

Example 1.2

When this is played in a 'dead-pan' fashion to listeners, some perceive the beat as coming on the first, third, fifth note, and so on; whilst others perceive the beat as coming on the second, fourth, sixth note, and so on. Both are valid interpretations which make reasonable musical sense. Of course, in a literate score, the two alternatives would be notated differently, as follows:

Example 1.3

Example 1.4

A good performer, confronted with one of these alternatives, would naturally play it in such a way as to make sure that listeners did not 'mis-hear' it as the alternative. In a reading situation, this would imply assigning to the passage, before playing it, one or other of the two alternative interpretations. This would then allow decisions about the duration, loudness, and quality of the various notes to be made. In this case, the cues which allow a reader to arrive at the correct interpretation are fairly straightforward. They include the placing of the bar-lines and the beaming of notes into pairs. There are, however, many examples where the assignation of a correct interpretation is less straightforward, and therefore demands greater literacy on the part of the performer. Take, for example, the second movement of the Schumann's *Phantasie* for piano, bars 141–157.

Example 1.5 Bars 141–157 from second movement of *Phantasie* for piano by Schumann.

Here, the bar-lines and the beaming suggest a conventional 4/4 beat. If, however, a performer attempted to place the beats on the first, third, fifth and seventh quavers in each bar, musical nonsense would result. The 'beats' are in fact on the second, fourth, sixth, and eighth quavers. The phrase marks suggest this to some degree, but it takes considerable reading skill to see that the disposition of notes themselves demands this interpretation. In essence it entails the knowledge that in the upper register of the piano, all other things being equal, the uppermost notes will constitute the psychologically dominant material, especially if separated from lower notes by a significant interval (cf. Dowling, 1973; Deutsch, 1977). Why then, one may ask, did Schumann put the bar lines where he did? Presumably because he wanted to instil into the music a slight metrical 'unease' as though there were a suppressed 4/4 metre going on underneath all the time. This theory is substantiated by the fact that five times during the passage, the underlying metre 'breaks through' in the form of an accented 5th quaver. To capture all this in a performance demands a highly intelligent reading of the score. Few of us, maybe, would be capable of picking all this up at a first playing, even if we were technically proficient enough to play the passage at all, but Schumann is within his rights to demand that we should be able to understand his intentions from the score.

The claim that readers should be able to interpret a score before playing it should not be confused with the claim that they should be able to hear what the music should sound like 'in the mind's ear'. This second claim may be true of particular individuals, but one would wish to call it literacy only if mediated by an appreciation of the musical meaning. Let us take a linguistic analogy. Any competent reader of English should be able to imagine what the following would sound like if spoken: *Homo factus est*. However, only if the reader understood Latin would we wish to say that he had displayed full literacy in the task. Similarly, we could imagine a musician raised on a diet of atonal music who might somehow be able to imagine the pitches associated with the following sequence:

Example 1.6

This would, I believe, not be taken as evidence of musical literacy unless it was coupled with a knowledge that the sequence implied a movement from tonic to dominant harmony in the key of A minor. Furthermore

I believe that we should wish to ascribe literacy to a music reader who displayed evidence of this knowledge even if he was not imagining the actual sounds. There is mounting evidence now that language reading does not always involve a sight to sound translation, but can take place by a direct transition from sight to meaning (Allport, 1979; Bradshaw, 1975; Patterson and Marcel, 1977; Saifran and Mann, 1977). I wish later to review some evidence which suggests that competent music readers may use a similar process.

Finally, nothing which has been said above about the skills which might be employed by performers implies that performers should have full conscious awareness of these processes. On the contrary, they may be largely unaware of what is going on when they read. The notion that highly practised perceptual skills are executed without the involvement of consciousness receives general support in the psychological literature (e.g. LaBergc and Samuels, 1974; Schneider and Shiffrin, 1977).

1.2 Introspections and conversations

It is a common experience among keyboard players in particular that page turners do not turn early enough. This author has, on several occasions, agreed in advance with a page turner that a head nod would signal the turn, only to find in performance that the nod was ignored. 'I couldn't believe that you wanted me to turn so soon!' is a typical post-mortem remark. This experience alone is enough to tell the seasoned performer that he reads further ahead than does the average page-turner. A similar thing occurs in choirs where a good and a less good reader are sharing the same copy. if the poor reader is controlling the copy he will invariably turn later than is comfortable for the good reader. Nonetheless, when one asks musicians to estimate how far ahead they customarily read, they usually have only the vaguest of ideas.

Nearly all instrumental teachers have to spend some time with their pupils on sight-reading, if only to prepare them for examinations. If my experience is typical, this vagueness about one's own sight-reading extends to all facets of it and makes the teaching of sight-reading an almost impossible assignment. I literally do not know what to say to a pupil who cannot sight-read. I do not remember having to *do* anything in particular myself to achieve my adequacy in reading. On the contrary I have often used my reading facility to cover up for far more intractable technical difficulties, or for lack of practice. I suspect that most good readers acquired their skill early in life without too much trouble, with the unfortunate consequence that those who sight-read best may well be the worst teachers of it. Teachers who in adult life have had to struggle to achieve a basic reading competence are probably in a far better position to impart useful hints to pupils. Nonetheless, it is of interest to discover what expert sight-readers have to say for themselves, and for this reason Wolf (1976) has performed a valuable service in interviewing four exceptional sight-readers of his acquaintance. Although only short extracts from the interviews are printed, some persistent themes emerge. One of these is the insistence that notes are seen in groups rather than singly. Nonetheless, some of the extracts suggest that introspection does not come easily. For instance, the following remark of Boris Goldovsky suggests that he is having to convince himself that a plausible statement actually finds corroboration in his own experience: 'When you read piano music, you see them (he staves) both simultaneously. You don't read them separately. The eye certainly covers both lines easily . . . I don't think I read the top line, then do the bass line. No, I'm quite sure that I see at least that much at once.' When Vladimir Sokoloff was asked what the principal problems involved in sight-reading were, his answer was: 'For me personally, there are none.' Although this is hardly useful for someone attempting to understand the sight-reading process, it is, I believe, an honest answer about a skill which, for him, is so highly overlearned that its execution requires almost no conscious effort.

Although, therefore, the comments of skilled sight-readers are of considerable interest as sources of hypotheses about the sight-reading process, it would be misleading to consider them descriptions of the processes involved. They are perhaps more like commentaries on their conscious experiences, or rationalisations of their own behaviour. Whilst such comments must be accounted for in a full theory of skilled music reading, they do not in themselves offer the means of achieving such a theory. This paper is motivated by the belief that only by direct observation of musicians engaged in reading tasks in the context of controlled experimental situations can one hope to achieve any substantial understanding of this complex skill. This belief has motivated much of the recent research on language reading (Williams, 1970), and the techniques and models developed there over the last 20 years have considerable relevance to the study of music reading.

1.3 Misreading

The phenomenon known as 'proof-readers' error' has been long familiar to cognitive psychologists (Vernon, 1931; Pillsbury, 1897; Huey, 1908). This occurs because of the tendency for incorrectly spelled words to be overlooked when the mis-spelling is slight. This is one of many observations which supports the view that reading involves 'top-down' or 'conceptually driven' processes, as well as 'bottom-up' or 'data-driven' processes (Runielhart and Siple, 1974; Smith, 1971; Kolers, 1970; Norman, 1976). In such processes a reader does not depend simply upon decoding of stimulus information to build up a mental representation of the text; he uses his prior knowledge and expectancy to supplement, or even replace stimulus information. Neisser (1967) enjoins us to characterise reading as 'externally guided thinking'. By looking at the kind of errors people make when reading, we can find out exactly what expectancies they have, and exactly what parts of the stimulus information they are using. For instance, it has been shown that readers are more likely to misperceive letters occurring in the middles of words than at the beginning or the end (Morton, 1964; Sloboda, 1976b). Thus, readers detect the mis-spelling in 'hwistle' much more readily than that in 'whitsle', suggesting that they identify words by identifying the exterior letters and then using the surrounding context and their knowledge of the language to pick the most appropriate word. Top-down processing is not confined to reading. It can be found in most types of perception: listening to speech (Marslen-Wilson and Welsh, 1978; Warren, 1970; Cole, 1973), looking at pictures (Palmer, 1975), perceiving chess boards (Chase and Simon, 1973).

The existence of 'proof-readers' error' in music has been demonstrated by the 'Goldovsky experiment' reported in Wolf (1976):

> a student whom Dr. Goldovsky describes as 'technically competent but a poor reader' prepared a Brahms *Capriccio* (Opus 76 no. 2) which she brought to her lesson. She began to play the piece through but when she arrived at the C sharp major chord on the first beat of the bar 42 measures from the end, she played a G natural instead of the G sharp which would normally occur in the C sharp major triad. Goldovsky told her to stop and correct her mistake. The student looked confused and said that she had played what was written. To Goldovsky's surprise, the girl had played the printed notes correctly—there was an apparent misprint in the music.

This misprint occurs in most standard editions of Brahms' piano music. It appears, therefore, that countless scores of musicians, let alone proof-readers and publishers, had never noticed this misprint. Goldovsky proceeded to test skilled readers by telling them that the piece contained a misprint which they were to find. He allowed them to play the piece as many times as they liked and in any way they liked. None of them ever found the mistake. Only when he narrowed the field down to a single bar did most readers spot the mistake.

Example 1.7 Bars 76–78 from *Capriccio*, op. 76, no. 2 by Brahms.

One may guess why this misprint was so difficult to spot. Firstly the chord occurred at the beginning of a bar. Skilled readers will be used to seeing C sharp major chords in other positions of a bar when the G sharp will have been signalled by an earlier note. Such chords may be visually identical to the 'misprint' in this case. Secondly the chord contains other accidentals. A quick glance at the chord may give the impression that one of them is actually attached to the G. Thirdly, and most importantly, we may suppose that most readers were expecting to find a C sharp major chord at that point. This expectancy, coupled with the fact that the printed chord was sufficiently similar to what was expected, led to the error. It is highly significant that the first person to notice the error was a poor reader. Perhaps one of the causes of poor reading is insufficient expectancy and the lack of top-down processing. Sloboda (1976b) studied misreading more systematically by introducing deliberate notational 'mistakes' into pieces of music which subjects were asked to read. Four excerpts from relatively little-known keyboard pieces by Marcello and Dussek were used. They were chosen for the unlikeliness of their having been encountered previously by the subjects used, and for their adherence to highly conventional harmonic and rhythmic devices. These excepts were copied out by hand, and had introduced into them a total of 72 copying errors distributed equally between the two staves and between the various positions within a musical phrase. Each error was produced by raising or lowering a note by one position on the stave, but transferring intact all accidentals, etc. The errors were chosen to be both playable and highly unlikely in the musical context as expressive of the composers' intentions.

These pieces were presented to a group of competent piano readers who were asked to sight-read each piece twice. Their instructions were to play exactly what was written with a view to seeing how much they could improve on the second play-through. Most subjects suspected that there might be something odd about the passages, and, having spotted one misprint, were consciously on the lookout for others. In spite of this, no subject managed to execute all the altered notes correctly. Instead, many of them were played as they appeared in the original score. Most subjects showed genuine surprise when some of the altered notes were pointed out to them. They had not noticed them, playing what ought to have been there rather than what was there. Not all altered notes were equally easy to spot. Hardest to spot were those in the middle of right-hand phrases. This corresponds rather well with the pattern shown when reading words.

Another interesting finding was that, although subjects made fewer errors on their second attempts at the pieces, they made more errors on the altered notes, playing even more of them as they appeared in the original correct score. This suggests that, as subjects began to become familiar with the structure of the pieces they used this knowledge to 'skim' even more. In general, their knowledge allowed them to predict correctly what notes should be played, but in the case of the altered notes this knowledge would predict the wrong course of action. Thus, it seems that good sight-reading is based, at least in part, on the ability to decide on probable continuations within an idiom. For conventional tonal music this implies a knowledge (explicit or implicit) of harmonic and rhythmic rules, and an ability to translate this knowledge into the movements necessary to produce the appropriate sounds. This does not necessarily mean that a good sight-reader must be technically expert. Many proficient instrumental readers will often sing a passage that they just cannot get their fingers round, or provide a harmonically acceptable substitute. In these cases it is clear that they know what they should be playing. Another hallmark of the good reader is the ability to correct mistakes rapidly and efficiently. For instance, it is easy, on the piano, to find oneself playing a key too high or too low. The good reader will often correct himself after playing only a single wrong note, whilst the poor reader will often continue at the wrong pitch for several notes. This does not so much suggest that good readers have 'good ears' (because most people can detect wrong notes when listening to someone else playing) as that they have the ability to monitor their own performances. The lack of this skill in beginners is widespread, and affects technical and interpretative skill as well. This lack may be due to the fact that the mental effort required to process the visual input and produce a response is so great that there is little attentional capacity left for monitoring.

It would be interesting to know at what level good readers monitor their performance. One possibility is that they listen to what they produce.

Another is that they monitor kinaesthetic feedback, or even the 'motor commands' themselves, so that they know even before hearing a note that they have played it wrongly. In studies of other forms of skilled performance there is compelling evidence that performers cannot be simply monitoring their output, since there is often not the delay in making correction movements which would follow if this were the case. In other words, they make corrections too quickly. Discussions of this issue are given by Broadbent (1977), Poulton (1957), Young (1969).

1.4 Reading span

One good way of enhancing one's reading performance is to obtain preview (Shaffer, 1975; 1976). If one is taking in visual information well ahead of the time when performance is required, one has time to decode the information and provide a steady flow of output in spite of temporary hold-ups along the information processing route. It follows that preview requires some form of memory storage in which notes that have been seen, but not yet played, can be held on a short-term basis. The greater the capacity of this store, the greater is the opportunity for preview, and the greater is the opportunity for making reasonable predictions about subsequent notes. Given six notes to go on, success in predicting the next note is more likely than if there are only two notes. A standard method of estimating the amount of preview in normal reading, and thus by inference the capacity of short-term memory store, involves measuring the 'eye-voice span'. This technique, and a modification of it suitable for application to music reading, has already been described in this journal (Sloboda, 1974). It was shown that better readers had larger spans for single line melodies. The best reader had a span of 6.5 notes, whereas the poorest reader had a span of only 3.5 notes. So the common advice to 'look ahead more' seems to be enacted by proficient readers. But looking ahead is no use to the reader unless he is able to remember what he has seen, so we must ask how it is that the good reader can memorise more of a musical score than a poor reader.

One clue is supplied by the observation that span is not constant but appears to 'jump' from one phrase boundary to the next, suggesting that readers are treating the phrase as some kind of 'unit'. This appears to be not simply a matter of picking out a visual boundary (like using gaps between words in prose reading (Hochberg, 1970), but of using the structure of the music itself to relate notes within a phrase to one another. This was shown by an experiment (Sloboda, 1977) in which musicians were asked to read musical passages, of which some conformed to the conventional rules of melodic progression, and others did not. It was found that span decreased for the unconventional melodies, as did the tendency for span to coincide with a phrase boundary (defined rhythmically). Thus we may conclude that one of the factors allowing good readers to hold larger 'chunks' of musical material in memory is their ability to organise the material into groups of notes having higher-order interrelationships. The effects of 'redundancy' on memory for linguistic material has been amply demonstrated in the psychological literature (Miller and Selfridge, 1950; Epstein, 1961; Marks and Miller, 1964). Thus, people read and remember less well items of the following sort—'of by method gravity is beer simplest the serving'—than items which conform to grammatical expectations, e.g. 'When eating spanners it is best to remove both feet'.

One may suppose that a lot of music is constructed according to rules which are similar to grammatical rules in that writing certain combinations of notes limits the range of notes which can follow them. For instance the sequence C–E–G–F–E–D suggests C, E or G as a probable continuation. B, on the other hand would be rather unlikely. Some writers (e.g. Pinkerton, 1956) have suggested that musicians learn a set of transitional probabilities between adjacent notes which makes certain intervals much more likely to be used than others. While this may be true, it is unlikely that it is the whole story. It is more likely that musicians learn that certain harmonic moves are more permissible than others within the tonal system (cf. Winograd, 1968; Sundberg and Lindblom, 1976; Longuet-Higgins, 1977), so that a melodic continuation is rendered acceptable if the implied harmonic progression allows it, regardless of the interval that it creates with the preceding note. Of course, musicologists devote much of their attention to the construction of musical grammars of considerable refinement (e.g. Forte, 1962; Cooper and Meyer, 1960). The question that concerns us here is how much of these grammars do musicians use (albeit automatically or unconsciously) to assist their reading? The word 'grammars' is deliberately put in the plural since it is clear that the rules of musical construction vary, if not from composer to composer, from period to period. It is likely that as we learn more about a particular composer, reading his music will become easier. Proficiency at reading Mozart only predicts proficiency in reading Messiaen insofar as their languages overlap.

While no experimental verification of this hypothesis exists, it is a common experience (among musicians who have to learn several works of a new composer writing in a consistent idiom) that it becomes easier to read the music as time passes. Chords which at first looked like meaningless jumbles of notes now start to 'lie under the fingers'. Rhythms which had to be pieced together note by note, now can be played 'as a pattern'. It is as if the reader is gradually learning new musical 'words' and entering them into the musical equivalent of a 'lexicon'. The reader seems to be acquiring new 'distinctive features' in a musical pattern recognition task (cf. Gibson, 1969; Uhr and Vossler, 1963).

1.5 The nature of musical memory

If reading ability depends upon rapid memorisation of notes in advance of their performance it becomes of central importance to determine the form in which the material is held. Is the representation acoustic (a set of imagined sounds), articulatory (a set of specifications for muscular movement), or what? A similar question has held centre stage in the study of language perception for several years (reviewed by Neisser (1967), and more recently by Bradshaw (1975), Henderson (1977), Allport (1979), Gibson and Levin (1975). One of the ways in which experimentalists have tried to solve this problem is to attempt to occupy the hypothesised storage-system with an extraneous task and observe whether there is a decrement in performance on the primary task (Allport, Antonis and Reynolds, 1972; Baddeley and Hitch, 1974). If there is no decrement, then it is often plausible to argue that the primary task cannot be using that particular memory system.

Using a technique of this sort (Sloboda, 1976a) it was found that subjects could memorise lists of letters, or sequences of tones, at the same time as performing a task in which they were required to write down a briefly exposed (2 sec.) segment of musical notation, without any significant detriment to either task. Nonetheless, musically trained subjects were significantly better at the notation transcription task than a control group of untrained subjects. This superiority could not be due to greater writing facility since the two groups of subjects did not differ in a condition where exposure was very brief (20 msec.). Thus it appeared that the musicians' superiority arose because of more efficient storage of the material in some non-verbal, non-acoustic type of memory. It seemed as though the visual input was obtaining direct access to some abstract form of representation which was not aurally based. The precise nature of this representation is yet unknown, although visual contour seems to be an important aspect of the input for musicians (Sloboda, 1978). In a sense, the independence of the reading system from vision-to-sound translation is not surprising. Proficient readers are always looking at one thing while listening to something else, simply because they read ahead. If they are occupying acoustic mechanisms by listening to what they are playing, visual input could not be passed through the same system, and another route would have to be developed. Of course, one cannot say that the sound system is *never* used in reading. In fact it probably is used when the reader is learning an unfamiliar idiom where no efficient procedures exist for determining the structure or 'meaning' of the music. It is probably the only way to sight-sing contemporary music efficiently. No tonal centre being present, each note has to be pitched as an interval from the preceding note, the pitch of the sound being matched to an internally generated image. Thus, the sound route must he available. The contention here is that it is not generally used by good sight-readers in conventional (tonally based) reading situations.

At the present time, it seems most plausible to suppose that the musical memory code is a representation of the visual input in abstract tonal and rhythmic space, consisting of a set of tonal centres, or harmonies, together with a more or less detailed specification of the structural-temporal relations between them. This representation may then be overlaid by visual specifications for frequently occurring sequences, such as scale passages. Thus the sequence CDEFGFEDC might be represented as 'C major (tonic+rising scale→dominant+falling scale→tonic)' in an hypothetical memory notation. Some such system would seem necessary to account for the mistakes made during attempts to memorise tunes (cf. Davies and Jennings, 1977). Such errors are generally tonally and rhythmically related to the stimulus, and are rarely haphazard. That such a memory system is directly involved in reading awaits experimental demonstration. A possible approach would be to look for interference between reading and a concurrent task which required tonal analysis.

1.6 Helping learners

The foregoing considerations lead to a number of suggestions for acquiring sight-reading proficiency, offered not because they have been tried and found to work, but rather in the hope that teachers might be encouraged to re-examine their teaching methods.

Firstly, the reader must build up the musical knowledge of form, style and 'language' to be able to make small-scale predictions about what is going to come next. This might be encouraged by making copies of scores in which, from time to time, one or two notes or chords have been left out. Students could attempt to play these scores, filling in with appropriate notes. Training in improvisation, providing continuations to given themes, keyboard harmony, and memory for melodies, should all help this ability.

Secondly, the reader must wean himself away from a direct association between a written note and a hand movement on the instrument. A good reader should appreciate the music 'in his head' without playing it at all. Sight-singing should help this skill, checking on an instrument afterwards to see if one is right. Reading 'a bar at a time' will also help: that is, looking at a bar, putting the music away, and attempting to play the whole of that bar. The size of chunks can gradually be built up as proficiency is acquired. Following the score of a work whilst listening to it on a record or on the radio should also help, attempting to keep a note or two ahead of the sound point and anticipating what the next notes will sound like. This exercise would be best begun with something simple (slow movement of a sonata or quartet) before symphonic works are tackled. Reading the score of a familiar work imaging the sounds of the music, but without actually playing them may help, as will learning a keyboard instrument— keyboard music makes explicit the harmony which is only implicit in a solo line, thus providing many more cues for the beginner to guess what is coming next.

Thirdly, sight-reading performed note-by-note is unlikely to improve however frequently practised. The music must be understood before it is played, using the actual sound to check out one's hypothesis. The main aid to this is a fascination with music itself, a desire to find out what a piece sounds like, It is therefore important to sight-read music that is liked. For many children this may mean a diet of pop-music transcriptions. In fact, these often make excellent sight-reading material, since they use basic harmonic patterns a great deal, and familiar rhythmic and melodic patterns. In the early stages, the reader should be encouraged to try to associate the sound with its written counterpart. Occasional stopping may facilitate this in the beginner by providing opportunity for thought about what has been played, or judgement of correctness.

Fourthly, it would seem reasonable to seek to attempt to develop musical sensibility before embarking on training in reading. No one would consider teaching a normal child to read while he was at a very early stage of learning spoken language. Yet it seems the norm to start children off on reading at the very first instrumental lesson without establishing the level of musical awareness already present. Without some musical knowledge a beginner has no expectancies which can be used in reading.

Fifthly, the teacher might advantageously create situations in which the learner needs to be able to read in order to fulfil musical or social aspirations. Membership of choir or a chamber music group will provide motivation for development of reading. Placing expectations of pupil's reading performance at a deliberately high level is also likely to enhance development. If we seek to improve standards, we must not let the poor reader hold us to ransom in an ensemble situation.

1.7 Improving musical text

In all that has been said so far we have assumed a perfect, immutable score which it is the reader's job to understand and execute. Many of the difficulties involved in reading, however, may be attributable to faults in the score itself, and not the reader.

The amount of psychological research on the presentation of printed language is considerable (Hartley and Burnhill, 1976; Poulton, 1959; Hartley, 1978; Watts and Nisbet, 1974), but it is doubtful how much of this is relevant to music, where both the reading environment, and the nature of the symbols used, are very different. There has been little research on factors of presentation in musical text which affect the ease and speed of reading, although practically every musician has come across examples of presentation practices which have seriously upset his reading performance. One can name just a few of these: crowding of ledger lines; inconsistencies in horizontal separation of notes; staves too close together, so that it is difficult to tell which stave a dynamic mark applies to; decrescendo signs which look like accents; notes which are not accurately centred on a line or a space; page turns in awkward places; notes, stems, stave lines which are too thick or thin for comfortable reading; unhelpful word underlay, etc.

Some of these difficulties are caused by lack of thought in preparation of the score, and can be prevented. Other problems are less easy to solve. How big should a stave be? Are clef changes preferable to ledger lines? How wide should a page of music be, and how many notes to the inch should a line contain on average? What is the best shape for note-heads? How thick should stems be, and how high should they be? Many of these questions seem to have been decided on the basis of engraving tradition, and, where explicit stipulations are made (e.g. Weaner and Boelke, 1966), there is little evidence that alternatives have been tried out, or even seriously considered. Nonetheless, if one takes several editions of practically any classical work, the differences in presentation are usually immense. Some of the differences may have only aesthetic import, but there is reason to suppose that not all differences are of this sort.

In the absence of substantial research into these matters, is there any general principle which could guide those concerned with the preparation of music which other people must play? One guiding principle must be to adopt any practice which makes it easier for the reader to perceive the structure of the music. To take an example, until recently it was the custom to join quavers and semiquavers in vocal music by beams only if the notes were sung to the same syllable. When a bar contained many short notes it was often difficult to see which notes came on a strong beat, and it was easy to overlook a single quaver amid many semiquavers. The modern practice of beaming the notes as in the manner of instrumental music clarifies the rhythmic structure of a vocal passage at no expense to other considerations (provided that the word underlay is set out intelligently). Another example concerns the use of accidentals. There are many examples of tonal music where, for several bars, a new key is established so remote from the original key that almost every note must be accompanied by an accidental of some sort. It would be perceptually and cognitively easier to change the key signature for the duration, since this would unambiguously signal the key change, so making the harmonic structure more apparent. The memory capacity of the average reader must also be taken into account. In a 12/8 piano bar containing 12 quaver chords with various accidentals, one should not expect the performer to be able to remember all through the bar that there was, say, an E sharp in the very first chord. If the last chord also contains an E sharp the accidental should be written again, even if the rules of notation do not strictly require it.

Many considerations of like kind are specific to a particular context, and demand knowledge of the particular work in question. For the serious student of music-presentation, there is no substitute for the detailed study of alternative editions of a work.

Those who produce instrumental parts which are to be played by professional orchestral musicians have, perhaps, the greatest need to consider psychological aspects of music reading. The amount of sight-reading required of professional instrumentalists (at least in Britain) is phenomenal. Slight blemishes in a part can waste valuable rehearsal seconds, and can contribute to faults in hastily rehearsed performances. A slight imperfection in a piano score which a solo performer has many months to study might not be important. In a part which may be seen by the performer only once, if at all, before the performance, such matters are of essential importance. It is, therefore, surprising to discover that the quality of many orchestral parts is very poor. Some sets of parts used by England's major symphony orchestras have to be seen to be believed.

Finally, a radical alternative to improving legibility of conventional notation is the devising of new notational systems (see Karkoschka, 1972). Some of these are necessary because the existing notation is incapable of specifying a composer's requirements, but others (e.g. Klavarscribo) have been proposed as improvements on conventional notation. These systems rarely offer advantages not available in conventional notation. They merely employ alternative symbols, which, their various proponents have claimed, assist reading in one way or another. None of these systems has gained wide adherence, but it would be presumptuous to suggest that they are all inferior to conventional notation. However, only when a set of objective criteria for the psychological efficacy of musical symbols is developed shall we have a way of judging between the numerous alternative notational systems which contemporary music is generating.

In conclusion, I hope to have shown that the psychological study of music reading is an important, if hitherto neglected, area of the psychology of music which nevertheless has bearing on central theoretical and practical issues in music. It offers one important route to a better understanding of the nature of musical cognition itself.

References

Allport, D. A. (1977) On knowing the meaning of words we are unable to report: the effects of visual masking. In S. Dornic (Ed.) *Attention and Performance VI*. Hillside, N.J.: Erlbaum Associates.

Allport, D. A. (1979) Word recognition in reading: a tutorial review. In H. Bouma, P. A. Kolers and M. Wrolstad (Eds.) *Processing of Visible Language* (proceedings of a conference held at the Institute for Perception Research, I.P.O., Eindhoven, Netherlands, September 1977).

Allport, D. A., Antonis, B., and Reynolds, P. (1972) On the division of attention: a disproof of the single channel hypothesis. *Quarterly Journal of Experimental Psychology*, **24**, 225–235.

Baddeley, A. D. and Hitch, G. (1974) Working memory. In Go Bower (Ed.) *Recent advances in learning and motivation VIII*. New York: Academic Press.

Bean, K. L. (1938) An experimental approach to the reading of music. *Psychological Monographs*, **50**, whole number 226.

Bradshaw, J. L. (1975) Three interrelated problems in reading: a review. *Memory and Cognition*, **3.2**, 123–134.

Broadbent, D. E. (1977) Levels, hierarchies, and the locus of control. *Quarterly Journal of Experimental Psychology*, **29**, 181–201.

Buck, P. C. (1944) *Psychology for Musicians*. London: Oxford University Press.

Chase, W. G. and Simon, H. A. (1973) The mind's eye in chess. In W. G. Chase (Ed.) *Visual Information Processing*. New York: Academic Press.

Cole, H. (1974) *Sounds and Signs: Aspects of Musical Notation*. London: Oxford University Press.

Cole, R. A. (1973) Listening for mispronunciations: a measure of what we hear during speech. *Perception and Psychophysics*, **11**, 153–156.

Cooper, G. W. and Meyer, L. B. (1960) *The Rhythmic Structure of Music*. Chicago: University of Chicago Press.

Critchley, M. and Henson, R. A. (1977) *Music and the Brain*. London: Heinemann.

Davies, J. B. (1978) *The Psychology of Music*. London: Hutchinson.

Davies, J. B. and Jennings, J. (1977) The reproduction of familiar melodies and the perception of tonal sequences. *Journal of Acoustical Society of America*, **61.2**, 534–541.

Deutsch, D. (1977) Memory and attention in music. In M. Critchley and R. A. Henson (Eds.) *Music and the Brain*. London: Heinemann.

Dowling, W. J. (1973) The perception of interleaved melodies. *Cognitive Psychology*, **5**, 322–337.

Epstein, W. (1961) The influence of syntactical structure on learning. *American Journal of Psychology*, **74**, 80–85.

Forte, A. (1962) *Tonal Harmony in Concept and Practice*. New York: Holt, Rinehart and Winston.

Gibson, E. J. (1969) *Principles of Perceptual Learning and Development*. New York: Appleton-Century-Crofts.

Gibson, E. J. and Levin, H. (1975) *The Psychology of Reading*. Cambridge, Massachusetts: MIT Press.

Hammer, H. (1963) An experimental study of the use of the teaching of melodic sight singing. *Journal of Research in Music Education*, **11**, 44–54.

Hartley, J. (1978) *Designing Instructional Text*. London: Kogan Page.

Hartley, J. and Burnhill, P. (1976) *Textbook Design: A Practical Guide*. UNESCO.

Henderson, L. (1977) Word recognition. In Sutherland, N. S. (Ed.) *Tutorial Essays in Experimental Psychology*, 1. Potomac, Md.: Erlbaum.

Hillbrand, E. K. (1923) *Hillbrand Sight-singing Test*. Yonkers, New York: World Book.

Hochberg, J. (1970) Components of literacy: speculations and exploratory research. In H. Levin and J. P. Williams (Eds.) *Basic Studies on Reading*. New York: Basic Books.

Huey, E. B. (1908) *The Psychology and Pedagogy of Reading*. Cambridge, Massachusetts: MIT Press, reprinted 1968.

Karkoschka, E. (1972) *Notation in New Music*. London: Universal Edition.

Kolers, P. A. (1970) Three stages of reading. In H. Levin and J. P. Williams (Eds.) *Basic Studies on Reading*. New York: Basic Books.

Kwalwasser, J. (1955) *Exploring the Musical Mind*. New York: Coleman-Ross Co. Inc.

LaBerge, D. and Samuel, S. J. (1974) Toward a theory of automatic information processing in reading. *Cognitive Psychology*, **6**, 293–323.

Lannert, V. and Ullman, M. (1945) Factors in the reading of piano music. *American Journal of Psychology*, **58**, 91–99.

Longuet-Higgins, H. C. (1972) Making sense of music. *Proceedings of the Royal Institute of Great Britain*, **45**, 87–105.

Longuet-Higgins, H. C. (1976) The perception of melodies. *Nature*, **263**, 646–655.

Longuet-Higgins, H. C. (1978) The perception of music. *Interdisciplinary Science Reviews*, **3**, 148–156.

Marks, L. E. and Miller, G. A. (1964) The role of semantic and syntactic constraints in the memorization of English sentences. *Journal of Verbal Learning and Verbal Behaviour*, **3**, 1–5.

Marslen-Wilson, W. D. and Welsh, A. (1978) Processing interactions and lexical access during word recognition in continuous speech. *Cognitive Psychology*, **10**, 29–63.

Miller, G. A. and Selfridge, J. A. (1950) Verbal context and the recall of meaningful material. *American Journal of Psychology*, **63**, 176–185.

Morton, J. (1964) The effects of context on the visual duration threshold for words. *British Journal of Psychology*, **55.2**, 165–180.

Neisser, U. (1967) *Cognitive Psychology*. New York: Appleton-Century-Crofts.

Norman, D. A. (1976) *Memory and Attention* (2nd edition). New York: Wiley.

Palmer, S. E. (1975) Visual perception and world knowledge. In D. A. Norman, D.E. Rumelhart and the L.N.R. Research Group, *Explorations in Cognition*. San Francisco: Freeman.

Patterson, K. E. and Marcel, A. J. (1977) Aphasia, dyslexia and the phonological coding of written words. *Quarterly Journal of Experimental Psychology*, **29**, 307–318.

Pillsbury, W. B. (1897) A study in apperception. *American Journal of Psychology*, **8**, 315–393.

Pinkerton, R. C. (1956) Information theory and melody. *Scientific American*, **194.2**, 77–86.

Poulton, E. C. (1957) On prediction in skilled movements. *Psychological Bulletin*, **54**, 467–478.

Poulton, E. C. (1959) Effects of printing types and formats on the comprehension of scientific journals. M.R.C. Applied Psychology Unit Report No. 346. Cambridge University, U.K.

Rumelhart, D. F. and Siple, P. (1974) The process of recognising tachistoscopically presented words. *Psychological Review*, **81**, 99–118.

Saifran, E. M. and Marin, O. S. M. (1977) Reading without phonology: evidence from asphasia. *Quarterly Journal of Experimental Psychology*, **29,** 515–525.

Schneider, W. and Shiffnin, R. M. (1977) Controlled and automatic human information processing. *Psychological Review*, **84.1**, 1–66.

Seashore, C. (1938) *The Psychology of Music*. New York: McGraw-Hill; reprinted by Dover Books: New York (1967).

Shaffer, L. H. (1976) Intention and performance. *Psychological Review*, **83.5**, 375–393.

Shaffer, L. H. (1975) Control processes in typing. *Quarterly Journal of Experimental Psychology*, **27**, 419–432.

Shuter, R. (1968) *The Psychology of Musical Ability*. London: Methuen.

Sloboda, J. A. (1974) The eye-hand span: an approach to the study of sight reading. *Psychology of Music*, **2**, 4–10.

Sloboda, J. A. (1976a) Visual perception of musical notation: registering pitch symbols in memory. *Quarterly Journal of Experimental Psychology*, **28**, 1–16.

Sloboda, J. A. (1976b) The effect of item position on the likelihood of identification by inference in prose and music reading. *Canadian Journal of Psychology*, **30.4**, 228–238.

Sloboda, J. A. (1977) Phrase units as determinants of visual processing in music reading. *British Journal of Psychology*, **68**, 117–124.

Sloboda, J. A. (1978) Perception of contour in music reading. *Perception*, **7**, 323–331.

Smith, F. (1971) *Understanding Reading: A Psycholinguistic Analysis of Reading and Learning To Read*. New York: Holt, Rinehart and Winston.

Steedman, M. J. (1977) The perception of musical rhythm and metre. *Perception*, **6**, 555–570.

Sundberg, J. and Lindblom, B. (1976) Generative theories in language and music descriptions, *Cognition*, **4**, 99–122.

Uhr, L. and Vossler, C. (1963) A pattern recognition program that generates, evaluates, and adjusts its own operators. In E. A. Feigenbaum and J. Feldman (Eds.) *Computers and Thought*. New York: McGraw Hill.

Van Neuys, K. and Weaver, H. E. (1943) Memory span and visual pauses in reading rhythms and melodies. *Psychological Monographs*, **55**, 33–50.

Vernon, M. D. (1931) Characteristics of proof-reading. *British Journal of Psychology*, **21**, 368.

Warren, R. M. (1970) Perceptual restoration of missing speech sounds. Science, **167**, 392–393.

Watts, L. and Nisbet, J. (1974) *Legibility in Children's Books*. Windsor, Berks.: NFER Publishing Company.

Weaner, M. and Boelke, W. (1966) *Standard Music Engraving Practice*. New York: Music Publishers' Association of the U.S., Inc.

Weaver, H. E. (1943) A survey of visual processes in reading differently constructed musical selections. *Psychological Monographs*, **55**, 1–29.

Weber, R. M. (1970) First-graders' use of grammatical context in reading. In H. Levin and J. P. Williams (Eds.) *Basic Studies on Reading*. New York: Basic Books.

Williams, J. P. (1970) From basic research on reading to educational practice. In H. Levin and J. P. Williams (Eds.) *Basic Studies on Reading*. New York: Basic Books.

Winograd, T. (1968) Linguistics and the computer analysis of tonal harmony. *Journal of Music Theory*, **112**, 3–49.

Wolf, T. (1976) A cognitive model of musical sight reading. *Journal of Psycholinguistic Research*, **5**, 143–171.

Young, L. R. (1969) On adaptive manual control. *Ergonomics*, **12**, 635–674.

CHAPTER 2

EXPERIMENTAL STUDIES OF MUSIC READING: A REVIEW

The psychological study of music reading is atypical of music perception studies in two ways. First, we can identify a clearly defined behavioral goal in most nonlaboratory music reading situations. This is not the case for many music listening behaviors. Second, the object of perception is visual, not auditory. The first of these features provides the investigator with some advantages; the second poses some problems. Both merit further comment.

2.1 Goals of music reading

The most common goal of music reading is the production of a coherent musical performance. The reader converts the visual input into a set of pre-scriptions for performance—he finds out which notes to play, in which sequence and combination they are to occur, and much else. His perform-ance provides the investigator with a continuous measure of the effectiveness of his reading procedures, and it is possible to specify some of the conditions that must be satisfied if a person can be said to have read the music effec-tively. We will examine some of these conditions in more detail later.

In contrast, it is not easy to define well-formed goals in most music listening situations, and few of them result in a behavioral measure that varies from note to note as performance does in respect of a score. In our culture the most common goal of listening is some degree of aesthetic satisfaction or affective response. It is enough for many listeners that the experience was enjoyable, or evoked some emotion. When investigators take music into the laboratory they typically ask subjects to reproduce, or make comparisons between short musical passages. Although such activities can be found in some 'natural' musical contexts (such as the transmission of vocal melodies by oral imitation) they do not typify the behaviorally 'inert' listening activities that are more commonly associated with, say, hearing a new piece of orchestral music in the concert hall. The question of how we study and understand such processes has not really been addressed by mainstream contemporary research into music perception: and it is clearly unsatisfactory, and unjustifiable, to suppose that the cognitive processes underlying the recognition and reproduction of simple melodies and chord sequences are the same as those underlying the activity of listening to a long contrapuntally organized composition. The problems of how to conceptualize the goals of listening, and how to measure the moment to moment cognitive processes that are deployed in service of those goals, urgently await solution. Luckily, in the study of music reading, these problems are, in outline, solved; at least for one central case. In this central case the goal is a performance that must satisfy certain conditions, and behavioral measures capable of shedding some light on the underlying cognitive processes can be derived from quantifiable aspects of the performance.

2.2 Music reading as a visual task

The advantages that are conferred on us by studying a perceptual activity with clear goals and a 'ready-made' behavioral measure are counterbalanced by the problems posed by the atypicality of the input medium. Principally, the onus is on the investigator to demonstrate that the activity of music reading is a species of *music* perception at all. The skeptic can argue that we are bound to hold a simpler hypothesis until data force us to reject it. This simple hypothesis is, in essence, that music reading is a visuo-motor task that does not engage any of the cognitive processes specific to and necessary to musical perception. On this hypothesis, visual signs are converted directly into prescriptions for action without any musical mediation. Thus, a particular symbol may be interpreted as a prescription for a particular movement pattern with respect to a particular instrument without any representation of the musical functions of the note (as, for instance, contributing to a particular harmonic or rhythmic structure). On this hypothesis, it is only *after* the notes have been produced, thereby allowing the performer to *hear* them, that any *musical* perception or cognition takes place. This hypothesis is falsifiable *only* by the demonstration that musical features of a score can be represented prior to performance and that these features can actually control performance in some systematic way.

At first glance, there appears to be an obvious falsifying counter-example to this null hypothesis. This is the case of people who claim to be able to read a score in complete silence, without mediation of instrument or voice. However, I choose not to make anything of this example here. There are several reasons for this. One is that there is no obvious way of assessing the claim. Another is that among the population of fluent music readers those who can read silently are statistically rare, and so, third they may be employing processes in silent reading that are not normally employed in reading for performance. For these reasons, I prefer to base the case for accepting music reading as a true species of music perception on the evidence from tasks where each note in the visual stimulus must be given its own response in a performance or transcription mode.

2.3 Principal themes in early studies

The experimental literature on the perceptual and cognitive processes under-lying music reading is not large. However, two important early studies exem-plify two major areas of concern that have contemporary relevance; differences in reading processes *between* subjects as a function of expertise; and differences in reading processes *within* subjects as a function of the nature of the stimulus materials.

Bean (1938) presented pianists with briefly displayed musical extracts, which they were then required to perform. Here, as in all the studies reported in this article, the notation used was the standard 'orthochronic' notation of conventional Western music. (For a discussion of its principal characteristics see Read, 1974 and Sloboda, 1981). He found that 'span of apprehension,' as measured by the number of correctly played notes, was greater for the more experienced pianists. This important result mirrors and anticipates the findings that have emerged in many, if not all, domains of cognitive skill—experts have immediate recall for notation which is superior to that of novices. Unfortunately, Bean's study does not allow us to pinpoint the causes of this superiority as precisely as we would like. Does the superiority arise because experts have more rapid perceptual coding processes; or because they have better and more economical ways of storing what they perceive in memory; or because they have more effi-cient motor programs to organize the response? All these stages are plau-sible locations for the superiority. Subsequent research has helped clarify the situation, as the next section will outline.

The studies of Weaver and associates (Van Nuys and Weaver, 1943; Weaver, 1943) were concerned with the measurement of eye movements

Figure 2.1 Notational patterns typical of (a) contrapuntal music and (b) homophonic or chordal music.

as pianists played extended excerpts of classical music from score. One of the most striking findings from these studies is that the sequence of fixations made depends upon the type of music being played. Contrapuntal music elicits more horizontal than vertical fixation sequences. Chordal music elicits the reverse relationship. However, this result does not allow us to know whether *musical* considerations are responsible for this difference, or whether the visual appearance of the scores could account for the result. For instance, the eye could be 'captured' by groups of notes connected with beams of stems. Figure 2.1(a) shows an example of notation often associated with contrapuntal scores; notations such as the one in Figure 2.1(b) are more typical of chordal scores. Considerations of continuity and connectedness make it plausible that (a) would elicit a horizontal scan, and (b) a vertical scan, regardless of musical significance. Nonetheless, Weaver's work is a valuable and ecologically valid precursor of more recent studies that have attempted to manipulate the stimulus material in a more controlled way. It is a great shame that, despite the large amount of contemporary research on eye movements in language reading and scene scanning, there has been, to my knowledge, no further published research on eye movements in music reading since Weaver's work.

We can profitably combine the concerns of these two studies to generate a two-dimensional 'schema' for research into skills such as music reading (Figure 2.2). Such a schema may, ideally, be incorporated into the factorial design of a single experiment, where subjects of at least two levels of skills are examined on at least two conditions of stimulus presentation. This allows the examination of interaction effects, which are often as telling as

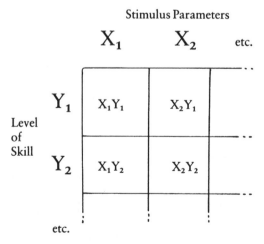

Figure 2.2 Basic factorial schema for skills research.

the main effects of experience or stimulus material. For instance, experts may exhibit a difference in behavior toward two stimulus conditions not shown by the novices. This can allow us to pinpoint more exactly in what respect experts are different from novices.

2.4 Musicians compared to nonmusicians

We began our examination of more recent studies by taking a few examples of experiments that conform to the schema given in Figure 2.2. There is a small group of such experiments that set out to compare absolute novices with experienced readers on some aspect of music reading. The particular problem these studies have had to face is that of finding a way to measure the reading behavior of novices. Clearly one cannot expect absolute novices to sit down at a piano and play what they are shown. We need a response measure that does not put the nonmusician at a disadvantage, while retaining the requirement that a discrete response should be made to every note in the display. The solution adopted by Sloboda (1976a, 1978a) and Salis (1980) is to ask subjects to *copy* highly simplified excerpts of music notation (e.g. Figure 2.3) onto a bare stave after a brief viewing period. This parallels the 'reconstruction task' used by Chase and Simon (1973) in their now classic studies on chess skill. The copying task can be taught in a few minutes, and most musicians have not had extensive practice at this task.

In Sloboda's (1976a) experiments, subjects were presented with stimuli containing between one and six randomly chosen pitch symbols in the format exemplified by Figure 2.3. Under one condition subjects were able to observe the displays for 2 seconds; under another condition the stimuli were displayed for only 20 msec. Subjects were required to make a response for each note in the display, even if only guessing, and their responses were scored in terms of number of notes correctly copied. The two main effects were highly significant: musicians are better at this task than nonmusicians, and subjects perform best in the 2-second exposure condition. The interaction of these two effects was also significant: musicians performed much better than nonmusicians in the 2-second exposure condition, but they were not significantly better than nonmusicians at 20 msec, where both groups performed very poorly.

Figure 2.3 Simplified notation for copying experiments.

These results tell us that musicians do not read better than nonmusicians simply because they have better response organization. Arguably, the copying response eliminates this particular advantage which the better musicians in Bean's study had. Thus, the advantage must relate to input coding or storage processes. The interaction also tells us that musicians are unlikely to have a highly speeded input scanning rate in comparison to nonmusicians. If they did, then we would expect superiority at the brief exposure in the number of notes correctly recorded. The results suggest, instead, that musicians have more efficient coding and storage mechanisms than nonmusicians, so that, with adequate viewing time, they are better able to retain the details of the display.

One obvious contender for the mechanism that gives musicians the advantage in this task is some specifically musical coding of the notes. Musicians might code the stimulus as a little tune, or as a series of pitch intervals. To test this hypothesis a further series of experiments was carried out (Sloboda, 1976a) using various attempts to interfere with musicians' supposed coding processes, so eliminating the advantage over nonmusicians. Thus, subjects carried out the task while listening to various kinds of music and speech; in one condition they even had to remember a short melody while doing the primary task. It was hypothesized that if musicians were using a specifically *musical* code in storing the visual display, then their performance should be selectively disrupted by concurrent musical interference. Disappointingly, the results gave no support for this hypothesis whatsoever. None of the interference conditions had the slightest detrimental effect on the performance of any subject; indeed, some subjects actually improved with interference.

Experiments using this copying paradigm have been carried out many times by students in Smith's laboratory, and it has been used as the basis of one of the laboratory workshops in the collection by Bennett, Hausfield, Reeve, and Smith (1981). Smith (personal communication) testifies that the principal results described above are robust and have been replicated many times by her students. It is particularly reassuring to have this confirmation, for the lack of interference effects is puzzling and counterintuitive. Halpern and Bower (1979, 1982) were equally puzzled by this finding, and their experiments examine the 'interference problem' further.

In the Sloboda (1976a) studies, the musical interference condition was as follows. The subject listened to a short tone sequence of a length preelected during training so as to ensure equal difficulty for all subjects. Immediately after the sequence ended the subject observed the visual display, and then made his attempt at reproduction. Finally he heard a second tone sequence which could either be identical to the first sequence or differ from it by one note. He then had to judge whether the two tones were the same or different. So he was required to hold the tone sequence in memory while carrying out the reading task. Halpern and Bower reversed this design. In their experiment, the subject first observed the visual display, then carried out an interfering task, and finally attempted to reproduce the visual display. So the subject was required to hold the visual display in memory while carrying out the interfering task.

Halpern and Bower *did* obtain interference effects. Musicians performed worse with interference, while nonmusicians were not affected by the interference. Musicians were equally affected by two interference conditions, a visual and an auditory one. In the visual condition subjects classified a random selection of single notes into one of four sets, quarter or half-note, and high (above the middle line) or low (below the middle line). In the auditory condition subjects classified a similarly random collection of played notes into one of four sets, combining long–short in duration with high–low in pitch.

The most plausible explanation for the difference between the two studies is that musical interference disrupts retention and rehearsal processes, but does not disrupt coding and storage for immediate output. In other words, interference disrupts memorization for recall (in Halpern and Bower's case, after 15 seconds), but does not disrupt reading for immediate transcription. A possible reason for this is that musicians have overlearned mechanisms for immediate transcription gained precisely from years of reading experience, although they do not have well-developed mechanisms for retaining sections of score for recall many seconds later. This latter task is novel to most musicians, and performance on it, arguably, does not tell us much about reading mechanisms. In general it seems that automated and overlearned tasks are less susceptible to interference than novel tasks. What the Halpern and Bower study does suggest is that memorization from score does involve specifically *musical* mechanisms since only the musicians were disrupted by the two interference tasks, both of which could have engaged musical knowledge. However, it is possible that such knowledge is only mobilized *during* the 15-second retention period and does not contribute to normal reading.

A further study (Sloboda, 1978a) returned to another rather puzzling feature of the first experiments' results, the lack of any difference between musicians and nonmusicians at the 20-msec exposure. This was not a floor effect, since subjects were all performing significantly above chance. The result is puzzling because there is a body of literature that demonstrates that subjects are able to identify more of the information contained in a very briefly exposed display when the constituents of the display are familiar than when they are not (Allport, 1968; Welsandt, Zupnick, and Meyer, 1973). Since musicians are much more familiar with music notation than nonmusicians, why do they not outperform the nonmusicians? One possibility is that they *do* outperform the nonmusicians, but that a more sensitive measure than number of notes correct is required to demonstrate that superiority. Accordingly, in the Sloboda (1978a) study, various methods of scoring were used, giving credit for nearness in pitch to the correct note and preservation of the up–down contour of the original. Sure enough, some scoring methods did yield the hoped for superiority. Most significantly, musicians were better than nonmusicians at retaining the correct up–down relationships between adjacent pairs of notes, even though not necessarily positioning either note of a pair on the right line or space. These results can be interpreted as showing that 20 msec is too short a time for accurate localization of notes on a stave, but that it *is* sufficient time for global attributes of contour and shape to be registered. This is consistent with our understanding of visual perception in other domains (e.g., Navon, 1977; Palmer, 1977) and does not necessarily implicate musical knowledge in the process. Familiarity with the visual characteristics of music notation could be a sufficient explanation of the musicians' superiority.

It is also noteworthy that, in contrast to studies of experts and novices in other domains like chess, musicians show a superiority over nonmusicians even when, as in the Sloboda (1976a, 1978a) studies, the stimulus notes are chosen at random and do not form musically coherent patterns (in that they do not represent common structures or sequences within the system of diatonic tonality). Why this should be is not at all clear. Maybe the complete absence in nonmusicians of any knowledge about the names or functions of the individual symbols puts them at a disadvantage in *any* situation involving music notation. In contrast, it is hard to find a novice chessplayer with similar levels of ignorance about chess notation. Nevertheless, it is still worth asking whether musicians gain an additional advantage over nonmusicians when the stimuli 'make musical sense.' Halpern and Bower carried out a second experiment that directly addresses this question. They used immediate recall without interference, thus making the task of more direct relevance to music reading, and found indeed that musicians performed better on 'good' than 'bad' melodies, whereas nonmusicians showed no difference between the melody types.

This result provides the strongest indication so far that musical knowledge is implicated in reading, even though the reconstruction task is not identical in its requirements to normal reading.

2.5 Good readers compared to poor readers

Nonmusicians are severely limited in the range of responses they can give to music notation. To make direct comparisons between musicians and nonmusicians we must grossly simplify both stimulus and response in comparison to the habitual fare of the performing musician. Accordingly, this line of investigation cannot take us very far. Fortunately, music reading skills are distributed very unevenly through the population of musicians. Some otherwise competent performers are very poor readers. Others excel at reading. The task on which differences emerge most strikingly is that of 'sight-reading,' where the performer is required to provide a coherent performance of a piece of music he or she has never seen before. Sight-reading is to be contrasted to the case where a performer uses a score to guide performance of an already learned piece. In the latter case, the performer is using the score (probably selectively) as an *aide-mémoire* rather than as the primary source of information about the music. One may often observe that a performer hardly looks at the music for pages at a time. Clearly, his primary source of information about the music is stored in his long-term memory. The score is used, from time to time, simply to act as a retrieval cue for the next section of music. Sight-reading is, in contrast, a 'cleaner' and 'simpler' case of reading. The performer must examine the great majority of, if not all, the notes, and the success of his performance is directly related to the knowledge gained from this examination, uncontaminated with long-term knowledge about the particular piece of music. Of course, long-term knowledge of a *general* kind may be implicated, as it is in prose reading, and the use of such knowledge is, as we will see, precisely what distinguishes the expert from the ordinary player. The remaining studies reviewed in this paper are all concerned with sight-reading. Other types of reading, important as they are, are not treated further.

In any continuous transcription task, such as copy typing, simultaneous interpretation, or music reading, there is a time lag between the perception of a symbol and its subsequent realization in output. When a particular symbol is being spoken or played, the eye or ear is already receiving input from a symbol further ahead in the input. A simple way of demonstrating the existence of this lag is to suddenly remove the stimulus while a reader is engaged with it. Typically, performance does not stop dead exactly simultaneously with the removal of the stimulus. The reader is able to produce a little more output. The average amount of extra output available is known, in prose reading, as the 'eye–voice span' or in typing or instrumental music reading the 'eye–hand span.' For normal prose the eye–voice span (EVS) is about five or six words in adult readers. For simple tonal melodies the average instrumental eye–hand span (EHS) is about five or six notes. In a series of studies (Sloboda, 1974, 1977) it was found that EHS varied with both expertise and the nature of the material to be read. In one study (Sloboda, 1974), reading ability was estimated by counting the number of performance mistakes in a large corpus of sight-reading performances. People who made many mistakes had lower EHS (3–4 notes) than those who made few mistakes (6–7 notes). In addition (Sloboda, 1977), it was found that performers had greater EHS when reading tonally coherent music than when reading music that broke rules of tonal progression. In both these studies the experimental design was such that subjects were deprived of the score at various distances prior to a musical phrase boundary. It was found that there was a greater than chance likelihood of EHS coinciding with a phrase boundary. This effect interacted with reading ability. The best reader ended his performance at a phrase boundary on 72% of occasions, the worst reader on only 20% of occasions. Thus, for good readers, the EHS was not constant; it expanded and contracted to accommodate a phrase unit.

Here is incontrovertible evidence that musical knowledge is implicated in sight-reading. How, otherwise, would a reader know that a particular note marked a phrase boundary, prior to having heard the music? It is, of course, true that much printed music contains visual signs marking phrase boundaries other than the notes themselves, just as printed text contains punctuation marks. But in these experiments all such signs were eliminated from the score, and in one condition (Sloboda, 1977) even the long notes which often mark phrase endings were eliminated, so that the reader would have no clue to phrase subdivision other than the melodic, harmonic, and rhythmic logic of the note sequence itself. We conclude, then, that good sight-readers are particularly attuned to important superordinate structures within a score, structures that link notes together into musical groups. They organize their perception and performance in terms of discovering these higher order groupings, with consequential economy of coding.

It does not seem likely that these results could be explained purely in terms of response factors, such as the tendency for experts to improvise phrase endings that were not seen, or to stop short at a phrase close. On the first count, there are several plausible ways to improvise an ending to most phrases, but the data show almost no instances of erroneous yet plausible responses among the better readers. Their performances were almost error free. On the second count, readers were under strict instructions to play *all* the notes they saw and *only* the notes they saw. The subjects believed themselves to have complied with these instructions.

In sum, then, the EHS studies show that good readers 'look farther ahead' than poor readers and are more sensitive to the musical structure of what they read than poor readers. It is plausible to infer that the latter phenomenon is, in part, responsible for the former.

Turning away from EHS, we may ask whether good readers differ from poor readers in the *type* of sight-reading mistakes they make, in addition to their frequency. This question has been examined mainly in relation to 'proofreaders' error,' the tendency for readers to misperceive small inaccuracies in text as the 'correct' or 'intended' sequences. In prose, many readers fail to see small spelling or typing errors. Do musicians also fail to see 'misprints'?

Wolf (1976) reports the experience of a distinguished piano teacher and sight-reader, Boris Goldovsky, who discovered a misprint in a much used edition of a Brahms *Capriccio* only when a relatively poor pupil played the (musically impossible) printed note at a lesson. Goldovsky stopped the pupil, thinking her to have misread, but soon discovered that it was *he*, and countless other pupils and colleagues, who had misread, inferring a sharp sign in front of a note because in the musical context it *had* to be a G sharp, not, as printed, a G natural. So struck was he with his misperception, that he devised the 'Goldovsky experiment', which consisted in telling skilled readers that there was a misprint somewhere in the piece and asking them to find it. He allowed them to play the piece as many times as they liked and in any way that they liked. No musician ever found the mistake. Only when he told his subjects which bar (measure) the mistake was in did most of them spot it. (The piece is Brahms' op. 76, no.2, and the mistake occurs in bar 78, which is reprinted in Sloboda, 1978b).

Misprints of this nature are, thankfully, rare in printed music. To ascertain the generality of this effect, it is necessary to construct scores with 'deliberate' misprints. This was the purpose of an experiment reported in Sloboda (1976b). In this experiment subjects were presented with pieces of piano music that were littered with misprints. The pieces of music were in conventional classical style, composed by lesser known contemporaries of Mozart, and each misprint mislocated a note by one scale step on the stave in such a way that the resulting sequence was blatantly out of character, in virtue of containing an unprepared and unresolved discord. The subjects were all competent pianists and they were asked to give two performances of each piano piece at sight, being particularly careful to play exactly what was written. Although the overall level of error in performance was very low for all subjects (2.9% for first performance, 1.7% for second performance) the level of error on the misprints was high (38% for first performance, 41% for second performance). All the misplayings of these misprints conformed to proof readers' error, that is, subjects substituted the original correct notes, although, of course, they had never seen or heard the original music.

It is noteworthy that, although overall errors decreased on a second playing, proofreading errors *increased*. This suggests that what subjects had learned from a first playing were *not* only individual notes, but also some things about the overall melodic and tonal structure in virtue of which the misprint became even less likely to be spotted, contradicting, as they did, the tonal coherence of the pieces. Here, then, is further evidence that musical knowledge is implicated in reading. The Goldovsky experiment suggests that it is skilled, rather than unskilled, readers who are most likely to be susceptible to proofreaders' error, presumably because they are more likely to be reading for superordinate structures.

2.6 Master readers compared to good readers

Studies on skill such as those of Chase and Simon (1973) have taught us that we must expect significant changes in the structure of skill beyond the point of mere proficiency. There are, in any skill domain, those practitioners who by virtue of their excellence and experience deserve the title 'master.' A factor correlating very strongly with mastery is quite simply the time spent practicing the skill in question. A master has probably spent upward of 10 000 hours engaged with his skill, whereas the merely proficient practitioner has probably only spent some couple of thousands of hours on the same skill. We may expect to find as many significant differences between the master and the merely proficient as we do between the proficient and the novice.

For sight-reading, such differences have been studied with respect to expressive aspects of piano performance (Sloboda, 1983). For a performance to be musically effective, it must do more than present a listener with the right notes at the right speed; the performer must modulate tempo and dynamic in such a way that he provides a coherent, and possibly novel, insight into the structure of the music. The level of structure I wish to concentrate on here is that specified by the meter of a piece of music. Most conventional notated music specifies a subdivision of the musical stream into bars (measures) each containing the same number of beats (pulses) of notionally equal duration. The first beat of each bar is marked for the highest prominence (stress) within that bar, and for a listener to understand the music he must be able to identify the metrical contour from the first few notes of a performance. Sometimes the notes themselves allow only one coherent metrical reading (Steedman, 1977) but often the music is metrically ambiguous until the performer adds some expressive content. The most ambiguous sequence of all would be one made up of the same note repeated over and over again. Unless the performer modulates such a sequence in some way a listener may infer any meter he likes. Here, then, is one condition which, it can be argued, must be satisfied if a performer is to be said to have read the music effectively. Metrical information specified by the score should be specified in the performance too.

Shaffer (1980, 1981) has devised a means whereby all the objective features of a piano performance can be recorded on computer. If we deny a pianist the use of the pedals, then he has only three dimensions of variation available for expressive performance; the loudness of a note, onset timing, and offset timing. Shaffer's equipment allows one to record all these features by means of photocells attached to the piano mechanism. Using Shaffer's system it was possible to obtain full records of the expressive devices used by a group of pianists asked to sight-read a metrically ambiguous melody, notated twice, with different placement of metrical stress. Meter was signified in the score by the placement of bar lines and beams, and in no other way. The second notation was generated from the first by shifting the bar lines and beams one semiquaver (eighth-note) to the right in the score.

Subjects were asked to play each melody at sight five times in a row. The melodies were embedded in a longer series of test melodies; and no subject noticed that the two melodies contained the same notes. The instructions encouraged the performers to give each melody some musical character, to be reproduced as exactly as possible on the five consecutive performances, but no mention was made of meter. In a second experiment, audio recordings of the performances were played to listeners who had to try and identify which of the two notated forms each performance came from.

The subjects themselves ranged considerably in playing experience. The least experienced subject had been playing for about 11 years, and the most experienced subject, a professional pianist, had been playing for more than 40 years. The results showed many significant differences as a function of experience. First, the number of notes where the performance of the two melodies differed increased with experience. The masters made the two performances more distinct from one another. Second, the types of expressive devices used increased in number with experience. In particular, the less experienced players tended to concentrate on loudness variations at the expense of timing variations. The more experienced players used loudness variations too (stressed notes louder than unstressed notes) but supplemented them with timing variations (such as the slight delaying in the onset of the note *following* a stress). Third, the most experienced player was significantly better at communicating meter than the least experienced player. Listeners identified many more performances correctly.

Expressive aspects of piano performance result from the detailed planning of finger movements in advance of sound production. The pianist must know how loud he wants a particular note to sound, when he wants it to sound, and for how long, *before*, not after, he actually hears it. If it can be shown, as I believe we have shown here, that his allocation of expressive variation is governed by a fundamental aspect of musical structure such as meter, then it seems indisputable that knowledge of such musical structure is a direct consequence of the reading process, so proving music reading to be a real species of, and window onto, music perception.

2.7 Summary

This review of the small literature on music reading has been concerned to show that music reading is a genuine species of music perception, by demonstrating the various ways in which musical structure affects performance in readers of varying levels of expertise. Written recall of notes is improved when the sequence to be recalled is tonally coherent (Halpern and Bower, 1979, 1982); the eye–hand span is sensitive to musical phrase structure (Sloboda, 1974, 1977); errors in reading tend to be musically plausible (Sloboda, 1976b; Wolf, 1976); and expressive aspects of sight performance respond to structural aspects of the noted music (Sloboda, 1983). In general, the effects of musical structure are most pronounced in the more experienced readers, suggesting increasing mediation of representations couched in terms of formalisms which define relationships between groups of notes. Such mediating representations are being discovered to play an essential part in many music perception tasks (cf. Deutsch, 1982), and it is to be hoped that a fuller articulation of the nature of these representations will be instrumental in advancing our understanding of the whole range of skills (such as composition and improvisation) that can properly be called musical (cf. Sloboda 1982, 1985).

References

Ailport, D. A. The rate of assimilation of visual information. *Psychonomic Science,* 1968, **12**, 231–232.

Bean, K. L. An experimental approach to the reading of music. *Psychological Monographs*, 1938, **50**, Whole number 226.

Bennett, A., Haustield, S., Reeve, R. A., and Smith, J. *Workshops in cognitive processes.* London: Routledge and Kegan Paul, 1981.

Chase, W. G. and Simon, H. A. The mind's eye in chess. In W. G. Chase (Ed.), *Visual information processing.* New York: Academic Press, 1973.

Deutsch, D. (Ed.) *The psychology of music.* New York: Academic Press, 1982.

Halpern, A. R. and Bower, G. H. Interference tasks and music reading. Unpublished manuscript, Stanford University, 1979.

Halpern, A. R. and Bower, G. I-I. Musical expertise and melodic structure in memory for musical flotation. *American Journal of Psychology,* 1982, **95**, 31–50.

Navon, D. Forest before trees: the precedence of global features in visual perception. *Cognitive Psychology,* 1977, **9**, 353–383.

Palmer, S. E. Hierarchical structure in perceptual representation. *Cognitive Psychology,* 1977, **9**, 441–474.

Read, G. *Music notation.* London: Gollancz, 1974.

Salis, D. L. Laterality effects with visual perception of musical chords and dot patterns. *Perception and Psychophysics,* 1980, **28**, 284–294.

Shaffer, L. H. Analysing piano performance: A study of concert pianists. In G. E. Stelmach and J. Requin (Eds.), *Tutorials in motor behaviour.* Amsterdam: North Holland, 1980.

Shaffer, L. H. Performance of Chopin, Bach and Bartok: Studies in motor programming. *Cognitive Psychology,* 1981, **13**, 326–376.

Sloboda, J. A. The eye–hand span: an approach to the study of sight reading. *Psychology of Music,* 1974, **2**, 4–10.

Sloboda, J. A. Visual perception of musical notation: registering pitch symbols in memory. *Quarterly Journal of Experimental Psychology,* 1976a, **28**, 1–16.

Sloboda, J. A. The effect of item position on the likelihood of identification by inference in prose reading and music reading. *Canadian Journal of Psychology,* 1976b, **30**, 228–236.

Sloboda, J. A. Phrase units as determinants of visual processing in music reading. *British Journal of Psychology,* 1977, **68**, 117–124.

Sloboda, J. A. Perception of contour in music reading. *Perception,* 1978a, **7**, 323–331.

Sloboda, J. A. The psychology of music reading. *Psychology of Music,* 1978b, **6**, 3–20.

Sloboda, J. A. The uses of space in music notation. *Visible Language,* 1981, **15**, 86–110.

Sloboda, J. A. Music performance. In D. Deutsch (Ed.) *Psychology of music.* New York: Academic Press, 1982.

Sloboda, J. A. The communication of musical metre in piano performance. *Quarterly Journal of Experimental Psychology,* 1983, **35A**, 377–396.

Sloboda, J. A. (1985) *The musical mind: An introduction to the cognitive psychology of music.* London: Oxford University Press.

Steedman, M. J. The perception of musical rhythm and metre. The perception of musical rhythm and metre

Van Nuys, K. and Weaver, H. E. Memory span and visual pauses in reading rhythms and melodies. *Psychological Monographs,* 1943, **55**, 33–50.

Weaver, H. F. A study of visual processes in reading differently constructed musical selections. *Psychological Monographs*, 1943, **55**, 1–30.

Welsandt, R. F. Jr., Zupnick, J. J., and Meyer, P. A. Age effects in backward masking (Crawford Paradigm). *Journal of Experimental Child Psychology*, 1973, **15**, 454–461.

Wolf, T. A. cognitive model of musical sight reading. *Journal of Psycholinguistic Research*, 1976, **5**, 143–171.

CHAPTER 3

THE USES OF SPACE IN MUSIC NOTATION

3.1 Introduction

In this article I want to describe how space is used in music notation. Music notation is unfamiliar to many people and so I have attempted to make what I say intelligible to the non-musician by defining all the technical terms I use. Music notation (score) is very different from language notation (text) and so some prefatory comparative remarks may help to place this notation in a wider context.

Perhaps the most fundamental difference between score and text is that a score must be able to specify different events as occurring simultaneously whereas text portrays a single sequence of events. The problem of how to link up parallel streams of information has thus been fundamental to the development of score. No analogous problem exists for text. A second difference concerns use. Score readers are mainly concerned with producing a musical performance. Text readers are more concerned with understanding and remembering what they read. This difference makes issues of layout of foremost importance in a score. The music reader cannot afford to lose his place or experience ambiguity even for a second if he is to maintain the flow of performance. This demand has expressed itself in intense and prolific experimentation with different ways of arranging score material over the centuries. In contrast, the solitary text reader is able to pace his own reading to accommodate deficiencies in layout. Thus there has not been the same historical incentive to experiment with layout. Unhelpful layout may be a nuisance: but it hardly ever leads to total breakdown. A third difference concerns the levels at which spacing and layout become important. Score material presents the reader with diverse spatial information at a microscopic level. Any two-centimeter square of a modern score will contain a rich array of symbols at varying distances and directions from one another. In contrast a similarly sized portion of text is most likely to contain evenly spaced letters in evenly spaced rows. Interesting spatial differentiations occur, if at all, at the macroscopic level, and concern such matters as how paragraphs are sited. Another way of putting this difference is to say that in a score there are complex spatial constraints which determine the positioning of each notational element with respect to its neighbors, whereas in text the determination of the position of one letter in relation to its neighbors is trivially simple. Thus, layout is an integral part of the music notation system. In language notation it is an optional extra.

There are, of course, many points one could make which would tend to blur the clear lines drawn up by these distinctions. There is not one use for scores any more than there is for texts. It would be fair, however, to claim that these differences do characterise broad and prevailing tendencies within the two systems.

What follows from these comparisons? Firstly, spatial considerations in music notation are more complex and multi-levelled (and arguably more interesting) than spatial considerations in text. Secondly, perhaps as a result of the complexity, there has been little, if any, controlled experimentation using different spatial arrangements of music. And so, thirdly, this article cannot draw on published psychological research. Rather its aim is to present an historical and conceptual perspective on some of the major motivations for, and problems with, using space as a notational tool. In this task I draw most heavily on the work of musicologists and music historians, in particular the monumental study of Apel (1953). Other useful source and background material has been provided by Abraham (1979), Cole (1974), Hyatt-King (1964), Karkoschka (1972) and Read (1974).

Western musical civilization of the last 1500 years has produced a bewildering multiplicity of notational systems devised in different contexts and for different purposes. Nonetheless, today we would recognize one particular system as central. This is, to adopt Read's (1974) terminology, the *orthochronic* system. Figure 3.1 shows a typical portion of this notation. It has been the major western notational system for over 400 years, holding its place against all competitors even in this [twentieth] century which has seen a mushrooming growth of new notations. As the discussion proceeds I shall touch on various aspects of orthochronic notation, looking both at their development and at notational systems which have used space in different ways to achieve similar ends. Also, since any notational system can only meet limited needs, it is necessary to compare orthochronic notation with systems whose aims are different. Differing aims place differing demands on the available space.

3.2 Directions for action

A most important fact about orthochronic notation is, apparently, negative. It is impossible to tell, just by examining a typical extract, which instrument

Figure 3.1 A section of orthochronic notation showing the principal notational features.

the extract is intended for. The central features of the notation are abstract. They specify pitch and rhythmic relationships between notes and groups of notes, *not* what keys are to be pressed on an instrument nor precisely how the notes are to sound. They are intended to convey something of the musical structure to a reader. Psychological implications of this fact have been discussed by Sloboda (1978a, 1982). This characteristic probably explains why orthochronic notation has retained its central position. It is a lingua franca for all musicians, as understandable to a violinist as to a singer.

The corollary of this is that each instrumentalist must have additional practical knowledge before he can actually play the music. For instance, orthochronic notation may tell a flautist to play the note D, but it does not tell him which fingers to place over which holes to achieve the D. The wish to have a more direct notational aid to performance has sometimes led to the development of notations based upon a different principle—that of specifying actions on a particular instrument. Such notations achieve this end at the expense of universality. A notation devised for the violin would be meaningless to a trumpet player.

One large sub-group of such systems are the tablatures. Figure 3.2 is part of a French lute tablature of the sixteenth century. The horizontal lines represent the strings of the lute. The letters designate frets on the finger-board. In this example, the frets are marked by the letters B to H, with A denoting an open string. Tablatures use letters or numbers to specify at least part of

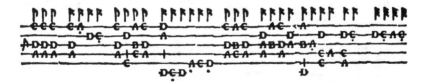

Figure 3.2 'Fortune a bien couru sur moi' from *Tres breve et familiere introduction pour entendre et apprendre par soy mesme a iouer toute chanson reduictes en la tabulature du Lutz.* Source: Apel (1953), p. 65.

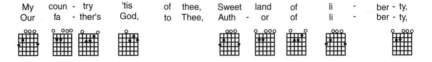

Figure 3.3 Chord sequence for 'My Country, 'tis of thee' (first line) in modern guitar notation.

the actions required. Some modern successors have eliminated alphabetic symbols completely in favor of graphic representation. A simple example of this is modern guitar notation (Figure 3.3) in which strings and frets are represented on a two-dimensional matrix, with dots to show the finger positions.

A more complex example is a modern system for the piano called Klavarscribo. In this system vertical lines represent the black keys on the piano, the spaces between representing white notes. The score is read from top to bottom, and the small circles represent the keys to be struck (unfilled circles are white notes). Figures 3.4 and 3.5 show the same extract from F. Chopin's Sonata op. 58 written in orthochronic notation and Klavarscribo. To the eye there is little to suggest that it is the same music in both cases.

When we go on to consider the detailed requirements of a developed music notation system, I shall wish to return to these examples to argue that the price paid for instrumental specificity is, in general too high, since it restricts the number of dimensions remaining for representing other important aspects of the music. An alternative approach which has worked very well for many instruments is to incorporate additional symbols into

Figure 3.4. A bar from F. Chopin, Sonata op. 58, in orthochronic notation. Source: Karkoschka (1972). p. 12.

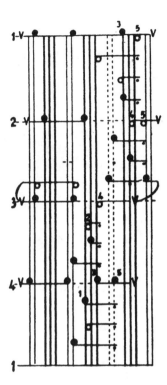

Figure 3.5 The same music as Figure 4 notated in Klavarscribo. Source: Karkoschka (1972), p. 12.

the orthochronic system without altering its basic characteristics. Thus, for instance, many piano scores contain small numbers over some of the notes, which prescribe fingering. There are also many simple symbols which can be placed over or under notes to specify such things as the nature of attack, loudness, phrasing. The spatial constraints here are rather indefinite. If there are too many of these additional symbols the score takes on a cluttered appearance, and there is a danger of overloading the reader with detail. Compare Figures 3.6 and 3.7 which are different editions of the same music. Figure 3.6 is crowded with specific performance directions. Figure 3.7 uses such directions sparingly. In general, editors must take a middle line between giving the performer no help at all (trusting to his own musical competence) and giving him so much that some of it is bound to be ignored. The trend recently has been towards the former approach, at least in respect to classical music. It is not coincidental that Figure 3.6 predates Figure 3.7 (a contemporary edition) by some decades.

Figure 3.6 Opening bars of 'Andante' from W. A. Mozart, Sonata in F, K. 533. (Ed. A. Zimmerman). London: Novello. Undated (c. 1900).

3.3 The staff

The most noticeable and characteristic feature of any segment of orthochronic notation is the grid of five horizontal lines on which the notes are placed. These lines are called staff-lines, with the five lines known, collectively, as a staff (plural staves). Unlike the tablatures, the function of the staff in orthochronic notation is to represent the pitch dimension. From earliest times pitch was seen as one of the most important aspects of music to notate. The earliest notations were alphabetic, dating at least as far back as pre-Christian Greece. In these systems each note of the scale was designated by a letter or other symbol. To notate a melody one simply wrote out the letters in the correct order. The first use of space to indicate pitch was the development of *neumes* in around the

Figure 3.7 The same music as Figure 3.6 (Ed. W. Lampe). München: Henle, 1955. Reproduced with the publisher's permission.

eighth century AD. These were used almost exclusively in the liturgy of the Christian Church to notate the plainchant melodies to which prayers were sung in religious communities. Figure 3.8 shows one of the earliest examples of neumes from a French manuscript c.871. The neumes are written above the Greek text and indicate the directions of pitch change. Thus ⟋ denoted a rise, ⟍ a fall, and ✓ a fall followed by a rise.

This system had no power to specify the extent of a pitch change, only its direction. Read (1974) comments 'Useful solely as a reminder to the singers, refreshing their memory of a general rise and fall originally learned by rote, the neumes provided only the over-all contour of the plainsong melodic line—not an exact map by which a novice might approach an unknown musical territory' (p. 7). This comment introduces a very important consideration, that of the context in which a notational system is used. Neumes did not do badly what orthochronic notation does better. They probably served the cultural and psychological requirements of their users better than modern notation would have done. They had an economy of symbolism which exactly served its purpose within monastic choirs, where novices would learn most of what they needed through repeated hearing of the same hymns. It was only, possibly, as chants elaborated and diversified that more precise mnemonic systems were necessary.

The next conceptual development was the use of vertical distance to indicate the extent of the pitch change. Figure 3.9 shows an early example from the tenth century which places neumes relative to a single horizontal line given a precise pitch (F below middle C in this example). The distance of a neume from this line gives an indication of its pitch distance from F.

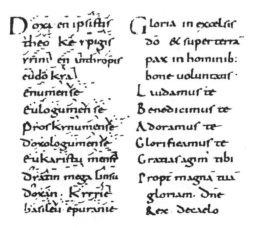

Figure 3.8 'Gloria' from a St. Amand manuscript c. 871. Paris: Bibliotheque Nationale, ms. lat. 2291. Reproduced with the Trustees' permission. Source: Abraham (1979), p. 62.

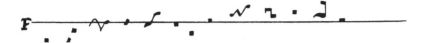

Figure 3.9 Tenth century neume notation (author unknown). Source: Read (1974), p. 10.

The difficulty with this, from a modern musician's point of view, is that the y-axis is not calibrated. A reader cannot easily tell what range of pitches is covered, nor the exact distance of any particular neume from the baseline. Both these problems were solved over the next two centuries by the addition of further horizontal lines denoting other precise pitches. By the 12th century the number of lines had reached four. This number seems to have been supported by two principles. One was that lines were provided for alternate pitches in a scale. Thus, the bottom line might represent A, the space above it B, the next line C, the next space D, and on. This principle remains in operation today in orthochronic notation. It means that the pitch of a note need never be estimated by reference to its physical distance from another point on the paper. It can be identified precisely by counting up the staff lines. For experienced readers, even this is not necessary. The position of the note is directly known by a kind of spatial subitising. The look of each position on a staff becomes so distinctive that no conscious counting is required.

The second principle was that the number of staff lines was tailored to the pitch span of the melodies. Most melodies could be encompassed within nine successive pitches of a scale. This span (about an octave) would be the comfortable range of an average untrained male voice. Even in the 12th century most notated music was church music sung exclusively by monks. As time passed, however, it became more customary for instrumental music to be noted on a staff. Instruments have larger pitch spans than voices, and so more lines were needed to encompass the melodies that could be played on instruments. Six lines were fairly common and up to fifteen were known. Somehow things settled down and the five lines of modern orthochronic notation became the norm. Although it is impossible to know this with certainty, it seems probable that one of the reasons why the five-line staff survived is that it represents the best compromise between good span and readability. Figure 3.10 presents a ludicrously extreme example of the readability problem. This is part of a composition by E. Brown (1952). There are fifty staff lines, and it is practically impossible for a reader to keep any bearings at all. Luckily for the performer, Brown does not intend the lines to be taken seriously, but

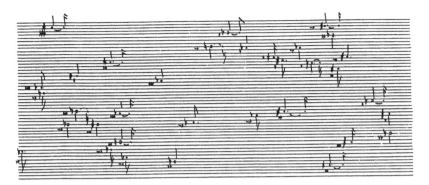

Figure 3.10 'November 1952' from Folio by E. Brown. New York: Associated Music Publishers Inc. Reproduced with the publisher's permission. Source: Karkoschka (1972), p. 90.

the moral is clear enough. There is a limit to the number of lines a staff can contain if a performer is to use it to rapidly identify the pitches of successive notes. This presents a problem within orthochronic notation when melodies span more than eleven notes of a scale, as frequently happens. The problem has been solved in three ways, all in common use today.

The first solution is to recalibrate the staff as the melody rises above or falls below the range of the staff. This is conventionally done by arbitrary symbols known as clef signs. The leftmost symbol in Figure 3.1 is the treble clef sign, and it indicates that the bottom line of the staff is to be read as the E above middle C. There are four or five such symbols in common use, and when one of them occurs in the course of a piece of music it instructs the reader to recalibrate everything from that point onwards until another clef sign is encountered.

For tunes which skip about a lot, clef signs are, however, rather unsatisfactory. If the clef must be changed every few notes the reader will spend as much time interpreting the clef symbols as the notes themselves. Another solution which is in common use is to temporarily extend the staff by ledger lines. The first note of Figure 3.1 is on a ledger line and the reader is asked to interpret it as if it were another staff line below the lowest one shown. In fact, the reader may imagine the staff is extending indefinitely both above and below its visible portion, but to avoid the problems associated with Figure 3.10 only that portion of it becomes visible which allows a single note to be identified. Thus, ledger lines extend only as far on either side of a note as to make them clearly visible. Most fluent readers become adept at rapidly interpreting up to five ledger lines. With more lines, problems of readability again develop. Figure 3.11 shows two

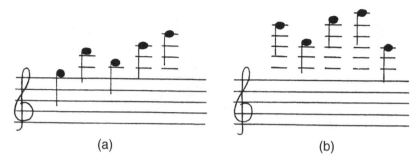

Figure 3.11 Two examples of the use of ledger lines: (b) is more difficult to read than (a).

extracts using ledger lines; (a) would be easily read by most competent readers today; (b) would not be fluently read.

At this juncture a comment about the vertical spacing of staff lines and ledger lines is pertinent. Although not logically necessary, it has always been standard practise to make the distances between adjacent staff-lines equal to one another. This has meant that the vertical distance between notes is an accurate measure of the pitch distance between them.

Although this information is technically redundant, it does provide readers with an additional analog cue to pitch which arguably supplements the 'digital' information supplied by the lines themselves. There is, for instance, some evidence that music readers can be aware of the contour of a notated melody before they can precisely identify the constituent notes (Sloboda, 1978b). It is unclear how much use competent musicians make of this information in performing situations, but one informal observation supports its importance. It sometimes happens that staves are printed so close together that there is a difficulty about placing a note on, say, the fifth ledger line. If the spacing of the ledger lines were to preserve the spacing of the staff lines, they would come too close to, or overlap, the adjacent staff. In such a situation the ledger lines are squashed closer together. This, of course, upsets the analog representation of pitch, and many musicians complain bitterly that such notes are very difficult to read, especially if the music is unfamiliar. In the best publishing houses this crowding of ledger lines never occurs. The solution is, of course, to move the staves further apart, but with fewer staves to the page, production expenses increase. This probably accounts for the persistence of this troublesome practice. An allied point concerns the size of a staff. This has both psychological and economic implications. If staff lines are too close together the reader has problems of discrimination, especially if he must be at some distance from the score when performing. Conversely, if the lines are too far apart then it may be impossible to see the stave clearly with a single fixation. Similarly, from the printer's point of view, closely spaced lines demand finer (and thus more expensive) printing. Widely spaced lines mean fewer staves per page and thus more pages. Engraving tradition seems to have settled on a between-staff-line distance of about 0.20 to 0.25 cm as suitable for most performing scores.

The third solution to the problem of increased melodic span we owe to the rise of polyphonic music in the middle ages. Polyphonic music is that where several streams of notes are performed simultaneously. This type of music can be vocal, where different singers take different melodies simultaneously. It can be for an instrumental group, where, for instance, different pipe instruments play different notes. Or it can be for a keyboard instrument played by one performer producing simultaneous sounds with different hands and fingers.

In all these cases, the notational problem is to indicate which person or hand takes which stream of notes. To put all the notes on to a single staff would be to overcrowd it hopelessly if more than a couple of parts were involved. So the solution arrived at fairly early was to give each part a separate staff. These staves were vertically aligned and joined in some way to indicate simultaneity. A typical example of this is given in Figure 3.4. This is part of a piano piece—the curved bracket at the left indicates that the two staves are to be played simultaneously, the upper by the right hand, the lower by the left hand. This arrangement is necessary when a single performer must read both staves simultaneously: the relevant portions must clearly be as close to one another as possible. It also provides an ideal vehicle for extending the span of pitches which can be notated. This is because the two staves can be calibrated differently by clef signs, as in Figure 3.4. Suitably calibrated, the piano score has over twice the pitch span of a single staff. In the notation of symphonic music this system can be extended indefinitely, twenty staves being a not uncommonly large number for a conductor's score. Of course, in this case many of the staves overlap closely in pitch calibration, or, indeed, are identical. Each staff is identified with the name of the appropriate instrument at the left of the page.

It remains to add that this score arrangement is not the only possible or desirable one for polyphonic music. When many performers are involved it often makes sense to arrange things so that each performer has primary access to his own part. Figure 3.12 shows in diagrammatic form the three major ways in which a polyphonic composition can be arranged in space. In this example three parts are shown, but the same principles can apply to any number. The full, dashed, and dotted lines represent the staves for the three

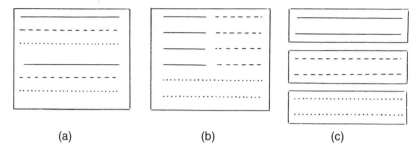

Figure 3.12 Three arrangements for polyphonic scores.

separate parts or instruments; (a) is the score arrangement just described, and would be typified by any organ score (separate staves for right hand, left hand and feet); (b) is an arrangement whereby each part is confined to a circumscribed area on the page. Although the other parts would be visible to a performer they would not get in his way. This arrangement is typical for one piano, three players music and for much medieval vocal music where each part was to be taken by one singer. In (c) each part is physically separate and can be distributed around the room among the various performers. This is the usual format for modern orchestral players where their own part may be one of as many as fifty different parts going on simultaneously. Of these systems, (a) is undoubtedly the oldest. It allows the reader to keep a direct check on the synchrony of the parts. Examples (b) and (c) make visual checks progressively more difficult. The survival of (c) depends upon the development of cues to synchrony. One, outside the scope of this article, is the conductor, who provides an external reference for a group of performers through his gestures. Probably more crucial was the development of methods for notating cues to synchrony and timing within individual parts. It is to this second major dimension that we now turn.

3.4 Bars, timing and rhythm

We have seen how orthochronic notation has commandeered the vertical dimension for notating pitch. It is only a first approximation to say that the horizontal dimension represents time. Temporal aspects are certainly represented, but not in any strict analog sense. Distance from left to right is not a direct measure of time elapsed. To understand how time notation works it is necessary to return to its beginnings in history.

As we have seen, most of the early notations were designed for singing liturgical chant. Thus there were two parallel notations—one giving the words in an orthography essentially that of today—the other, usually above the words, giving musical directions. In addition, the early music was all homophonic. No matter how many people sang, they all sang the same melody. It would not be unfair to say that up to about the thirteenth century the only timing information explicitly supplied by the musical notation was that of order; the order of the successive words and the pitches to which they were to be sung. If there were differences in the duration of the notes then these were possibly suggested by the flow of the words, or were part of an oral tradition of timing which had grown up in particular communities. Thus, while pitch notation continued to develop towards the modern staff system, the temporal aspect remained undeveloped until the thirteenth century. At that time notational distinctions between long and short notes began to be made.

For some reason, the strategy of using space to indicate time was not adopted. A compelling explanation for this is that scribes felt themselves constrained by the parallel vocal text. From the appearance of Figure 3.13 one could guess that the scribe had written out the words before embarking on the music. The spacing of the letters and the words is very regular; that of the notes is quite irregular. Clearly, the main consideration was to ensure that the right notes fell over the right syllables. This is what determined the spacing of notes, and so timing had to be indicated in some other way. In general, this was done by altering the shapes or appendages of the notes. In this example, from a thirteenth century French manuscript there are three types of note: squares with stems, squares, and diamonds, denoting long, short and shorter notes respectively. It is along this path that rhythmic notation continued to develop despite the fact that much notated music now came to be instrumental, and so without constraint of words.

The history of the subsequent development of rhythmic notation is of some complexity, but certain principles emerged which have remained with us to the present day. One was that note durations were conceived as simple multiples of each other. The other was that simple combinations of durations would often recur several times thus setting up a rhythmic grouping. A simple example of this, as apposite to the twentieth as to the thirteenth century, is given in orthochronic time notation in Figure 3.14(a). In this example the white (unfilled) notes have twice the duration of the black (filled) notes. If the duration of the black note is taken as one unit, then we can see a repeating pattern every three units. This is expressed today by saying that a triple metre is being used. When the rhythm is more elaborate, it is not so easy to determine what the repeating grouping should be just by examination of the note values. Sometimes a sequence

Figure 3.13 'Ave beatissima' from the Codex Montpellier (thirteenth century). Montpellier: Bibliotheque de l'Ecole de Medicine. MS. H 196, p. 93. Reproduced with the Trustees' permission. Source: Apel (1953), p. 291.

can be grouped in more than one way. In these cases, some notational means of specifying the grouping directly is required. It is required because rhythmic groupings have important performing implications. For instance, the first note in each rhythmic group is typically accented in some way (e.g. played louder). This is particularly important for communicating the rhythmic structure to a listener. A direct and visually compelling

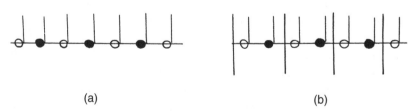

(a)   (b)

Figure 3.14 Rhythmic notation.

cue to rhythm is particularly useful when the musician is reading unfamiliar music 'at sight'. Under these conditions he will not have time to work out the rhythmic structure from the note sequence itself. In more leisured study circumstances, or where the music is already partly familiar, direct cues are not so crucial. In modern times sight-reading is required of musicians in many circumstances. The same was not true 700 years ago. The possibility of effective sight-reading has rested upon the emergence of two notational devices.

The first of these is an indication, at the beginning of a sequence, of the number and type of notes in each metrical grouping. This is achieved by two numbers (see Figure 3.1). The upper number tells the reader whether the recurring grouping is 2, 3, 4 or whatever number of units. The bottom number specifies the unit. These two numbers together comprise the time signature of a piece, and in Figure 3.1 this signature indicates a triple meter, with the filled note (known as a quarter-note in America) as the unit.

The time signature, however, leaves a very important question unanswered, for it does not tell the reader which note is the first, accented, note in each group. One cannot simply assume that the first note printed is given the accent. Many tunes begin on an unaccented note. Furthermore, it would be quite difficult for a reader to keep track of the meter through a long piece without dropping a note. A recurrent cue is required. This is supplied, in orthochronic notation, by bar lines. These are vertical lines, running the extent of a staff, which precede the first note in each metrical unit. A bar is the space between two adjacent bar lines, and so each bar contains a complete metrical unit with its first, accented, note at its leftmost edge. The correct barring for Figure 3.14(a) is shown in Figure 3.14(b).

Regular metrical barring did not become widespread until the sixteenth century, but when it did if offered a number of cues to synchronization. The first is the use of bars as a tally in part performance (Figure 3.12(c)). If a performer knows the meter and the speed he can keep track of the music by counting the bars. In symphony orchestras a primary responsibility of a conductor is to maintain the beat, moving his arms in such a way as to clearly indicate the timing of the first note in each bar (the down-beat) and the regular progression of metrical units during each bar. Performers may then tally each downbeat with a bar on their score. In addition, many parts actually number the bars so that in rehearsal performers can agree to 'start from bar 50'.

The second cue to synchronization is available only in parallel score arrangements (Figure 3.4 and 3.12(a)). This is achieved by vertically aligning bar lines in the separate parts. In many instances the bar line will be ruled right down the whole system of parallel staves to make more salient the points of synchrony. Figure 3.15 shows an early example from Italy (Naples, 1603), transcribed using modern conventions in Figure 3.16. Two features are of note. One is that when some parts contain many short notes the bars must be widened to accommodate them legibly. Thus bars are not of regular size. The trend in modern orthochronic notation has been to attempt to minimize difference in size between successive bars, although it is not possible to eliminate it entirely. In some music, a bar may contain so many notes that it requires the whole width of a page. To maintain this width for bars containing only one or two notes has little psychological advantage, and severe economic disadvantage. The other feature is that the distance between adjacent notes in parallel parts cannot be kept constant if the bars are to be aligned. The clearest example of this in Figure 3.15 comes in the third bar, where the top two parts have many closely spaced notes, whilst the bottom two parts contain only few notes. In this example, and in general up to at least the eighteenth century, no consistent method for spacing out the notes within a bar was adopted. Thus, although bar-lines provided conceptual points of synchrony for a reader, one could not drop a plumb-line at any other point within a bar and expect any synchrony between the notes encountered in the various parts. The time dimension from left to right was stretched and contracted quite arbitrarily within each bar. It is worth noting that in some early scores the bar lines were not even straight. What appears to have happened is that bar-lines became so useful to musicians that scribes often went back over old un-barred scores to put the bar-lines in. In these older scores there was often no attempt whatsoever to maintain vertical alignment of parts, and scribes were apparently too hard-pressed to write out the music afresh. So one finds examples like the splendid British keyboard

Figure 3.15 From A. Mayone *Primo libro di diversi capricci per sonare* Naples, 1603, p. 70. Source: Apel (1953), p. 17.

Figure 3.16 Transcription of first three bars of Figure 3.15 using the conventions of modern orthochronic notation.

score (circa 1540) in Figure 3.17, where the clumsy barring indicates the extent of the visual splits which early keyboard players were required to perform. Notational clarity apart, a modern keyboard performer would find it impossible to sight-read such a score. I suspect that a sixteenth century player would have found it equally difficult, and it suggests that such a score would have had rather different purposes—perhaps archival, perhaps as an aid to a performer attempting to memorize a piece, or perhaps as a starting point for an improvisation.

It was not really until the nineteenth century that what we now see as a logical corollary of bar-lines, namely proportional spacing of notes, came to be widely accepted. It is now standard notational practice to make systematic use of the space within the bar. Two main principles summarize this practice:

Firstly, notes which begin simultaneously must be vertically aligned. This has the useful consequence for, say, a pianist, that all the notes he

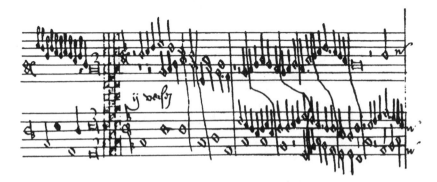

Figure 3.17 From a keyboard manuscript. London, 1540. British Museum, Ms. Add. 29996, p. 117. Reproduced with the Trustees' permission. Source: Apel (1953), p. 11.

must play simultaneously can be seen from a single vertical slice of score. This supersedes an earlier, intermediate, principle of spacing whereby a note occupied the centre of the time-space allotted to it, rather than the left-hand boundary of that space. This meant that a keyboard player had to scan horizontally as well as vertically to find the notes which had to be played together. Figure 3.18 shows a small extract from a score of a Handel organ concerto; (a) is an early printed score (c. 1800?); (b) is a modern reprinting. The clearest example of the change can be seen at the beginning of the second bar. In (b) the three notes to be played simultaneously are precisely aligned; in (a) there is considerable divergence, particularly for the top note, which, because it lasts for the whole bar, is placed almost in the middle of the bar.

Secondly, the space between a note and the following note must be proportional to the time between their respective onsets. This has always been interpreted rather loosely. It is not necessary that the space following a particular note need be twice that of a note with half its duration, only that the space be discernibly larger to the reader. This principle, in fact, follows as a necessary consequence of the first principle applied to parallel staves.

Figure 3.18 (a) From G. F. Handel, Organ concerto Op. 4 No. 3. Publisher unknown, c. 1800. Source: Cole (1974), p. 58. (b) The same music as (a). Ed. K. Matthaei. Kassel: Barenreiter, 1956, p. 59. Reproduced with the publisher's permission.

It is, however, used nowadays, even in cases where the constraints of alignment do not strictly require it. Thus, as in the pitch dimension, analog spatial information about timing is available to the reader as a formally redundant cue. Again, what psychological evidence exists is consistent with the idea that, at least in some circumstances, readers make use of proportional spacing of notes in organizing their perception of the score (Sloboda, 1977). To illustrate the principles of proportional spacing in an extended orthochronic example, I offer as Figure 3.16 my own transcription of the example in Figure 3.15 (first three bars).

3.5 How well does music notation use space?

The preceding sections outlined the principal spatial characteristics of orthochronic notation and its forbears. In this final section I wish to turn to questions of greater generality: to look at music notation not from the point of view of musical history, but from that of the formal study of symbolic systems. This shift in perspective allows us to focus less on questions of development and more on questions of information content, symbolic structure and psychological effectiveness. Any musical notation system must code certain types of information about the music. It uses particular symbols in particular spatial arrangements to represent this information, and has a greater or lesser effectiveness in conveying this information to the reader in a manner consistent with his requirements. These issues can be examined without reference to the historical context of particular notational systems. What follows is an outline of the way in which these issues may be expanded and articulated to form a conceptual framework within which systematic scientific evaluation of alternative notations could be carried out. It is necessary, I believe, to say something about these three issues separately, although the overall goodness of a system will be the result of a combination of factors from the three levels.

(a) *Information content.* The information conveyed by different musical systems can vary in two major respects: how specific the information is, and what type of information is conveyed. The notion of specificity is best conveyed by two extreme examples. Figure 3.19 is the score of a contemporary composition in which the performer is asked to contemplate what he sees and play anything that the pattern suggests to him. No detailed rules are supplied for interpreting the various elements. Thus there is no sense in which particular elements of the display correspond to particular sounds or features of the music. At the other extreme are notations which almost totally specify each sound. Some modern electronic compositions achieve such specificity by giving the precise details of all the oscilators,

Figure 3.19 Sheet 3 of A. Logothetis, *Cycloide*. Munich; Edition Modern, MusikVerlag Hans Werwerka, 19. Reproduced with the publisher's permission. Source: Karkoschka (1972), p. 129.

filters, etc. Orthochronic notation is specific in that it provides information about each note in a piece of music. Of course, even in such a case, specificity can vary according to how much information about each note is provided. Sometimes only one or two dimensions of the sound (e.g. pitch and duration) are notated. Sometimes many more dimensions of the sound are specified. The need for specificity poses certain formal problems for a notation system. One is how to represent the order of events. Another is how to correlate the elements in the various dimensions which refer to the same note. How do we show, for instance, that a given note has a pitch x, a duration y, and an intensity z?

At a given level of specificity there can be further variation in the *type* of information represented. One distinction of type was mentioned in Section 3.2, that between systems which notate actions (e.g. the tablatures) and those which notate aspects of the sound. If any consideration were to limit the number of dimensions which could be notated, then the different types of information would have to be traded of against one another. Increased specificity in one area would imply decreased specificity in another.

(b) *Symbolic structure.* By structure is meant both the nature of the symbols chosen and their spatial arrangement. Design of the structure becomes a formal problem when some degree of specificity is required.

There are a whole set of solutions to this problem which we could characterize as essentially non-spatial. As an example, we could assign each event a number (1 being the first event, 2 being the second, and so on) and then make certain statements about the various characteristics of each event (e.g. '2 has a pitch of 565 Hz', '7 has an intensity of 65 dB', etc.) These statements could be arranged on the page in an arbitrary order. One's immediate feeling that such a system would be pointless (i.e. ineffective) does not invalidate it as a perfectly consistent and correct way of symbolizing the specified dimensions of the music. Nonetheless, a notation system could utilize the space provided by the writing surface in a more systematic fashion. The most primitive use of space is to order the elements in some way. With music, the ordering is nearly always temporal. Information about the first note is spatially adjacent to information about the second note, and so on. This is, presumably, because temporal order is the dimension which *makes* music. In the example just given, one could achieve this characteristic by grouping all the statements about event 1 together at the top of a page, with all the statements about event 2 following immediately below, and so on. This could be structurally described as a list. The next advance on a list is a matrix. Here, the two spatial dimensions of a page are utilized systematically. Thus, for instance, the horizontal dimension might represent the temporal order of events, with the various characteristics of each event separated out vertically down the page. So, for example, reading across one row would give the pitches of successive notes, reading across another row would give their intensities, and reading down a column would give all the features of a single event. (I owe much of my conceptualization of structure and some of the terminology to Twyman (1979).)

A different use of the two dimensions might be called 'co-ordinate'. Here, both horizontal and vertical dimensions represent ordinal axes on which some 2-dimensional function may be plotted. Orthochronic notation can be seen, in part, as a graph of the pitch (y)–time (x) function, each note plotted as a point on the graph. Matrix and co-ordinate notations can be made very powerful by the use of two other supplementary devices, partition and clustering. In partitioning, one divides the page up into discrete areas where space may serve a different function. Thus, for instance, in Figure 3.15 the pitch dimension is not represented continuously in the vertical dimension. It only operates within each staff, recalibrated for each. The space between the staves has no pitch implications at all, and so other, pitchless information may be placed here. In some modern scores, for instance, a rising and falling line between staves is given to indicate increases and decreases in speed. A most imaginative use of partitioning is shown in Figure 3.20. This is the second page of Busotti's *Siciliano*. Here, vertical space within staves is interpreted conventionally, but the slant of a staff indicates the degree of acceleration or deceleration of speed. Dotted vertical lines indicate points of synchrony.

Clustering refers to the practice of representing several dimensions of an event, not by separate symbols, but by different aspects of a composite symbol. Thus, a note's position could indicate its pitch, whilst its shape indicated its duration, and its color indicated its intensity. This is a useful economy of space, which allows one to compact several rows or columns of a matrix into one.

These strategies, in their detailed operation, would seem to account for most of what one could say about the possible structures of music notation

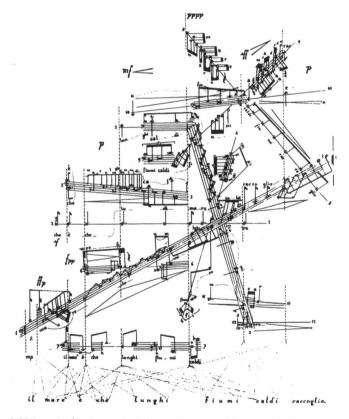

Figure 3.20 Page 2 of S. Bussotti, *Siciliano*. Florence: Aldo Bruzzichelli, 1962. Reproduced with the publisher's permission. Source: Karkoschka (1972), p. 94.

systems. When a combination of all the strategies is available there would seem to be very few formal limits on the number of specific dimensions which could be represented by a symbolic system. If questions of how well space is used have significance at this level, it is with respect to the economy of space. A system which allows clear representation of twenty pieces of information has a claim to greater efficiency than one which allows representation of only ten pieces of information within the same area of space. But for a criterion of what constitutes a clear representation, we must turn to the final, psychological level of analysis.

(c) *Psychological effectiveness.* Music notations are for use by readers. Their effectiveness is the extent to which readers are able to retrieve the information about the music which they supply. Effectiveness is not simply a function of the symbolic structure of the score, nor of the information it contains, but of the conditions under which a reader is expected to retrieve the information. These conditions may include general factors of human psychological functioning; they certainly include factors specific to the particular reading situation. All I am able to do here is to enumerate a representative sample of issues pertaining to psychological effectiveness. Although these issues are all empirically determinable, almost none have received rigorous empirical treatment.

A fundamental issue I have already referred to is the extent to which a reader is expected to provide a coherent performance of the music at first sight. Clearly, the more the reader must do without prior knowledge, the more constraints are placed upon what is an acceptable notation. Some of these constraints are straightforward matters of legibility. Even within a single notational system clarity and consistency can vary greatly according to the care with which a score is laid out and the nature of the reproduction process. It is distressing to discover that many of the parts which players in major symphony orchestras must use (at least in Britain) are shockingly presented and reproduced. Figure 3.21 shows a not untypical example of the kind of thing an orchestral player must put up with. It has not been determined how much this upsets performance. Certainly the players themselves complain bitterly. A major difficulty is spatial uncertainty. This can occur when staff lines are badly printed, or too close together. In this case it is sometimes difficult to see which line a note is centered on. A similar problem occurs when noteheads are too large with respect to the staff lines. A different type of spatial uncertainty is caused when ancillary marks are not properly aligned with the notes, or when they are too far from the staff to allow easy estimation of their alignment.

These considerations lead to the wider issue of discriminability. When a notation system uses a large number of different symbols, two different

Figure 3.21 Extract from an orchestral part used by a British symphony orchestra, date and publisher unknown.

symbols can often look very much alike. If a reader is expected to discriminate the symbols at speed, then he will arguably be helped by symbols which are as different as possible in appearance. On the other hand, if he is to perceive relations between different notes then he will also arguably be helped by symbols which preserve that relationship (e.g. symbols for notes close in pitch will be more like one another than symbols for notes not similar in pitch). The analog representations of pitch and time in orthochronic notation are based directly on this latter principle. Here, closeness in space maps directly on to closeness in pitch and time. When space is the notational dimension then it is possible to achieve increased discriminability simply by expanding the axes (i.e. make the staves larger and the notes farther apart). But to do this raises problems in a different area, that of the visual span and eye-movements.

If a reader is to use the score to organize immediate performance then he must take in all the information required for a particular action with as few fixations as possible. An average rate of performance for a moderately demanding piano piece might be ten notes per second (some of them executed simultaneously). It would be difficult to achieve more than four or five separate fixations in this time, and so the information required must necessarily be contained in a small area. Expanding the dimensions of the symbols would increase the number of fixations required to read the same number of symbols. Thus an effective notational system also has to be compact, and this poses problems when more than one dimension of the same event must be notated. The conventional matrix would be unhelpful because different aspects of one note could be spread right down a page. The device which arguably saves orthochronic notation is the clustering described in the previous sub-section. By using different visual aspects of the same symbol (position, shape) to indicate different sound aspects of the same note (pitch, duration) one can increase the visual density of the information at little expense to clarity. In general, a system such as the staff system would seem to be able to support about five different dimensions of sound without difficulty. For instance, the two spatial dimensions could represent pitch (vertical) and order (horizontal). Shape of note is a third dimension which could be used to represent duration. Ancillary symbols above and below the note could represent intensity and phrasing. There is, however, clearly some limit to the number of dimensions which could be usefully added in this way. This shows itself in lute notation (Figure 3.2) where note shape is used to designate which fret to touch, at the expense of a means of signifying duration. Klavarscribo fits in an extra dimension only because the arrangement of keys on a piano is isomorphic with the pitch dimension. Thus, the same horizontal information specifies both pitch and which key should be pressed (Figure 3.5).

A final requirement of a system that is to be read at sight is universality. One can only become proficient at reading any system if one encounters a large body of music written in that notation. Many contemporary notation systems are ruled out on this count because they are designed by the composer with a particular composition in mind, and are used only for this composition. Thus, Brown's fifty-line staff (Figure 3.10) has never been used before or since his one composition. Many contemporary notations are designed with the expectation that a performer will devote considerable time to a study of the particular score and its notation before a performance is possible. It would be inconceivable to arrange a performance of Busotti's *Siciliano* (Figure 20) at sight. Neither he nor his performers would wish for that. Similarly no notational system devised prior to about 1500 would have been read at sight. Musical culture just did not require it.

Today, musicians accustomed to reading orthochronic notation at sight become very sensitive to slight changes in notational practice. One simple spatial example concerns the positioning of note-stems (the vertical lines attached to notes). The modern convention is that descending stems are attached to the left edge of a note-head, ascending stems to the right. Some earlier scores reversed this convention. Informationally and structurally this has absolutely no consequences at all, but it is psychologically disruptive. Such scores are more difficult to read at sight, and the subjective impression is of something quite wrong about them.

Even when reading at sight is not required, a score's primary function is to assist a musician in performance. In such cases the score may be used to elicit learned response patterns in the correct sequence. This means that the performer must be able to keep place in the score, even if he does not use all the information in it. When detailed prompting is required, he must be able to find the appropriate information rapidly and effectively. Thus, many of the psychological considerations pertinent to reading at sight remain important in less extreme reading situations. Compactness and discriminability are still necessary. Consistency in positioning of information is also important. A reader must be able to know exactly where to go for particular types of information, even if he does not always need them. For instance, in a conventional orthochronic score, information about intensity is always to be found below the staff.

Two concluding remarks are in order. First, I hope to have shown that spatial factors in music notation are of some complexity and importance, and that there are several frameworks within which empirically determinable questions about efficiency of alternative arrangements may be asked. Second, I need to emphasize that nearly all my remarks about the psychological aspects of music reading are based on personal experience and accounts of other musicians rather than on rigorous investigation. Although it is to be hoped that serious empirical work will be undertaken. I should perhaps finish by firing one warning shot across the bows. Efficiency can only be meaningfully estimated where a reader is as familiar with the system in question as he is with the accustomed system with which the experimental system is being compared. Failure to find an immediate effect of some notational change does not imply that there will be no effect after the months or years of familiarization that has been received by the accustomed system. Any evaluation of notational reform is going to be a long-term process, and one which will require a considerable commitment from musicians who are required to learn and operate with new systems. Any short-term experimentation is almost bound to lead to the erroneous conclusion that orthochronic notation as it now stands is the best of all possible systems.

References

Abraham, G. *The Concise Oxford History of Music.* London: Oxford University Press, 1979.

Apel, W. *The Notation of Polyphonic Music 900–1600.* Cambridge, Massachusetts: The Mediaeval Academy of America (fourth Edition), 1953.

Cole, H. *Sounds and Signs: Aspects of Musical Notation.* London: Oxford University Press, 1974.

Hyatt King, A. *Four Hundred Years of Music Printing.* London: Trustees of the British Museum, 1964.

Karkoschka, E. *Notation in New Music.* London: Universal Edition, 1972.

Read, G. *Music Notation.* London: Victor Gollancz, 1974.

Sloboda, J. A. Phrase units as determinants of visual processing in music reading. *British Journal of Psychology*, 1977, **68**, 117–124.

Sloboda, J. A. The psychology of music reading. *Psychology of Music*, 1978a, **6.2**, 3–20.

Sloboda, J. A. Perception of contour in music reading. *Perception*, 1978b, **7**, 323–331.

Sloboda, J. A. Music performance. In D. Deutsch (Ed.) *Psychology of Music*. New York: Academic Press, 1982.

Twyman, M. A schema for the study of graphic language. In P. A. Kolers, M. E. Wroistad, H. Bouma (Eds.) *Processing of Visible Language 1*. New York: Plenum Press, 1979.

CHAPTER 4

IMMEDIATE RECALL
OF MELODIES

4.1 Introduction

The primary purpose of this chapter is to present musical transcriptions of the attempts of eight adult subjects to recall part of a folk melody that was repeatedly presented to them. We also present the results of some analyses of these transcripts, which seem to point particularly clearly to the involvement of structural knowledge in musical memory.

4.1.1 Problems of transcription

The study of free recall in music has not commended itself to many researchers. This is understandable: For one, there is no generally accepted criterion for what counts as a reliable transcription. The conventional notation of Western musical culture forces the transcriber to translate what may be a fluctuating and richly variable signal into a limited set of pitch and time categories prescribed by the notation. Much information is inevitably lost in the process. This is, of course, true of linguistic transcription, too, but the problems are less acute because it is often possible to assume that the speaker intends to address the categories the notation embodies (e.g. he or she intends to utter words contained within a shared natural language). In music, it is less clear to what extent a singer *intends* a performance to be interpreted within the categories of tonal music. The problem arises largely because the intentions of a musical performer are not bound by *practical* constraints in the way that they usually are in language. Linguistic communication is embedded in an extralinguistic context, and it is often easy enough to discover when a speaker's intentions have been misinterpreted. Music is not a communication system in the way that language is. It is relatively self-contained and has no major consequences for domains of cognition beyond music.

How, then, can we know when a singer intends his or her performance to be interpreted by a listener within the categories supplied by conventional notation?

We think there are at least three factors that should be taken into consideration:

1. If a Western listener *hears* the bulk of a performance as fitting the pitch/time categories of tonal music, then it is likely that the performer intends it to be heard this way. In other words, if a performance *makes sense* tonally, then it is probable, though not completely certain, that such sense was intended by the performer, especially if the performance is fairly long. There are so many degrees of freedom for a musical performance that it would be coincidence indeed if a sequence generated non-tonally had consistent and strong tonal implications. Successful transcription is in itself some indication that an intention exists to address the categories embodied in the notation.

2. There is evidence that children immersed in a musical culture (such as our own) internalize the structures that are implicit in the bulk of music they hear (e.g. Gardner, 1981; Zenatti, 1969). We therefore, feel that most adults, conceive of music in terms of these enculturated structures. This is as true of performance as it is of perception.

3. Given positive indications on the preceding two counts, a performance is most likely to address intentionally the normal categories of the culture when its context encourages this. One such context involves the presentation of an unambiguously well-formed musical sequence for recall. We may argue that if a singer *hears* the music as tonal, then he or she will attempt to reproduce it as tonal.

These criteria raise particular problems for the transcription of the performances of children or of people from cultures whose musical structures are different from those of the transcriber. It is especially difficult to interpret transcriptions of songs by very young children (e.g. Dowling, 1982; Moog, 1976) or of songs from specialized or isolated subcultures (e.g. the Serbo-Croatian folk songs transcribed by Bartok and Lord, 1951). We are not concerned with resolving these difficulties here. Rather, we argue that our own data do not fall foul of these difficulties and are, therefore, optimal for transcription into conventional notation.

The foregoing does not entirely dispose of the problems associated with making transcriptions. One very important and well-documented fact about performance is that, even when the intention is unambiguously directed towards the categories of pitch and time enshrined in our notation, performance deviates significantly and systematically from the notated ideal. Conventional notation is not up to the task of recording the expressive variation that is present in any musical performance. Furthermore, such variations are not reliably diagnosed as variations by listeners. This means that whereas variations may contribute to the sense of musical life or articulation and may even help a listener to assign the intended tonal or metrical structure (Sloboda, 1985), they are unlikely to be capable of reliable transcription by ear, even if a notation were available to represent them. They are reliably captured only by mechanical transcription that records the exact timing and pitch parameters of successive notes (e.g. Seashore, 1938; Gabrielsson, 1974; Shaffer, 1981).

If the primary concern of an empirical study is with such expressive variation, then, clearly, conventional transcription is of little use. If, however, the primary concern is with the basic pitch and timing structures on which expressive variations operate, then there is some merit in a transcription process that necessarily discards much of these variations. Only when a variation is so large as to cause some uncertainty about which category a note should be assigned to (e.g. crotchet or quaver, G or G#) does it need to find its way into a transcription. If the performance is, indeed, one based on the structures inherent in our culture, then the proportion of variations causing uncertainty should not be large. If it is, we can hardly say that the performance strikes the ear as unambiguous. Such a performance does not fulfil the first of our criteria for transcription. In our own data, subjects produced a total of 1069 notes. We judged 62 (5.8%) of these to be ambiguous in the time domain and 33 (3.1%) in the pitch domain. Of this small proportion, many timing deviations were apparently due to the taking of a breath that distorted an established metre; and several pitch deviations were associated with large pitch leaps, suggesting response programming problems rather than intrinsic deviations from tonality as an explanatory cause.

We are satisfied that our transcriptions do not misrepresent the performance in any way that is germane to the issues under discussion. We do not rule out, however, the possibility that we—and other potential transcribers—are subject to systematic perceptual distortions. For instance, the effects of categorical pitch and time perception will almost inevitably be to render transcriptions more coherent than they might be. One merit of transcription in conventional notation is, of course, that it is immediately comprehensible to literate musicians. More literal transcriptions, in terms of precise performance parameters, are invaluable for some purposes, but they must be interpreted into something approaching conventional notation before they can be understood as music. Formal procedures for translating between numerical performance parameters and conventional notation (e.g. Longuet-Higgins, 1976; Steedman, 1977) have not yet solved the full range of problems presented by real auditory signals. We believe that, for the type of research reported here, there is, at present, no viable alternative to aural transcription by musically trained listeners.

4.1.2 The analysis of recall data

A different reason for the paucity of empirical work on musical recall is the lack of agreed upon and well-motivated methods of describing and analysing the content of a performance in relationship to an original model. It is clear that crude measures such as number of notes correct tell us little of interest about the nature of the recalls.

The recent study of recall processes in language provides some pointers to the type of analysis that might be appropriate (Bower, 1976; Kintsch, 1977). We know that verbal recall is rarely word-for-word correct, but it matches the original at a higher level of meaning and structure. We find substitution and inference, selective loss of information, and other distortions, but preservation of essential meaning and structure. We do not wish to be constrained by the details of recall analysis methods in language, but we are concerned to explore methods of musical analysis that provide information at an analogous level of abstraction. This makes certain conditions necessary. First, the music to be remembered must be long enough to contain within it a variety of the types of structural progressions and relationship that characterize the typical music of the culture; we have chosen the folk song or popular song melody as such a typical structure. Second, the music to be remembered must be short enough to allow for the possibility that subjects can encode it completely at some level of abstraction within a single hearing; pilot observations suggest that a melody containing about 30 notes fulfils these conditions. It is worth pointing out that most contemporary research on musical memory has used some form of recognition procedure (e.g. asking subjects to judge whether two melodies are the same or different) and has used sequences containing much fewer than 30 notes.

4.1.3 Recall versus recognition

Recall and recognition testing both have a long and well-established history within the study of memory. Both have strengths and weaknesses, and to a large extent, complement one another. Recognition studies are particularly amenable to factorial hypothesis-testing designs in which a high degree of stimulus control is exercised. By restricting subjects' responses to a few preordained categories, it is possible to obtain precise answers to preformulated questions. Yet, as many, including Newell (1973) and Allport (1975) have noticed, such research strategy can be counterproductive. In many cases, the binary theoretical choices that this forces one to make are naive and ill-conceived. Successive refinements and elaborations can lead one away from what was important about the original question, so that the research, although technically sound, sheds little light on the most salient aspects of the phenomenon under study.

There are other reasons for being cautious about the overextensive use of the recognition paradigm in music research. In many instances, subjects are required to do things that are not familiar to them and that find no parallel in their normal musical behaviour. Experiments which, for instance, use the probe technique of extracting a small segment from a longer one for recognition are of doubtful ecological validity, as are those requiring recognition of any short, decontextualized musical fragments. The most prevalent type of natural recognition behaviour involves the identification of the name of a piece of music or the feeling that 'I have heard this before,' where 'this' can be as long as a whole movement or as short as a theme in context (Halpern, 1983; Pollard-Goit, 1983).

Recall studies provide more 'messy' data, since subjects' responses are not confined to preordained categories. Although hypothesis testing is still possible. the amount of behaviour left unaccounted for is much larger. This is the price that many researchers are prepared to pay for data that bear on integrated sets of complex processes and that reflect more directly the exercise of preexisting skill. Recall data provide many more opportunities for abrasive contact between theoretical preconceptions and reality. They are also, perhaps, the most appropriate kind of data to gather when theory is relatively unrefined. One is less likely to overlook some vital aspect of the behaviour in question when faced by a rich data base than when restricting oneself to the impoverished behaviour that is the typical outcome of recognition experiments.

A particular difficulty with the recall method as applied to music is that many subjects have no well-practised response mode, have no instrumental skill, and may be totally inept at vocal techniques such as singing, humming, or whistling. Such ineptitude naturally predisposes the researcher toward recognition testing. We wonder, however, whether psychologists of music have sometimes made too pessimistic assumptions about the ability of untrained subjects to retain material and make coherent responses. With a methodological and theoretical predisposition toward recognition studies, such assumptions may not have been as critically examined as they should have been. We have been pleasantly surprised by the quantity, quality, and coherence of the data we have obtained from committed but relatively untrained subjects.

Our investigation was prompted by the wish to provide a data base of musical recalls. We began with no strong hypotheses about what we would find, other than the intuition that high-level structures would be implicated. Rather than present a rational reconstruction that embeds our data in theoretical preconceptions, we proceed roughly historically, describing first our method of data collection, then our results and some of the analyses performed, and finally, theoretical comments. This seems the most appropriate way to proceed in a study that has a strong component of natural history.

4.2 Method

Our subjects were eight students drawn from a volunteer pool in the Department of Psychology, City of Liverpool College of Higher Education. All were females between the ages of 19–22. Four of the subjects had not had any special musical training but enjoyed listening to music. These we will call the 'non-musicians'. The other four subjects were musically trained and were active performers of classical music.

We recorded piano performances of several sequences taken from folk-song melodies. Each subject was asked to listen to each sequence six times in a row, providing an attempt at sung recall after each hearing (to 'la' or any other chosen syllable). Each recall was recorded for subsequent analysis. After preliminary examination of the recall data, it was decided to discard the results for all sequences other than the first one presented. This was because material from the first set intruded massively into subsequent recalls. Sometimes, the first recall of the second sequence was almost identical to the last recall of the first sequence, even though the presented melodies were quite different. It was surprising for us to obtain this high degree of intersong contamination, and the finding is intriguing in itself. It is also something that only a recall study could have shown. However, we decided to leave it aside in this context as an unnecessary complicating factor.

Accordingly, the data we present are from the six recalls of the first sequence given to the subjects alone. The sequence, given in Example 4.1, was played at a speed of about two crotchets per second. It comprises the first three phrases of the Russian folk song, ~Sailor,'' contained in a collection of Russian songs (O'Toole, 1974). This song was not known to any of our subjects. The sequence contains 29 notes, subdivided into three phrases (11 + 9 + 9). There are multiple cues to this phrase subdivision: (1) the rests after Notes 11 and 20, (2) the fact that each phrase occupies an identical metrical slot of two bars, and (3) the fact that Note 13 begins a repetition of the melodic and rhythmic pattern that starts the sequence (Note 12 is an added upbeat). In terms of traditional analysis, the sequence shows an A_1A_2B form, where A_1 and A_2 are variants of the same material

Example 4.1 The stimulus sequence used in the study.

and *B* introduces new material. In fact, the *B* phrase shares features with *A* as well as differs from it. Notes 25–28 repeat the rhythmic pattern of notes 6–9 at an equivalent point in the metrical structure (third half-bar). Harmonically, the *A* phrase implies a I–I–V–I movement in D minor, and the *B* phrase is best interpreted as V–I–V–I in F major. In the full song, *B* is followed by a repetition of *A*, to bring the verse to a close in D minor.

We believe that the melody is highly unambiguous in that most listeners within the Western tonal culture hear the structural groupings we have informally assigned, in strong preference to other possible groupings. We base this belief on our own musical intuitions, but also on the formalizations provided by Lerdahl and Jackendoff (1983), Longuet-Higgins (1976), and Steedman (1977). These formalizations embody heuristics for assigning metrical and harmonic structure to note sequences in a way that appears to match the intuitions of experienced listeners. As we understand them, such heuristics provide unanimous support for our parsing.

The appendix to this chapter provides complete transcriptions of the six recall attempts by each of the eight subjects. Subjects 1–4 are the non-musicians, subjects 5–8 are the musicians. The recalls are numbered in sequence so that, for instance, 3.4 denotes the fourth recall of Subject 3. The transcriptions use conventional notation, but with certain differences and additions:

1. All recalls are transcribed in D minor/F major even when, as in a few cases, subjects transposed their response to a new key (usually a semi-tone up or down). We may take such transpositions to be unintentional and of little interest in the present context, except to show that subjects are coding in terms of pitch relationships rather than absolute pitches.

2. We have not given metrical interpretations above the level of the crotchet beat. Thus, bar lines are omitted.

3. The symbols × and o denote approximations to notated duration and pitch, respectively. When we were in doubt about which pitch or time

category was nearest to the note sung, we assigned the note to the category that best preserved a consistent metrical and harmonic interpretation. Although this does make the transcriptions look more coherent than arguably they ought to be, the proportion of notes involved is small enough to make us feel that this is not a serious problem.

4. The curved slur mark encloses notes sung within a single breath.

5. The symbol v denotes a slight but discernible pause that bends rather than disrupts an established metre. It is usually associated with the taking of a breath.

4.3 Results of data analyses

4.3.1 Melodic contour analysis

The first analysis is a fairly low-level one. It measures the degree to which the melodic patterns of the original are retained in the recalls. For this purpose, we derived a melodic contour for Example 4.1 that shows the pitch movements within the three phrases without regard for duration or contiguous repetition. This is shown in Example 4.2.

Example 4.2 The melodic contour of Example 4.1.

We then obtained the melodic contour of each recall by the same method. For instance, the melodic contour of 1.1 is given in Example 4.3, and that of 1.6 in Example 4.4. When the subject sang one phrase or less, we looked across the entire contour in Example 4.2 for the best-fitting phrase. Thus, 1.6 was evaluated against the contour for the second phrase of Example 4.2, on account of the D–A movement at the beginning. When

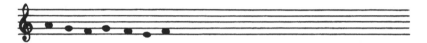

Example 4.3 The melodic contour of Recall 1.1.

Example 4.4 The melodic contour of Recall 1.6.

a subject provided two or more phrases, as in most cases, then the first phrase sung was matched against the first phrase of the original, and so on.

Within each phrase, a recall scored 1 for each of its notes that formed part of a melodic pattern (of two or more notes) found in the original. For example, Example 4.3 scores 6, because the first six notes match the first six notes of Example 4.2. Recall 1.2 provides a more difficult example. Its contour is given in Example 4.5. To score this recall, one has, in effect, to slide the original contour along the recall contour. Thus, the first six notes of the original are found at Notes 1–6 in Example 4.5. Notes 7–10 do not match anything in the original, but then Notes 11–12 match Notes 7–8 of the original. Therefore, this recall scores 8 on 14 for this measure.

Example 4.5 The melodic contour of Recall 1.2.

A final example of our scoring procedure is given for Recall 8.4. The melodic contour of its first phrase is given in Example 4.6. In this case, we find no match to the beginning of the original, so we move through the original contour until we find a match. Notes 7–9 of the recall match notes 7–9 of the original, so this phrase scores 3 on 9.

Example 4.6 The melodic contour of Recall 8.4.

Table 4.1 presents summary data from this analysis. Column 1 gives, for each subject, the melodic contour score summed over the six recalls; Column 2 gives the total number of melody notes in the recall contours; and Column 3 expresses 1 as a percentage of 2. These percentage data show wide individual differences ranging from 0% for Subject 6 to 88% for Subject 5. Is there any particular reason for the exceptionally low scores of Subjects 4 and 6? Our view is that these two cases can be explained, but differently. Let us take Subject 6 first. If we examine a recall such as 6.5, we experience a strong intuition that, despite its low melody score, it is *very* similar to Phrases 1 and 2 of the original. We argue later that its perceptual similarity is based on a shared underlying metrical and harmonic structure; that this subject has constructed a new melody

Table 4.1 Melodic contour analysis, by subject

Subject	Contour score	Total pitch movements	Contour score as percentage of pitch movements
1	32	62	52
2	45	158	28
3	66	145	46
4	2	116	2
5	84	96	88
6	0	60	0
7	72	140	51
8	86/387	120/897	72/43

which in effect, *means* the same thing as the original. Subject 4's recalls demand a different explanation. Visual and aural inspection make it fairly clear that the first two phrases of these recalls are based, not on Phrases 1 and 2 of the original, but on Phrase 3; and that Phrase 3 of the recall is variable, sometimes resembling the original Phrase 3 (e.g. 4.6), sometimes Phrase I (e.g. 4.1), and sometimes neither (e.g. 4.5).

A new structure has been composed by rearranging the phrases of the original, possibly encouraged by a recency effect that favoured memory for Phrase 3 at input. If we rescore this subject, allowing for her phrases to be matched to the original phrase that they most resemble, then her score rises to 67 on 118 (57%). What is particularly striking about these data is the extreme resilience of the new recall schema, once established. There is no move towards a more faithful reproduction of the original over its six repetitions. This persistence of an initial erroneous schema is evident in the recalls of other subjects, although on a smaller scale. It is most evident in the discarded data for subsequent melodies.

We may ask a different question of the data provided by this scoring. To what extent do subjects improve in melodic recall over trials? Table 4.2 presents melody scores summed over subjects for each of the six trials. Although the number of notes matching the original melodic contour rises from 54 to 98 over the six trials, the total number of melody notes produced increases too, so that the *proportion* of accurate melodic recall stays fairly constant at around 50%. Thus, the failure of this scoring method to account for much of what subjects do is not simply a matter of poor performance in early trials. Later trials show the same freedom from exact imitation as do the earlier trials. A two-way (ANOVA) on the percentage score of each subject for each trial confirms this picture. Although there are

Table 4.2 Melodic contour analysis, by trial

Trial	Total produced	Score	Percentage
1	109	54	50
2	144	74	51
3	135	56	41
4	162	77	48
5	162	91	56
6	181	98	54

highly significant differences between subjects ($F(7, 35)$ 18.34, $p < 0.0001$), the trials factor is not significant ($F(5, 35) = 039$).

4.3.2 Metrical analysis

The freedom suggested by the melody scores contradicts our intuitions that these recalls are often highly constrained by the original. Our second analysis is aimed at capturing one portion of those intuitions. This is a score of metrical consistency. We assigned a score of 1 to each crotchet beat of a recall over which an unsyncopated and uninterrupted quadruple metre was maintained. This was done by attempting to assign bar lines, either by counting from the first beat in fours or, if appropriate, from the second beat with the first beat as an upbeat. We noted the points at which such a process yielded a barring at odds with our perceptions of metrical stress. We believe our intuitions match those formalized by Steedman (1977), although we have not subjected the recalls to a computer program based on Steedman's rules.

Example 4.7 shows the results of one of our analyses (on Recall 1.2). The first eight beats of this can be unambiguously interpreted in a quadruple metre with primary stresses on Beats 1 and 5. However, the events on Beats 9 and 10 do not fit such a metrical interpretation; therefore, this recall scores 8 or 10. Another case is shown in Example 4.8 (Recall 5.5). The first 16 beats, encompassing the first two phrases, are straightforward. If, however, we take Beat 17 as the first beat of the next bar, we obtain a pattern of double quavers on strong beats and crotchets on weak beats. It is, in fact, almost impossible to hear Beat 22 as weak. The barring that

Example 4.7 Metrical analysis of Recall 1.2.

Example 4.8 Alternative metrical analysis of Recall 5.5.

matches the metrical feel of this sequence most exactly is given in Example 4.9. This makes Beat 17 into an additional upbeat, enlarging Bar 4 to contain five beats. This beat is, therefore, scored as anomalous, as is Beat 20, which is noticeably longer than the consistent metre would predict. This recall scores 23 on 25.

Example 4.9 Alternative metrical analysis of Recall 5.5.

Table 4.3 presents summary data from this analysis for each subject. Not only is the total percentage of metrical consistency very high, it is also high for each individual subject. Whatever subjects are doing with the details of the melody, they are, on the whole, ensuring that their recalls use the metre of the original.

Table 4.3 Metrical analysis

Subject	Total beats played	Metre score (beats)	Score as percentage of total
1	45	43	95
2	135	108	80
3	146	137	94
4	14/1	120	86
5	102	92	90
6	54	46	85
7	145	112	77
8	112/889	115/773	94/88

4.3.3 Rhythmic analysis

One possible reason for the high scores on the metrical analysis is that subjects have accurate memories for the rhythmic patterns of the original, if they correctly reproduce most of the rhythms, then it automatically follows that they will reproduce the metre. Accordingly, we assessed the degree of rhythmic reproduction by awarding each half-bar of a recall 1 point if it matched the rhythm at the same position in the original. Summary results of this analysis are shown in Table 4.4. Fewer than 50% of rhythms are exact copies of the original rhythmic sequence. It seems, therefore, that metrical consistency cannot be explained in terms of rhythmic reproduction. Rather, subjects are creating new rhythmic combinations within an underlying quadruple metre.

Table 4.5 presents the rhythmic reproduction analysis summed across subjects for each trial. Like the melodic reproduction scores, these scores do not seem to increase across trials. A two-way ANOVA on the percentage data factored by subject and trial shows a significant effect of subject ($F(7, 35)$ = 3.09, $p < 0.02$) but not of trial ($F(5, 35 = 2.27, p > 0.05)$. If subjects do improve across trials, their improvement is not due to more accurate rhythmic recall.

4.3.4 Breath analysis

We now turn to some scoring measures that try to take direct account of the phrase structure of the recalls. We first examine the way that subjects group notes by breathing. In this analysis, a score of 1 is given for each audible breath between notes or groups of notes. We partitioned the recalls into two unequally sized segments: (1) the last notes in Phrases I and 2, and (2) all other notes. Those in the first group were determined by examining the barring assigned to recalls in the metrical analysis. The last note of Phrase 1 was defined as the last note in Bar 2 whose duration (including

Table 4.4 Rhythm analysis, by subject

Subject	Total produced	Score	Percentage
1	27	10	37
2	62	14	23
3	66	36	55
4	66	29	44
5	47	31	66
6	24	10	42
7	64	33	52
8	56/412	25/188	45/46

Table 4.5 Rhythm analysis, by trial

Trial	Total produced	Score	Percentage
1	55	21	38
2	66	31	47
3	62	26	42
4	75	40	53
5	77	35	45
6	77	35	45

any subsequent rest) was a crotchet or longer. The last note in Phrase 2 was similarly defined for Bar 4. The only recall where this gave a result at odds with our intuitions was 7.5. Our procedure places the phrase boundary after the crotchet F (Note 10), whereas we would view it as occurring after the D quaver (Note 11). This uncertainty presents no problems in the present analysis since neither note is associated with a breath.

Table 4.6 presents summary data from this analysis, showing the percentage of breaths following notes in Categories (1) and (2) for each subject. Almost all phrase endings were followed by breaths, but less than 10% of other notes were followed by breaths. This is overwhelming evidence that subjects are choosing to breath at phrase ends rather than at other places.

4.3.5 Phrase structure analysis

Our next analysis attempts to quantify the degree to which subjects construct their phrases using the patterns of melodic and rhythmic imitation present in the original. That is, do they preserve the A_1A_2B phrase structure? To answer this question, we need a measure of the degree to which Phrases 2 and 3 imitate Phrase I. If subjects are reproducing this aspect of the original,

Table 4.6 Breath analysis

Subject	Percentage of breaths at phrase endings	At other places
1	100	0
2	91	10
3	92	1
4	100	7
5	100	0
6	100	6
7	92	10
8	90	5

Table 4.7 Percentage match of phrase analysis

Subject	Phrase 1 to Phrase 2	Phrase I to Phrase 3
1	79	–
2	71	70
3	69	41
4	73	44
5	78	22
6	88	–
7	70	11
8	58	44
Mean	71	41
Original	63	13

then we predict that the similarity of Phrase 3 to Phrase I is significantly less than the similarity of Phrase 2 to Phrase I. Accordingly, we compared each beat in one phrase with the corresponding beat in the other phrase, awarding a score of 1 if the pitch(es) in the two beats were identical and a score of 1 if the timing pattern was the same. These scores, represented as a percentage of total possible score, are given in Table 4.7. The missing data occur because Subjects 1 and 6 did not provide a third phrase in any of their recalls.

All six subjects for whom comparison is possible show a greater match between Phrases 1 and 2 than between Phrases 1 and 3. Nonetheless, most still show a considerable degree of similarity between Phrases 1 and 3. Applying our scoring technique to the original melody yields the percentage values given at the bottom of Table 4.7. It is apparent that most subjects make Phrases 1 and 3 more similar than in the original. This suggests two things: (1) Subjects do reproduce the $A_1 A_2 B$ schema of the original, and (2) there is a tendency to make the recall more consistent than the original. Memory tends towards structural simplification.

4.3.6 Harmonic analysis

Our next analysis concerns the harmonic structure of the recalls and the degree to which they match the harmonic structure of the original. The original has a simple and unambiguous harmonic structure that is primarily conveyed by harmonic notes falling on the strong beats in each bar (Beats 1 and 3) with passing notes falling on weak beats (2 and 4). The harmonic implication of each two-beat segment is determined by its strong beat and is shown as follows:

// I I / V I// I I /V I // V I / V^7 I //
(D minor)   (F major)

We scored the recalls by counting the number of half-bars that began with a note drawn from the chord of the harmonic sequence prescribed at that point for the original. For example, the first note of Bar I had to be D, F, or A for it to be scored positively. This scoring matched our intuitions about the harmonic structure of the recalls in all cases except the recalls of Subject 2, where it seemed to us that the E that began the fourth half-bar functioned as an appoggiatura to the following D and thus fulfilled a tonic function. This was therefore allowed as a correct harmony.

Table 4.8 shows the percentage of harmonic replication for each subject, broken down over phrases. We observe a great difference among subjects on this measure, ranging from 8% to 97%. The distribution of scores across phrases is, however, also highly variable, with Subjects 4 and 7 representing the two extremes of a distribution. The only previous analysis that showed such intersubject variability was the melodic contour score previously discussed. The possibility exists that the harmonic score might represent simple differences in melodic contour recall. One may argue that high melodic contour recall will necessarily lead to an improved harmonic score. If this is so, we might expect a high positive correlation between the two measures. Accordingly, we computed Spearman's rho and found a non-significant positive correlation of .429. Inspection of Tables 4.1 and 4.8 shows striking dissimilarities. For instance, Subject 6 scores lowest on melodic contour recall (zero) but scores highest on harmonic recall (93%). Her recalls show that she has constructed a new melody on the harmonic and rhythmic structure of the original. Although this subject demonstrates the most wholesale use of this strategy, it crops up in the other subjects, too. Good examples are found in Recalls 1.6, 3.1, and 8.4. Even subjects who show poor harmonic retention overall display isolated pockets of retention. Recall 2.3, for instance, shows a good harmonic match in Phrase 3, even though the previous two phrases show an odd amalgam of

Table 4.8 Percentage of replication of harmony analysis

Subject	Phrase 1	Phrase 2	Phrase 3	Total
1	63	100	–	70
2	38	39	36	38
3	83	100	13	66
4	0	0	25	8
5	92	75	82	84
6	91	100	–	93
7	79	83	0	56
8	100	100	90	97
average	68	67	37	

Phrases 1 and 3. Likewise, Subject 4 seems to have been totally dominated by Phrase 3 of the original (as remarked upon previously). If we allow her data to be matched against the harmonic structure of Phrase 3 in all cases, then her score rises to 82%.

4.3.7 Between-subjects analyses

Our final analysis constitutes a sweep over all the previous analyses to ask whether any shows a clear difference between musicians and non-musicians. Table 4.9 presents the mean percentage score for non-musicians and musicians on each measure, and the result of two-way ANOVA carried out on the percentage scores factored by subject group and trial. The only analysis yielding any significant differences is that on the harmonic retention scores. Musicians as a group do significantly better on this measure than non-musicians.

There are doubtless many other analyses that these results could afford. For instance, it is possible to examine the degree to which crude contour (up–down movement) is retained even when precise melodic imitation is lost (e.g. the start of Recall 6.5 has the same contour as the start of the original—two downward steps). One may assess the degree to which general stylistic features of the original (such as characteristic pitch or timing intervals) are reproduced in the recalls. Some of these features may be perceived as particularly salient by some subjects and overdone in the recalls. For instance, Subject 2 overuses the octave leap from the beginning of Phrase 3 of the original. One might also try to ask whether themes and motives from a subject's wider musical knowledge are incorporated into the recalls. For instance, Recalls 3.1–3.4 suggest a contribution from this subject's knowledge of another tune that resembles the original. This is the Christmas carol, 'We Three Kings of Orient Are'. Example 4.10

Table 4.9 Comparison between musicians and non-musicians

Analysis	Non-musicians	Musicians	F-ratio	p
Melodic contour	32	52	.935	NS
Metre	89	87	.441	NS
Rhythm	39	51	1.342	NS
Breaths[a]	94	94	.175	NS
Phrase match[b]	14	43	1.131	NS
Harmony	45	82	18.718	.0001

[a]Proportion of phrase endings followed by a breath (omitting Subjects 1 and 6 for missing data).

[b]Percentage match of Phrases 1 and 2 minus percentage match of Phrases 1 and 3. Trials 5 and 6 only. Subjects 1 and 6 omitted for missing data. See Table 4.7.

Example 4.10 The carol, 'We Three Kings,' compared to Recall 3.1.

gives the first three phrases of this carol above Recall 3.1. The recall resembles the carol's melodic structure more than that of the experimental sequence, particularly at Bars 2 and 5. Other analyses will no doubt suggest themselves. Our data present a small but rich base of material against which to test future hypotheses, and we make no claim to have provided an exhaustive account of the data here. Nonetheless, we feel that the analyses performed so far allow us to draw some quite definite conclusions.

4.4 Conclusions

Let us summarize our main findings:

1. Recall of this simple melody is never note-for-note perfect, even in the best case.

2. The exact recalls provided by these subjects are highly related to the original in many respects.

3. The most fundamental feature that is preserved in this melody is the metrical structure. Almost all the recalls are interpretable as maintaining a quadruple metre. This suggests that metre is a primary structural frame for melodic comprehension and recall.

4. Most subjects articulate the metrical frame at a level higher than the bar. The stimulus sequence is coded into two-bar phrases, and the recalls show overwhelming evidence of being governed by this phrase subdivision. Subjects breathe more often between phrases than in other places and reproduce the melodic and rhythmic imitations between phrases that preserve an A_1A_2B structure.

5. Within the metrical phrase structure, subjects do not reproduce the exact rhythms of the original. Rather, they substitute metrical equivalents in about half of the cases.

6. Subjects vary significantly in the degree to which their recalls match the harmony and melodic pattern of the original. This suggests that

listeners can attain a metrical representation independently of attaining a harmonic representation. Memory for harmonic structure seems to be related to musical expertise.

7. There is evidence that harmonic structure may be coded even when exact melodic structure is lost. On some occasions, this leads to a radically new melody, although, more commonly, subjects make small variations on the original melody that are harmonically and metrically consistent.

8. Musicians and non-musicians differ significantly on only one of our measures. This is the ability to retain the harmonic structure of the original.

9. Subjects do not show an improvement in performance over the six trials on any of our measures. Some recalls get longer, but they do not get any better.

What do these results tell us about memory for music? They point toward the notion that memorizing simple, well-formed tonal melodies involves building a mental model of the underlying structure in which not all of the surface detail is necessarily retained. Recall involves processes akin to improvisation, which fill in structurally marked slots according to general constraints about what is appropriate to the piece or genre. We have evidence that different levels of structure are available to people with differing amounts of musical expertise. Musicians code harmonic relationships that seem less accessible to non-musicians. in both groups, however, there is evidence of a great amount of common processing. Subjects seem to share the pool of basic melodic and rhythmic building blocks. Contiguous movements up and down scales and chords of the key account for much of the melodic content; and simple dactylic or equal interval rhythms for almost all of the timing content.

It is not our intention to make detailed theoretical proposals for the nature of the representational system implied by these results. However, we notice that our results fit quite well with the system proposed by Sundberg and Lindblom (1976) for generating Swedish nursery tunes (whose structures are similar to our own material). In their system, a hierarchical metrical tree is generated, which specifies binary subdivisions of a piece into phrases, bars, and beats. Harmonies and rhythms are assigned to terminal elements on the basis of their status within the tree structure, and pitches are chosen to satisfy the harmonies and rhythms specified. To account more precisely for our results, we need to modify the system to allow for the possibility of only *part* of a tree being generated, and we also need to construct a melodic generation process that samples some lexicon of possible melodic patterns. Some individual differences could be accounted for by a weighting system that makes it more likely that a frequently encountered pattern will be chosen for any particular role. It would also be necessary to build in some real-time constraints. The speed at which a melody is presented clearly has an important bearing on the detail of representation achieved, although we are not in a position to make detailed predictions.

We see the development of theory in this area as working towards a formal system, embodied in a computer program, which takes melodies like ours as its input, and models the type of recall obtained as its output. Sundberg and Lindblom's (1976) system provides the most detailed sketch of a possible output generation system. Several theoretical approaches are relevant to the input procedures. At the level of the individual note, the notions of tonal space developed by, for instance, Sheperd (1982) and Krumhansl (1983) might be used to predict the kind of individual pitch error most likely to find its way into recalls. Our intuition is, however, that such simple relationships will often be overridden in extended melodic representation by factors relevant to melodic shape and imitation and to the preservation of metrical and harmonic structure. We look, therefore, to theories of music perception that generate temporally extended hierarchic structures by means of parsing procedures (in particular, Lerdahl and Jackedoff, 1983; Longuet-Higgins, 1976; and Steedman, 1977).

It may be argued that musical recall data cannot directly disconfirm these theories, because a particular unpredicted recall can always be accounted for by some additional factor ignored by the theory (e.g. the freedom exercised by an individual to preserve some linear or statistical feature of the music at the expense of harmony, metre, and hierarchical structure). It would, however, be disconcerting for such theories if a significant proportion of recall distortions could not be accounted for under their assumptions. Nonetheless, we may wish to see recall data not so much as detailed testing grounds for existing theories, but rather as pointers to aspects of memory and representation for which, as yet, no well-developed theory exists. There is no psychological theory of melodic or thematic identity; neither is there any detailed theoretical framework in terms of which we could articulate the nature of the intrusion errors that we noted.

Whatever view one takes about the relationship between recall data and theory testing, we believe our data to be a more concrete and appropriate explanandum for the development of theory than the oft-appealed-to 'intuitions of experienced listeners,' concerning which there can be legitimate and unresolvable dispute.

Appendix

This appendix contains transcriptions of six recall attempts by each of eight subjects aurally presented with Figure 4.1. The following are the special symbols used; details of interpretation are given in the text.

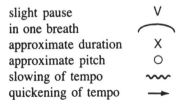

slight pause	V
in one breath	⌒
approximate duration	X
approximate pitch	O
slowing of tempo	⌇
quickening of tempo	→

Subject 1

Subject 6

Subject 7

Subject 8

References

Allport, D. A. The state of cognitive psychology. *Quarterly Journal of Experimental Psychology*, 1975, **27**, 141–152.

Bartok, B., and Lord, A. B. *Serbo-Croatian folk songs.* New York: Columbia University Press, 1951.

Bower, G. H. Experiments in story understanding and recall. *Quarterly Journal of Experimental Psychology*, 1976, **28**, 511–534.

Dowling, W. J. Melodic information processing and its development. In D. Deutsch (Ed.), *The psychology of music.* New York: Academic Press, 1982.

Gabrielsson, A. Performance of rhythm patterns. *Scandinavian Journal of Psychology.* 1974, **15**, 63–72.

Gardner, H. Do babies sing a universal song? *Psychology Today,* 1981, **14**(4), 18–27.

Halpern, A. Organization in memory for music. *Bulletin of the British Psychological Society*, 1983, **36**, A124.

Kintsch, W. On comprehending stories. In M. A. Just and P. A. Carpenter (Eds.), *Cognitive processes in comprehension.* Hillsdale, NJ: Erlbaum, 1977.

Krumhansl, C. L. Perceptual structures for tonal music. *Music Perception,* 1983, **1**, 24–58.

Lcrdahl, F., and Jackendoff, R. *A generative theory of tonal music.* Cambridge, MA: MIT Press, 1983.

Longuet-Higgins, H. C. Perception of melodies. *Nature*, 1976, **263**, 646–653.

Moog, H. *The musical experience of the pre-school child* (C. Clarke, Trans.). London: Schott, 1976.

Newell, A. You can't play 20 questions with nature and win. In W. G. Chase (Ed.), *Visual information processing*. London: Academic Press, 1973.

O'Toole, L. M. *The Gateway Russian song book*. London: Collets, 1974.

Pollard-Gott, L. Emergence of thematic concepts in repeated listening to music. *Cognitive Psychology*, 1983, **15**, 66–94.

Seashore, C. E. *The psychology of music*. New York: McGraw-Hill, 1938.

Shaffer, L. H. Performance of Chopin, Bach, and Bartok: Studies in motor programming. *Cognitive Psychology*, 1981, **13**, 326–376.

Shepard, R. N. Structural representation of pitch. In D. Deutsch (Ed.), *The psychology of music*. New York: Academic Press, 1982.

Sloboda, J. A. *The musical mind: The cognitive psychology of music*. London: Oxford University Press, 1985.

Steedman, M. J. The perception of musical rhythm and metre. *Perception*, 1977, **6**, 555–570.

Sundberg, J., and Lindblom, B. Generative theories in language and music descriptions. *Cognition*, 1976, **4**, 99–122.

Zenatti, A. Le développement génetique de la perception musicale. *Monographs Français de Psychologie*. No. 17.

CHAPTER 5

COGNITION AND REAL MUSIC: THE PSYCHOLOGY OF MUSIC COMES OF AGE

The past ten years have seen such qualitative and quantitative changes in the psychology of music that it is tempting to make a provocative claim. The claim is that until about ten or so years ago there was no scientific discipline which deserved the title 'psychology of music'. Books had been written with this name. Research into music had been carried out using the techniques of experimental psychology. But something essential was lacking. I would loosely adopt Kuhn's (1962) thinking and say that only in the last ten years has the basis for normal paradigmatic science in the psychology of music emerged.

I believe that there are five important characteristics of a healthy paradigm: an agreed set of central problems; agreed methods for working on these problems; agreed theoretical frameworks in which to discuss them; techniques and theories which are specific to the paradigm; research which is appropriate to the whole range of phenomena in the domain being studied.

Although parts of this recipe have been present in different research endeavours, the full set has only recently emerged at one time and within a research community who intercommunicate their ideas and results.

How and why such a discipline should emerge at this particular point in time is a question for sociologists and historians to pursue. Nonetheless, it is abundantly clear that public foci such as conferences and journals have played a crucial part in sustaining the paradigm. Journals such as *Music Perception* and regular conferences, (e.g. Clynes, 1982) have been, and continue to be vitally important to the health of the discipline.

Let us take each of the five characteristics of a paradigm in turn, and elaborate on them in the context of the psychology of music.

5.1 The agreed problem

There seems to be a growing consensus that a central problem for the psychology of music is to explain the structure and content of musical experience. This is not to deny the importance of studying the processing of musical material, but this approach puts the emphasis onto the endpoint of processing—what the processing is supposed to achieve. This involves examining two major questions: a. What is the nature of musical knowledge or representation?; b. How does music have aesthetic and emotional effects?

Both questions are of central importance, but the majority of research has focused on the first of these two questions. I would judge that this definition of the problem excludes much that has been loosely called psychology of music. It, for instance, excludes many studies in music education where the prime aim is to test a teaching method, and where the prime research measure is some measurement of the technical improvement of the learner. I am not denying that music learners have musical experiences, nor that the nature of these experiences contributes to the nature of the learning. It does seem, however, that much research in this area either ignores, or makes simplistic assumptions about, the nature of the experience.

There are, however, research studies in other apparently more cognitively oriented programmes which I would also want to claim are somewhat peripheral to our major concerns. These are the studies which derive their data from musical situations, but which do not attempt to explain their musical significance. Such findings are certainly important and worthy of discovery, but they do need considerable interpretation before they contribute to the psychology of music. Research by Vos and Rasch (1982) that I much admire illustrates this well.

They have shown that perceived onset of a musical note is related to its rise time. The slower the rise, the later the onset appears to be. This has practical implications. For instance, instruments with slower rise times will have to play earlier than others if they are to sound simultaneous. But these findings generalize to any generated sounds whatsoever, musical or not. What might be the specifically musical significance of synchrony and asynchrony? McAdams (1982) has shown that perceived onset asynchrony encourages us to hear two sounds as separate, whilst synchrony encourages fusion. This now begins to relate to musical issues. Perhaps asynchrony is a way of emphasizing polyphony, whilst synchrony encourages perception of homophony. We may then begin to ask questions about what other features of a musical stimulus contribute to the experience of polyphony or homophony. And now we begin to move into the realm of core psychology of music. The questions which we would want to answer in this are: What effects on the musical experience do different types of synchrony patterns have? Why do musical performers choose particularly large or small asynchronies at particular points? Can we identify structural features of music which we would predict to be associated with certain asynchrony patterns? And so on.

One of the seminal publications in our young discipline was Longuet-Higgins' (1976) paper in *Nature*. Longuet-Higgins wrote a computer simulation which took a sequence of pitches and durations as input, and produced a sensibly notated version as output. His thesis was that a central part of experiencing any music as music is the assignation of sounds to positions in tonal and metrical space. This involves determining the key of the melody and its principal stresses. The heuristics in the program are embodiments of strong psychological hypotheses about an experienced listener's processing mechanisms. This research is central to the psychology of music not only because it directly addresses the central problems, but also because the analyses it provides actually accord well with 'the intuitions of experienced listeners', and thus have a strong claim to be an empirically verified account of music experience. The insights of Longuet-Higgins have found echoes at the core of several more recent theoretical enterprises (e.g. Balzano, 1980; Lerdahl and Jackendoff, 1983).

5.2 Agreed methods

Some of these methods have been around for a long time. Maybe no one is specific to psychology of music, but recent years have seen researchers exercising a greater freedom to use many different methods to complement one another. In particular, many researchers are eschewing the strait-jacket of traditional methodologies such as the same–different recognition experiment, and are exploring a whole range of methods:

1. Direct recording of performance parameters. This has seen a recent renaissance following the explosion of availability of computer technology for handling and analysing such data (Clarke, 1985; Gabrielsson, 1974; Michon, 1974; Rasch, 1979; Shaffer, 1981, 1984).

2. Computer synthesis of sound patterns to test perceptual hypotheses, sometimes coupled with prior analysis of music with method 1 (Gabrielsson, 1985; Sloboda, 1985a; Sundberg, Askenfelt and Fryden, 1983).

3. Measurement of memory performance. Recognition measures, usually of computer synthesized stimuli, are common (Cuddy, Cohen and Miller, 1979; Deutsch, 1982; Dowling, 1978; Edworthy, 1985; Tan, Aiello and Bever, 1981). Less common are studies of musical recall (Deutsch, 1980; Sloboda and Parker, 1985).

4. Studies of verbal behaviour connected with music, such as judgements about qualities of music, and protocols. These have been most

particularly connected with aesthetic aspects (Crozier, 1974; Smith and Cuddy, 1986), but also such processes as composition (Reitman, 1965; Sloboda, 1985b).

5. Studies of physiological correlates of musical experience. These include evoked potentials, heart rate and other autonomic measures, also studies of hemispheric differences (Davidson and Schwartz, 1977; Harrer and Harrer, 1977; Hirshkowitz, Earle and Paley, 1978, McKee et al., 1973).

6. Simulations of aspects of music perception (Longuet-Higgins, 1976), performance (Sundberg and Fryden, 1985), or generation (Sundberg and Lindblom, 1976; Ulrich, 1971).

A principal concern of all these methods is increasingly to measure or control the *microstructure* of the music or the behaviour, investigators are concerned to discover how the specific actions and events contribute to the global phenomenon. It is no longer adequate, for instance, to simply record the number of errors in some task. We wish to know exactly what errors were made and where.

5.3 Agreed theoretical frameworks

A convergence is detectible in the central assumptions made by researchers working in this discipline. Some of these are: Music is constructed according to grammar(s) (Sundberg and Lindblom, 1976); representation is often hierarchic (Deutsch and Ferowe, 1981; Martin, 1972); tonality, metre, and rhythm are psychologically real organizing principles (possibly instantiations of musical universals) (Lerdahi and Jackendoff, 1983); different processes (composition, performance, perception) access the same core representations (Sloboda, 1985b).

This by no means shows that theoretical agreement has been reached, but it does prescribe the kind of things that are theoretically interesting to researchers. In particular, it is arguable that those who hold the above assumptions will particularly want theory to account for: errors in performance, their nature and position; distribution of expressive parameters in performance; differential memorability of musical passages; differential perceived salience of musical events; judgements of well-formedness by listeners; cultural differences in music perception; processes of enculturation and learning, and skill-level differences; structural determinants of musical meaning.

5.4 Specificity of the activity

There has been a tendency among researchers to become interested in music because it is a good example of something else: e.g. a complex motor skill; a language-like phenomenon; a complex auditory phenomenon; a set-theoretic entity.

Of course, music is all these things, and it is important to bring in ideas from other areas to elucidate music; but it is possible that many of us, including myself, have been too eager to see music through the spectacles of our own extra-musical preoccupations, and underplay its uniqueness.

It is most precisely at the point where our studies characterize music as wholly unlike anything else that we may be most secure at establishing a real psychology of music. We may locate this uniqueness of music at the confluence of three aspects: 1. Music creates a non-referential world; 2. It does so through the psychological dimensions of tonality and metre; 3. Despite the lack of reference, music has deep emotional significance.

Rhythm and metre are, of course, concepts which have parallels in other domains, such as speech (Martin, 1972). Tonality, however, seems something quite unique to music. The study of scales, harmony, melody, and key seems to be what gives our subject its specificity and its heart. We have begun to unravel the rich and complex structure which makes the tonal system such a fruitful medium for building interesting forms (e.g. Longuet-Higgins, 1972; Balzano, 1980). We have done less to relate tonality to the emotions, but it is becoming much more respectable to pose this as a question for research effort (e.g.Minsky, 1982).

5.5 Appropriate research

1. Music psychology demonstrates its maturity by starting to address the range of activities properly described as musical. Although the majority of research relates to perception, increasing research effort is devoted to examining such activities as performance (Clarke, 1985), memory (Sloboda and Parker, 1985), composition (Lerdahi, 1988) and improvisation (Davidson, 1985; Pressing, 1988).

2. Music psychologists are becoming more concerned to use real music in their investigations instead of impoverished music-like stimuli. It is being realized that certain aspects of music will not be understood unless materials of some complexity are used. This does not entail giving up stimulus control; however, more researchers use relatively long sequences (two or more phrases) (Sloboda and Gregory, 1981;

Tan *et al.*, 1981). ensure that both rhythmic and tonal structures are present (DeLiege, 1985), and try to use 'composed' material rather than 'constructed' material where feasible (Pollard-Gott, 1983). This is part of the move towards greater 'ecological validity'.

3. Music psychology increasingly employs subjects in behaviours that are close analogues of common musical activities, such as memorizing for recall (Sloboda and Parker, 1985), sight-reading (Sloboda, 1984), extended listening (Pollard-Gott, 1983), improvising (Sagi, 1988).

4. Music psychology has come to address issues which are not simply of interest to psychologists, but to practitioners of the various arts and skills of music (performers, music theorists, etc.). We find increasing numbers of professional musicians undertaking psychological research, often in collaboration with psychologists (Rosner and Meyer, 1982; Sternberg, Knoll and Zukofsky, 1982). Collaboration of various kinds has been particularly encouraged by such bodies as the Institut de Recherche el de Coordination Acoustique/Musique (IRCAM) in Paris.

5.6 The coming of age

The title of this paper commits me, if I am serious about my analogy, to identify a precise historical moment which signified the coming of age of our discipline. I have no doubt at all about what this moment was. It was the publication in 1983 of Lerdahl and Jackendoff's *Generative Theory of Tonal Music*. This is for several reasons:

1. It must be one of the most comprehensively reviewed books in music/psychology (Cady, 1983; Child, 1984; Clarke, 1986; Longuet-Higgins, 1983; Peel and Slawson, 1984; Rosner, 1984). The avid interest with which it was awaited and then devoured by a very wide constituency signals the community of concern around the problems it addresses. It was recognized that the authors had articulated a core problem for music theory and psychology, and had attempted an ambitious answer.

2. It has the problem of the structure of musical knowledge as its main theme.

3. It is explicit and detailed. It offers rules for understanding the perceived importance of each note in an extended piece of music.

4. It is 'universal'. It can account for anything from a small fragment of music right up to a symphonic movement. It also attempts to be universal in another sense, in proposing that culturally specific rules are special cases of culture free rules which apply to all music.

5. It is ambitious. It tries to offer a complete theory which will cover most real music.

6. It is specific. Although many of the structures are borrowed from other domains, notably generative linguistics, the way they are applied to music is unique for a. the notion of several independent but interactive structural analyses of the same passage, b. the distinction between well-formedness rules and preference rules, c. the proposal of special rules to deal with such music-specific events as cadences.

7. It is empirically oriented. The authors claim that specific predictions of the theory may be tested.

8. It is written with the contribution of a highly trained working musician who is prepared to use his own musical intuitions and insights as the basis of theory.

These features do not necessarily imply that Lerdahl and Jackendoff have produced a theory without flaws. The longer we live with it the more apparent its shortcomings are. This is not the point. The mere existence of the theory has significantly accelerated the amount of thinking and research around the problems it addresses (Deliège, 1985; Narmour, 1983; Todd, 1985). In 'coming out' the authors have undoubtedly laid their heads on many chopping blocks, but had they not done so, fewer people would have been motivated to sharpen up the particular hatchets. Lerdahl and Jackendoff are to be congratulated for making themselves so explicit that criticism of them is relatively easy and fruitful. By seeing what they do not do, we should be able to make rapid progress in developing better theories. Any discipline which cannot produce a steady stream of theories of the clarity, complexity and elegance of Lerdahl and Jackendoff, is certainly not to he judged mature. We may have come of age, but we still have a long way to go.

It is particularly heartening to see that Lerdahl and Jackendoff have stimulated diverse type of endeavour. Music theorists have held it up against other theoretical and analytical perspectives (see Clarke, 1986). Scientists have started to conduct empirical studies aimed at testing certain of its predictions. For instance, work carried out in Shaffer's laboratory (Todd, 1985) shows that the pattern of timing deformations in expressive playing can be predicted quite closely from patterns of prominence derived from a Lerdahl–Jackendoff analysis.

Although some studies have arisen specifically with reference to Lerdahl and Jackendoff's theory, many more have been carried out within the general climate that has been responsible for the intense interest in their work. I would like to illustrate this point with reference to two studies that I have been recently involved with (Sloboda and Parker, 1985; Sloboda, Hermelin and O'Connor, 1985). They both concern a 'real' musical task, that of memorizing composed music for subsequent recall. One study looks at 'normal' processes in relatively unselected subjects. The other study looks at a single case of 'exceptional' memory. In each study a principal concern is with the type of representation which must be postulated to account for memory distortions.

5.7 Recall of folk tunes

Although memory has been a major concern of the psychology of music, almost all the serious research has been conducted using a recognition method. Subjects are presented with two short music-like sequences and they are required to detect some difference.

David Parker and myself decided to explore a more direct approach, of playing a real tune to subjects and asking them to attempt to recall, by singing, what they could remember (see Sloboda and Parker, 1985 for further details). The study was devised as a preliminary step on the road to investigating how musicians go about memorizing long pieces of music, a topic we know almost nothing from the viewpoint of empirical science.

Secondly, it seemed to us that a memory recall would provide the most detailed, rich, and explicit clues to the nature of the structures and representations that people use when dealing with tonal music. In particular, an analysis of the type of error made should tell us a great deal about the structures being picked up.

Thirdly, extensive literature search failed to discover any similar analysis of a corpus of recalls.

The data were collected as follows. Short but unfamiliar folk melodies were played on the piano and tape recorded. Subjects were tested individually by listening to each melody and then trying to sing it back to 'la' or any other convenient syllable. Each melody was repeated six times in succession, and so six consecutive recalls were obtained.

Figure 5.1 shows the melody to which we have devoted our major attention. It is the first 12 bars of a Russian folk song called 'Sailor'. It contains 30 notes. None of our subjects had heard it before.

Figure 5.1 Stimulus melody in Sloboda and Parker (1985) study.

Figure 5.2 shows transcriptions of the six recalls of a single subject on repeated presentation of the tune. This set of recalls displays features typical of the corpus as a whole. Firstly, the recalls are remarkably coherent and definite. This makes them easy to transcribe and analyse. We had fears of vague mumbled hummings which would be impossible to transcribe. Our fears were groundless. Second, not a single recall in our whole corpus is note perfect. Third, everyone who has heard these recalls agrees that the subjects display real memory for the music.

We have subjected the data to a number of analyses which have corroborated these intuitions. First we showed that subjects do not retain a large proportion of the actual melodic and rhythmic sequences present in

Figure 5.2 Transcriptions of six consecutive recalls of a typical subject in Sloboda and Parker's (1985) study.

Figure 5.3 Example of recall of phrase 1 in Sloboda and Parker's (1985) study.

the original. Even when we give considerable latitude in the positioning of material average scores are still low. Expressed as a percentage of total notes recalled, only 43% of the notes matched the melody given, and only 46% matched the rhythm given. One interpretation to place upon this would be that for about half the time subjects were improvising at random to sustain the melody. We have evidence, however, that their productions were constrained by high-level features of the original melody.

The first of these features is the metrical structure. We found that we could satisfactorily parse 88% of the recalls as in consistent 4-beat metre, like the original, by applying the kind of parsing rules formalized by Lerdahl and Jackendoff, and others. In other words, subjects were extracting the metre of the original as a frame for their recalls.

The second of these features is harmony. In this case we found quite wide subject differences. Half of our subjects were music students, the other half were just interested in music. In the case of the music students 81% of the material was harmonically appropriate. That is to say, whilst the material was melodically and rhythmically new, it used notes from the chords implied in the original. We scored the recalls by looking at the notes subjects chose to begin each half-bar, giving a score of 1 if the note came from the chord prescribed by the original at that point. Figure 5.3 gives an example of memory which is harmonically and metrically perfect but contains almost none of the actual notes of the original.

A third higher-order feature of these recalls concerns phrases. It should be clear that the original melody falls into three phrases of two bars each. The second phrase rather closely imitates the first, but the third phrase introduces new material. Subjects showed awareness of this structure in two ways, through breath positions, and through imitative relations between phrases:

1. *Breaths.* In each subject's recall we defined the end of phrase 1 as the last note in bar 2 whose duration was a crotchet or longer. The end of phrase 2 was similarly defined as the last long note in bar 4. We then compared the number of times subjects breathed at a phrase end to the number of times they breathed elsewhere. Almost every phrase

end was associated with a breath, and almost no other point was. Subjects made the phrase structure explicit through their breathing.

2. *Imitative structure.* We asked whether subjects preserved the imitative relationships between phrases 1 and 2, making the third phrase different. To do this we took each recall, and compared phrase 1, beat by beat, with phrase 2, awarding a score of 1 if the pitches were identical, and a score of I if the rhythms were identical. We found that phrases 1 and 2 had a 71% match, whereas phrases 1 and 3 had only a 41% match. So, as in the original, subjects preserved the closer relation of phrases 1 and 2.

How do we summarize our findings? They show that a trivially simple ecological technique coupled with appropriate data analyses yields good insights into structural aspects of musical memory. They suggest that memory of a tonal melody involves building up a model of the underlying structure in which not all of the surface details are necessarily retained. Recall involves a reconstruction process which fills in structural slots according to general constraints. The type of structure noticed depends to a certain extent on experience. In our sample only the musically trained show a majority retention of harmonic structure. All the subjects were able to access the metrical and phrase structure.

5.8 An exceptional musical memory

The second study I wish to report is of a much more dramatic and sensational kind. We saw in the previous experiment that ordinary people, even those with musical training, are not very good at retaining exact details of even a short melody. Yet musical folklore abounds with stories of people gifted with quite exceptionally accurate musical memories. The most famous story probably concerns Mozart's exploits with Allegri's *Miserere* (Anderson, 1966). However trustworthy we believe the observers of this feat of memory to be, the actual record of the attempt does not survive. It would be of considerable interest to examine a contemporary musician with memory powers equal to that claimed for Mozart.

A rigorous examination of such a memory would not only be of intrinsic fascination, it would also have theoretical significance. We could ask whether a prodigious musical memory is the result of some abnormal mode of representing music (such as a vivid 'eidetic' store) or whether it comes about through the same kind of structural assimilation as more mundane memory.

If the former, then we would expect it hardly to matter whether the material to be remembered was easily assimilable to well learned structures. If the latter, however, we would expect music containing familiar structures to be remembered better than music lacking some of these structures. We would also expect any errors that did occur to be predominantly structure preserving.

In 1984, an opportunity presented itself to examine a young man of allegedly remarkable memory powers for piano music (see Sloboda, Hermelin and O'Connor, 1985 for further details). He had been discovered during a large scale study of *idiots savants*. These are people of low intelligence, often mentally handicapped. who appear to have an isolated pocket of intellectual excellence. A small number of such people excel in music. Sometimes their excellence is only relative to their mental age; and the skill would not be unusual in a normal person with some musical training. This particular man, who we shall call NP, was particularly interesting because his alleged memory skill was far in excess of any normal accomplishment. The claim was that he could memorize an extended movement in two or three hearings.

NP was 22 years old at time of testing. He lives in a home for the autistic, and displays the typical range of autistic symptoms, including language deficiency, social withdrawal, gaze aversion, and obsessive behaviour patterns. His major obsession is music. He spends as much of every day as possible playing the piano or listening to music.

Prior to the experimental sessions, a number of piano pieces were pre-recorded on tape. In the event, we were able to expose NP to two of them, neither of which, to our knowledge, he had learned before: 1. a lyric piece by the nineteenth-century Norwegian composer Edward Grieg (*Melodie* Opus 47 no 3): 2. a short atonal piece by the twentieth-century Hungarian composer Bela Bartok ('Whole Tone Scale' from *Mikrokosmos* Book 5).

Neither piece was technically virtuosic, and well within the technical capacity of the subject. In the trials, NP simply listened to the recordings. At no stage did he see anyone visually demonstrating the appropriate motor movements on the piano, nor did he have the chance to examine a score. NP heard each entire piece through, then heard it in shorter sections, as judged appropriate from the signals he gave, and his moment to moment capacity. After each presentation of the piece (or section) he was asked to try and play what we had heard. The whole session was recorded on tape, and all recall attempts were transcribed for analysis.

We found that NP learned the Grieg piece to almost note-perfect criterion in about 12 minutes, during which time he heard no more than four repetitions of any section of the piece. The piece is 66 bars long and contains

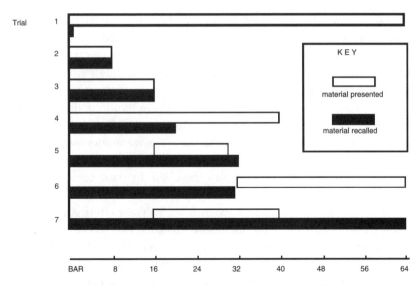

Figure 5.4 Learning history for subject NP on Grieg Op. 47 no. 3 (from Sloboda, Hermelin and O'Connor, 1985).

310 notes (discounting adjacent repetitions of the same chord). Figure 5.4 shows a summary learning history. The upper white bar of each pair shows what NP heard on a given trial. The lower black bar shows what was recalled. Although recall was never 100% perfect, the deviations from score were very minor; an occasional omission or addition of a subsidiary note which hardly changed the character, and never the structure.

Table 5.1 shows some summary quantitative data. The top figure is the number of notes whose recall was attempted over all trials. The second figure is the number of wrong notes (sum of notes omitted which should have been played and notes played which should not have been). The third figure is the number of times that there was a stumble, pause, or backtrack. The fourth figure represents the wrong notes and stumbles as a percentage of notes attempted, to give a gross error rate.

Table 5.1 Summary quantitative data of the exceptional musical memory study

| | **NP** | | **AS** | |
	Grieg	**Bartok**	**Grieg**	**Bartok**
Notes attempted	798	277	354	153
Notes wrong	54	137	265	12
Stumbles, pauses	11	37	19	10
Total % error	8	63	80	14

Table 5.1 includes data from a number of comparisons that help us to understand better the nature of NP's achievement with the Grieg. The second column shows data from NP's attempt to recall the Bartok piece. Although shorter than the Grieg, and with just as simple a rhythmic and formal structure, the reproduction attempts were hesitant, error-prone and unconfident. For instance, in four attempts to recall the first 51 notes of the piece, NP never played more than 36 correctly, and each time with frequent stumbles. Although many fewer notes were attempted overall, the error rate was a massive 63%. It appears that NP cannot function at a high level outside the framework supplied by conventional tonal harmony.

A second comparison summarized in Table 5.1 comes from the attempts of a professional pianist AS to memorize the same two pieces. AS was an approximate age and experience control for NP. Figure 5.5 shows the learning history for the Grieg piece in the same format as Figure 5.4 for NP. The hatched bars are recalls containing large numbers of errors.

This shows that good recall was obtained for the first eight bars alone. When further material was attempted, even the original level of performance on the first eight bars was lost. It was clear that AS was simply overwhelmed by the amount of material in the Grieg. Although some of the right hand melody was reproduced reasonably well, the accompanying

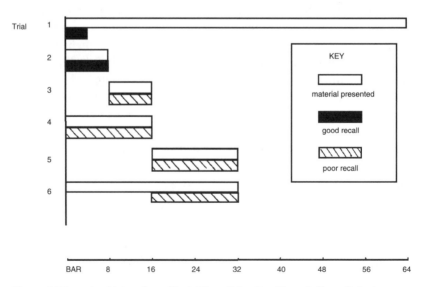

Figure 5.5 Learning history for subject AS on Grieg Op. 47 no. 3 (from Sloboda, Hermelin and O'Connor, 1985).

chords bore no resemblance to the original for significant portions of the recalls.

The Bartok, in contrast, showed negligible error. This was partly due to the brevity of the section attempted (first eight bars only), but it was clear that the atonality did not disrupt AS to anything like the extent that it did for NP. Like many contemporary musicians, AS had considerable experience of this kind of music.

A third comparison was obtained by looking at the results of some simple tests of NP's verbal memory. This was found to be consistent with his general level of intellectual functioning. He had a forward digit span of 5 (as compared to an average of 7) and a backwards span of 4 (as compared to an average of 6). He was able to recall simple 7-word sentences haltingly but correctly, but could only recall 4 out of 7 words when word order was jumbled. There was no evidence of any exceptional memory capacity outside the realms of tonal music.

It is quite clear from these data that NP is not the possessor of some primitive but high-capacity 'echoic' or 'mimicking' memory, but has a narrow but intensely highly-developed window of 'normal' memory which operates, as in most known cases of expertise, by representing material in terms of familiar higher-order structures. This ability, like other exceptional skills, has been developed through many thousands of hours of practise over many years, in conjunction with an intense degree of absorption with the material concerned, and an unusually high degree of motivation to succeed at this particular task (cf. Chase and Ericsson, 1981).

In sum, these two studies illustrate how naturalistic musical situations may be exploited to provide insights into the nature of musical representation. They accord well with the theoretical perspectives formalized by Lerdahl and Jackendoff, in that they suggest overlapping structured hierarchic representations of music (rhythmic, metrical, tonal, etc.), where higher levels have greater 'durability' than lower levels.

5.9 Conclusions

The type and range of endeavours summarized in this paper convinces me that our discipline of psychology of music has indeed come of age, and that we can happily take risks. We no longer need to convince a sceptical psychological world that we have rigour, scientific respectability and relevance. Rather, we should boldly extend the frontiers of our subject by tackling some of the outstanding difficult issues head-on.

Lerdahl and Jackendoff have set new standards for comprehensiveness and boldness in theory. Let us hope that they stimulate not only criticism but other, even bolder, theories. Many empirical workers have broken new ground in subject matter. The upsurge in performance studies is a most impressive development of the last five years or so. It is particularly heartening to see people attempting to systematically observe some real phenomenon just because it is there to be examined, and has inherent importance. A favourite study of mine is one by Gruson (1988), who had the courage to tackle the question of what goes on when people practice the piano. Do people of different skill level do different things? Her painstaking analysis of session tapes showed that indeed there are important and reliable differences across skill levels. The study raises as many questions as it solves, but it is a fine example of the pioneering work which will move our discipline forwards.

I would like to conclude by mentioning some areas which I believe are ripe for an intensification of psychological investigation. Firstly, it would be good to see many more psychological studies on the processes of composition and improvisation. Secondly, we would benefit from more studies on the processes of musical communication in ensembles, examining, for instance, the role of the conductor. Thirdly, we need more studies which give information on the mental processes that take place when listening to extended music. There are a whole range of unanswered questions about the type of memory representation which is built up, particularly in early listening, about the role of imagery and the emotions. Fourthly, we need systematic investigation of large scale memorization skills in professional performers and others.

Early attempts will be unsophisticated and much criticised, but the territories must be claimed. So, I invite those who are committed to bringing about the true maturity of our subject to tackle precisely those questions that their caution tells them are much too difficult. That is the way forward, I am sure.

References

Anderson, E. (Ed.). (1966) *The letters of Mozart and his family*. London: Hutchinson.

Balzano, G. J. (1980) The group-theoretic description of twelvefold and microtonal pitch systems. *Computer Music Journal*, **4**, 66–84.

Cady, H. L. (1983) Review of a generative theory of tonal music. *Psychomusicology*, **3**, 60–67.

Chase, W. G. and Ericsson, K. A. (1981) Skilled memory. In J. R. Anderson (Ed.). *Cognitive skills and their acquisition*. Hillsdale, N.J.: Erlbaum.

Child, P. (1984) Review of *A generative theory of tonal music*. *Computer Music Journal*, **8.4**, 56–65.

Clarke, E. F. (1985) Structure and expression in rhythmic performance. In P. Howell, I. Cross and R. West (Eds.). *Musical structure and cognition.* New York: Academic Press.

Clarke, E. F. (1986) Theory, analysis and the psychology of music: A critical evaluation of Lerdahl, F. and Jackendoff, R., *A generative theory of tonal music. Psychology of Music,* **14**, 3–16.

Clynes, M. (Ed.). (1982) *Music, mind and brain: The neuropsychology of music.* New York: Plenum.

Crozier, J. B. (1974) Verbal and exploratory responses to sound sequences varying in uncertainty level. In D. E. Berlyne (Ed.). *Studies in the new experimental aesthetics: Steps toward an objective psychology of aesthetic appreciation.* Toronto: Wiley.

Cuddy, L. L. Cohen, A. J., and Miller (1979) Melody recognition: The experimental application of musical rules. *Canadian Journal of Psychology,* **33**, 148–157.

Davidson, L. (1985) Tonal structures of children's early songs. *Music Perception,* **2.3**, 361–374.

Davidson, R. J. and Schwartz, G. E. (1977) The influence of musical training on patterns of EEG asymmetry during musical and non-musical self-generation tasks. *Psychophysiology,* **14.1**, 58–63.

DeLiege, I. (1985, August). The concept of preference in the constitution of groups in music perception. Paper presented at the Fifth Workshop on Physical and Neuropsychological Foundations of Music, Ossiach, Austria.

Deutsch, D. (1980) The processing of structured and unstructured tonal sequences. *Perception and Psychophysics,* **28**, 381–389.

Deutsch, D. (1982) The processing of pitch combinations. In D. Deutsch (Ed.). *The psychology of music.* New York: Academic Press.

Deutsch, D. and Feroe, J. (1981) The internal representation of pitch sequences in tonal music. *Psychological Review,* **86**, 503–522.

Dowling, W. J. (1978) Scale and contour: Two components of a theory of memory for melodies. *Psychological Review,* **85**, 341–354.

Edworthy, J. (1985) Melodic contour and musical structure. In P. Howell, I. Cross and R. West (Eds.). *Musical structure and cognition.* New York: Academic Press.

Gahrielsson, A. (1974) Performance of rhythm patterns. *Scandinavian Journal of Psychology,* **15**, 63–72.

Gabrielsson, A. (1985) Interplay between analysis and synthesis in studies of music performance and music experience. *Music Perception,* **3.1**, 59–86.

Gruson, L. (1988) Rehearsal skill and musical competence: Does practice make perfect? In J. A. Sloboda (Ed.) *Generative processes in music. The psychology of composition, improvisation and performance.* London: Oxford University Press.

Harrer, G. and Harrer, H. (1977) Music, emotion and autonomic function. In M. Critchley and R. A. Henson (Eds.). *Music and the brain. Studies in the neurology of music.* London: Heinemann.

Hirshkowitz, M., Earle, J., and Paley, B. (1978) EEG Alpha asymmetry in musicians and non-musicians: A study of hemisphere specialization. *Neuropsychologia,* **16**, 125–128.

Kuhn, T. S. (1962) *The structure of scientific revolutions.* Chicago: University of Chicago Press.

Lerdahl, F. and Jackendoff, R. (1983) *A generative theory of tonal music.* Cambridge, MA: MIT Press.

Lerdahl, F. (1988) Compositional systems and psychological reality. In J. Sloboda (Ed.). *Generative processes in music: The psychology of composition, improvisation and performance.* London: Oxford University Press.

Longuet-Higgins, H. C. (1972) Making sense of music. *Proceedings of the Royal Institute of Great Britain,* **45**, 87–105.

Longuet-Higgins, H. C. (1976) Perception of melodies. *Nature,* **263**, 646–653.

Longuet-Higgins, H. C. (1983) All in theory—the analysis of music. *Nature,* **304**, 93.

Martin, J. G. (1972) Rhythmic (hierarchical) versus serial structure in speech and other behaviour. *Psychological Review,* **79**, 487–509.

McAdams, S. (1982) Spectral fusion and the creation of auditory images. In M. Clynes (Ed.). *Music, mind and brain: The neuropsychology of music.* New York: Plenum.

McKee, G., Humphrey, B., and McAdam, D. W. (1973) Scaled lateralisation of alpha activity during linguistic and musical tasks. *Psychophysiology,* **10**, 441–443.

Michon, J. A. (1974) Programs and 'programs' for sequential patterns in motor behaviour. *Brain Research,* **71**, 413–424.

Minsky, M. (1982) Music, mind and meaning. In M. Clynes (Ed.). *Music, mind and brain: The neuropsychology of music.* New York: Plenum.

Narmour, E. (1983) Some major theoretical problems concerning the concept of hierarchy in the analysis of tonal music. *Music Perception,* **1.2**, 129–199.

Peel, J. and Slawson, W. (1984) Review of *A generative theory of tonal music. Journal of Music Theory,* **28.2**, 271–294.

Pollard-Gott, L. (1983) Emergence of thematic concepts in repeated listening to. music. *Cognitive Psychology,* **15**, 66–94.

Pressing, J. (1988) Improvisation: methods and models. In J. Sloboda (Ed.). Generative processes in music: *The psychology of composition, improvisation and performance.* London: Oxford University Press.

Rasch, R. A. (1979) Synchronization in performed ensemble music. *Acustica,* **43**, 121–131.

Reitman, W. R. (1965) *Cognition and thought.* New York: Wiley.

Rosner, B. (1984) Review of *A generative theory of tonal music*. *Music Perception*, **2.2**, 275–290.

Rosner, B. and Meyer, L. B. (1982) Melodic processes and the perception of music. In D. Deutsch (Ed.). *The psychology of music*. New York: Academic Press.

Sagi, M. and Vitanyi, I. (1988) Experimental research into musical generative ability. In J. Sloboda (Ed.). *Generative processes in music: The psychology of composition improvisation and performance*. London: Oxford University Press.

Shaffer, L. H. (1981) Performance of Chopin, Bach, and Bartok: Studies in motor programming. *Cognitive Psychology*, **13**, 326–376.

Shaffer, L. H. (1984) Timing in solo and duet piano performances. *Quarterly Journal of Experimental Psychology*, **36A**, 577–595.

Sloboda, J. A. (1984) Experimental studies of music reading: A review. *Music Perception*, **2.2**, 222–236.

Sloboda, J. A. (1985a). Expressive skill in two pianists: Style and effectiveness in music performance. *Canadian Journal of Psychology*, **39**, 273–293.

Sloboda, J. A. (1985b). *The musical mind: The cognitive psychology of music*. London: Oxford University Press.

Sloboda, J. A. and Gregory, A. H. (1981) The psychological reality of musical segments. *Canadian Journal of Psychology*, **34**, 274–280.

Sloboda, J. A.., Hermelin, B., and O'Connor, N. (1985) An exceptional musical memory. *Music Perception*, **3.2**, 155–170.

Sloboda, J. A. and Parker, D. H.H. (1985) Immediate recall of melodies. In P. Howell, I. Cross and R. West (Eds). *Musical structure and cognition*. New York: Academic Press.

Smith, K. C. and Cuddy, L. L. (1986) The pleasingness of melodic sequences: Contrasting effects of repetition and rule familiarity. *Psychology of Music*, **14.1**, 17–32.

Sternberg, S., Knoll, R. L. and Zukofsky, P. (1982) Timing by skilled musicians. In D. Deutsch (Ed.). *The psychology of music*. New York: Academic Press.

Sundberg, J., Askenfelt, A., and Fryden, L. (1983) Music performance: A synthesis by rule approach. *Computer Music Journal*, **7**, 37–43.

Sundberg, J., and Fryden, L. (1976) Teaching a computer to play melodies musically. In *Analytica. Studies in honor of Ingmar Begtsson*. Publication no 47 issued by the Royal Swedish Academy of Music, 67–76.

Tan, N., Aiello, R., and Bever, T. G. (1981) Harmonic structure as a determinant of melodic organization. *Memory and Cognition*, **9**, 533–539.

Todd, N. (1985) A model of expressive timing in tonal music. *Music Perception*, **3.1**, 33–58.

Ulrich. J. W. (1977) The analysis and synthesis of jazz by computer. *Proceedings of the 5th International Joint Conference on Artificial Intelligence*, pp. 865–872.

Vos, J., and Rasch, R. (1982) The perceptual onset of musical tones. In M. Clynes (Ed.). *Music, mind and brain: The neuropsychology of music*. New York: Plenum.

CHAPTER 6

PSYCHOLOGICAL STRUCTURES IN MUSIC: CORE RESEARCH 1980–1990

6.1 Selecting the core topics

The 1980s saw a huge increase in the quantity and quality of psychologically oriented investigations into music. A full account of recent advances would fill several books. A brief chapter like this must make drastic selections if it is to be more than an annotated bibliography. It seems important to make the selection on explicit and rational bases, rather than on personal whim, and so I devote the first section of this chapter to outlining my method for selecting what to include.

In 1983 I completed a major review of the field of psychology of music as I saw it at the time. This was published as a book (Sloboda 1985a). In this book I paid as much attention to underdeveloped areas of study that I believed deserved attention (such a composition and performance) as I did to well-studied areas (such as the perception of brief musical fragments). My intention for this essay is to complement the earlier book by concentrating on work published since 1983, and by focusing on the central themes that emerge from this work. This means that if a topic is poorly represented in the central literature, I will not deal with it here.

It is always difficult to define what counts as central work, but my task has been made easier by the inauguration in 1983 of the journal *Music Perception* under the inspired and dedicated editorship of Diana Deutsch. This journal has rapidly established itself as the flagship of the psychology of music confraternity. Its bias is experimental and theoretical, seeking to understand the basic perceptual and cognitive processes that underlie musical behaviour; and it is the only psychological journal that attracts significant contributions from music theorists as well as psychologists. Because of its unrivalled pre-eminence, it seems entirely sensible to confine my review to the issues raised within the pages of that journal (volumes 1–5, 1983–8).

Even this, however, is too wide a brief, since the first five volumes contain over 100 contributions. To determine which papers could be classed as relating to core issues, I undertook a citation analysis of all the papers in the first five volumes. Table 6.1 shows the ten most cited publications

Table 6.1 The ten most frequently cited publications in Volumes 1–5 of
Music Perception

Author	Date	Title and source	Number of citations
Deutsch, D. and Feroe, J.	1981	The internal representation of pitch sequences in tonal music', *Psychological Review, **88**, 503–22.*	17
Lerdahl, F. and Jackendoff, R.	1983	*A Generative Theory of Tonal Music,* Cambridge, MA: MIT Press.	17
Dowling, W. J.	1978	Scale and contour: two components of a theory of memory for melodies. *Psychological Review, **85**, 341–354.*	15
Krumhansl, C. L.	1979	The psychological representation of musical pitch in a musical context. *Cognitive Psychology, **11**, 346–374.*	15
Schenker, H.	1979	*Free Composition,* trans. E. Oster, New York: Longman. Originally published as *Die freie Satz* (1935).	12
Helmholtz, H.	1954	*On the Sensations of Tone as a Physiological Basis for the Theory of Music,* trans. A. J. Ellis, New York: Dover. Originally published 1863.	12
Krumhansl, C, L. and Kessler, E.	1982	Tracing the dynamic changes in perceived tonal organisation in a spatial representation of musical keys. *Psychological Review, **89**, 334–368.*	12
Shepard, R. N.	1982	Structural representations of musical pitch. In: D. Deutsch (ed.) *Psychology of Music.* New York: Academic Press.	11
Krumhansl, C L. and Shepard, R. N.	1979	Quantification of the hierarchy of tonal functions within a diatonic context. *Journal of Experimental Psychology: Human Perception and Performance, **5**, 579–94.*	10
Meyer, L. B.	1973	*Explaining Music,* Berkeley: University of California Press.	9

summed across all contributions to the journal. These ten key publications were then used as a 'sieve' to select papers from the journal to form the basis of this review. The criterion adopted for inclusion was that the paper should cite at least three of these ten key publications. Table 6.2 gives a list of the nineteen papers selected in this way. They are listed in citation

Table 6.2 Nineteen core articles from Volumes 1–5 of *Music Perception*

Author(s)	Volume	Number of items from Table 6.1 cited by author
Rosner, B. S. and Meyer, L. B.	4.1	8
Lerdahl, F.	5.3	8
Krumhansl, C. L.	1.1	7
Brown, H.	5.3	7
Deutsch, D. and Boulanger, R. C.	2.1	6
Roberts, L. A. and Shaw, M. L.	2.1	6
Bharucha, Jj.	5.1	6
Kessler, E. J., Hansen, C., and Shepard, R. N.	2.2	5
Hantz, E.	2.2	5
Cuddy, L.	2.3	5
Lerdahi, F. and Jackendoff, R.	1.2	4
Butler, D. and Brown, H.	2.1	4
Swain, J. P.	4.1	4
Krumhansl, C. L., Sandell, G. J., and Sergeant D. C.	5.1	4
Cross, I., West, R., and Howell, P.	2.3	3
Todd, N.	3.1	3
Stoffer, T. H.	3.2	3
Deliège, I.	4.4	3
Cook, N.	5.2	3

order, so that the paper citing the largest number of the ten key references appears at the top.

6.2 The psychological approach to music

The fundamental characteristic that distinguishes the psychologist of music from the music theorist or analyst is the former's concern with empirical measurement of musical behaviour or response. A secondary concern is with 'generalizability' (both across listeners and across pieces). Psychologists are concerned to discover commonalities of response that hold across members of a population. Let us take a hypothetical example of what this would mean in practice.

Theorist X, writing about musical passage Y, states that a certain sequence leads to a sense of resolution at point Z. This statement is primarily based on the theorist's own informed intuitions. He or she has listened to the passage in question, has compared it to other passages, and has applied to it formal descriptions that may or may not be drawn from historically established modes of musical discourse. It is up to other readers to agree or disagree with the analysis offered.

Psychologist A, wishing to verify this statement, would begin by asking whether the notion of 'resolution' can be operationalized. Is the meaning of the term clear enough that a task can be devised that would allow judgements of 'resolution' to be measured in an objective and unambiguous way? A typical psychological operationalization of such a concept might be embedded in an instruction such as this: 'please listen to each of the following short musical sequences and rate, on a scale of 1 to 10, the degree to which you perceive each sequence as coming to an acceptable close (i.e. the degree to which the sequence sounds 'finished'). Award the mark of 1 if you hear the sequence as not at all closed, and 10 if you hear it as perfectly closed.'

Let us suppose, for convenience, that passage Y contains twelve chords, and that the theorist proposes the eighth chord in the sequence as point Z (the point of maximum resolution). A possible tactic for the psychologist would be to construct a set of sequences made up of between one and twelve chords, each starting on chord 1 of Y but ending on a different chord of the sequence. A psychological verification of X's statement would be obtained if a random sample of an appropriate population rated the sequence ending on chord 8 as significantly more closed than other sequences. Typically, sample size would be twenty to forty individuals, drawn from student populations with general musical interests but little formal theory or analysis training.

Problems of operationalizing musical responses are not trivial ones. These problems explain, to a significant degree, why psychologists have made so little progress in exploring the higher levels of musical response, including the emotional and aesthetic aspects of the response. Even if all such problems were solved, however, it would not make psychological work easy. There are just too many statements in the music literature for psychologists to verify each one of them. The work required to verify the single sentence uttered by Theorist X concerning passage Y could easily keep a psychological researcher busy for weeks, if not months. At the end of the research, all that would have been accomplished would be a verification of X's acumen with respect to that passage.

The selection of research topics must be guided by further considerations, and these considerations are ones that psychologists and music theorists probably share. Both professions are centrally concerned with explaining responses to music. So if X's views on Y are to be accorded any professional weight they should contain reference to some general principles by virtue of which the specific judgement is made (i.e. Z is the point of closure because it has formal properties K, L, M, etc.). It is proposed that closure is generally signalled by such properties within a musical genre.

Given such potential explanations the psychologist is now in a much better position to carry out useful research. Musical passages may be collected (or constructed) in which the presence or absence of the various formal features K, L, M, etc., is systematically manipulated, and listeners' responses to these passages measured in some way. This activity will commend itself to psychologists, particularly when the features so defined are common to a whole range of music, rather than a small sub-set of pieces or genres. For this reason, the central topics in psychological research have been concerned with aspects of musical structure that are common to the widest body of music for which there exists a formal literature of theory and analysis: Western tonal music, whether art, folk, or popular.

This concern is reflected in the citation orientation of contemporary psychological research (as shown in Table 6.1). More psychologists take Schenker or Meyer, or Lerdahl and Jackendoff as their analytic reference point than, say, Babbitt (who rates sixty-fifth in the citation ranking, with only three out of one hundred authors referring to him). This does not simply reflect the musical conservatism (or populism) of psychologists (although this may be a contributing factor), but a genuine scientific concern to explain historically and culturally pervasive aspects of music before looking at forms that inhabit a more prescribed and closed domain.

The other thing that is abundantly clear from Table 6.1 is the predominance of pitch (over rhythm, metre, timbre and form) as a dimension for psychological investigations. Only one of the top ten citations (Lerdahl and Jackendoff) deals with rhythm, metre, or large-scale form in any substantial way.

6.3 Krumhansl's research: a benchmark

Table 6.1 shows that the work of Carol Krumhansl and associates has achieved an unrivalled pre-eminence in the field, with three out of the top ten citations going to work from her laboratory. This work provided a solid benchmark for the whole field of psychology of music for the 1980s. It is not necessarily the most adventurous or far-reaching research, but it represents a secure platform of scientific achievement which has undoubtedly raised the general standards and expectations of the field to new levels, and against which any new development must be compared.

Krumhansl's work (ably summarized in Krumhansl 1983) is essentially an experimental verification of traditional theoretical notions about tonal relationships (between notes, chords and keys). It is common in many formal and informal theories of tonality to refer to the keys of C major and F# major as 'distant', whilst C major and G major are 'close'. Similarly, the third and fifth degrees of the major scale are held to be musically closer to the tonic than the second degree (which is actually closer in pitch). Do these, and other theoretically accepted statements, have good grounding in the actual responses of theoretically naive listeners?

Krumhansl's method for investigating such questions is to use experimentally constructed 'minimal' stimuli which are usually computer generated. This means that all aspects other than the ones under investigation can be strictly controlled (duration, loudness, attack, etc.). Each stimulus consists of two parts: (a) a tonal context, which could be a scale, a tonic chord, or a perfect cadence in the relevant key, (b) a test stimulus, which could be a note, a chord or a pair of items. When the test stimulus is a single item, listeners are asked to rate the degree to which it fits with or completes the context. In the case of pairs of items, listeners may be asked to rate the similarity or closeness of the two items to one another in the context. In all cases, such ratings are made on a numerical scale.

6.3.1 Rating of notes in a tonal context

A specific example of this approach is a study by Krumhansl and Kessler (1982) which asked adult listeners to rate each note of the chromatic scale for how well it fitted, in a musical sense, with the key-defining context. The listeners had a moderate to high level of musical experience, but no explicit instruction in music theory. Figure 6.1 shows the mean results for the major and minor key contexts (averaged over all keys as if in C). The results are clear and unequivocal. Notes of the tonic triad were given the highest rating, followed by notes of the diatonic scale, with chromatic notes being given the lowest rating. This exactly confirms traditional music theory.

Thinkers about music have long been concerned to offer explanations for why certain pitch relationships (such as the octave and the fifth) seem particularly privileged. The appearance of Helmholtz high in the citation rankings signals psychologists' recognition of his seminal contribution in this area. He pointed to the fact that many pitch combinations that we judge most consonant or harmonically central have a strong coincidence of harmonic overtones. So, for instance, the first (and usually strongest) non-octave harmonic of a natural tone is the fifth degree of the scale, the next is the major third, and so on.

Although overtone consonance is a probable factor in the historical development of musical scales, it has a number of shortcomings as a psychological explanation. For one thing, consonance rankings do not match Krumhansl's rankings in a minor scale context, as Figure 6.1 shows. In particular, the

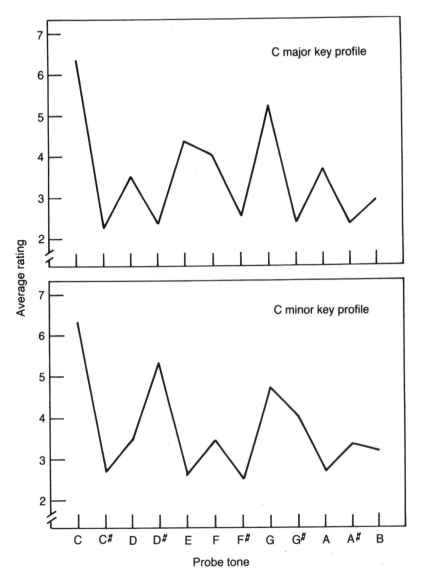

Figure 6.1 The major and minor key profiles obtained by Krumhansl and Kessler. The profile for the major key (upper graph) is the average rating given each of the twelve notes of the chromatic scale following a tonic triad chord or a cadence in a major key. The minor key profile (lower graph) is averaged over the minor tonic triad and minor cadences. The profiles are shown with respect to C major and minor, respectively. Source: Krumhansl and Kessler 1982. (© 1982 the American Psychological Association, reprinted by permission)

minor third is a less consonant interval than the major third, yet the minor third degree of the scale is judged more fitting than the major third in the minor context.

Another sign of the inadequacy of the consonance explanation is the existence of individual differences between listeners based on their degree of musical experience. For instance, Krumhansl and Shepard (1979) tested adults with negligible musical instruction on a pitch-rating task, and found that these subjects based their ratings primarily on pitch height rather than harmonic relatedness. Even more dramatically, Kessler, Hansen and Shepard have undertaken cross-cultural work using similar tasks, comparing the responses of Balinese adults who have rarely heard Western music to the responses of those familiar with Western music (Kessler *et al.* 1984*).

Although there were some similarities in response across groups, the results supported the notion that listeners are more likely to rank notes in terms of tonal relationships when the stimuli are based on scales with which they are familiar, in comparison with those with which they are not familiar.

A third source of evidence against consonance-based explanations is recent work by Krumhansl, Sandell and Sergeant, in which the probe-tone technique was applied to twelve-tone serial music (Krumhansl *et al.* 1987*). In a complex series of experiments, the authors show that listeners familiar with twelve-tone music made judgements that could be predicted from formal constraints of this idiom. For instance, they were more likely to judge a note as fitting the context of a preceding partial tone-row if it had *not* occurred in the context.

These are simply three examples from many which show that important perceptual responses to music are learned as a result of exposure to music (see Hargreaves 1986; Sloboda 1985a). Responses based purely on physical consonance should, arguably, be little affected by experience.

A more promising line of psychological explanation is based on the proposal that musical works of a genre contain within them statistical and sequential regularities which allow listeners to build up relatedness profiles for pitches and chords. For instance, note counts on melodic lines in a corpus of non-modulating tonal music (see Youngblood 1958; Knopoff and Hutchinson 1983; Krumhansl 1990) show that the tonic, third and fifth degrees of the scale are the most frequently repeated notes, followed by the diatonic set, with chromatic notes occurring least often. The correlation between these counts and the ratings in Krumhansl's own experiments is high (over 0.85). When counts include all notes in a piece (not just the melodic lines) and accord notes a weighting according to their duration (e.g. Hughes 1977, also cited by Krumhansl 1990), then the correlation becomes almost perfect (0.969).

However, the demonstration that such regularities exist in the music is not a demonstration that the listener can necessarily pick them up during normal music listening, nor does it lead to a proposal for a mechanism for doing so. A logical next step in this research would be the construction of a computer program that embodies a proposed learning mechanism, is then exposed to a large body of music in a particular idiom, such as Western tonal music or Balinese music, and ends up responding to Krumhansl-like tasks as appropriate human listeners respond. A principal problem for such a mechanism would be how to store the information in such a way that data from pieces in different keys could be combined. If the combination were to be done on grounds of absolute pitch, then the pre-eminence of particular pitches would probably be destroyed. If the combination were to be done relative to the tonic of each piece, then a mechanism is required for determining what is the tonic. If that mechanism itself depended on the outcome of a note frequency count, then it is not clear that circularity could be avoided. The issue of tonic determination is examined in more detail below (see section 6.4).

6.3.2 Rating of chord pairs in a key context

A different set of music theory statements evaluated by Krumhansl concerns the relationship of chords and keys. Within a key, traditional music theory proposes that the chords of IV and V are particularly closely related to I (because of their closeness in the cycle of fifths, and their shared notes). An experiment by Bharucha and Krumhansl (1983) verified such statements by asking listeners to rate how closely related a pair of chords sounded when preceded by an orienting tonal context. The context could be either C major or F# major, and the pair of chords could also be either chords based on the C major or F# major scale. In order to avoid complications raised by inversions, voice leading, or pitch height (see Deutsch and Boulanger 1984), the chords were computer generated according to a technique first developed by Shepard (1964). Each pitch of the chord was duplicated at each audible octave, with a tailing-off in amplitude towards each edge of the audible range. This effectively destroys pitch height information, leaving 'pure' harmony as the only discriminable factor.

Within the experiment, listeners were exposed to every possible combination of pairs of chords within each key, and preceded by each key context. This allowed the application of two particularly powerful statistical techniques to the data: multi-dimensional scaling (Kruskal 1964) and hierarchical cluster analysis (Johnson 1967). These provide alternative representations of the psychological closeness of each item of a set to each other item. Figure 6.2 shows the basic results of such analyses applied to the chords of a single key within that key context. The left-hand box

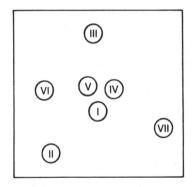 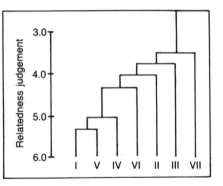

Figure 6.2 The multidimensional scaling solution (left panel) and the hierarchical clustering solution (right panel) of the relatedness ratings of chords in the basic set of harmonies of a key (1–VII). Source: Krumhansl *et al.* 1982b. (© 1982 the American Psychological Association, reprinted by permission)

shows a two-dimensional scaling solution where relatedness is given by spatial proximity. The right-hand box shows a cluster analysis, where relatedness is given by the level at which the branches for two chords meet. The lower the level, the higher the relatedness. Both analyses yield very similar pictures, confirming the high relatedness of I, IV and V within a key context.

One of the most important demonstrations of Bharucha and Krumhansl's study (1983) is that the perception of such relatedness is fragile and dependent on an appropriate key context. When chord pairs in C major were preceded by a C minor context, relationships like that in Figure 6.2 were discovered. When, however, the same chord pairs were preceded by an F# major context, their perceived relatedness dropped dramatically, and the privileged relation of I, IV and V disappeared. In informal musical language, the sudden key shift caused listeners to 'lose their tonal bearings' and be unable to interpret the new chords in a consistent tonal framework. The extent of this disruptive effect turns out to be directly related to key distance as measured round the cycle of fifths. A similar experiment by Krumhansl, Bharucha and Castellano, where chords in C major were preceded by a G major context, showed almost no disruption of the pattern obtained in Figure 6.2 (Krumhansl *et al.* 1982a). Listeners are able to retain tonal orientation provided that key shifts are small steps round the cycle of fifths. In such small steps, chords and notes are shared between the two keys, and these may perform some pivotal function (see also Lerdahl 1988*).

The key-distance effect is relatively robust, and can be found using several different tasks. An example of this is a study by Roberts and Shaw (1984*). They asked their subjects to judge whether or not two chords were of the same type (major, minor, diminished or augmented). Judgement was easiest when the two chords were from keys close to one another on the circle of fifths, although this effect was only apparent for highly trained musicians.

Similar effects were also found in a series of experiments reported by Bharucha (1987*) where, for instance, judgements about the intonation of a probe chord were fastest when preceded by a chord context from a relatively close key. Bharucha uses such data to construct a connectionist model of harmony, where notes, chords and keys are conceived of as nodes in a hypothetical 'neural' network. A web of connections between nodes means that when one node is activated, activation spreads through the network to nearby nodes. Such activation forms the basis of tonal expectation, and the model accounts neatly for data from a number of different sources. It is, however, a model for the hypothesized nodes and connections of an experienced listener. A satisfactory account of how such a network is developed from a primitive starting point has yet to be constructed. Also, as Bharucha is quick to point out, the model does not yet incorporate non-harmonic influences (e.g. voice leading) or activation patterns caused by the recollection of specific pieces of music. What is particularly important about Bharucha's work is the application of connectionist models to music. Connectionism is having a profound effect on theorizing in many other domains of psychology, and even though intense debate still rages about the ultimate usefulness of the approach, it is good to know that music is as good a testing ground for its assumptions as any other domain of cognitive functioning.

6.3.3 Limitations of Krumhansl's approach

The experimental approach outlined above has many merits from the scientific point of view. It provides rigorous quantified answers to questions of deep theoretical interest, and shows that the precision of a basically psychophysical approach need not be limited to single isolated stimuli, but can be used to study musically interesting phenomena such as the effects of key context.

None the less, like all single approaches, it has difficulties and shortcomings. A major problem is the unusualness and unspecificity of the judgements required from listeners. Most normal musical listening does not require overt judgements of the similarity or relatedness of simple events, and it is possible that such judgements may be dissociated from deeper and more automatic modes of musical processing. In addition, the instructions allow listeners a great deal of freedom to choose what dimensions of the sound they will include in their judgements of relatedness. This freedom may be exercised in arbitrary, or highly task-dependent ways. This consideration becomes particularly important when different groups of listeners (by age or culture) are examined. Differences in response may be due to differences in understanding of what is being asked, rather than in the organization of musical perception. This second problem is to a certain extent reduced as stable and consistent patterns emerge from the application of this technique across a wide variety of people on a wide variety of different tasks.

A different kind of objection has recently been raised by Butler (1989). He suggests that the ratings of a single tone in a tonal context might be an artefact of the specific context stimuli used in Krumhansl's experiments. The note profile of Figure 6.1 closely resembles a profile derived from the relative frequency of each note in the immediately preceding contexts. It is, therefore, possible that Krumhansl's results derive from short-term activation of specific notes rather than from an enduring internalized tonal schema. Butler's criticisms clearly merit examination and empirical substantiation. Whether or not the criticisms turn out to be well-founded they point to the dangers of relying too heavily on any one methodology as a basis for strong theoretical claims. The best validation of any theory is the discovery of converging evidence from different methods of enquiry. In this case, such evidence does exist, particularly from the study of musical memory tasks.

There are a large number of studies that have used a memory paradigm to investigate structural factors in music perception. Most of these studies have used recognition memory, in which listeners are required to say whether two musical sequences are the same or different. Generally these studies show that different sequences are most likely to be judged the same when the substituted item is close to the original along one of the metrics defined by Krumhansl's data. So, for instance, listeners detect a diatonic substitution (for example, E for G in C major) in a melody less well than a chromatic substitution (for example, F# for G in C major) (Cuddy *et al.* 1979). Similar results have been obtained for chord sequences (Bharucha and Krumhansl 1983).

A final shortcoming of Krumhansl's approach which relates particularly to the multidimensional scaling and cluster analysis techniques is that one has to test every possible pair of items in a set. This makes for a combinatorial explosion as the set size increases, and makes it very difficult to run experiments on large sets or on long musical passages. The issue of length also places limits on what can be included in recognition memory experiments as well. An alternative, but less well used technique is recall or reproduction, where listeners hear a musical passage and are asked to sing or play it back. Where it has been tried (e.g. Sloboda and Parker 1985), it has yielded data that are congruent with the recognition studies, but that display a variety of richer features that cannot be captured by the ecologically sparse response categories of the more typical experiment. In addition, such tasks are more musically natural, resembling, as they do, the way in which much music is actually learned.

There has, in fact, been a valuable interplay between those who start from the basis that strict experimental controls are paramount and those who start from the assumption that musical realism is paramount. On the first count, it is notable how Krumhansl's most recent work has moved towards greater musical realism (e.g. Palmer and Krumhansl 1987). That particular study used Bach fugue subjects as its stimulus materials and subjected them to ingenious experimental manipulations. On the second count, it is apparent that work based on realistic situations (such as performance) has become increasingly sophisticated in terms of the controls and theoretical models applied to the situation. This progression can be seen by comparing a relatively early study such as that by Gabrielsson (1974), which simply measures timing variations in free performance and attempts to induce some underlying regularities, with studies by Clarke (1988) and Sloboda (1983, 1985b) which manipulate performance materials in controlled ways in order to test specific theoretical ideas. This marrying of scientific control with musical realism is one of the factors which has led me to suggest (Sloboda 1986) that the psychology of music as a scientific discipline has now 'come of age'. Clearly, however, the tensions between these conflicting requirements are still strong, and will continue to act as a spur to new developments.

6.4 How do listeners establish a tonal centre?

The work of Krumhansl and others has shown that, with a suitable tonal context, listeners rate musical stimuli with respect to that context in accordance with many of the traditional tenets of music theory. Several investigators have sought to examine a further question: what is it that determines whether a context will or will not establish a strong sense of key or tonal centre? This is an immensely important issue for all tonal music because arguably listeners must establish the key of a piece within the first few bars (if not notes) if they are to code and store the musical material appropriately.

Hantz (1984*) raises this issue from the perspective of a music theorist, and suggests that some psychologists' views of what constitutes a tonal sequence are too naive. In particular, it is incorrect to suppose that a pitch sequence made up of notes from a single diatonic set will necessarily have strong tonal implications. The converse is also true: sequences with chromatic notes may have very strong tonal implications.

Butler and Brown (1984*) have suggested that one important factor facilitating identification of tonal centres is the detection of rare pitch intervals within the diatonic set. The rarest interval is, of course, the tritone (e.g. C–F#). Any given tritone can be found only in two major keys (in the case of C–F#, the keys are G major and C# major). Any added third note will specify a unique key (since the scales concerned share no other notes than the particular tritone). In contrast, a common interval like a perfect fourth (e.g. C–F#) can be found in five keys (C, F, B<flat>, E<flat>, A<flat> and D<flat>), and most additional single notes will not eliminate the ambiguity completely. Butler and Brown verified this hypothesis in an experiment where musicians were asked to listen to a three-note sequence and specify a tonic for the sequence. Where the sequence included a tritone, listeners consistently agreed on the correct tonic (which was not necessarily present in the stimulus sequence). Where the sequence did not contain a tritone, listeners did not agree, even when one of the three notes present was a possible candidate for tonic.

The order in which notes appear is also important, a finding confirmed and extended by Brown (1988*). She took short extracts from classical compositions which contained a variety of pitch sets, ranging from those containing too few pitches to specify uniquely a key ('unspecific'), through those uniquely specifying a single key ('specific'), to those containing pitch sets that could not be contained within a single key ('incongruent'). Examples of each type of extract are given in Figures 6.3, 6.4 and 6.5. In one part of the experiment, subjects heard the untransformed extracts and were asked to identify the tonic. Not surprisingly, there was greatest agreement in the case of the specific extracts.

Brown then constructed tone sequences—three for each extract—which contained one (and only one) of each of the pitch classes contained in each extract (see Figures 6.3–6.5). The A sequences were designed strongly to evoke the tonal centre of the corresponding music excerpt; B sequences were designed to evoke some tonal centre other than that of the corresponding excerpt. In both cases this was done by making the rarest interval from the diatonic set of the chosen key prominent in the sequence and supporting it with other notes that could be interpreted in the same key. This can be seen clearly in Figure 6.5, where the A sequence makes the B<flat>—E tritone prominent, while the B sequence makes the G—C# tritone prominent. The C sequences were designed to be ambiguous by obscuring and de-emphasizing rare intervals. The figures beneath the notes show the percentage of listeners choosing each note as tonic. In each case, the results showed strong effects of order on the choice of tonic. In the case of the 'specific'

Figure 6.3 Sample of Brown's stimuli with 'Unspecific' tonal content (Bartok: 85 pieces without octaves for children, 'Romance', mm. 8–12). Response percentages are shown for pitch strings (A) ordered to promote C major, local tonic of musical excerpt) (B) ordered to promote key of G major, and (C) ordered to promote tonal ambiguity. Source: Brown 1988. (© 1988 the Regents of the University of California, reprinted by permission)

extracts such as Figure 6.4, Brown's A sequences actually provoked more unanimity amongst listeners than did the original extract.

The work of Brown and Butler is a salutary reminder of the dangerous gap that can develop between theoretical formalisms and what listeners actually do. Listeners operate in real time and are subject to memory and other processing limitations. Many influential theories of musical structure are time—independent and assume no processing limitations. At a theoretical level, a pitch sequence may be tonally unambiguous. As a listener processes it from left to right, it may appear locally ambiguous, or even unambiguous in a different key. Such local perceptions may (and arguably often do) colour the perception of the whole passage.

Related work reported by Cross, West and Howell confirms this general point in a rather different way by demonstrating that the effects obtained also depend crucially on the task required of listeners (Cross *et al.* 1985*). In one of their experiments, listeners were asked to detect 'wrong notes'

Figure 6.4 Sample of Brown's stimuli with 'Specific' tonal content (Schubert: Sonata, D.664 (III), m. 49). Response percentages are shown for pitch strings (A) ordered to promote D major, local tonic of musical excerpt, (B) ordered to promote key of G major, and (C) ordered to promote tonal ambiguity. Source: Brown 1988. (© 1988 the Regents of the University of California, reprinted by permission)

in sequences. Wrong notes were notes that could not be contained in the scale(s) implied by the previous notes of the sequence. They found that wrong-note detection was better after sequences such as C–F–G than after sequences containing the tritone, such as B–F–G. On first examination this seems to contradict Brown and Butler. Surely the tritone B–F creates the strongest key sense, making the wrong note 'stand out' most strongly. Cross *et al.* argue convincingly that the better detection of a wrong note in the first sequence is a function of its uniqueness. There is only one note, F#, that is incompatible with any major scale that contains C–F–G. There are five possible wrong notes with respect to the B–F–G sequence (C#, D#, F#, G# and A#). So an F# in the first sequence sounds more wrong than an F# in the second sequence.

Salutary as the work of Brown and Butler is, it also has some puzzling aspects. A straightforward application of their findings suggests that tonal music compositions should contain the fa–te tritone (to use sol-fa terms) in

Figure 6.5 Sample of Brown's stimuli with 'Incongruent' tonal content (Mozart: Sonata, K.570 (I), m. 49). Response percentages are shown for pitch strings (A) ordered to promote F major, local tonic of musical excerpt, (B) ordered to promote key of D major, and (C) ordered to promote tonal ambiguity. Source: Brown 1988. (© 1988 the Regents of the University of California, reprinted by permission)

the first few notes if listeners are to identify the key most efficiently. The reality is that almost no tonal pieces start in this way, yet listeners are still able to identify the key extremely well. Figure 6.6 shows the opening bars of Mozart's piano sonata K.576 in D major. Although I do not have experimental data, I would be very surprised if a large majority of listeners did not identify the tonic as D, even though the tritone is absent. Although it is theoretically possible that the piece is in G major or A major, it is psychologically impossible for me to hear it that way. It has to be in D.

A number of investigators have attempted to tackle the issue of key identification from a purely theoretical perspective by constructing algorithms

Figure 6.6 Mozart: Sonata, K.576 (1), bars 1–2.

that take the early notes of a piece as input, and produce candidate keys as output (e.g. Longuet-Higgins and Steedman 1971; Krumhansl 1990). These algorithms work from left to right through a sequence, and their output is therefore sensitive to pitch order. The Longuet-Higgins and Steedman algorithm takes single-line melodies as input and discards all information except pitch-class order. As it moves from left to right through the melody, it successively eliminates keys within which the notes heard so far cannot be contained. When this process fails to come up with a unique key (or eliminates all keys) there is a fall-back procedure that looks at the very first note of the sequence to see if it is the tonic of one of the candidate keys remaining (or eliminated last). If not, the first note is assumed to be the dominant of the correct key. This algorithm assigns the correct key to all forty-eight of the Bach fugue subjects from the *Well-Tempered Clavier*. It is apparent straight away that this algorithm will be greatly helped by encountering a tritone early in the sequence, thus supporting Brown and Butler's data. It would, however, fail to reach a conclusion concerning Figure 6.6 above.

Krumhansl's algorithm combines pitch-class information with durational information so as to compute a running duration total for each note of the chromatic set. This yields a duration profile which is correlated with the prominence profile for each major and minor key obtained in the Krumhansl and Kessler (1982) study (see Figure 6.1 above). The algorithm does not yield a unique key, but assigns to each of the twenty-four keys a relative likelihood rating, which can be updated from note to note, as the piece progresses. It is clear from Figure 6.1 that this algorithm will be helped most by early emphasis on the primary harmonic notes of the scale, particularly tonic and dominant. By note 2 of Figure 6.6, the correlations to D major and D minor should be well above all other values, with note 5 (F#) pushing D major further ahead. The system also handles the tritone reasonably well, not because a tritone produces high correlations to the two candidate keys, but because it produces even lower correlations for all other keys. If we suppose that it is not the absolute level of correlation that counts psychologically, but relative differences in correlation across the twenty-four key 'monitors', with keys that 'stand out' from the others being considered as candidates, then Krumhansl's algorithm appears to be a much more satisfactory one than that of Longuet-Higgins and Steedman.

Neither algorithm, however, is entirely plausible as a psychological mechanism. The Longuet-Higgins and Steedman algorithm places too great a load on short-term memory, since the system must hold the first note of the piece together with a list of keys eliminated (or not eliminated).

The memory of the first note will be particularly important when the sequence does not establish an unambiguous tonal centre early on. But, as Deutsch (1970) and others have demonstrated, memory for pitch is most fragile precisely in that situation, and is unlikely to survive more than a handful of intervening notes.

Similarly, the memory of the Krumhansl algorithm is probably too good. If it accumulates all information about pitch frequency from the beginning of a piece, then it will accumulate great tonal inertia, and will not hear a modulation as establishing a new key until the new notes have been heard as often as the ones left behind. However, this problem could probably be quite easily 'fixed' by building in a time-decay function to the pitch-duration counters. My intuition is that the best decay function would be exponential, with a rapid early decay, but a lingering residual. This would allow for reasonably rapid establishment of new keys after modulations, but would allow for an advantage of returning to the 'home' key after a tonal excursion.

A more fundamental shortcoming of all such algorithms is that they operate entirely without respect to other structural cues, such as rhythm and metre, dynamics, articulation and timbre. It is evident that these factors interact in the psychological determination of key. For instance a note placed on a metrical accent or played at a greater intensity than its neighbours is more likely to be considered as a candidate for tonic than an unaccented passing note.

6.5 Hierarchies as psychological structures for the representation of music

One of the reasons why music appears interesting and comprehensible is that it contains various kinds of structure that the human mind is capable of apprehending. It has often been claimed that making sense of music *is* the process of discovering and representing its structure. An important class of such structures is the class of hierarchical structures. Rather than attempt a definition of hierarchies, I will give examples of two major types of hierarchic structure which I will call *reductional* hierarchies and *grouping* hierarchies. These are not exclusive categories. A given hierarchy can be of both types, but it is difficult to imagine a hierarchical structure that is of neither type.

A good example of a reductional hierarchy is that proposed by Deutsch and Feroe (1981—the most cited reference in *Music Perception*). In Lerdahl's adaptation of their model (Lerdahl 1988*) the chromatic set of pitches is represented as a five-level hierarchy (see Figure 6.7). Each level describes

level 1:	C											(C)
level 2:	C							G				(C)
level 3:	C				E			G				(C)
level 4:	C		D		E	F		G		A		B	(C)
level 5:	C	Db	D	Eb	E	F	F♯	G	Ab	A	Bb	B	(C)

Figure 6.7 The pitch space orientated towards the tonic chord of C major as postulated by Lerdahl. Source: Lerdahl 1988. (© 1988 the Regents of the University of California, reprinted by permission)

an 'alphabet' (i.e. an ordered functional pitch set). Level 1 contains notes related to one another at the octave; level 2 adds the open fifth space; level 3 adds the notes of a diatonic triad; level 4 adds the remaining notes of the diatonic set (in this example the major diatonic scale), and level 5 adds the remaining chromatic notes.

What makes this a reductional hierarchy is the fact that as one progresses from lower to higher levels, elements are dropped from the representation. Only the most 'important' or 'salient' elements survive to higher levels. In this model, the alphabets are defined culturally, and so may be different for different groups of people or types of music.

A major psychological prediction of the Deutsch and Feroe model is that sequences that can be represented in terms of stepwise movements up or down any (or several) of these alphabets will be easier to represent (and thus remember) than other types of sequence. Such movements tend to produce repeating patterns of a type very common in classical tonal music, and experimental evidence (e.g. Deutsch 1980) supports the prediction that such sequences are easy to remember. Figure 6.8 gives one such sequence, and shows how it can be represented as a chromatic turn (one step down and one step up at level 5) repeated at four successive descending positions at level 3.

Lerdahl (1988) also points out that the model accounts for some of the implicative characteristics of melody suggested by Meyer (1973). A stepwise movement at any level of the hierarchy seems to create an implication for further movement at that level. The implication is strongest when the initial movement is on to a note that is not represented at the next highest level. For instance, in C major, a move from C to D strongly suggests a movement to E, because D is not contained in level 3, but E is. The implication for further movement to F is not so strong, because E serves as a structural resolution to the sequence.

An example of a grouping hierarchy is provided by Lerdahl and Jackendoff (1983, 1984). In their theory, which will be discussed more fully below, it is claimed that an experienced listener parses a musical sequence into non-overlapping groups of events, which are given such standard musical names

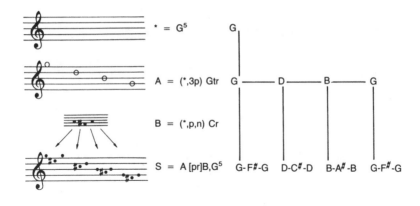

Key:
* reference note;
p downward movement of one step within an alphabet;
n upward movement of one step within an alphabet;
Gtr alphabet of the G major triad;
Cr alphabet of the choromatic scales;
A[pr]B the application of pattern B to each element of pattern A.

Figure 6.8 Formal representation of a hierarchically organized tone sequence after Deutsch and Feroe. Source: Sloboda 1985a. (© 1985 Oxford University Press, reprinted by permission)

as *motifs*, *phrases*, and *sections*. A specific set of grouping preference rules is provided, which is claimed to capture intuitions about the musical features that incline a listener to place notes together in the same group, or to place a group boundary between them. An example of a grouping hierarchy produced by this theory is given in Figure 6.9.

The grouping mechanism produces a hierarchy because the groups formed at a basic level are then grouped into 'groups of groups', and so on, until the final level is reached where the whole piece is a single group. Unlike a reductional hierarchy, the grouping hierarchy includes all elements at every level. What changes is their degree of relatedness. At the top level, every element is related to every other element in the same way by being a member of the same group (the piece). At lower levels an element is most strongly related to other elements in its own group, progressively less related to elements in more distant groups.

We will consider the psychological evidence for this grouping hierarchy below. But first, we should note the contrast between the two hierarchies just described. The reductional hierarchy of Deutsch and Feroe (1981) is not a grouping hierarchy. For instance the relationship of C# to its neighbours C and D is not specified in the hierarchy. It forms a group with neither of them. Lerdahl and Jackendoff's grouping hierarchy is not reductional.

Figure 6.9 The grouping structure of Bach: 'Ich bin's, ich soilte bussen' from
St Matthew Passion. Source: Lerdahl and Jackendoff 1984. (© 1984 the Regents of the
University of California, reprinted by permission)

It does not nominate a sub-set of elements from a lower level to be given
prominence at a higher level. Some hierarchies, however, can be both
reductional and grouping. In these cases, groups are formed, but a single
item from each group is nominated as the head member of the group, and
goes forward to form an element at the next highest level. An example
of such a hierarchy is the *time-span reduction* of Lerdahl and Jackendoff
(1983, 1984).

Hierarchies are very appealing to human beings. The vast majority of
social structures depend upon them, and many of our theories of how the
world is and works are couched in hierarchic terms. Many children enjoy
writing their address as, for instance, 35 Any Street, Newtown, Overshire,
England, Europe, The World, The Solar System, The Milky Way, The
Universe. In doing so they are building a grouping hierarchy of physical

locations. The command chain of any organization usually represents a reductional hierarchy.

Because hierarchies are so appealing they bring with them a danger. People tend to impose hierarchical explanations to an extent that may be inappropriate. In particular, what works well at a local level may not necessarily translate to higher levels, and vice versa. There is a satisfying elegance to complete hierarchic descriptions of entire pieces of music (such as those supplied by Schenker (1979) and Lerdahl and Jackendoff (1983)), but many observers, including psychologists, have pointed out that the ability to describe something in hierarchic terms does not necessarily mean that listeners represent what they hear according to such descriptions (see, for instance, Rosner 1984).

6.5.1 The psychological status of Lerdahl and Jackendoff's theory

Lerdahl and Jackendoff's generative theory of tonal music (Lerdahl and Jackendoff 1983)—henceforth GTTM—is the most ambitious attempt to date at a complete theory of what a listener knows when he or she knows a well-formed piece of tonal music. In the words of Lerdahl and Jackendoff (1984) the theory

> takes the form of explicit rules that assign, or 'generate', heard structures from musical surfaces. By 'musical surface' we mean, broadly, the physical signal of a piece when it is played. By 'heard structure' we mean all the structure a listener unconsciously infers when he listens to and understands a piece, above and beyond the data of the physical signal.

GTTM has a number of self-confessed limitations. It represents the supposed understanding of an experienced listener who knows a piece well. It does not attempt to construct a model of how such a representation is built up in real time and over repeated hearings. As justification for this limitation the authors appeal to Marr (1981) and others, who argue that one cannot sensibly investigate mechanism until one knows the endpoint that the mechanism is meant to achieve. A second limitation is its failure to deal with non-hierarchic aspects of music, or polyphonic counterpoint. GTTM is unique in a number of ways. It goes beyond the reductional approach of Schenker in specifying explicit rules for moving from lower levels of the hierarchy to higher ones. It also captures the intuition that musical awareness is multidemensional. GTTM proposes not one hierarchical reduction but four, which proceed independently, although they interact at higher levels. In addition to *grouping structure* mentioned above, there is *metrical structure, time-span reduction,* and *prolongational reduction.* Metrical structure is the hierarchy of repeating patterns of strong and weak beats. GTTM proposes that metrical structure is only extracted up to inter-mediate levels, spanning a few seconds. This accords with the intuition that we do not hear large-scale timing regularities as metre. Time-span reduc-tion creates a tree-like hierarchy for the whole piece. At each level, the most prominent element (defined metrically or harmonically) is chosen as the head element to be represented at the next higher level. Such reduc-tion often ends with the Schenkerian *Ursatz* (I–V–I) at the higher level. Prolongational reduction is analogous to time-span reduction, but attempts to capture the flux of harmonic tension and resolution within a piece.

GTTM is also unique in proposing that most of the rules determining the formation of these hierarachies are *preference* rules. They do not specify mandatory decisions, but incline the decision in one way or another. Grouping rules may conflict with one another. In such situations, the music may be heard as ambiguous. Lerdahl and Jackendoff arrange the preference rules in a rough weighting order by specifying that some pref-erences are 'strong' and others are 'weak', but they do not attempt to quantify these rules by assigning numbers to the weights. They do, however, present the preference rules as empirically testable, and explicitly invite experimental verification.

This challenge has been taken up by a number of researchers, notably Deliège (1987*) and Todd (1985*). Deliège focused on the local Grouping Preference Rules (see Figure 6.10) by asking musician and non-musician subjects to listen to brief musical excerpts and mark the positions of group boundaries. In a first experiment using recorded performances of classical instrumental music, Deliège found that the majority of musicians' choices (77%) were in accordance with GTTM rules. Choices not in accordance with the rules were of several types. For instance, some subjects did not group according to the length rule (Figure 6.10, Rule 6, right-hand example) but included the first long note in the same group as the shorter notes pre-ceding it, suggesting that, in real time, such sequences are likely to be inter-preted under proximity rules (Figure 6.10, Rule 2). Other results suggested the need for new rules. For instance, some subjects placed a boundary at the point of change in direction of melodic contour or of underlying harmony.

In a second experiment using constructed nine-note sequences, Deliège intro-duced features that would lead to conflicting segmentations on two different grouping rules. An example of such a sequence is given in Figure 6.11. Grouping by dynamic difference would produce a segmentation after note 3, but grouping by timbre would produce a segmentation after note 4.

Proximity Rules

Rule 1: Slur or Rest — Type 1

Rule 2: Attack-Point — Type 1

Change Rules

Rule 3: Register — Type 2

Rule 4: Dynamics — Type 2

Rule 5: Articulation — Type 1

Rule 6: Length — Type 1

Rule 7: Timbre — Type 2

Figure 6.10 The grouping preference rules of Lerdahi and Jackendoff. Source: Deliège 1987. (© 1987 the Regents of the University of California, reprinted by permission)

Subjects were allowed to choose only one grouping boundary in each sequence. The results were not simple, but were in general accordance with a higher-level grouping rule of GTTM (Symmetry) which says: 'Prefer grouping analyses that most closely approach the ideal subdivision of groups into two parts of equal length'. Subjects in Deliège's experiment showed a tendency to choose the grouping that most nearly divided the sequence into two equal halves. A general problem affecting the interpretation of Deliège's results is that the grouping preference expressed may depend on the relative magnitude of conflicting musical cues (for example,

Figure 6.11 Example of conflict between two rules: (a) segmentation for rule 4 (change in dynamics); (b) segmentation for rule 7 (change in timbre). Source: Deliège 1987. (© 1987 the Regents of the University of California, reprinted by permission)

a large dynamic contrast may 'win' over a small timbral change, but the preference may be reversed if the small timbral contrast is increased).

Todd's work (1985) stems from the now well-established position that expressive variation in musical performance is systematic, and performs the funtion of reinforcing a structural interpretation of the music. For instance, my own work (Sloboda 1983, 1985b) has shown how the local deviations in timing and loudness of pianists assists listeners to extract the intended metre of a musical passage. Shaffer (1981) has shown how such deviations tend to be stable over repeated performances by the same musician, not just at a local level, but also at more global levels, as indicated through the use of rubato or dynamic progressions. Todd focused on the expressive slowing at phrase and segment endings that is a characteristic of the performance of much Classical and Romantic music. His basic argument is that the degree of such slowing should represent the relative importance of that particular boundary in the time-span reduction of GTTM. Boundaries of major units (represented at high levels in the hierarchy) should receive greater amounts of slowing than lower-level boundaries. Todd incorporated these suppositions into a mathematical model, and Figure 6.12 shows the predictions of the model for a sixteen-bar phrase with the time-span reduction given at the top of the figure. The height of the line on the lower graph is an indication of the degree of deviation from tempo. Data from performances of the theme of Mozart's A Major Sonata (K.331) fit the predictions of the model extremely well. Since the time-span reduction of GTTM depends in part on identifying points of greater or lesser harmonic stability, an unambiguous reduction structure is less likely for music where the tonality is not so well defined. This is reflected in data from performances of Chopin's Etude No. 3 from *Trois Nouvelles Etudes*, where slowings are sometimes determined by local harmonic tensions and relaxations (prolongational structure) rather than the time-span reduction. This reflects the tonal instability of the central section of this piece. On the whole, however, the fit to GTTM is remarkably impressive. Todd's work is particularly encouraging because it shows that performance data can be

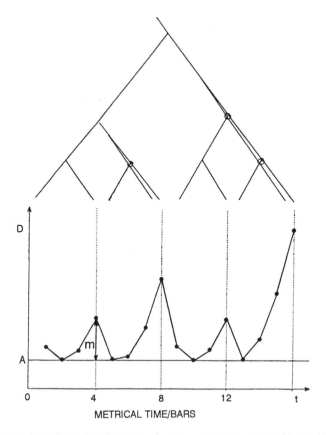

Figure 6.12 A hypothetical performance duration structure generated by Todd with the given time-span reduction above. Source: Todd 1985. (© 1985 the Regents of the University of California, reprinted by permission)

applied to the larger-scale aspects of GTTM. It is rather difficult to see what kind of listening tests could provide equally compelling evidence of large-scale awareness. Indeed, Rosner (1984) suggests that such levels are available only to musicians who can study the score of a piece, and are therefore represented in the minds of analysts, but not necessarily other listeners.

The amount of empirical work stimulated by GTTM is not yet large. One unexplored area is in respect of Lerdahl and Jackendoff's claim that many of the rules of GTTM are universal (i.e. they embody general facts about human perceptual and cognitive propensities and capacities, not just contingent facts about certain genres). It follows that music of all cultures and periods should be susceptible to analysis by modified versions of GTTM, and that cross-cultural data should support such analysis.

6.5.2 Other empirical investigations into structural perceptions

Although there have been few direct empirical tests of GTTM, a number of investigators have taken more general and less precise music-theoretic proposals as the basis for psychological investigation. For instance, Cook (1987*) investigated whether listeners were capable of perceiving large-scale tonal closure within a movement. To this end, he 'adjusted' a number of classical piano pieces so that they ended in a different key to that in which they started. University music students listened to both versions and were asked to rate them on a number of dimensions, including coherence and completion. For pieces lasting less than one minute, students rated the 'correct' version higher, but on longer pieces, there were no consistent differences between pieces. Cook argues that such data are damaging to many theories that attempt to explain the appeal of classical tonal music in terms of the tonal journey which starts and ends in the same key.

Rosner and Meyer (1986*) looked at the influence of melodic form (AA' vs. AA'B) on the perception of musical structure that has generally been held to have perceptual salience. In one of Rosner and Meyer's experiments (Experiment 5) melodies also differed in what the authors call 'melodic process'. This idea, originated by Meyer, 'specifies the principal motions by which a melody leaves its main starting point and finally achieves closure'. For instance a *gap fill* process 'has a large early skip, usually upward, of a fourth or more, followed by a more or less stepwise return to a point of closure'. In contrast an *Adeste Fideles* process, like the Christmas carol after which it is named,

> always involves two characteristic skips. The first spans a fourth and the next one a fifth. Both usually occur in the first half of the melody; the second skip leads to upward motion to the third or fourth of the scale, followed by downward resolution often to the tonic. (Meyer 1973: 19)

Examples of these two types of melody are given in Figure 6.13.

Rosner and Meyer asked listeners to rate all possible pairs of melodies within their experimental set for similarity. This allowed a multidimensional scaling to be produced (of a similar sort used by Krumhansl—see p. 126 above). A difficulty with using multidimensional scaling in this context is that it is not possible to compare all possible pairs in the universe under consideration: the universe is too ill-defined. And so there is a certain amount of 'ad-hoccery' in the choice of stimuli to include. This is in contrast to the studies of Krumhansl, which tend to sample every element of a given universe (for example, the chromatic set, the diatonic chord set).

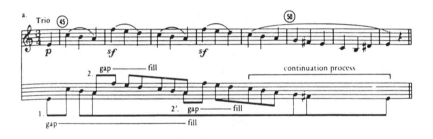

Figure 6.13 (a) Melody from Beethoven's Piano Sonata in A, op. 2 no. 2 (III) bars 45–52 with gap-fill processes shown in lower staff. (b) Melody from Handel's Flute Sonata in G, Op. 1 no 5 (V) bars 1–4 with Adeste Fideles process indicated on lower staff. Source: Rosner and Meyer 1986. (© 1986 the Regents of the University of California, reprinted by permission)

However, the broad results of this analysis showed that listeners grouped melodies in terms of melodic process but not in terms of form. In all their experiments, however, there were 'rogue' melodies that seemed to be classified on the basis of prominent local events. Rosner and Meyer argue that although analysts typically conduct their analyses in terms of large-scale features of the music, listeners are actually more likely to construct a representation that is primarily based on local features, although they do not rule out the possibility of achieving higher-order representations.

Implicit in the work of Cook and of Rosner and Meyer is the notion that there are processing limits on human cognitive capacity that limit what can be extracted from music, at least on early hearings (Swain 1986 makes this point more explicitly). Their findings do not show that people cannot hear out large-scale structure. They simply show that they do not usually do so in early listening *given the experimental tasks required of them*. This last caveat is important, because competence is sometimes tied quite firmly to particular tasks, and does not show itself in other tasks. With longer exposure and/or different tasks, it is still quite possible that we may find evidence of large-scale psychological representations. At the very least, the existence of unusual individuals who can reproduce large musical structures from memory after one or two hearings (see Sloboda *et al.* 1985) is a finding to put on the other side of the balance sheet.

The search for appropriate measures of structural awareness has led some researchers down what seem at first to be rather curious avenues. For instance, Stoffer (1985*) asked listeners to detect the location of clicks superimposed on musical sequences. This follows work in language (Fodor and Bever 1965) and music (Gregory 1978; Sloboda and Gregory 1980) showing that clicks are more accurately located when they occur at phrase boundaries. Indeed clicks near to phrase boundaries seem perceptually to migrate towards the boundary. The explanation for this phenomenon is that listeners try to organize their perception so that the extraneous event (the click) falls between the two structural units (the phrases). Stoffer's particular contribution was to extend the technique so that it could be used with non-musicians (the earlier studies relied on the ability to read a score to mark the click location). In his second experiment listeners were simply required to press a button as soon as they heard a click. The prediction was that reaction times would be faster at phrase boundaries since, in some sense, listeners were 'expecting' the click to fall there. This prediction was confirmed for both musicians and non-musicians, although the effects were stronger for musicians. The studies also show that 'simple' explanations of the skill are not sufficient. For instance, one possibility is that listeners simply divide melodies into two equal halves. Stoffer showed that when a phrase boundary occurred after one-third of a passage, the click judgements moved accordingly. Another possibility is that listeners identify phrase boundaries on the basis of some gross physical cue like a long note or a gap. Stoffer ruled out this explanation by making all notes of equal length and intensity. Phrase awareness must have been dependent on melodic or harmonic factors.

What is particularly interesting about this technique is that subjects are not required to make any judgement about the music at all, yet their 'subconscious' analyses reflect structural awareness in the absence of any formal knowledge about phrase structure. In this respect the technique resembles reproduction, but it does not depend (as reproduction does) on the practical musical accomplishment of the experimental subject. We need more 'indirect' measures of this sort to probe structural awareness in ordinary untrained listeners. Evidence from cognitive and perceptual psychology suggests that this 'back door' approach can often yield a richer picture of what is known than a direct judgement would suggest. A dramatic example of this is the work on subliminal perception. A stimulus of which a subject can give no conscious report can none the less measurably affect performance on some other task (Dixon 1981).

6.6 Concluding remarks

In this chapter I have attempted to give a fairly detailed picture of some central preoccupations of psychologists of music as represented through a citation-based selection of papers from the journal *Music Perception*. By any account these preoccupations relate to core issues in music. Tonal music is claimed by many analysts to gain its power and appeal from the complex structures that tonality can support, both on a small and a large scale. Psychologically based investigations have demonstrated the psychological reality of some of these structures, particularly those operating on a small scale. The investigations have been more equivocal in relation to larger structures. This may be because such structures reside only in the heads of specialists who analyse and write about music; but it may also be because we have not yet developed measuring techniques capable of capturing large-scale awareness.

Although the topics of this chapter are central, they do not by any means exhaust the psychology of music. The wide range of perceptual and cognitive topics studied by music psychologists is well illustrated in books such as Deutsch (1982), Howell *et al.* (1985), Dowling and Harwood (1986), Sloboda (1985a, 1988). These topics range from the nature of absolute pitch (Ward and Burns 1982), through the measurement of ensemble playing in chamber music (Rasch 1988) to the connections between musical structure and emotional response (Dowling and Harwood 1986). There is also a large body of research on developments and educational aspects of musical skill (e.g. Shuter-Dyson and Gabriel 1981; Hargreaves 1986). Most of the research reported in this chapter relates to adults familiar with a musical idiom. The story of the acquisition of this familiarity over the first years of life is a fascinating one which must be brought together into an overall account of the psychology of musical perception and performance.

Although I began the chapter with an undertaking to confine myself to contemporary achievements rather than hopes for the future, I cannot resist ending without choosing one area that I believe should see a substantial growth throughout the 1990s. This is the study of psychological functions of music. The studies outlined in this chapter show that human beings go to a great deal of cognitive effort to build up complex structured representations of the music they hear. The studies give very few clues, however, as to why people do this, what psychological purposes are fulfilled. Many volumes have, of course, been filled by commentators on music setting forward their own philosophies and hunches. What we have lacked is any really convincing empirical work on, for instance, the links between musical structure and emotional response. Work has started in one or two places, and my hope is that future work will be able to provide a sketch of an answer to the question that many of us cannot even answer articulately for ourselves: why do we devote so much of our lives to these organized sounds we call music?

Note: * denotes a core article listed in Table 6.2.

References

Bharucha, J. (1987) Music cognition and perceptual facilitation: a connectionist framework. *Music Perception,* **5**, 1–30.

Bharucha, J. and Krumhansl, C. L. (1983) The representation of harmonic structure in music: hierarchies of stability as a function of context. *Cognition,* **13**, 63–102.

Brown, H. (1988) The interplay of set content and temporal context in a functional theory of tonality perception. *Music Perception,* **5**, 219–50.

Butler, D. (1989) Describing the perception of tonality in music: a critique of the tonal hierarchy theory, and a proposal for a theory of intervallic rivalry. *Music Perception,* **6**(3), 219–42.

Butler, D. and Brown, H. (1984) Tonal structure versus function: studies of the recognition of harmonic motion. *Music Perception,* **2**, 6–24.

Clarke, E. F. (1988) Generative principles in music performance, in J.A. Sloboda (ed.) *Generative Processes in Music: The Psychology of Performance, Improvisation and Composition.* London: Oxford University Press.

Cook, N. (1987) The perception of large-scale tonal closure. *Music Perception,* **5**, 197–206.

Cross, I., West, R., and Howell, P. (1985) Pitch relations and the formation of scalar structure. *Music Perception,* **2**, 329–44.

Cuddy, L. L., Cohen, A. J., and Miller, J. (1979) Melody recognition: the experimental application of musical rules. *Canadian Journal of Psychology,* **33**, 148–57.

Deliège, I. (1987) Grouping conditions in listening to music: an approach to Lerdahl and Jackendoff's grouping preference rules. *Music Perception,* **4**, 325–60.

Deutsch, D. (1970) Tones and numbers: specificity of interference in short-term memory. *Science,* **168**, 1604–5.

Deutsch, D. (1980) The processing of structured and unstructured tonal sequences. *Perception and Psychophysics,* **28**, 38 1–9.

Deutsch, D. (ed.) (1982) *The Psychology of Music.* New York: Academic Press.

Deutsch, D. and Boulanger, R. C. (1984) Octave equivalence and the immediate recall of pitch sequences. *Music Perception,* **2**, 40–51.

Deutsch, D. and Feroe, J. (1981) The internal representation of pitch sequences in tonal music. *Psychological Review,* **88**, 503–22.

Dixon, N. F. (1981) *Preconscious Processing*. Chichester: Wiley.

Dowling, W. J. (1978) Scale and contour: two components of a theory of memory for melodies. *Psychological Review*, **85**, 341–54.

Dowling, W. J. and Harwood., D.L. (1986) *Music Cognition*. New York: Academic Press.

Fodor, J. A. and Bever, T. G. (1965) The psychological reality of linguistic segments. *Journal of Verbal Learning and Verbal Behaviour*, **4**, 414–20.

Gabrielsson, A. (1974) Performance of rhythm patterns. *Scandinavian Journal of Psychology*, **15**, 63–72.

Gregory, A. H. (1978) Perception of clicks in music. *Perception and Psychophysics*, **24**, 171–4.

Hantz, E. (1984) Studies in musical cognition: comments from a music theorist. *Music Perception*, **2**, 245–64.

Hargreaves., D. J. (1986) *The Developmental Psychology of Music*. London: Cambridge University Press.

Helmholtz, H. von (1954) *On the Sensations of Tone as a Physiological Basis for the Theory of Music* (1863). trans. A. J. Ellis, New York: Dover.

Howell, P., Cross, I., and West, R. (eds) (1985) *Musical Structure and Cognition*. New York: Academic Press.

Hughes., M. (1977) A quantitative analysis, in M. Yeston (ed.). *Readings in Schenker Analysis and Other Approaches*. New Haven: Yale University Press.

Johnson, S. C. (1967) Hierarchical clustering schemes. *Psychometrika*, **32**, 241–54.

Kessler, E. J., Hansen, C. and Shepard, R.N. (1984) Tonal schemata in the perception of music in Bali and in the West. *Music Perception*, **2**, 131–65.

Knopoff, L. and Hutchinson, W. (1983) Entropy as a measure of style: the influence of sample length. *Journal of Music Theory*, **27**, 75–97.

Krumhansl, C. L. (1979) The psychological representation of musical pitch in a musical context. *Cognitive Psychology*, **11**, 346–74.

Krumhansl, C. L. (1983) Perceptual structures for tonal music. *Music Perception*, **1**, 28–62.

Krumhansl, C. L. (1990) *Cognitive Foundations of Musical Pitch*. New York: Oxford University Press.

Krumhansl, C. L. and Kessler, E. (1982) Tracing the dynamic changes in perceived tonal organization in a spatial representation of musical keys. *Psychological Review*, **89**, 334–68.

Krumhansl, C. L. and Shepard, R. N. (1979) Quantification of the hierarchy of tonal functions within a diatonic context. *Journal of Experimental Psychology. Human Perception and Performance*, **5**, 579–94.

Krumhansl, C. L., Bharucha, J. J., and Castellano, M. A. (1982a) Key distance effects on perceived harmonic structure in music. *Perception and Psychophysics*, **32**, 96–108.

Krumhansl, C. L., Bharucha, J. J., and Kessler, E. J. (1982b) Perceived harmonic structure of chords in three related musical keys. *Journal of Experimental Psychology: Human Perception and Performance*, **8**, 24–36.

Krumhansl, C. L., Sandell, G. J., and Sergeant, D. C. (1987) The perception of tone hierarchies and mirror forms in twelve-tone serial music. *Music Perception*, **5**, 31–78.

Kruskal, J. B. (1964) Nonmetric multidimensional scaling: a numerical method. *Psychometrika*, **29**, 28–42.

Lerdahl, F. (1988) Tonal pitch space. *Music Perception*, **5**, 315–50.

Lerdahl, F. and Jackendoff, R. (1983) *A Generative Theory of Tonal Music*. Cambridge, Mass.: MIT Press.

Lerdahl, F. and Jackendoff, R. (1984) An overview of hierarchical structure in music. *Music Perception*, **1**, 229–52.

Longuet-Higgins, H. C. and Steedman, M. J. (1971) On interpreting Bach. *Machine Intelligence*, **6**, 221–41.

Marr, D. (1981) *Vision*. San Francisco: Freeman.

Meyer, L. B. (1973) *Explaining Music*. Berkeley: University of California Press.

Palmer, C. and Krumhansl, C. L. (1987) Independent temporal and pitch structures in perception of musical phrases. *Journal of Experimental Psychology: Human Perception and Performance*, **13**, 116–26.

Rasch, R. A. (1988) Timing and synchronization in ensemble performance, in J. A. Sloboda (ed.) *Generative Processes in Music: the Psychology of Performance, Improvisation, and Composition*. London: Oxford University Press.

Roberts, L. A. and Shaw, M. L. (1984) Perceived structure of musical triads. *Music Perception*, **2**, 95–124.

Rosner, B. S. (1984) Review of *A Generative Theory of Tonal Music* by Fred Lerdahl and Ray Jackendoff. *Music Perception*, **2**, 275–90.

Rosner, B. S. and Meyer, L. B. (1986) The perceptual roles of melodic process, contour, and form. *Music Perception*, **4**, 1–40.

Schenker, H. (1979) *Free Composition*, trans. E. Oster. New York: Longman, originally published as *Die freie Satz* (1935).

Shaffer., L. H. (1981) Performance of Chopin, Bach, and Bartok: studies in motor programming. *Cognitive Psychology*, **13**, 326–76.

Shepard, R. N. (1964) Circularity in judgements of relative pitch. *Journal of the Acoustical Society of America*, **36**, 2346–53.

Shepard, R. N. (1982) Structural representations of musical pitch. in D. Deutsch (ed.) *Psychology of Music*. New York: Academic Press.

Shuter-Dyson, R. and Gabriel, C. (1981) *The Psychology of Musical Ability*, 2nd edn. London: Methuen.

Sloboda, J. A. (1983) The communication of musical metre in piano performance. *Quarterly Journal of Experimental Psychology*, **A35**, 377–96.

Sloboda, J. A. (1985a) *The Musical Mind. The Cognitive Psychology of Music.* London: Oxford University Press.

Sloboda, J. A. (1985b) Expressive skill in two pianists: style and effectiveness in music performance. *Canadian Journal of Psychology,* **34**, 274–80.

Sloboda, J. A. (1986) Cognition and real music: the psychology of music comes of age. *Psychologica Belgica,* **26**, 199–219.

Sloboda, J. A. (ed.) (1988) *Generative Processes in Music: The Psychology of Performance, Improvisation, and Composition.* London: Oxford University Press.

Sloboda, J. A. and Gregory, A. H. (1980) The psychological reality of musical segments. *Canadian Journal of Psychology,* **34**, 274–80.

Sloboda, J. A. and Parker, D. H. H. (1985) Immediate memory for melodies, in P. Howell, I. Cross, and R. West (eds) *Musical Structure and Cognition.* London: Academic Press.

Sloboda, J. A., Hermelin, B., and O'Connor, N. (1985) An exceptional memory. *Music Perception,* **3**(2), 155–70.

Stoffer, T. H. (1985) Representation of phrase structure in the perception of music. *Music Perception,* **3**, 191–220.

Swain, J. P. (1986) The need for limits in hierarchical theories of music. *Music Perception,* **4**, 121–48.

Todd, N. (1985) A model of expressive timing in tonal music. *Music Perception,* **3**, 33–58.

Ward, W. D. and Burns, E. M. (1982) Absolute pitch. in D. Deutsch (ed.) *Psychology of Music.* New York: Academic Press.

Youngblood, J. E. (1958) Style and information. *Journal of Music Theory,* **2**, 24–35.

CHAPTER 7

REVIEW OF *LANGUAGE, MUSIC, AND MIND* BY DIANA RAFFMAN

Are there things about musical experience that we know but cannot say? This is the central question that this important book unpacks in the light of philosophical and psychological analysis. The question throws into stark opposition two quite distinct philosophical positions. On one side is the conviction that much knowledge, particularly aesthetic knowledge is ineffable. This position is well expressed by the following remark of John Dewey:

> If all meanings could be adequately expressed by words, the arts of painting and music would not exist. There are values and meanings that can be expressed only by immediately visible and . . . audible qualities, and to ask what they mean in the sense of something that can be put into words is to deny their distinctive existence.

On the other side is the view, championed most vociferously by Daniel C. Dennett, that all conscious knowledge is propositional in form, capable of expression in verbal form if only we attended closely enough and possessed the necessary vocabulary. This 'bracingly Spartan' view of consciousness leads Dennett to assert that:

> There are no colours, images, sounds, gestalts, mental acts, feeling tones or other Proustian objets trouvés to delight the inner eye: only featureless—even wordless—conditional-intentions-to-say-that-p for us to be intimately acquainted with.

Raffman is broadly in sympathy with Dennett's minimalist agenda. In particular she shares with him the rejection of phenomenological 'raw feels', but believes that music provides a good example of something that challenges his strict propositionalism. The basic thrust of her argument is that musical knowledge involves a level of representation that is necessarily non-propositional. There is, in other words, a type of musical knowledge that is not, even in principle, expressible in words.

Raffman's book cogently and meticulously maps out the territory that provides the intellectual underpinnings of her position, from which she is able to define and articulate three different types of musical ineffability. These are not only philosophically exact, but psychologically plausible, and are used to elucidate a number of secondary, but equally important issues, particularly the nature of musical meaning, and the possible role of emotion as a vehicle for musical meaning.

The enterprise is deeply imbued with the 'cognitivism' that characterizes most of the influential work in music psychology of the last two decades. Drawing on the general computational approach of Fodor and others, as exemplified in music psychology through the seminal theorizing of Lerdahl and Jackendoff, Raffman's premise is that 'conscious musical perception or experience results from the unconscious computation of a series of increasingly abstract mental representations of an acoustic signal.' (p. 4) In order to understand her proposals for musical ineffability, it is necessary to sketch an outline of Raffman's characterization of these representations.

At the lowest, or shallowest, level is a representation of the sound in terms of the finest pitches, durations, timbres and loudnesses that we can discriminate (although Raffman, for the purposes of establishing her arguments talks mainly about pitch). Such a representation is inferred from outputs of auditory transducers of physical stimulation. Such outputs are (in the case of pitch) a function of acoustic frequency. This level is called by Raffman, the N-level, or *nuance* level, of representation, because it is a non-structural representation, which captures as much as possible of the richness of the original acoustic stimulus. In language perception, an analogous level of representation might be the level that carries information about the voice of the speaker, accent, intonation and modulation, speed, etc.

At the next level is a representation of the music as a collection of pitch and duration classes within a symbolic system, which Raffman calls the mental score because of its close isomorphism with an actual conventional score. The mental score represents music in terms of such description as can be cashed by trained listeners in verbal expressions such as C#, F, tonic, crotchet, quaver, etc., which Raffman designates collectively as chromatic-pitch-events. This level is the lowest or shallowest at which the representation can be said to be structural or grammatical, in that it is composed of a finite set of tokens or elements out of which all legitimate pieces of western tonal music can be constructed. The linguistic analogy might be phonemic representation.

Chromatic-pitch events are inferred from the N-level representation via mental schemata, built from experience, which represent certain 'institutionalized' relationships obtaining among pitches, intervals, chords, etc.

These schemata are generally designated as 'tonal schemata' within the psychological literature, and their psychological reality has been attested by a large number of experimental studies. They assign n-level events to differentiated classes of event such as the twelve steps of the chromatic scale, chromatic intervals and chord types. With this level of representation, a listener should, at least in principle, be able to take down a musical excerpt from dictation even if, in the sense to be articulated below, the music is not understood.

The third level of representation allows a listener to represent a musical work not simply as a collection of successive notes with tonal and rhythmic/metrical 'names', but as an articulated hierarchical structure in which certain events have greater or lesser importance along a number of dimensions. Raffman designates this level the M-grammatical level (musical grammar). Lerdahl and Jackendoff's *Generative Grammar of Tonal Music* is the most comprehensively worked out proposal for the kinds of structural description that underlie the musical intuitions of experienced listeners of tonal music. The details of their grammar need not concern us here. It has many features analogous to the generative linguistic grammars proposed by Chomsky to underlie syntactic competence, and like Chomsky's grammar, relies for its operation on certain supposedly universal constraints on human cognitive functioning, including in the case of music, gestalt principles of perceptual grouping. Raffman's interest is more in the function of this level of representation (p. 19):

> You, the experienced listener, have unconscious knowledge of certain rules for musical analysis. As you hear an incoming musical signal, you unconsciously represent it and analyse it according to those rules: that is to say, you assign it a structural description. *Ex hypothesi* it is in virtue of assigning a structural description that you have the conscious experience you do—that you hear or, as we often say, *feel* music as you do. For example, it's in virtue of assigning such an analysis that you feel the tonic as being the most stable pitch in a scale, or an accent as being relatively strong in its metrical context, or a harmonic progression as being 'tense' or 'relaxed.' As Lerdahl and Jackendoff will put it, having the right sort of musical structure in your head is what *understanding* the music consists in.

Raffman argues, I believe correctly, that all three levels of representation are potentially available to consciousness. She reviews, with clarity and fairness, the 'categorical perception' data, and concludes that subcategorical information from the n-level cannot be suppressed as fully as it sometimes is in language perception. We hear both that a note is C (chromatic pitch event) and that it is mistuned (n-level event), and that it elicits, in this particular context, a sense of relaxation or repose (M-grammar).

Although Raffman outlines the above distinctions with admirable clarity, in doing so she has largely reflected a mainstream psychological 'received view', which in itself is not something to get hugely excited about, although it is admirable and unusual for a philosopher to be so clear and up-to-date about both psychological and musical thinking. Where Raffman makes her distinctive and original contribution is in tackling the following key question: in what sense might any of these levels be supposed to involve *ineffable* or unsayable knowledge?

As remarked earlier, Raffman articulates three different types of musical ineffability. The first she calls *structural ineffability*, and it relates to limitations in the ability to verbalize outcomes of representing music according to the M-grammar. She provides some examples of experiences falling into this category, which will be recognizable to many experienced musicians (pp. 31–2):

> Having easily reported the pitches, rhythms and time-signature of a heard piece, along perhaps with some of its local grouping, time-span, and prolongational structures, a listener (perhaps even a highly expert one) finds himself at a loss: 'I am feeling that E-natural in a certain distinctive way, but I can't say just how. I know it's the leading tone, and that it's preparing the return to the tonic, and I know it's a weak prolongation of the E-natural in the previous bar . . . but somehow I feel there is more going on.' Or a performer feels himself compelled to play a certain passage in a certain way (e.g., to slow down, or to get louder, or to increase the vibrato speed)—consciously feels, knows, that it must be played thus, and yet cannot say why . . . What I want to suggest is that unconscious structural representations – in particular, relatively global levels of representation – are 'making themselves felt' in our conscious experience, yet their contents elude our verbal grasp.

The proposed cause of this type of ineffability is simple and intuitively plausible. At more global levels of M-grammar assignation, there will be much more variability of structural assignment across listeners and across hearings (due to training and listening history and performance variation) than there will be at local levels. Thus, the psychological conditions for generation of descriptive language are adverse. This does not mean, however, that verbal descriptions of these ineffable intuitions are impossible. A lot will depend on the experience of the listener, and on the efforts made to infer an appropriate description. Sometimes, as Raffman suggests (p. 32) 'the structural ineffability dissolves, or anyway seems to dissolve, with explicit music-theoretic analysis: one applies pencil to score and discovers an element of the musical architecture that seems, intuitively, to account for the character of the experience.'

Raffman has pinpointed a real phenomenon that deserves more serious psychological study than it has received. However, she claims that structural ineffability is relatively uninteresting from a philosophical point of view. Examples of structural ineffability certainly do not meet the stringent criterion of being necessarily non-propositional: they are only contingently so for a particular person at a particular time.

The second type of musical ineffability is characterized by Raffman as *feeling ineffability*. This comes about because of the essential sensory-perceptual or experiential nature of music. Knowing a piece of music involves, along with other things, knowing what it sounds like. 'A person deaf from birth cannot know a piece of music.' (p. 40) This does not mean that a trained musician has to hear a particular new piece of music to know it. It is possible to compute what it sounds like (at least to some degree of specification) by examining a score, provided that one has a rich enough base of prior musical experience to fall back on. But without this sensory underpinning there is no possibility of full knowledge.

This type of ineffability is by no means unique to music. All sensory experiences, from sunsets to 'the taste of last night's chicken curry' have the same ineffability. They require 'actual occurent sense-perception of the relevant stimuli at some point' (p. 4). Yet, according to Raffman, there seems to be a special quality to the feeling ineffability of musical knowledge that commands our particular attention in the way that last night's curry does not. Her thought is that it is the grammatical structure of music that (mis)leads us to expect something effable as an end result of 'following' a piece of music. 'Music's grammatical structure may mislead us into semantic temptation' (p. 41) in a unique way not brought about when we observe a sunset, or even a painting. This comes about because of music's formal similarity to language.

These considerations allow a lengthy but extremely useful digression into the possible nature of musical meaning. Raffman argues that there is a sense in which to experience a class of peculiarly musical feelings (feelings of beat strength, metrical stress, prolongational tension, and so forth) is to understand the music. These feelings serve something of the same function as linguistic meanings do with respect to structural representations of language. For instance, experienced listeners by and large cannot help but recover these feelings when listening to music, and there is a sense in which these feelings can be determined as 'right' or 'wrong'. 'If a person fails to feel the C-natural in a C-major scale as the most stable pitch in the collection . . . then we will be justified in saying that he has misunderstood the music, that he ought to listen more carefully—or, perhaps, that he does not yet 'know the language.' (p. 54) Also, such musical feelings are arguably the basis of musical communication in that 'the performer's mission is to sculpt the nuances of pitch, duration, loudness, and the rest in such a way that his listeners feel the music in the same way he does'. (p. 55)

There is, however, in Raffman's mind a key distinction between linguistic semantics and the 'quasi-semantics' of music described here. 'Whereas the relation of a linguistic string to its meaning is a more or less conventional one, the relation of a musical string to the relevant feelings is nonconventional: we are presumably just *wired* in such a way as to have these feelings upon tokening those mental representations. Not surprisingly, the tie between music and feelings is considerably tighter than the tie between a sentence and its meaning.' (p. 55)

From this perspective, Raffman sheds interesting new light on the proposal that the meaning of music is somehow tied up with the emotional responses it evokes. Basically she claims that emotions are not the basis for musical meaning because, contingently, musicians do not take emotional responses as normative. That is, they are not open to dispute. I may be surprised if you find the last movement of the Jupiter Symphony morose and life-negating, but I cannot say you are wrong. On the other hand, musicians can and do argue about the correct way to feel a particular note in terms of its stability or prominence (p. 59):

> Such disputes may prove unresolvable . . . as when listeners 'hear the music differently' owing to disparities in their unconscious structural descriptions. But such disputes, far from undermining the normativity of the judgments at issue, are possible only in its presence. . . . Musicians argue about phrasings and dynamics and resolutions. They do not argue about the emotions they feel or otherwise ascribe to music.

Raffman also brings to our attention an ambiguity in the use of the term 'meaning', which sometimes refers to content (as in "Bachelor" means unmarried man') and value (as in 'your support means a lot to me'). 'No doubt music means something to us, in the sense of being important or valuable. . . . Perhaps the valuing of musical works for their emotive properties, in concert with their apparent possession of grammatical structure, fosters the mistaking of those emotive properties for musical *contents.*' (p. 60) It seems to me that this simple but profound distinction probably renders obsolete libraries full of conceptually confused writing on musical meaning!

Insofar as this second type of ineffability attaches to knowledge of musical structure (in principle verbalizable), it also fails to meet the stringent criterion of necessary non-propositionality. For this, we will need to show that a further ineffability also attaches to other levels of musical knowledge incapable of full verbalization. According to Raffman, there is such a level: it is the N-level, and so her third and final type of ineffability is *nuance ineffability*.

This type of ineffability comes about because we do not have categorizations or schemas as fine-grained as the stimuli we can discriminate. For this to lead to the strong conclusion of necessary ineffability, Raffman needs to establish that it is impossible that we could acquire such schemata. Her arguments are basically psychological. First she argues that 'it is hard to see what point there would be to a schema whose "grain" was as fine as that of perception. Indeed the C-interval schemas presumably serve to reduce the information load imposed precisely by the nuance representations of the N-level'. In other words, human processing limitations make total effability of the N-level a psychological impossibility. Second she argues that the just noticeable distinction (JND) for perceptual properties varies with stimulus and observer characteristics (including alertness, health, etc.) Such inconsistencies make it hard to see how long-term mental representations of the required sort could be established. Thirdly, she argues that the perception of, for instance, out-of-tune intervals as out-of-tune (rather than as in-tune instances of microtonal n-intervals) is necessary for us to establish structural awareness at all. If every nuance were recognized and categorized 'we would not be hearing the music as tonal: tonal music just is music whose melodies and harmonies soar out from the background welter'. (p. 86)

I have to say that I find the first and third of these arguments rather less convincing than the second. The first seems to be an unverified assumption. We simply do not know how fine-grained a schema could be developed with adequate experience. Clearly such a schema would not produce in a person possessing it an awareness of music as tonal, in the sense we now understand. Probably new types of music would need to be written to train and exploit this type of schema, but I don't find it inconceivable that, for instance, a microtonal schema or a timbral schema could form the basis of coherent and comprehensible musical structures.

The second argument seems much more powerful. If there is inherent instability in our perceptual discriminations at or around the JND, then the conditions for acquiring schemata of an appropriate grain can never be established. There will, therefore, always be a residual ineffable component in any conceivable representation of music. As Raffman poetically describes it, musical experience will always be characterized by 'an evanescent corona shimmering around the structural frame of the piece'. (p. 96)

But a final problem remains. If we don't have schemata for nuances, then 'there is an important sense in which we do not know what N-pitch or N-interval we are hearing at any given moment. If that is so, then what is it that we know but cannot say? In other words, what do we know ineffably?' (p. 87) Raffman's solution is to propose that (p. 88):

> you hear (n-events) as nuances, and therein know that they are nuances (as opposed to, say, C-pitches); it's just that, for lack of interval schemas sufficiently fine-grained to permit type identifications, you don't know *which* nuances they are. Hence although in hearing the nuances you know how they sound, there will be nothing you can say, no report you can make, that could, by itself serve to reproduce that knowledge in the mind-brain of another listener. On the contrary, your only hope of getting him to know what you know is to ostend the signal: he must hear it for himself.

I am fully in agreement with Raffman's conclusion that the only way to communicate nuance is by demonstration. This is why so much of music performance teaching is a matter of demonstration: at the end of the day, a teacher has to show what she wants through performance and hope that the pupil can pick it up—'play it like this'. But I think that Raffman is overly pessimistic in believing that musicians do not, or cannot, know which nuances they are experiencing. Indeed, if there is no possibility of identifying and remembering nuances at some level, then there is no possibility of learning by imitation. Recent research has shown that musical performers can retain and reproduce substantial portions of the nuances of heard performances (for instance, rubato and other timing deformations below the level of the smallest note-length). Therefore, they must know, at least in broad outline, which nuances they are experiencing. It is simply that this knowledge informs performance programs more directly and explicitly than it informs verbal consciousness.

Again, if listeners really were incapable of knowing which nuances they were hearing, there would be little possibility of identifying particular performers or performances. But it is common knowledge that connoisseurs can tell Gilels from Schnabel, or even two different Gilels performances from one another. So, although a listener may not be able to identify a nuance in the language of tonality (e.g. 'a slightly prolonged up-beat'), he may be able to identify it as symptomatic of a style (e.g. 'late Rubenstein'). Thus, he not only knows that he heard a particular nuance, but can identify that nuance as part of one performer's expressive repertoire, rather than that of another performer.

What does all this have to say about the original Dewey–Dennett opposition? It seems to me that Raffman's challenge to Dennett's strong propositionalism is upheld. The JND argument clinches for me that there will always be a residual ineffable 'corona'. Where I think more work needs to be done is in a deconstruction of the n-level, which is more complex than Raffman would have us believe. Even taking the pitch domain alone (and there are many interesting considerations in the time, timbre, and loudness domains which Raffman does not address), then it seems to me that there are certain aspects of nuance knowledge that can be, as it were, gathered up into a kind of 'proto-effability' which may be parasitic on structural representations of music. These are probably the grosser nuances which can be used to 'mark' the c-level representations. So, for instance, we don't just know that this note is an F#—we also know that it is significantly sharpened, lengthened, and softened, relative to its neighbours. We don't necessarily have available the vocabulary to capture all of this, but our ability to imitate or recognize style shows that, in some sense of the term, the knowledge is, indeed, propositional, in the sense that it is symbolic and computable, and can be brought into conscious awareness, even if it is not always there.

The performance research of recent years suggests that the degree of proto-effability of particular nuances is heavily dependent on the cognitive economy with which they can be represented. Nuances that have the effect of heightening the impact of legitimate structural representations are much better assimilated than those that have an arbitrary relationship to structural factors. This is what I mean by saying that the representations are parasitic on structural representations. Another way of saying this is that it is the existence of global maps of the musical territory that allows us to get a fix on some of the local detail. There would be no way of capturing nuance 'from the bottom up'.

There are many aspects of this excellent book to which I have not done justice, in particular a detailed analysis of the impact of Raffman's thinking on our understanding of Nelson Goodman's seminal work on the nature of aesthetic understanding. Whether or not Raffman's conclusions are ultimately defensible does not really matter. What she has done is set a new agenda for the interdisciplinary study of music—at the interfaces of philosophy, psychology, and music analysis—and has set impeccably high standards in the posing and critical analysis of fundamental questions. There is a strong tendency in the study of music perception for fragmentation of aims. Psychologists pursue goals that are unrelated to major questions in music or philosophy, and vice versa. This leads to mutual accusations of triviality or irrelevance. Our discipline needs particularly strong work at the disciplinary interfaces to ensure that it continues to be 'progressive' rather than 'degenerative', in Lakatosian terminology. Raffman's book provides the proof that such work can still be done. It deserves to be read by anyone who has a serious interest in the study of music cognition.

References

Raffman, D. (1993) *Language, Music, and Mind*. Cambridge, MA: MIT Press.

CHAPTER 8

DOES MUSIC MEAN ANYTHING?

8.1 Introduction

In 1985 I gave a paper to the Belgian Psychological Society entitled 'Cognition and real music: the psychology of music comes of age' (Sloboda, 1986). It was an optimistic paper, focusing on what I then saw as the best and most promising signs of our young and growing discipline. At that point in time, when we were still basking in the afterglow of Lerdahl and Jackendofi's ground-breaking *Generative Theory of Tonal Music* (1983), it seemed that music psychology had, at last, reached paradigmatic status, in Kuhnian terminology. We were no longer a rag-bag of eccentrics operating at the unfashionable fringes of psychology, but a proper sub-discipline with a programme! I proposed that there were five important characteristics of a healthy scientific paradigm: an agreed set of central problems; agreed methods for working on those problems; agreed theoretical frameworks in which to discuss them; techniques and theories specific to the paradigm; research which is appropriate to the whole range of phenomena in the domain being studied.

In 1985 I believed I had identified at least one central problem or task for music psychology: that was 'to explain the structure and content of musical experience', which could be further elucidated by two more specific questions:

1 What is the nature of musical knowledge or representation?

2 How does music have aesthetic and emotional effects?

Both of these questions still seem to me to be fundamental to music psychology and are absolutely central to the enterprise of determining if, and in what ways, music might be said to mean something. If the mental representation of music is not simply a copy (however reduced the 'grain') of the original acoustic signal, and if this representation is in some respects shared by composer/performer and listener, then such a representation might be held to comprise the 'meaning' of the music. This would be analogous to saying that the meaning of a sentence is to be found, not in its acoustic or visual characteristics, but in the underlying proposition which speaker intends and listener recovers.

But many commentators have resisted the apparent linguistic analogy, on the grounds that whatever the nature of mental representations of music, they do not and cannot carry referential meaning of the sort carried by sentences. I believe this resistance to be correct. Music is unlike a natural language in many ways, and because it does not have to serve practical communicative functions, there can be much looser coupling between the representations of different individuals. An alternative view of 'music as a language of the emotions' has received expressions of varying degrees of cogency and clarity. According to this view, the meaning of music is somehow tied up with the emotional states it evokes or reminds of.

The interfaces of philosophy and psychology are natural environments to attempt to clarify these two questions, and I will sketch the broad parameters of a 'received' direction in which answers to the two questions above have been framed within the discipline of psychology, illustrating some of these directions from my own research. In doing so, I am very aware that psychology of music has, to a large extent, progressed independently of developments in musicology, and that some of the positions articulated here may appear musicologically naive or off-centre. However, a short paper of this sort cannot go about rectifying the divergences of a generation of scholars, and makes no attempt to do so.

8.2 The nature of musical representation

The book by Lerdahl and Jackendoff (1983) remains the paradigmatic expression of the 'received' view on representation of tonal music (which has been taken by most psychologists as the paradigm example of a musical language). It is grounded in the following assumptions:

- **music is constructed according to grammar(s)**—i.e. sets of explicit or implicit rules or constraints determining the legality or 'well-formedness' of musical sequences
- **representation is often hierarchic**—i.e. grammars determine elements within a musical sequence which control or subsume neighbouring elements, and this process is recursive so that lead elements at one level become subsumed at the next higher level (metre is probably the simplest example of this)
- **tonality, metre, and rhythm are psychologically real organising principles (possibly instantiations of musical universals)**—i.e. these

music-theoretic descriptions correspond to the natural tendencies of perceivers to 'parse' acoustic input

- **different processes (e.g. composition, performance, perception) access the same core representations,** i.e. there is a unified representational substrate which all explicit activities feed on, even if there are additional representational modes specific to the activity (e.g. motor representations of performance).

Lerdahl and Jackendoff's main achievement was to deliver a set of specific operations which, if applied to a piece of tonal music, would yield a complete description of that music, in which each event was marked as being more or less prominent in one of several hierarchical systems. Such descriptions yielded strong empirical predictions about perception and memory (e.g. listeners would recall prominent events more readily than subsidiary ones, would hear prominent events as more important or accented, would hear unstable events as subsumed by more stable ones, etc.).

A strong claim that could be made on the basis of this type of programme is that to have understood a piece of music is to have parsed it according to the principles embodied in some representational theory which is shared within a community of composers, performers and listeners. Although there may be areas for legitimate dispute (indeed the interest of music analysis is often exactly in assessing plausible alternative parsings), there are some key characteristics of pieces which could not be represented in a radically different way which had any real claim to be a meaningful representation of that piece. If anyone were to propose that the most prominent notes in the opening theme of Mozart's Symphony no 40 (E<flat> D D E<flat> D D E<flat> D D B<flat>) were (in descending order) the 2nd, 5th and 8th notes we would be strongly inclined to say that he or she didn't understand the music. Most of us would agree 3, 6, and 9 in ascending order. Without going into detail, much perceptual and cognitive research in this area can be seen as showing that there are, indeed, large areas of agreement between individuals about such matters. These agreements often transcend different levels of training, and sometimes transcend cultures.

If the strong claim were to be true, the search for musical meaning must stop at the level of structural description. Everything else would be, as Stravinsky and others have claimed, irrelevant noise.

8.3 Shortcomings of the representational approach

Any musician presented with the above type of account of the meaning of music is likely to complain that, however real the processes and representations described above are, they miss out the core of what makes a musical experience musical. A structural description is merely the skeleton and framework on which flesh and blood must be put. To have constructed a structural representation is only a small part of musical understanding. One could characterise this response as proto-Searlian. Everything described above could be put inside Searle's Chinese Room (Searle, 1980).

I once had the privilege to study a young autistic man, Noel Patterson, who was a rather clear example of a person who could do everything implied by the strong claim but who failed to demonstrate 'musical understanding' in some very important sense (Sloboda, Hermelin, and O'Connor, 1985). He was able to memorize heard tonal (but not atonal) piano music rather quickly, and reproduce it with a high degree of accuracy. His recall errors were 'structural', in that omissions tended to be subsidiary elements (as characterized by such theories as that of Lerdahl and Jackendoff) and substitutions were structurally appropriate. But after a very short time his performances became stripped of all expression (even that contained in the original from which his performance was derived) so that there was nothing of interest in his performance for an audience. He played totally mechanically. From a musician's point of view it is almost as if Noel Patterson had 'missed the point' of bothering to play the music at all.

8.4 Feelings as the dynamic aspect of music

What is this 'point' that both the strong claim and Noel Patterson's performance leave out? It is that the structures underlying music animate an experience which is *dynamic*. The experience involves sensations of tension and resolution, anticipation, growth and decay. One account of this would hold that such experiences *depend* upon having assigned a particular structural analysis to a sequence. We feel the music as increasing in tension towards a particular point *in virtue* of its being assigned a structural importance, but the structural description does not in itself *incorporate* that feeling. The structural description is a precondition for the feeling. Another account would have the experience of dynamism as an essential precondition of a listener recovering the structural description, given that there is no proof that an analysis such as that offered by Lerdahl and Jackendoff can be carried out algorithmically on the basis of information presented in a score. We may need the dynamic feelings to bootstrap the parsing process. Lehrdahl and Jackendoff, whilst acknowledging that there is a relationship between some of their structural descriptors and dynamic experiences (e.g. of tension or resolution) did not seek to establish a direction of psychological causality. Either way, it is not at all clear that the feelings we are speaking of here are identical with those feelings that we characterize as emotions or moods in other contexts. Emotions and moods are valenced (positive or negative) feelings where one's own orientation to the object of the emotion is a key component (like–dislike, approve–disapprove, happy–unhappy, etc.; cf. Frijda, 1986). We may indeed feel such emotions and moods to music (and these feelings are the stuff of our aesthetic and other responses to music, determining the importance or personal significance of our experience—a different kind of meaning, as Raffman (1993) has so clearly pointed out), but the dynamic feelings or sensations of tension are essentially unvalenced. Given a particular structural understanding of the music feelings of tension or resolution are just a correlate of that understanding (whether I like them or not).

So, a musical performance could be one in which the performer recognizes the dynamic implications of the structure and enhances the acoustic signal in such a way as to boost or highlight those implications. Returning, for instance, to the initial theme of Mozart 40, one 'musical' performance response to this would be to make each of 3, 6 and 9 a little louder and a little more prolonged than the previous element. How does a performer know that this is a good or appropriate way to highlight the dynamic characteristics of the passage? And how does a performer choose appropriate levels of loudening and slowing? A number of theorists are converging on the notion that this knowledge is a consequence not only of the structural characteristics of a given piece of music but also of a whole range of other signals that impinge upon humans and can be mapped, by processes of analogy, onto the musical process. In other words, it is the whole process of being a biological human inhabiting a physical and social world that provides the fuel and the impetus for a dynamic understanding of music. Putative non-human sentient beings would have a hard job understanding music in the way we do, because their set of mapping analogies would be so different.

The analogical mapping we are speaking of is entirely different from the iconic or associative process whereby musicians can imitate real-life sounds, such as birdsong. That is a rather uninteresting mimicking of surface characteristics. What is implied in the above proposal is somewhat deeper and more abstract. Imagine, for instance, that I come to a swinging door in a corridor. I push it, and it doesn't yield. I push again, a little harder. Still it doesn't quite yield, but I sense that a third push will do it. I push for a third time, harder still, and the door suddenly swings open, propelling me through to the next corridor. This is just one of many concrete examples of a dynamic process which involves repeated application of increasing force and a sudden release of whatever was holding the obstacle in place.

One reading of the opening theme of Mozart 40 (and, of course, there are many others) could assign it to this dynamic shape, representing something that has got stuck at a particular level, here represented by the small semitone movements from D to E<flat>. As the force is repeated, the obstacle is overcome and the music is 'freed' to fly up to the B<flat>. The increasing force is well represented by louder and longer sounds because this would be the exact consequence of reproducing this sequence of actions on the bow of a violin, for instance. The actual bodily process of interacting with an instrument in a real physical environment makes this analogy directly available to the performing musician. Incidentally, this is probably why computer music often sounds 'inhuman'. Its creators are not bound by the constraints that bind musicians interacting with real instruments in real time using real human bodies!

If this line of argument is accepted, then it follows that a major task for those concerned with explaining how we understand music is to analyse and describe the whole range of analogies of the above sort that are available to musicians. The notion that the instantiation of music practice in actual bodily movements may profoundly affect its structure and our conceptions of it, has been forcefully championed by Baily (1985), Blacking (1995) and Cuniming (1997) among others. Suggestions by a number of researchers (e.g. Clynes, 1977; Sundberg and Verillo, 1980; Todd, 1995) indicate the type of analogies which might be available to even the most unsophisticated listener. The results presented by Watt and Ash (1998), in which music is reliably ascribed characteristics such as male–female, good–evil, may come about through the integration of clusters of appropriate basic analogies into 'virtual persons'. But this is not the only, or even a necessary, consequence of dynamic awareness of music. The type of ascriptions that listeners are prepared to make on the basis of musical experience will undoubtedly be determined by a range of cultural and contextual factors.

8.5 Physical manifestations of emotion as core unvalenced reactions to music

It is commonplace knowledge, although rather little researched, that music evokes in people physical concomitants of emotion. Music 'moves people to tears' with great reliability and regularity. Although I wouldn't have used precisely this terminology at the time, it struck me some years ago that such concomitants were rather attractive candidates for one major class of 'unvalenced dynamic sensations'. My own subjective experience of such sensations is often of noticing them first, interpreting them (at an aesthetic level) second. For instance, there comes a tightening or pricking sensation at the back of the throat which has an increasing intensity over a number of seconds. I then notice sensations behind my eyes. As sensations increase, I notice my eyes watering. A point of maximum tension is reached, then the feeling ebbs and subsides. Whether I like or value this feeling depends upon a very large range of considerations. Do I think the music is profound (or maudlin)? Am I alone or with others? Am I performing this music, and will indulging these sensations help or inhibit the performance, etc.? All of these later evaluative processes are part of the aesthetic experience. The raw 'tears' seem much closer to the form of the music itself. It is also interesting to note that it is sometimes quite difficult to ascribe a particular emotion to such an experience. Often it seems neither sad nor happy in a straightforward way.

Many musicians report having experienced these raw manifestations rather early in life (Sloboda (1989) found them beginning at around age 7–8), and musicians often claim that these experiences had a profound effect on their motivation for future involvement with music (similar findings are reported in a series of studies on 'strong emotions to music' by Gabrielsson and Lindstrom, 1993). Over 90% of respondents in a survey claimed to have cried to music in the last 5 years (Sloboda, 1991).

To substantiate the hunch that these feelings are tied to musical structure, it is necessary to plot the exact time-course of the feelings and see if there is any systematic link to structure. Waterman (1996) played a variety of listeners the same musical extracts (in individually testing sessions) and asked them to indicate by pressing a button whenever they 'felt something'. He found significant agreement between listeners in location of button presses. There was also within-listener agreement when the same pieces were played one year later. This suggests that these reactions are stable and locatable within specific portions of the musical structure.

To widen the range of musical materials included, Sloboda (1991) surveyed 75 individuals and asked them to identify specific pieces of music that had reliably elicited physical reactions such as tears, shivers down the spine and gooseflesh, or racing heart. All examples supplied were of western tonal music, but ranged from Bach to contemporary pop and jazz. Musical analysis of those segments which participants could identify precisely (within a measure or phrase) yielded an interesting and unexpected correlation. Tears were associated with melodic or harmonic sequences, appoggiaturas and suspensions, and downward harmonic movement through the circle of fifths. Shivers were associated with enharmonic changes and other harmonic, textural, or dynamic discontinuities. Racing heart was associated with syncopation, and other forms of accentual anticipation. These effects were insensitive to style, and examples of all these effective structures were found in both classical and pop music. This is another indication that these responses are 'pre-aesthetic'.

While a detailed explanation for the specific feeling-structure linkage has not yet emerged, it is clear that the features of music associated with these feelings are features of the sort that would be marked as more or less prominent within a Lerdahl and Jackendoff type of analysis, yielding appropriate responses of tension-resolution (e.g. appoggiatura) or violation of expectancy (e.g. enharmonic change, syncopation). This is a vindication for the structurally-based explanations of emotional response to music pioneered by L. B. Meyer (1956, and his followers, e.g. Narmour, 1977).

I do not wish to claim that such sensations as described above constitute a level of meaning for music over and above the structural. They are, however, intense symptoms of the operation of such a level. This level can, no doubt, be investigated using other techniques (for instance monitoring of brain and physiological response, or continuous manual response of the kind used by Madsen, *et al.* 1993). Such techniques all share the feature that they measure essentially non-propositional or 'hot' cognitions, rather than the 'cold' cognitions of the propositional level. It is also important to re-emphasize that these sensations or feelings are not specific emotions, although they may easily give rise to specific emotions if appropriate contexts or associations are to hand. In this respect I believe that the absolutist position on emotion (as, for instance, argued by Meyer, 1956) may be more robust than some of us might have thought!

8.6 Summary

Mapping from language to music might be an overplayed tactic, but the above analyses suggest that there is a way of doing it which doesn't do too much injustice to either form. Insofar as linguists still allow a division between syntax and semantics (and I am not fully conversant with the latest thinking), it seems to be that one could see the structural description of the music as a form of syntax, and the dynamic sensations of flux, tension, expectations fulfilled or violated as the semantics. This is because the structural description does not refer to anything outside the music, while the dynamic aspects do so refer, if only by analogy. Dynamic awareness of music involves reading the music as an embodiment of something else, and my proposal for that something else is, broadly, the physical world in motion, including that very special sub-class of moving objects, the living organism. But this analogical linking up is not at the level of specific mimicry of the auditory signals of that moving world, but at various deeper levels concerned with the underlying forms of these motions as initiated, experienced, and mediated by the conscious human agent. Specifying what is included in this, and finding a principled reason for excluding what should be excluded is a task hardly yet begun.

References

Baily, J. (1985) Music structure and human movement. In P. Howell, I. Cross, and R. West (Eds.) *Musical Structure and Cognition*. London: Academic Press.

Blacking, J. (1995) *Music, Culture and Experience*. Chicago: University of Chicago Press.

Clynes, M. (1977) *Sentics: the Touch of Emotions*. New York: Doubleday.

Cumming, N, (1997) The subjectivities of 'Erbarme Dich'. *Music Analysis*, **16.1**, 5–44.

Frijda, N. (1986) *The Emotions*. Cambridge UK: Cambridge University Press.

Gabrielsson, A. and Lindstrom, S. (1993) On strong experiences of music. *Jahrbuch der Deutschen Gesellschaft für Musikpsychologie*, **10**, 114–125.

Lerdahl, F. and Jackendoff, R. (1983) *A Generative Theory of Tonal Music*. Cambridge: MIT Press.

Madsen, C. K., Byrnes, S. R., Capperella-Sheldon, D. A., and Brittin, R. V. (1993). Aesthetic responses to music: musicians versus non-musicians. *Journal of Music Therapy*, **30**, 174–191.

Meyer, L. B. (1956) *Emotion and Meaning in Music*. Chicago: University of Chicago Press.

Narmour, E. (1977) *Beyond Schenkerism The Need for Alternatives in Music Analysis*. Chicago: University of Chicago Press.

Ortony, A, Clore, G. L., and Collins, A. (1988) *The Cognitive Structure of the Emotions*. New York: Cambridge University Press.

Raffman, D. (1993) *Language, Music and Mind*. Cambridge, MA: MIT Press.

Searle, J. R. (1980) Minds, brains, and programs. *The Behavioural and Brain Sciences*, **3**, 417–457.

Sloboda, J. A. (1986) Cognitive psychology and real music: the psychology of music comes of age. *Psychologica Belgica*, **26.2**.

Sloboda, J. A. (1989) Music as a language. In F. Wilson and F. Roehmann (Eds.) *Music and Child Development*. St Louis, Missouri: MMB Press Inc.

Sloboda, J. A. (1991) Music structure and emotional response: some empirical findings. *Psychology of Music*, **19.1**, 110–120.

Sloboda, J. A., Hermelin, B., and O'Connor, N. (1985) An exceptional musical memory. *Music Perception*, **3**, 155–170.

Sundberg, J. and Verillo, V. (1980) On the anatomy of the ritard: a study of timing in music. *Journal of the Acoustical Society of America*, **68**, 772–779.

Todd, N. P. McA. (1995) The kinematics of musical expression. *Journal of the Acoustical Society of America*, **97**, 1940–1949.

Waterman, M. (1996) Emotional responses to music: implicit and explicit effects in listeners and performers. *Psychology of Music*, **24.1**, 53–67.

Watt, R. and Ash, R. L. (1998) A psychological investigation of meaning in music. *Musicae Scientiae*, **2.1**, 33–53.

EMOTION AND MOTIVATION

CHAPTER 9

MUSIC AS A LANGUAGE

9.1 Introduction

I guess that all of us are here because, in one way or another, we love music. It is that love which has led us to become teachers, performers, researchers, concerned to deepen our awareness and effectiveness in ensuring that music and musicians are held in high esteem by society and given society's best resources.

But as well as bringing love with us, most of us also probably carry a deep puzzlement; despite our deep familiarity with it, music still remains at many levels a mystery to us. We don't really understand what music is, how it comes to have such a profound effect on us, why it moves us, fascinates us, brings us back to it again and again.

To many of us, the mystery is part of the love. As in any love affair, it is the sense of never ending discovery which gives impetus to the love. Once we feel that we have found everything out about the other, the love dries up. It is, I am sure, for this sort of reason that many of us have a deep aversion to the scientific analysis of music. It seems that if we could reduce music to a set of explicit categories or formulae, if we could derive an all embracing theory, then music would lose its mystery and power.

I very much respect this intuitive aversion. I think scientists labour under a constant temptation to replace what they are studying with theories about what they are studying, and then talk about their theories as if they were the total reality of the situation. To overcome this tendency to narrow the sights, I believe that every scientist who studies music has a duty to keep his or her love of music alive, and be constantly aware of what escapes the net of particular theories.

On the other hand, I believe that science has much to offer musicians. One thing that it does is attempt to make theoretical assumptions explicit, and thus open to discussion and test. Everybody, whether scientist or not, is operating on theories and assumptions. Whatever else scientists may or may not do, they can offer people new ways of looking at old issues.

And sometimes these new ways are more profitable. They can also offer hard data to replace speculations.

Let me give one example of what I mean. Recently I attended a conference on what in Britain we call 'ear training' or 'aural training.' There was a lot of talk among the teachers there about 'developing a good ear' for music, and some rather sterile controversy about whether some people had better ears than others. As a psychological scientist, I was able to remind them that the ear as such is not the problem. Most people's ears function excellently, and there is nothing anyone can do to enhance their functioning. Everyone's ear is constantly sending to the brain highly sophisticated, fine grain information about all sounds received. It is what the brain does with it that determines musical differences between people.

As a result of a large amount of experimentation and theorizing in cognitive psychology, we are now able to say rather precisely what needs to happen to produce the behaviour that musicians would associate with 'a good ear.' First, the relevant dimensions of the sound have to be *attended* to, then the listener requires some method of *coding* or *categorizing* the individual sounds. Thirdly, the listener must be able to hold the various sounds together in some *structure* or *pattern*. Finally, the listener must be able to translate what has been received into some form of *response*. Many unfortunate people have been labelled 'tone deaf' because they can't sing in tune. The analysis just outlined shows that the problem could be entirely one of response; the other stages may have been completed perfectly.

I believe that the four stage theory of musical awareness is more useful to practitioners than an unarticulated theory about 'the ear.' It allows us to ask at what stage a problem might be occurring, and it gives us better ideas about what we might do to overcome the difficulty. All these stages are known to be susceptible to profound alteration through learning and experience. The theory does not solve all a practitioner's problems. The business of teaching and learning is still largely an art; but I contend that the availability of such ways of thinking will enhance a practitioner's functioning, by providing better and more varied tools to tackle particular problems.

It is in the same spirit that I offer some observations on music as a language. I do not claim that thinking of music as a language is a completely satisfactory way of accounting for everything about it. Indeed, some of the most important things about music seem to arise from the ways it is different from a language. But it offers a way of thinking about music which is, I believe, useful and illuminating.

Like music, the primary medium of language is sound. We can capture and measure the various physical dimensions of speech sounds through the many sophisticated measuring instruments we have. In themselves, however, these sounds are just sounds, with various physical characteristics such as pitch, amplitude, and timbre. They are not language. What makes them language is what human brains do with them. And it seems that what human brains do is to attempt to map these sounds onto internal structures. When some kind of match has been made with these structures, then language can be said to have come into existence. These internal structures seem to be divided into these types: *phonological, syntactic,* and *semantic.* Generally, some contact has to be made at each level for speech to be understood or created.

9.2 Phonology

Phonology describes the way in which the brain parcels up continuously varying sounds into discrete and separable units. These units constitute the basic building blocks of a language. It seems clear from studies on language that phonology is learned. Different cultures place phonological boundaries in particular places. What are taken as two separate speech sounds by users of one language are heard as the same by users of another.

There are some dramatic scientific demonstrations of the way that phonological mechanisms transform the raw sound. One of these is the phenomenon of *categorical perception*. We can take two naturally occurring speech sounds, such as 'da' and 'ba,' and artificially synthesize them. We discover that what distinguishes them physically is the frequency of the initial burst of sound. When it is high we hear 'da'; when it is low we hear 'ba.' What happens if we synthesize a series of sounds which move from 'da' to 'ba' through small steps of frequency change? How are they heard? The common sense view would be something like this. The sound definitely starts as 'da.' Gradually it becomes more and more ambiguous until a point is reached where it sounds like neither, or an amalgam of the two. Then it gradually becomes more and more like 'ba'.

Experimental evidence (e.g., Liberman *et al.,* 1961) shows that this common sense view is wrong. What actually happens is that we hear a series of apparently indistinguishable 'da's', and then, quite suddenly, the perception flips, and the experience is of 'ba'. Our brains categorize intermediate sounds, and make it very difficult for us to notice any difference between two sounds falling within the same category. Then, as some internal boundary is crossed, the perception quite suddenly changes, as the sound is assimilated to a new category.

What, then, of music? The best evidence we have (Locke and Kellar, 1973) is that similar categorization processes go on for most of us. That is, we tend not to perceive every slight change in sound dimensions, but assimilate to broad categories. One example of this is the musical scale. If we take a major triad, and change the third note of the chord in several equal small steps from major to minor, then many people experience an effect analogous to the language experiment. There seems to be a rather sudden shift from major to minor somewhere in the middle of the sequence.

We can find analogous effects in the time domain. If, for instance, we ask people to reproduce rhythmic patterns, there is a tendency for the reproductions to be inexact but categorical. That is, if the ratio of two notes in the original is roughly 2 : 1 then the reproduction will tend to be roughly 2 : 1. We have internalized categories which tell us that durations tend to be whole number multiples of one another. We find it hard to hear truly ambiguous rhythms as ambiguous. We try to fit them to one or other definite category.

When comparing to language, we need to make two important caveats. One is that the degree of categorization tends to depend on musical experience. In most of the published studies 'musicians' (however defined) tend to show stronger categorization effects than 'non-musicians'.

The second caveat is that even when we do categorize, we are still able to be aware of the differences within a category. So, for instance, a musician will be able to say 'that C# is flat.' This shows both categorization (an identification of the note as in the category C#, and the awareness that the note differs from an ideal central pitch. Sometimes we are simply aware that two notes within the same category differ in some way, without being able to consciously identify the difference. So one finds musicians who say 'I know that the note is badly pitched, but I can't tell whether it is sharp or flat' (Siegel and Siegel, 1977). The same phenomenon also explains why we are able to find two performances of the same notes different. We judge performance A to be livelier, clearer, more satisfying, than performance B, but cannot precisely identify what it is that makes them different. In general, these differences are due to minute expressive deviations within categories.

9.3 Syntax

The second level of structuring in language is syntax. This concerns the ordering of the basic phonological building blocks. In all languages, and in music, it is not enough to notice which sound categories (be they phonemes or notes) are present; their combination and ordering contains the crucial information. Most languages (and many musical styles) seem, at least in principle, describable by a grammar. This is a set of rules which is capable of generating (or recognizing) all sequences which are acceptable, and fails to generate (or rejects) sequences which are not acceptable.

There are many types of evidence that people handle language through syntactic structures. One is that it is much easier to remember word sequences that conform to grammatical order than the same sequences that have their order scrambled. This is so, even when the sentences make little or no sense. For instance, it is easier to remember *Colourless green ideas sleep furiously* than *sleep green furiously ideas colourless.*

In music, it is easier to remember sequences which conform to conventional rules of tonality than those that don't. This is increasingly so as one becomes more experienced with a particular musical culture. For instance, there are studies which suggest that the memory advantage for tonal sequences does not develop until about age seven in the average child (Zenatti, 1969).

In my own research (Sloboda, 1985) I have been interested in the growing ability of children to reject what we would judge to be illegal musical sequences. At age five, most children I tested seemed unable or unwilling to reject gross chordal dissonance as wrong. By the age of nine, they were overtly laughing or screwing up their faces at the 'wrong' chords, and scoring at an adult level. In another test, each chord was tonally coherent in itself, but the ordering of the chords could be either tonally conventional (e.g. ending with a cadence) or scrambled (e.g. ending without resolution). On this test children did not achieve adult levels of performance until the age of 11. I was particularly interested to find that these abilities seemed to develop regardless of formal music tuition. Children who had regular lessons did not develop these abilities earlier than other children. It seems that mere exposure to the standard musical culture is enough for children to build grammatical structures.

9.4 Semantics

I take semantics to be the systematic set of processes whereby the symbols of a language are able to be mapped onto, or represent, objects, states of affairs, and events that are not part of that language. To be a full language user it is not enough to recognize a sequence as grammatical; one has to understand it. This means at least two things: identifying what the individual words refer to, and identifying what kind of event or proposition is being described.

I see semantics as the driving force behind language acquisition. Children don't learn the meaning of their first words until they are already familiar with the objects and states that the words represent. Similarly they cannot learn to express relationships between objects (such as wants, movements) until they know and experience such relationships.

Their map of the world and their understanding of it undoubtedly develops as a result of becoming language users, but the whole process would never start unless they first had something there before language.

There was once a belief, generated through some of Chomsky's ideas, that children might have a 'language acquisition device' which would build up competence through mere exposure to language. Most experts would now reject this idea, emphasizing instead the necessity of a child's embeddedness in the social and physical worlds as the major stimulus to language development.

The study of semantic aspects of language development has proved rather fruitful. This is because it is relatively easy to determine a child's understanding through practical behaviour. We know that the child understands the concept 'under' if she is able to carry out the request to 'put the green block under the red one.' We all know the domain (or one important domain) onto which language has to be mapped. It is the public world of social and physical action that we all inhabit.

When we come to music, we have a difficulty. I think we would find it very difficult to agree on a set of criteria for demonstrating that a person had 'understood' some music. The domain, if there is one, onto which music maps is not wholly (and some may argue not even partly) public. Although there is general agreement that it has in some way to do with emotion, feeling, or affect, there are scant hard data to constrain our theorizing.

What little research has been done has tended to focus on the ability of listeners to verbally identify the general character of different pieces of music. Hevner's (1936) pioneering work still stands as the major contribution in this area. She showed that within our culture, adults tend to generally agree which adjectives best describe the character of a musical excerpt, that is, whether it is happy or sad, lively or solemn, restful or agitated. Gardner (1973) has more recently shown that this ability develops slowly through childhood and into adolescence.

The ability to describe and talk about music is clearly an important aspect of the awareness of musical meaning, but it is not primary. Anyone who has had any significant musical experience will know that the words to describe it are not always at hand. This will be particularly so for children. We should not take what children say about music to fully reflect their experience of it.

Another thing which limits many studies is their mode of data collection. Subjects are played several brief extracts in an experimental context. In contrast, real musical experiences are embedded in rich social and personal context. If we wish to understand more about how musical meanings are acquired, we need to turn to the everyday real-life acts of musical involvement that make up a child's musical life.

With substantial resources, I guess one would want to observe directly many children over many years. With fewer resources, I have had to adopt a different approach, but one which is nonetheless turning out to be rich and promising.

9.5 The autobiographical memory study

I have been asking people to write down the details of any autobiographical memories they could access which involved music in any way, from the first 10 years of their life. To date I have collected 113 usable memories from about 70 adults, ranging from professional musicians to people with little or no current involvement in music.

Despite the apparent indirectness of this approach, it allows us to answer questions not addressed by earlier research. First, we get the responses of people to the naturally occurring musical events of their lives, rather than to contrived experimental situations where a response is forced. Secondly, we can get some indication of the effect of such events on subsequent musical development. Thirdly, adults often have the words to describe, in retrospect, an experience that as a child he or she would have been inarticulate about.

It seems to me that for there to be any kind of consensus in a culture about musical meaning there would have to be fairly general kinds of experiences with music shared by large numbers of children in a culture. Furthermore, these experiences should be expected to generate regularly the same kinds of affective responses. I would not, for example, expect crucial experiences to occur very often within formal musical training. Such training is only given to a minority of children and could not account for wider cultural patterns.

I am aware of two great shortcomings of my study. One is that few people are able to access specific memories before the age of three or four. If the crucial experiences occurred in the first three years of life then my study will not capture them. The second shortcoming is that memory is selective, biased and inaccurate. I cannot guarantee that this sample of memories would necessarily give the same picture as a sample of observations on the subjects of children.

It is however, possible to argue that a memory study actually highlights the kind of event we are looking for. This is because memory for specific events very often seems linked to a high emotional tone. For instance, almost everyone of an appropriate age remembers exactly what they were doing when they heard the news of John F. Kennedy's death. If the meaning of music is connected to affect, then specific memories related to the acquisition of this meaning should be high in affect, so more likely to be remembered. Memory should act as a sort of filter or concentrator.

Although my volunteers were asked to write freely, I offered them 10 questions as cues:

1 How old were you?

2 Where did the experience take place?

3 Of what event did the music form a part?

4 Who were you with?

5 Can you identify the piece of music, or say anything about it.

6 If you can identify it, have you experienced it recently, and do you know it well?

7 What significance or meaning did the experience have for you at the time?

8 Did the experience influence your subsequent behaviour or attitudes in any way?

9 How often, if at all, does this memory come to you?

10 Any other comment.

After subjects had finished the recall task, they were asked to provide information on:

1 Current level of involvement with music.

2 Amount of formal music tuition received prior to the age of ten.

3 The degree to which experiences such as that reported determined current level of involvement with music.

4 The number of other memories available which were not written down.

On examination of the results, a coding scheme was devised so that quantitative statistical analysis could be carried out. It very quickly became clear that events could have two distinct types of significance. Firstly, the music itself could have some effect on the person. This I have called the *internal* significance of the event. Secondly, the context in which the music was taking place could have some effect. This I have called the *external* significance.

In the initial classification, I coded each memory on each of these two dimensions according to whether the significance was positive, neutral, or negative. Table 9.1 shows the frequency breakdown for all combinations of internal and external significance. Several points are of interest. First, there are almost no cases of negative internal significance. People rarely remembered events where the music itself was disliked or aroused negative affect. This is not simply a reluctance to recall negative experiences or some form of repression, since plenty of memories with negative external significance were recalled.

Secondly, the number of events having neutral classification on both dimensions was rather small (17% of the total). Thirdly, there are almost no cases of positive internal significance where the external significance is negative. One way of interpreting this is to say that you can't enjoy the music when you are not enjoying the circumstances in which it takes place.

I would like to give a few examples of specific memories illustrating the main categories of response. Here is one which shows positive internal significance but neutral external significance.

Subject 42: age twenty; regular private performer; tuition from seven

> I was seven years old, and sitting in morning assembly in school. The music formed part of the assembly service. I was with my friends Karen, Amelia, Jenny, Allan. The music was a clarinet duet, classical, probably by Mozart. I was astounded at the beauty of the sound. It was liquid, resonant, vibrant. It seemed to send tingles through me. I felt as if it were a significant moment. Listening to this music led to me learning to play first the recorder and then to achieve my ambition of playing the clarinet. Playing the clarinet has altered my life; going on a paper round and saving up to buy my own clarinet; meeting friends in the county band. . . . Whenever I hear clarinets being played I remember the impact of this first experience.

Table 9.1 Rated significance of 113 memories

Internal	External Positive	Neutral	Negative
Positive	16	25	3
Neutral	25	19	24
Negative	0	1	0

I would like to give one further example in this category to make a specific point:

Subject 49: age nineteen; regular private performer; tuition from six

> I was about ten years old, at school with the teacher and the other kids. The music was a very sad song about the loneliness of the people which we learned in a music lesson. The music made me very sad. I haven't heard it recently and don't know it well. I loved this piece so much that I bought some music instruments and played them every night. I used to think of this song very often, but then I forgot it almost totally until this experiment.

What this memory shows is that sadness in music can be a positive and sought-after experience, even for children. The next example shows positive external significance, but neutral internal significance.

Subject 23: age twenty; occasional private performer; tuition from seventeen

> I was about ten years old. I was singing in the school choir for the school carol concert. We were in the school hall. The carols were some more unusual ones. I can't remember them now. I remember being pleased at missing history lessons, and also because it was a really cheerful occasion. This memory returns occasionally, but I don't think the event had any particular influence on me.

The final example shows negative external significance with neutral internal significance. It is sadly by no means unique in this set of memories.

Subject 31: age fifty; occasional listener; tuition from seven

> I was five years old. I was at the local Infant School, and a music lesson was being taken by the Infant Head Teacher, Miss Linkler. She played a piece of music. I have no idea what it was called. I don't think I was ever told the name of the piece. The class had to listen to the music, and then beat out the time. Suddenly the teacher pounced on me, screaming that I was beating 3/4 time to a 4/4 piece of music. She then produced a battledore and gave me six smacks on the back of my thighs. At the time I ran home, and my mother had the greatest difficulty in making me go to school

after that. As far as the music goes, I have always considered that
I am not musical, and for many years I refused to sing or do anything connected with music. . . .

Since most volunteers provided a wealth of information about the social
context of their memories, it has been possible to isolate factors which are
associated with positive internal significance. The most significant of
these are:

- *Place:* When in a concert hall, church or at home, over 60% of the memories had positive significance, as opposed to only 29% of events at school.
- *Event:* 59% of events where the subject was listening to music were
  positively significant but only 17% of events where the subject was
  performing were positively significant.
- *With:* When with family and friends, 50% of memories were positive;
  when with teachers only 27% were positive.

All this suggests that the occasions when significant meaning was trans-
mitted were mainly informal, relaxed occasions when the person was not
being evaluated, and was in the company of loved ones. A stepwise discriminant analysis revealed that the event was the only one of these variables to
enter into the discriminant function. This suggests that listening is the
crucial factor. It just so happens in our culture that opportunities to listen
to music are provided more often away from school and teachers.

Positive internal significance is also predictive of indices relating to
subsequent behaviour:

- *Status:* 53% of people currently claiming to be regular performers of music
  produced a memory of positive internal significance; whereas only 26% of
  those not regularly performing did so.
- *Influence:* Positive memories were recalled by 68% of those who claimed
  that the memory had an enhancing influence on their subsequent musical involvement. Such memories were only recalled by 14% of those
  who claimed a neutral or negative subsequent effect.

It seems, therefore, that children experiencing events with positive internal significance were more likely to pursue a high level of involvement with
music in later life. Interestingly, this was not true of external significance.
Positive external significance did not go with a higher level of subsequent
involvement in music. People will not pursue musical activity just because
they have experienced positive events around music. The positive experience
has to come from the music itself.

Finally, it turns out that the amount of formal music tuition received before the age of ten relates weakly to experience of positive internal significance. If, however, we compare the age of the positive experience to the age of starting lessons, we find that the experience often precedes the start of lessons. Of the 36 events for which full information was available, only 9 (25%) occurred after the beginning of formal music tuition. It looks as though such experiences are spurs to a child seeking lessons, rather than the lessons providing a basis for such experiences.

On the sample I have so far it is hard to conclude a great deal about specific types of music eliciting these experiences. Sometimes people could not name the piece in question, and when they did, they covered a vast range of classical, folk, and popular pieces. The one thing which has emerged so far is that memories of nursery rhymes, hymns, and carols (of which there were a significant number) almost never carried positive internal significance. My explanation for this is that it seemed to be usually the *first* experience of a piece which led to the most profound effects. Many of the rhymes and hymns will have been repeated many times in the child's life, and the first experience of them may well have been before the age of concrete memories.

A similar analysis was carried out to see what factors seemed to be responsible for *external* significance. The picture here is simple. Negative significance is most often associated with performing situations (56% of cases), almost never with listening (4% of cases). It often occurs in a formal educational setting with teacher and/or other children present and almost never with parents or friends. Experiences with positive significance are spread roughly across all categories of occurrence.

The main negative experiences are of nervousness, embarrassment, humiliation, and criticism (either feared or actual) associated with the performing situation. These negative events almost invariably (85% of cases) had a negative influence on the subsequent involvement of these subjects with music, inhibiting either performing or listening involvement. These results will not be surprising to anyone familiar with the research literature on motivation, but they do remind us of the immense care that teachers need to take when asking children to perform. They confirm the reports of a recent British study which roundly condemned music competitions for their damaging effects on the development of young talented musicians.

To conclude the brief treatment of these results, I would like to turn back to the data on internal significance and look more closely at the content of these experiences. What kinds of things did respondents say about the musical experiences? I found that people's statements were of two kinds; statements about the *feelings* that the music evoked in them (e.g. 'The music made a deep impression on me,' and *judgements* about the characteristics of the music itself (e.g. 'the music was very lively'). I tabulated such statements according to similarity of meaning, and also according to the age at which the music was experienced. A statistically significant age progression was found on both the feeling and the judgment dimensions.

Adults who reported no particular feeling associated with the music had an average age of 4.8 years at the time of the memory. An *enjoyment* cluster (including words such as *love, like, enjoy, excited, elated, happy*) came from children with an average age of 6.2. Then followed a cluster which I have categorized as *wonder*. (It includes such words as *enthralled, incredulous, astounded, overwhelmed, awe-struck*, etc.) The average age associated with such feelings was 8.1. Finally a small cluster of sad feelings (e.g. melancholy, sad, apprehensive) was experienced by children with an average age of 8.7 years.

A similar progression was observed in *judgements*, although fewer memories contained judgement elements overall. The average age for events containing no judgment element was 6.7. A cluster of memories used what I have called *emotional neutral* descriptive words (e.g. *fast, loud, simple*, and the anodyne *nice*). The average age of such events was 4.8. The remaining memories all occurred at an average age of around eight years. They were mainly *emotional/sensual* (e.g. *beautiful, romantic, liquid, funny*) but with a few memories mentioning particular imagery or qualities of the performance itself.

Although the number of memories is as yet rather small for definite conclusions, a suggestive pattern has begun to emerge. At around four years of age, children begin to remember music for its general level of activity (*fast, loud, simple*). Such characteristics are capable of evoking memories of general excitement (*happy, enjoy, elated*) by around six years of age. By the eighth birthday, children are remembering music for its sensual and expressive characteristics (*liquid, funny, beautiful*), and by the age of nine are regularly remembering feelings of wonder or sadness as a result.

It looks as if the memories I have gathered reveal an evolutionary process in the acquisition of musical meaning. Music has meaning at many different levels. Excitement at the activity, movement, and energy of music seems to precede wonder at the sensuous and expressive qualities of music. The age of seven seems to signal the progression to the new awareness. It is useful to look at what other changes in the awareness of music as a language are taking place at this age. Evidence mentioned earlier suggests that the age of seven is when the grasp of tonal syntax becomes particularly apparent. It is at this age that a memory advantage of tonal music emerges, as well as the ability to reject non-tonal chords. I suspect that the syntactic and semantic developments are not unrelated.

This study has been exploratory. It has shown a number of things:

1 The autobiographical memory technique is a rich and workable one.

2 Significant musical experiences are most likely to occur in particular contexts (relaxed, informal listening).

3 Such experiences have long-lasting effects on musical behaviour and involvement.

4 Negative environmental factors generally preclude the possibility of the music itself acquiring positive significance, and can inhibit the level of subsequent involvement with music.

5 Positive environmental factors do not in themselves lead to an increase in involvement with music.

6 The general nature of the experiences does not seem to depend upon the amount of prior formal tuition. Most memories with high internal significance precede formal tuition.

7 Changes occur between the ages of six and eight in the nature of the emotional and judgmental responses to music. They move from responses related to energy and excitement towards ones of wonder and beauty.

We have a long way to go before we can explain precisely what features of music are capable of eliciting these early significant responses, but we now know they are common, deeply influential, and we know something about the situations likely to encourage them. I think this is crucial information for any attempt to build an understanding of musical semantics.

References

Hevner, K. (1936) Experimental studies of the elements of expression in music. *American Journal of Psychology*, **48**, 246–68.

Gardner, H. (1973) Children's sensitivity to musical styles. *Merrill-Palmer Quarterly of Behavioural Development*, **19**, 67–77.

Liberman, A. M., Harris, K. S., Kinney, J. A., and Lane, H. (1961) The discrimination of the relative onset time of the components of certain speech and non-speech pattern. *Journal of Experimental Psychology*, **61**, 379–88.

Locke, S. and Kellar, L. (1973) Categorical perception in a non-linguistic mode. *Cortex*, **9**, 355–69.

Siegel, J. and Siegel, V. (1977) Categorical perception of tonal intervals: musicians can't tell sharp from flat. *Perception and Psychophysics*, **21**, 399–407.

Sloboda, J. A. *The Musical Mind: The Cognitive Psychology of Music*. Oxford University Press, London, 1985.

Zenatti, A. (1960) Le développement génétique de la perception musicale. *Monographs Français Psychologique*, **17**.

CHAPTER 10

MUSIC PSYCHOLOGY AND THE COMPOSER

10.1 Introduction

According to one participant at a recent conference where composers and psychologists were both present, the level of mutual interest and communication was not high. It seemed that 'whenever a psychologist spoke the composers left the room, and whenever a composer spoke the psychologists left the room'! This is not a unique phenomenon for psychology. Psychology lays great claims to being relevant in every sphere of human activity, but psychologists are not always able to convince practitioners that their researchers deserve attention. Some of this may be attributable to resistances in the practitioners, but much is also to be laid at the door of the psychologist who, typically, is not good at interpreting the implications of his or her research to practitioners, or indeed directing the research towards questions which are of direct relevance to practitioners.

This paper attempts to outline some of the issues which may prevent psychologists and composers achieving a profitable meeting of minds, examines some aspects of a framework for mutual activity, and, through this framework, attempts to point to the type of psychological findings which might be truly relevant for composers.

10.2 Is music psychology credible to composers?

One sobering fact for psychologists is that composers have managed very well without them for hundreds of years. Masters of composition, from Machaut through Mozart to Messiaen, have achieved profoundly significant and lasting art without the slightest help from professional psychology. Indeed modern psychological research itself would support the view that the factors that help make a good composer are (among other things) long hours of practice at composing (from as early an age as possible), belief in self, perseverence, unwillingness to accept the first solution as best, exposure to the products of other composers, the existence of mentors and supportive but searching critics, etc. Academic knowledge, be it of music theory, philosophy, history or whatever has not had any proven effect on compositional ability. Why expect psychology to be any different?

One factor which may propel contemporary composers to search outside their own discipline for enlightenment is the breakdown of cultural consensus and traditions concerning the most basic parameters of music, its form, its instruments, its functions. Art music has broken free of longstanding constraints imposed not only by culture, but also by technology. Anything is now possible, and faced with almost infinite possibilities composers must generate their own constraints and discipline. They may rightly ask, 'is there anything that psychologists can tell us about the limits of human perception, cognition, or aesthetic and emotional response which can tell us that one avenue of exploration is more profitable than another'. In terms of theories of problem solving, composers must somehow 'reduce the search space'.

If some brave composer were to turn to the literature on psychology of music, there would be several immediate barriers to the discovery of useful Information. For instance, the vast majority of research is concerned with the way in which people perceive and handle conventional tonal music. Also, the research is mainly concerned with microstructural factors occurring within fragments of a few seconds of length. The question of large scale architecture is almost unstudied. Overarching all this is the fact that none of the research literature is *addressed* to the composer, but normally to other psychologists (who are, rightly, concerned with statistical correctness, methodology, and the development of detailed models of single aspects of a complex phenomenon).

It is not to be expected that psychology will provide composers with any ready made answers to questions which may be unasked, or even unformulated. Some mutual work is required. Composers must be able to formulate questions in precise and unambiguous ways. In their turn, psychologists must be prepared to accept composers' preoccupations and priorities without immediately rejecting them as 'unscientific' or 'too difficult'. These are not easy or trivial preconditions. What is required is a common framework.

10.3 What model of music is appropriate for composer–psychologist dialogue?

Some (maybe all) composers obtain satisfaction from their compositional work. The mere act of self-exploration or self-expression, the intense manipulation of compositional materials to achieve a personally meaningful end, can be quite enough motivation for the composer. Some would go further to say that such satisfaction is the only thing that can guide a composer.

Given this view, then a piece of music may be seen as an *expression* of the craft, effort, and personality of the composer. If we take such a view, then the only and ultimate arbiter of the work, its value and its purposes is the composer himself. The work's value is simply its value to the composer. Within such a framework a psychologist's role becomes rather limited— explaining how compositional activity can provide satisfaction to the composer, and, maybe, help the composer to obtain more satisfaction. This starting point, whilst logically feasible, is socially and ethically flawed. What makes it worthwhile investing effort and resources in composers (or any other creative artists) is that their work has value for others.

The exact opposite of this approach treats music entirely in terms of its *effects* on listeners. It is almost a *pharmaceutical* mode, ascribing to the music a mandatory power of bringing about certain perceptual, cognitive, or emotional responses in a listener. The question then becomes to discover what aspects of music have what effects and under what conditions. Such an approach is tempting for a psychological or physiological scientist, who can then treat music as a causal agent in the manner of the physical sciences. It does, indeed, underly much perceptual research on music in more or less explicit ways. It, however, reduces the composer to a technician manipulating the responses of a passive potential audience. This view is equally flawed, and has its uglier outcomes in the work of such agencies as the Muzak corporation, where social and behavioural control is the explicit purpose of their activities.

Neither of the above models provides a wholesome or productive meeting ground for composers and psychologists. The first makes it hard for the psychologist to make an authentic contribution, the second makes it equally hard for the composer. What alternatives do we have?

A model which many, including myself, have tried to develop in recent years is that of music as a *language*. This has worked particularly well in developing notions of music as structure (syntax), with the listener conceived of as decoding or analysing an acoustic surface into categorial elements which are then placed in hierarchically organized groups. This analysis has proved interesting and useful, at least for tonal music (see Sloboda, 1985; Lerdahl and Jackendoff, 1983). It is an advance on the pharmaceutical model because it frees the listener from the passive role of someone on whom music has 'effects', and allows that s/he may or may not learn the underlying rules of a particular genre of music: thus the existence of cultural and developmental differences.

However, the model fails in many places, particularly in the arena of semantics. It assumes that music has a 'meaning', intended by the composer and received by the listener. Success, on this model, is achieved if the listener reconstructs the composer's underlying intention, so as to 'understand what the composer was trying to communicate'. In doing so it possibly ascribes an unrealistically tight coupling between the composer's activity and that of the listener.

I wish to propose a different model as a potentially useful meeting ground for psychologists and composers, and this is the analogy of music as *architecture or artefact*.

10.4 Music as architecture

We will conceive of a composer as an architect of a structure (a musical composition). Beyond him we have a range of 'middle men' who perform the function of making the achitect's plan into reality. In building work, they are the surveyors, builders, manufacturers. In music they are the publishers, performers, and instrument makers. The customer of all this work is the 'user', in music's case, often, although not always exclusively, the listener.

The steps in the creation of an artefact such as building are usually, (a) determine the function(s) the building may perform, (b) design a structure that can serve that function, (c) choose materials which will allow the structure to be made. (b) and (c) often interact, in the sense that the structure can be to a certain extent determined by the available materials.

Psychologists and composers can only begin to fruitfully interact if the composer will agree to be explicit about intended functions of this work. A composer who refuses to do this is in effect reverting to the expressive model, claiming a right to do what he likes without having to specify any outcome for others. A psychologist can be of no use to an architect if the architect does not care what use people make of his building. Some really useful dialogues have taken place between psychologists and real architects. The psychologist's contribution has sometimes been to say 'you may have intended that people would use your building in such-and-such a way. Well, I have to tell you that, because of various properties of your building, and various characteristics of the people who inhabit them, the buildings are not serving their intended function'. On some occasions the psychologists may be able to suggest relatively minor changes which make the buildings usable; in other cases it may turn out that the building is so unworkable that it has to be demolished (as happened in the case of many high-rise apartment developments of the 1960s).

But there is another side to the issue of function. An architect can never entirely predetermine all the uses that people will make of his building. Users to a certain extent choose what use to make of a building. A building may have been designed to live in, but someone decides to run a business from it. A church may have been designed for worship, but later users turn it into a museum or concert hail. The best the architect can do is provide *affordances* (salient features) which offer opportunities for certain kinds of use. There are always degrees of freedom for a user. This is true of music too.

Psychologists may have a role to play in this respect in providing knowledge of people's ability to pick up certain kinds of affordance, and the likelihood of their doing so given their motivations, background, and

ite of multiple affordances. Different people use
sterile debate about 'the' meaning of a piece of
ooking at the music as an artefact which can be
ach listener chooses what use to make of it in
:eived affordance and his or her own agendas.
<e satisfaction in designing music which can be
luding unplanned for ways, but this does not
negate the requirement to design the music with some uses in mind.

10.5 Psychologists as reactionaries or realists?

The typical psychologist of music will be less concerned with grand designs than components. If we translate into architectural terms, he is more likely to be studying staircases than elevations. An imaginary psychologist of staircases might tell a story something like this. 'Staircases have a structure, Involving recursive incremental platforms. People exposed to this structure are able to learn to move up and down it. A skilled staircase user will adjust leg and body movements quite finely to the features of the steps—s/he is therefore highly sensitive to the structure. People build up certain kinds of expectancies. You can show this by devising a staircase which violates recursive rules (e.g. has steps of different unpredictable sizes—see Figure 10.1A below). People take longer to get up such steps and tend to trip over. People are also sensitive to higher-order recursive structures (e.g. landing placements). if landings are placed at regular intervals (Figure 10.1B) people show awareness of them (by, for instance, taking pauses more often at these places than elsewhere). Some psychologists go even further and claim that there is an optimum step size for staircases which is determined by characteristics of the human body, and that this configuration is likely to remain an invariant characteristic of all usable staircases into the indefinite future. This proposal is resisted strongly by some avant-garde architects who claim that different step sizes will provide new challenges and possibilities to users (Figure 10.1C).

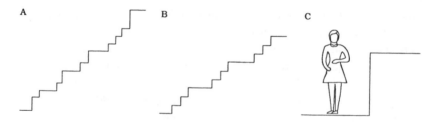

Figure 10.1 Steps of different sizes.

This somewhat 'tongue in cheek' parody of psychological studies of, say scales and tonality, nevertheless has a number of serious points. In order to make any contribution, the psychologist has to analyse the situation with respect to function (at some level). In the absence of knowledge of any explicit statement from the architect he may take a rather low level function, such as 'going up or down a staircase'. Considerations of why a person might not want to go up or down a staircase are left to one side. In music, psychologists tend to work at a functional level of 'perceiving similarities or differences' or 'being able to remember' or 'forming perceptual groups', showing what factors in music promote or hinder such functions. The question, 'why should the music need to be remembered?' is not often asked. Some composers may not intend that the details of a composition be remembered by a listener, but even where they do, we need to know why. What higher functions is memory in music serving? On these grounds it would seem essential for psychologists to be enquiring of composers 'What are you hoping that your music will allow people to do with it?' and of listeners 'Why are you listening to this music, what are you using it for?' Few psychologists I know of are doing this. Ethnomusicologilsts such as Merriam (1964) have come closest to systematic treatment of this area, although Merriam's distinction between functions and uses of music may not be a particularly useful one for psychological analysis. In this paper, I am using the two words interchangeably.

Another point of the parody is to show that psychologists are more able to assess human performance than human competence. They look at what people do. This is realistic. If you want to change people you need to know where they are starting from. It may also be reactionary, in that there is a strong temptation to use what people are currently doing to draw strong inferences about what they are able to do. Thus you will find psychologists of music claiming that the tonal system is the best possible system of pitch organization, the human voice is the best possible instrument, etc. I take a middle view. Change is possible, but it proceeds slowly and incrementally, each step being only a small change from the preceding one. So called cultural revolutions are, in fact, surface perturbations which conceal underlying continuities. Change through evolution seems to characterize almost every historical phenomenon from the differentiation of species to the growth of ideas. Psychologists may be able to remind composers that people need preparation before they can handle radical change.

10.6 The functions of music

Given the above argument, it follows that the functions of music will be relatively stable over time. New functions will arise, and old ones will drop out, but at a slow rate. Functions will be largely determined by cultural and psychological requirements of listeners. Composers may be able to invent radically new forms and structures: they are hardly capable of inventing new functions. Of course, we are here talking of generalized functions. Each specific composition (building) has unique features which may be related (or may not be related) to the precise requirements of its location, intended users, etc. This is why there is always new work for composers (and architects). Thus, at a given cultural point, functions of music are not arbitrary, but maybe (in principle) enumerated by observation. This is an empirical process in which a composer has no particularly privileged position.

Functions, or goals, are also capable of indefinite hierarchical embedding. Disagreements about ultimate functions can legitimately arise. For one composer, it may be a satisfactory goal to have some listeners like his composition. Others will argue that a person only likes something if it is fulfilling some further function, and that we cannot build for liking without understanding what that further function is. By analogy, it may be argued incoherent to say that a person likes his house without being able to specify in what way it fulfils useful functions for him. I take the latter view, and see as non-explanatory any account of music which posits as ultimate function the achievement of affective or aesthetic states (such as liking, pleasure, or the experience of some emotion). Affective states are concomitants or symptoms of processes of behavioural or cognitive adaptation and change, and have no value in themselves.

This may be made clearer by an example. It is very likely that music has served mnemonic functions in many cultures. That is, the music serves as a means of structuring the recall and organization of some other behaviour. The use of music to help recall of words is a paradigm example of this. Songs aid retention of culturally important material, particularly in non-literate or semi-literate societies. The ability of the music to guide or remind or help the user anticipate, will lead to a sense of satisfaction or pleasure in the music. A composer will need to know what features promote music's mnemonic functions if he is to compose apppropriate music for this purpose. A person's aesthetic or emotional reaction to the music in respect of this function will be entirely based on the degree to which the function is satisfactorily fulfilled. My strong claim is that all such reactions are contingent on their fulfilling some psychological function. There is no such thing as 'just' liking a piece of music.

Of course, many functions of music may be grasped by composers and listeners only intuitively and implicitly. It is not expected that a full formal description will always be forthcoming. A listener may gain intense value from a musical experience without necessarily being able to articulate and explain the basis of this value. In other cases, the listener may be clear enough about the outcome (e.g. 'It renewed my sense of hope') but be unable to articulate the mechanism by which this outcome was achieved. Psychology in general (and cognitive psychology in particular) has much experience in formalizing and uncovering those processes which seem to be hard to consciously report.

There are two main reasons for self-report limitations. One is that the processes are truly subconscious, rapid and automatic. Examples of this are mechanisms of reading and perceptual analysis. They can be uncovered by relating task performance to structural factors in controlled stimuli. Another reason is that the listener quickly forgets the precise sequence of mental events. This is true particularly of complex time-extended activities such as problem-solving, day-dreaming, and, arguably, listening to music (see Ericsson and Simon 1980). A few music psychologists, including myself, are beginning to explore ways of allowing people to report on their experiences during extended music listening, either retrospectively or concurrently. I am looking at listener's ability to report either retrospectively or concurrently on moments of high emotional 'charge' during pieces of music. This is being linked to structural analysis of these moments. Preliminary work is confirming the insights of Meyer (1956) and others, that patterned or motivated tension and resolution seem to promote significant psychological outcomes for listeners. Indeed, an initial analysis of a small data-base of musical 'moments' which provoke strong physiological reactions shows strong and systematic relationships between the type of reaction (tears, shivers, or racing heart) and specific structural features of these moments. Full details of this research will be reported in due course.

One important line of psychologically informed theorizing is being undertaken by Lerdahl (1988), who is trying to articulate the defining characteristics of music that is capable of being grasped as structure (and thus as capable of supporting motivated tension and resolution). He arrives at a number of general postulates which would include tonal music but exclude serial music such as Boulez' *Le Marteau sans Maitre*. The postulates would not, however, exclude all novel compositional forms and devices, and he himself is exploring the possibility of using *timbre* in ways which are consistent with his postulates (Lerdahl, 1988).

Another equally important line of thinking is the attempt by some psychologists (e.g. Dowling and Harwood, 1986; Gayer and Mandler, 1987; Ortony, Clore and Collins, 1988) to articulate general theories about the cognitive antecedents and consequences of emotion. This work promises the opportunity of establishing formal links or analogies between musical events which promote emotion and non-musical life events which have similar effects. It may be easier to see the functions of the emotions in 'external' life events than in the 'internal' world of music.

10.7 Emotions in music serve non-trivial personal purposes for listeners

Taking the assumptions of modern cognitive science that many emotions serve rational purposes rather than being embarrassing lapses from functionality, it is possible to make a number of assumptions about emotional functions in music.

(a) *Each emotion experienced in response to music is matched by an identical emotional response to a (potential) analogous non-musical situation.* This statement is asserting that there are no emotional response which are unique to music. It is also asserting that a particular non-musical analogue is not necessarily experienced frequently (or at all) by a given individual. For instance, music may be accompanied by a sense of relief from anxiety that is seldom experienced in the extra-musical life of a particular individual.

(b) *The experience of emotion arises when substantial cognitive re-appraisal is required, and accompanies such re-appraisal.* This statement asserts that emotions function with respect to a cognitive system which is monitoring situations for changes of various sorts. They signal the detection of particular classes of change and are, in some yet to be fully understood ways, implicated in mobilizing further cognitive resources to handle these changes.

(c) *The need for re-appraisal is precipitated by the violation of current goals, plans, or assumptions. The situation will continue to be emotion bearing until such re-appraisal is complete.* This statement defines important types of change that are likely to be emotion-bearing. Such violations can be either negative (the death of a loved one) or positive (winning a lottery).

(d) *Such re-appraisal is promoted by any context which suggests the possibility of an alternative or a resolution to the precipitating situation.* It is a common observation that a small kindness can often restore the morale of some-one who is discouraged or disillusioned. It is not that the kindness itself solves the major problems, but it reminds the recipient of 'another world', and can motivate a renewed effort to tackle the problem. In a similar way, many prisoners of war (or conscience) have testified to the immense value of tiny scraps of Information or encouragement from the outside world in reviving hope and energy. Some formal therapies are based on a systematic application of this phenomenon.

(e) *Such contexts are typically less available than complete re-appraisal would require. People, therefore, accumulate a backlog of unfinished business.* A col-loquial way of expressing this statement is that life events leaves most people with emotional scars. If, for instance, a person continues to feel hurt or angry about some long past event, this signals that the individ-ual has not yet been able to deal successfully with all the consequences and implications of that event.

(f) *People will seek and use appropriate subsequent context to continue the unfin-ished re-appraisals. Such context will contain (a) some reminder or analogue of the initial emotion-provoking disturbance and (b) a demonstration of the resolution of that disturbance.* A clear example of such a context would be the 'story with a happy ending'. A huge number of the world's most loved and retold stories are based on the theme of an individual or group struggling against adversity to win through to a goal.

(g) *Certain musical structures meet these criteria. Cultural or pan-cultural common-alities of experience tend to make such structures widely effective, rather than individualistically so.* The discovery and specification of such musical structures is a task for the future. This statement suggests that few emotional responses to music are 'pure'. In the sense of being detached from an individual's life experiences. However, it relates life experiences to emotional response in a completely different way to the 'associationistic' model, where a person re-experiences the same emotion that he or she happens to have felt at the time of an earlier hearing of the music. Such associations certainly occur and are used by composers, but many, perhaps most of these responses, are com-pletely individualistic and cannot be systematized. It suggests, rather, that people will look to different pieces of music at different times of life and in different situations because they contain material relevant to particular types of re-appraisal.

(h) *Engagement with music can thus be seen as Important and purposeful work. Conceptions of music as recreation or diversion are short sighted and incomplete.* To make explicit connections between music and non-musical ends is not in any way to devalue the composer's work. For one thing, music may supply contexts which are rare or unavailable in other situations. Secondly, as stated before, music can serve multiple purposes, and no one purpose exhausts music's significance. Music is, therefore, not a substitute for or 'just like' something else.

10.8 Conclusion

I have suggested that a fruitful point of contact for musicians and psychologists is the architectural analogy, which focuses on articulating the functions of a composition, and then specifying the characteristics of the affordances which may allow these function to be fulfilled. Some functions may necessitate the possibility of the listener making discriminations and comparisons, of classifying events along dimensions (of relative tension or prominence), and of recalling earlier events. Psychologists are in a good position to formalize for composers the properties of sound structures which encourage or do not encourage such activities, and also to help assess the degree to which listener actually respond in intended ways. It is, however, up to psychologists to prove that their work is relevant and powerful enough to replace or supplement the time-honoured strategy of composers whereby they use themselves and their own responses as the means of assessing the adequacy of what they are doing. This may require a more intimate and personal relationship between individual composers and psychologist than has up to now been achieved, and conferences such as this may be an important catalyst to the development of such relationships.

References

Dowling, W. J. and Harwood, D. L. (1986) *Music Cognition.* Academic Press, New York.

Ericsson, K. A. and Simon, H. A. (1980) Verbal reports as data. *Psychological Review*, **87**, 215–251.

Gayer, W. W. and Mandler, G. (1987) Play it again Sam: on liking music. *Cognition and Emotion*, **1**, 259–282.

Lerdahl, F. and Jackendoff, R. (1983) *A Generative Theory of Tonal Music.* MIT Press, Cambridge, Mass.

Lerdahl, F. (1988) In: Sloboda J (ed) *Generative Processes in Music. The psychology of performance, composition, and improvisation. Cognitive constraints on compositional systems.* Oxford University Press, London.

Merriam, A. P. (1964) *The Anthropology of Music.* Northwestern University Press, Chicago.

Meyer, L. B. (1956) *Emotion and Meaning in Music.* University of Chicago Press, Chicago.

Ortony, A., Clore, G. L., and Collins, A. (1988) *The Cognitive Structure of the Emotions.* Cambridge University Press, New York.

Sloboda, J. A. (1985) *The Musical Mind: The Cognitive Psychology of Music.* Oxford University Press, London.

CHAPTER 11

EMPIRICAL STUDIES OF EMOTIONAL RESPONSE TO MUSIC

There is a general consensus that music is capable of arousing deep and significant emotion in those who interact with it. In a study of autobiographical memories of musical events (Sloboda, 1989a), one subject recalled the following event from the age of 7:

> I was sitting in morning assembly at school. The music formed part of the assembly service. . . . The music was a clarinet duet, classical, probably by Mozart. I was astounded at the beauty of the sound. It was liquid, resonant, vibrant. It seemed to send tingles through me. I felt as if it was a significant moment. Listening to this music led to me learning to play first the recorder and then to achieve my ambition of playing the clarinet. . . . Whenever I hear clarinets being played I remember the impact of this *first* experience. (p. 37)

This study asked a wide variety of adults to recall any memories from the first 10 years of their lives that involved music in any way. There was no attempt by the experimenter to suggest particular types of memory. Forty-four out of 113 memories so produced (39%) shared an important characteristic with the aforementioned example: a valued emotional experience that was derived from an awareness of some aspect of the musical sound itself. Although there were other memories in the sample where the emotional tone of the experience (positive or negative) derived from the context in which the music took place, the study showed that sustained involvement with music was more likely in those subjects who could recall a musical event of the positive type.

Because such experiences are widespread and seem to be important motivators for engagement with music, the study of these experiences deserves a more central position in the psychology of music than it currently enjoys. The purpose of this chapter is to explore how empirical science may study this type of phenomenon and to summarize some of what is known about it.

11.1 The cognitive content of the emotional experience

11.1.1 Free verbal response—adult experience

In a previously unpublished study, I asked 67 regular listeners to music to describe in their own words the nature of their most valued emotional experiences of music. Although every account was different in detail, some common themes emerged. The most commonly mentioned concept was that of music as *change agent (n = 41)*. Some common comments were:

- 'Music relaxes me when I am tense and anxious'
- 'One feels understood and comforted in pain, sorrow, and bewilderment'
- 'Involvement in music detaches me from emotional preoccupations'
- 'Through hearing emotions in someone else's music, it is possible to feel that emotions are shared and not your burden alone'
- 'Music motivates and inspires me to be a better person (e.g. more agreeable and loving).'

Common to these examples is the characterization of music as offering an alternative perspective on a person's situation, allowing him or her to construe things differently.

A second cluster of responses focused on the notion of music as promoting the *intensification* or *release* of existing emotions *(n = 34)*. These responses included:

- 'Music releases emotions (e.g. sadness) that would otherwise be bottled up'
- 'Music helps me discover what I am actually feeling'
- 'Music reconnects me to myself when my emotions are ignored or suppressed'
- 'Music makes me feel more alive, more myself'
- 'Music can provide a trigger for the outlet of my emotions concerning memories of pleasurable or painful experiences in my past.'

Common to these examples is the notion that music does not create or change emotion; rather it allows a person access to the experience of emotions that are somehow already 'on the agenda' for that person, but not fully apprehended or dealt with. Gabrielsson (1989) reports a similar finding in a study where he asked 149 people to describe the 'strongest (most intense, deep-going) experiences' they ever had to music. A significant number of respondents reported 'feelings that this music deals with myself; it reflects or clarifies my feelings and situations.'

11.1.2 Free verbal response—childhood experience

Gardner (1973) has demonstrated an age progression in the kind of adjectives children spontaneously use to describe the character of music they hear. Children aged 6 to 14 were asked to say whether or not two musical extracts came from the same composition and were then asked to verbally justify their choices. The 6-year-old children tended to base their justifications on such simple dimensions as fast/slow or loud/soft. Eight-year-olds used metaphors drawn from outside music, such as 'peppy,' 'dull,' 'churchy,' and so forth. Neither this study nor any other known to the author has directly asked children to describe their emotional experiences to music.

The previously mentioned retrospective study of Sloboda (1989a) provides some indirect evidence of an age progression in the nature of emotional response to music. For each memory, adults were asked to describe the nature and significance of the event and also to recall the age at which the experience had occurred. Many subjects spontaneously used emotion words or concepts to describe their experiences. The emotion words were divided into three broad categories: an *enjoyment* category (including love, like, enjoy, excited, elated, and happy), a *wonder/surprise* category (including enthralled, incredulous, astounded, overwhelmed, and awestruck), and a *sadness* category (including melancholy, sad, and apprehensive). There was a significant difference in the mean age associated with the recalled experiences relating to these categories. For enjoyment experiences the mean age was 6.2 years, for wonder/surprise experiences the mean age was 8.1 years, and for sad experiences 8.7 years.

This study also provided independent corroboration of Gardner's (1973) results. Descriptions of the music in terms of simple characteristics (e.g. fast, loud) were associated with experiences at a mean age of 4.8. Descriptions in terms of metaphor and character (e.g. liquid, funny, romantic) came at a mean age of 8.0. Gardner's results may have been partly due to the expanding vocabulary of the children he tested rather than a fundamental change in experience. However, the Sloboda data—coming as they do from adults with sophisticated vocabularies—are less plausibly explained in a similar way. It appears increasingly likely that there is a fundamental change in the experience of emotion to music and in its cognitive construal between the ages of 6 and 8. At the heart of this change is a heightened response to aspects of music which strike children as surprising or unexpected. This may be related to a widely reported increase in sensitivity to aspects of tonality at about this age (Dowling, 1982;

Imberty, 1969; Thackray, 1976; Zenatti, 1969). The more one has under-stood and internalized the implicit 'grammar' or 'rule system' of a musical language, the greater the possibility for surprise at novelty.

11.1.3 Forced verbal response—adult experience

The great majority of studies on emotional characteristics of music have asked subjects to ascribe such characteristics to pieces of music by choosing an adjective from a checklist (e.g. Hevner, 1936; Scherer & Oshinsky, 1977; Wedin, 1972). These studies show that, by and large, adults in a given musical culture agree on the broad characterization of a musical passage. The relevance of these studies to emotional *experience,* however, is not proven. It is possible to make character judgments on the basis of con-ventional characteristics without experiencing any emotion whatsoever.

A study by Waterman (personal communication, March 1990) approached the issue more directly by asking 76 college students to indicate on a checklist of emotions which ones they have actually experienced to music. The checklist consisted of 25 emotion words or phrases, each rep-resenting a major emotion type in the theory of Ortony, Clore, and Collins (1988). This theory proposes that experienced emotion arises through cognitive appraisal of situations construed as either *events, actions of agents,* or *objects.* Until such construal takes place, no emotion is possible. The most undifferentiated emotion arises from simply placing a positive or negative valence on a situation so appraised. The basic event-related emotion pair is PLEASED–DISPLEASED. The corresponding pair for actions of agents is APPROVE–DISAPPROVE, and that for objects is LIKE–DISLIKE.

Within the theory, other emotions are produced by appraising the situation to finer levels of differentiation. For instance, within the event branch, an event can be appraised as relevant to oneself or relevant to someone else. It can be further appraised as a present event or one in the future. Each level of differentiation is achieved by the consideration of an additional variable: The more variables added, the more specific is the emotion and the more specific the eliciting situation. A relatively unspecific event-based emotion is that of being DISPLEASED at the occurrence of an event judged UNDESIRABLE. A typical word for such emotion would be SADNESS. A more spe-cific event-based emotion is that of being DISPLEASED at the nonoccurrence of a event whose PROSPECT was judged as DESIRABLE for ONESELF. A typical word for such an emotion would be DISAPPOINTMENT.

Waterman found that the emotions reported most often did not fall under any one appraisal category (events, actions of agents, or objects). People frequently experienced emotions relevant to appraisals of music as event (for instance, 72% of the subjects reported experiencing HOPE in response to music), action of agent (53% experienced ANGER), and object (92% experienced LIKING). However, there was a significant negative correlation between the proportion of subjects experiencing an emotion and its specificity in the theory, in terms of the number of cognitive variables requiring appraisal. Less specific emotions such as JOY (71%) were experienced more often than more specific emotions such as RESIGNATION (33%). The full list of emotion labels used in the study is given in Table 11.1, together with the percentage of respondents experiencing that emotion and the number of local appraisal variables relevant to that emotion in Ortony *et al.*'s theory.

Table 11.1 Proportion of subjects who have felt each emotion to music, and the number of local variables influencing the intensity of each emotion, according to Ortony, Clore, and Collins (1988). Data are from Waterman (personal communication, March 1990)

Emotion	%	Number of local variables influencing emotional intensity			
		1	2	3	4
Sadness	96.2	■			
Joy	93.4	■			
Liking	92.1	■	■		
Appreciation	86.8	■	■		
Dislike	81.6	■	■		
Satisfaction	78.9	■	■	■	■
Suspense	77.6	■	■	■	
Hope	72.4	■	■		
Anger	52.6	■	■	■	
Hopelessness	52.6	■	■	■	
Disappointment	52.6	■	■	■	■
Pride	51.3	■	■	■	
Relief	50.0	■	■	■	■
Sympathy	48.7	■	■	■	■
Happiness for	46.1	■	■	■	■
Resignation	43.3	■	■	■	
Fear	42.1	■	■		
Remorse	39.5	■	■	■	■
Gratitude	32.9	■	■	■	
Resentment	30.3	■	■	■	■
Self-satisfaction	30.3	■	■	■	■
Fears confirmed	23.7	■	■	■	■
Shame	17.1	■	■	■	
Reproach	15.8	■	■	■	
Gloating	13.2	■	■	■	■

Waterman's data demonstrate that most adults have experienced a range of emotions to music and that frequency of response is less a function of the type of cognitive appraisal underlying the emotion than of its cognitive specificity. There are, however, major problems with any empirical approach which limits subjects' responses to a set of experimenter-determined categories. A more direct way of eliciting data would be to ask subjects to specify a nonmusical situation in which they have experienced the same emotion as during a particular episode of music listening. It may then be possible to map formal characteristics of the nonmusical situation directly onto formal characteristics of musical events without any need to employ the vocabulary of emotional terms at all. This approach is currently being explored.

11.2 The antecedents of emotional experience

11.2.1 Factors external to the music

It is clear that the same event, be it musical or otherwise, does not always result in the same emotional experience. For example, I can listen to the same recording on two different occasions and be moved to tears on one of them, while remaining completely detached on the other.

There are several possible reasons for this inherent variability. One is that the same piece of music may be appraised on different criteria. A musical passage appraised as event may incline a listener to an event-based emotion such as sadness. The same piece appraised as the action of an agent may incline a listener towards an emotion such as gratitude.

Another possibility is that one's prevailing mood determines the extent to which a piece of music will lead to strong emotional experience of particular sorts. It may be hard to experience grief or sadness in response to music when one's prevailing mood is cheerfulness, even though one is carrying out the relevant cognitive appraisals of the music, which in other circumstances would lead to sadness.

A third possibility is that there may be some emotional or mood states which simply preclude any relevant appraisal-based emotion to the music from occurring at all. One of the most striking features of the Sloboda (1989a) study was the almost complete absence of differentiated responses to the music itself when the context was being appraised as negative. The most typical negative context was a situation of threat, anxiety, or humiliation, brought about by being placed in a situation where one's performance was being assessed. Such situations included singing or playing in front of an audience or a teacher. They often included fear of verbal or physical punishment (and sometimes its realization). For many subjects these contexts had long-lasting effects, leading to 'refusing to have anything to do with music' or 'considering myself completely unmusical.'

The evidence of the study is that the likelihood of experiencing positively valued emotional responses from music is a direct function of the degree to which the subject feels relaxed and unthreatened. If someone is feeling frightened, anxious, or under threat, this usually means that there are factors in the environment which are dominating the appraisal system, probably because they impinge on significant personal goals (e.g. preservation of self-esteem). Under these circumstances the music itself will not be likely to yield appraisal-based emotions. This may be because the appraisals are not undertaken at all (the attention is on the threat-provoking context) or because the appraisals are in some way 'blocked' from access to the system which produces emotional experience.

11.2.2 Factors intrinsic to the music

Although it is well established that people respond emotionally to music, little is known about precisely what it is in the music that they are responding to. A recent study (Sloboda, 1991) attempted to establish something about the specific types of musical events that are associated with physically based concomitants of emotional response to music. Physical reactions such as crying, shivering, a racing heart, and so forth avoid some of the problems associated with verbal emotion labels that were discussed previously. It is very difficult to be mistaken about whether you cried or not to a piece of music. Such reactions are stereotyped, memorable, distinct from one another, and shared by all humans regardless of culture and vocabulary. They are arguably more closely connected to the experience of emotion than verbalizations which may be infected with rationalizations.

In a study by Sloboda (1991), subjects were asked to specify particular pieces of music to which they could recall having experienced any of a list of 12 physical manifestations commonly associated with emotion. Having identified such pieces, they were then asked to specify the location within the music that provoked these reactions. They were encouraged to do this, where possible, with reference to a score or a recording, but since this was a postal questionnaire study, no direct check on method was made. Surprisingly, and in contradistinction to Meyer's (1956) misgivings, a significant proportion (about one third) of the people were able to locate their reaction within a theme or smaller unit. Those specific segments for which a published score was available (i.e. the classical citations) were classified according to the musical features they contained, and according to the emotional reaction they provoked.

Table 11.2 Music-structural features associated with physical-emotional responses

Feature		Number of musical passages provoking a response		
		TEARS	SHIVERS	HEART
1	Harmony descending cycle of fifths to tonic	6	0	0
2	Melodic appogiaturas	18	9	0
3	Melodic or harmonic sequence	12	4	1
4	Enharmonic change	4	6	0
5	Harmonic or melodic acceleration to cadence	4	1	2
6	Delay of final cadence	3	1	0
7	New or unprepared harmony	3	12	1
8	Sudden dynamic or textural change	5	9	3
9	Repeated syncopation	1	1	3
10	Prominent event earlier than prepared for	1	4	3
Total number of musical passages		20	21	5

From *Music Structure and Emotional Response: some Empirical Findings,* by J. Sloboda, *Psychology of Music,* 1992. Copyright 1991 by Society for Research in Psychology of Music and Music Education. Adapted by permission.

Table 11.2 shows the main results of this analysis. Twenty musical passages provoked the cluster of responses labeled TEARS (i.e. crying, lump in the throat). The majority of these passages contained melodic appoggiaturas and melodic or harmonic sequences. Twenty-one passages provoked the cluster of responses labeled shivers (i.e. goose pimples, shivers down the spine). The majority of these contained a new or unprepared harmony. Only 5 passages provoked HEART reactions (i.e. racing heart and pit-of-stomach sensations). These were associated with repeated syncopations and prominent events occurring earlier than prepared for.

A more recent unpublished analysis of the popular and jazz citations (by transcription from audio tracks) has confirmed this basic picture. The same features tend to be operative, although the picture is somewhat obscured due to the fact that combined physical reactions are more common in these passages than in classical music. That is to say, subjects frequently reported TEARS, Shivers, and HEART reactions simultaneously to the same segment of music.

Figure 11.1 shows an example of an excerpt that provoked tears. It is the opening passage from Albinoni's *Adagio for Strings.* Note that the first 7-note melodic phrase contains 3 consecutive appoggiaturas, C–B<flat>, A–G, G–F#. The phrase is then repeated in sequence form (exact repetition at one higher scale step). This is followed by a second phrase which is repeated twice more in sequential fashion. What seems to characterize this, and other TEARS-provoking passages, are the successions of harmonic tensions or dissonances which are created and resolved within a structure which has a high degree of repetition and implication-realization (see Narmour, 1977). In general terms, an implication is set up when a musical segment contains within it some parameter, such as a pitch movement. The implication is realized if the parameter is repeated. For example, in Figure 11.1 the initial scalar movement D–C sets up implications for further downward scalar motions, which are realized. A sequence realizes implications that a theme, once stated, will be repeated. If the first repetition is at a certain pitch distance from the first statement, then the implication is that a second repetition will repeat this pitch jump. Psychologically, passages with strong implication-realization are to some extent predictable. In cases like that of Figure 11.1 it is possible that the predictable but repeated appoggiaturas, which 'tease' the sense of consonance, are responsible for the particular form that the emotional response takes.

Figure 11.2 shows an example similar to an excerpt that provoked SHIVERS (copyright restrictions preclude citing the actual example). It is characterized by a sudden key shift from E to C# in the context of a rising sequential pattern based on E, then F#, and then G#. In terms of music analytic theories of expectancy/implication (see, for instance, Meyer, 1956, 1973; Narmour, 1977; Schmuckler, 1989), the sequential progression E–F# sets up an implication for a progression G# (which is fulfilled). At the same time the harmonic progression (successive chords within E-major tonal space) sets up an implication for further chords within this tonal space (which is violated). This dual characteristic of an event being both expected (at one level or according to one criterion) and unexpected (at another level or on another criterion) seems to be shared by several of the SHIVERS-provoking passages. For example, an enharmonic change fulfills one

Figure 11.1 Opening theme from Albinoni's *Adagio for strings*.

Figure 11.2 An example similar to an excerpt that provoked shivers.

expectancy (melody note stays the same) while violating another (harmonic function of melody note changes). In other cases, the response seems to be associated with a significant change in some characteristic of the music at or near a major structural boundary (e.g. new phrase or verse in a 32-bar song). If there is some psychological dissociation or independence between the various mental analyses that may be carried out on music, then it could well be that some emotional responses come about when there is a mismatch between the output of two processing units or 'modules.' The boundary may be expected according to the computations of one 'module' (e.g. a rhythmic/metrical analyzer assigning events a hierarchical position within a phrase-structure tree), but the specific parameter change can still 'surprise' another 'module' (attuned to, say, texture or dynamic).

Figure 11.3 shows a passage provoking heart reactions. This is bar 191 from the last movement of Beethoven's *Piano Concerto No. 4* in G major, op. 58. Here the phrase structure of the whole movement is built on multiples of even numbers of bars (2, 4, 8, etc.). The piano solo starting at bar 184 reinforces this. A new phrase starts at 188, and there is an implication that the next phrase will commence at bar 192. Instead it arrives at 191 with a sudden increase in dynamic. Each phrase beginning functions as an accent within the phrase structure. Here, then, is a case of an expected accent arriving earlier than it 'should.' This is also the principal feature of syncopation, another provoker of heart reactions.

In each case, it is clear that expectancies and violations of expectancy are playing a major part in the promotion of emotional reactions to the music. These results are an empirical vindication for the music-theoretic tradition whose main inspiration is L. B. Meyer. However, what the data demonstrate is that the nature of the emotional experience depends on the particular character and pattern of an interlocking set of implications and their realization or nonrealization. A major task for the future is therefore the specification of the precise way in which emotions map onto different kinds of musical events. A theory providing at least the differentiation of Ortony *et al.*'s will be necessary.

Figure 11.3 Main features surrounding bar 191, last movement, in Beethoven's *Piano Concerto No. 4* in G major, op. 58. From *Eulenberg score no. 705*. Copyright by Ernest Eulenberg, Ltd. Adapted by permission.

11.3 Conclusions

The empirical study of emotional responses to music is in its infancy, despite several recent attempts to construct a theoretical framework for considering emotions in music (e.g. Dowling and Harwood, 1986; Sloboda, 1989b). The subject poses serious methodological and theoretical problems. Since there is no generally accepted theory of the emotions and how they interact with cognition, I believe that open-ended empirical investigations with a strong element of natural history continue to be the most profitable way of exploring this area at this time. Music psychology is already a successful interdisciplinary study, with major advances at the junctions of music theory and cognitive science. A satisfactory incorporation of the study of emotion into this work will require methods and theoretical approaches drawn from a wider range of subdisciplines. I hope this chapter has given at least a hint that this is a promising area ripe for further development.

References

Dowling, W. J. (1982) Melodic information processing and its development. In D. Deutsch (Ed.), *The psychology of music.* New York: Academic Press.

Dowling, W. J. and Harwood, D. L. (1986) *Music cognition.* New York: Academic Press.

Gabrielsson, A. (1989) Intense emotional experiences of music. In *Proceedings of the First International Conference on Music Perception and Cognition* (pp. 371–376). Kyoto, Japan: The Japanese Society of Music Perception and Cognition.

Gardner, H. (1973) Children's sensitivity to musical styles. *Merrill-Palmer Quarterly of Behavioural Development*, **19**, 67–77.

Hevner, K. (1936) Experimental studies of the elements of expression in music. *American Journal of Psychology*, **48**, 246–268.

Imberty, M. (1969) *L'acquisition des structures tonales chez l'enfant* [The acquisition of tonal structures in the child]. Paris: Klinksiek.

Meyer, L. B. (1956) *Emotion and meaning in music.* Chicago: University of Chicago Press.

Meyer, L. B. (1973) *Explaining music.* Berkeley: University of California Press.

Narmour, E. (1977) *Beyond Schenkerism: The need for alternatives in music analysis.* Chicago: University of Chicago Press.

Ortony, A., Clore, G. L., and Collins, A. (1988) *The cognitive structure of the emotions.* New York: Cambridge University Press.

Scherer, K. R. and Oshinsky, J. S. (1977) Cue utilization in emotional attribution from auditory stimuli. *Motivation and Emotion,* **1**, 331–346.

Schmuckler, M. A. (1989) Expectation in music: Investigation of melodic and harmonic processes. *Music Perception,* **7**, 109–149.

Sloboda, J. A. (1989a) Music as a language. In F. Wilson and F. Roehrnann (Eds.), *Music and child development.* St. Louis, MO: MMB, Inc.

Sloboda, J. A. (1989b) Music psychology and the composer. In S. Nielzen and O. Olsson (Eds.) *Structure and perception of electroacoustic sound and music.* Amsterdam: Elsevier.

Sloboda, J. A. (1991) Music structure and emotional response: Some empirical findings. *Psychology of Music,* **19**, 110–120.

Thackray, R. (1976) Measurement of perception of tonality. *Psychology of Music,* **4**, 32–127.

Wedin, L. (1972) A multidimensional study of perceptual–emotional qualities in music. *Scandinavian Journal of Psychology,* **13**, 1–17.

Zenatti, A. J. (1969) *Le développement génétique de la perception musicale* [The genetic development of musical perception] (Monographie Françaises de psychologie No. 17). Paris: Centre Nationale des Recherches Scientifiques.

CHAPTER 12

EMOTIONAL RESPONSE TO MUSIC: A REVIEW

12.1 Introduction

The reason that many people engage with music, as performers or listeners, is that it has power to evoke or enhance valued emotional states. Studies supporting this general assertion are reviewed in Section 12.2. In the light of this one might have expected the study of emotion to be central to the psychology of music. This has not been the case. There are conceptual and methodological reasons for this. Conceptual issues are discussed in Section 12.3, of which the primary issue is the inherent variability of emotional response, from listener to listener, and within the same listener on different occasions. Section 12.4 addresses some of the methodological issues, arising primarily from difficulties of measurement.

Notwithstanding the difficulties inherent in research on this topic, some progress has been made, and Section 12.5 outlines some major findings, including some evidence that a major subset of emotional responses are cued by confirmations and violations of expectancy within the musical structure, in line with the predictions arising from the theoretical proposals first articulated by L. B. Meyer (1956).

12.2 The importance of emotions to music participants

12.2.1 Music listeners

Music has the power to evoke strong and significant emotions in a wide cross-section of the general population (Gabrielsson and Lindstrom, 1993). For instance, in a survey of the crying behaviour 331 North American adults (Frey, 1985) it was discovered that 63 (8%) of the 800 crying episodes reported were triggered by music.

When 67 regular listeners of music were asked to describe the nature of their most valued responses to music (Sloboda, 1992), two common themes emerged. The first theme was of music as change agent, in which it helped the individual to move from a less desirable to a more desirable psychological state. This was evident in statements such as 'music relaxes me when

I am tense and anxious', 'music motivates and inspires me to be a better person (e.g. more agreeable and loving)'. The second theme was of music as promoting the intensification or release of existing emotions. This was indicated by statements such as 'Music helps me discover what I am actually feeling', and 'Music reconnects me to myself when my emotions are ignored or suppressed through sheer busyness'.

12.2.2 Music performers

In an ongoing project on communication of emotion in piano performance, ten professional pianists were asked to what extent their own emotional reactions to the music they performed were important in helping them determine their own interpretation. All of them judged their own responses to be important. One pianist said 'I choose repertoire that I can put my whole emotional energy into. I couldn't play without it'. Another judged the effectiveness of a performance by taping it and listening to it 'as audience' to see if it had the intended emotional effect.

Strong emotional responses to music appear to underlie the decisions of many individuals to commit to careers in music. A study of childhood musical experiences (Sloboda, 1989a) showed that individuals reporting intense positive experiences to music were more likely to continue to engage with music over the lifespan. In a therapeutic study (Brodsky, 1995) it was discovered that professional musicians may even use their emotional involvement with music as some compensation for perceived deficiencies in human relationships. For instance, one violinist said 'when I am playing the violin I have a deeper relationship and experience than any human could offer'.

12.2.3 Psychological functionality of music

The above findings suggest that music serves a major psychological function in many people's lives, closely connected to the explicit purposes of many forms of psychotherapy. Musical engagement can thus become a form of self-administered therapy (Sloboda, 1989b). Conceptions of music as 'entertainment' or 'diversion' grossly underestimate the seriousness of many people's engagement with music.

12.3 Conceptual issues

12.3.1 Definitional problems

The psychological literature on emotion contains a number of unresolved problems. For instance, which psychological states are to be counted as emotions? One proposal would include only positively or negatively valenced states ('anger', 'joy', etc.) and exclude unvalenced or neutral states (such as 'alertness' or 'surprise'). Another would make a distinction between emotions (acute reactions to time-limited events) and moods (chronic prevailing affective states engendered by the internal functioning of the organism). Yet again, researchers disagree about whether there are some emotions which are more basic than others (Frijda, 1986; Ortony and Turner, 1990). Research with music cannot resolve these problems. Indeed it may seem that music renders all these distinctions harder to make. Emotions to non-musical events can often be clarified by their behavioural consequences—e.g. if a person runs away then he or she is likely to be feeling fear. The behavioural consequences of emotional response to music are likely to be less tangible and less immediate. Emotions, moods, and other affective states may thus be less distinct from one another than in non-musical settings. In particular, it remains an open question as to whether emotional responses ascribed to specific time-limited musical events are independent of and clearly delineated from 'moods' evoked by whole pieces.

12.3.2 Between-person variation

A particularly acute problem presented by the study of emotion is its variability between individuals, and across time within individuals. There are some indications that cultural differences account for much of the between-person variance. Developmental studies (e.g. Gardner, 1973) confirm that knowledge of the conventions and structures of a musical culture are acquired over time, and influence the kind of emotional responses that are possible. Concepts of music as some form of universal 'language of the emotions' are probably without foundation (although one study—Pinchot Kastner and Crowder (1990)—has shown that US children as young as 3 years old can reliably map the major–minor distinction onto the happy–sad dimension).

A further source of between-person variability comes from the biographical associations from particular pieces of music. Musical stimuli, like olfactory ones, appear to have a particular power to evoke memories of earlier situations in which the same music was experienced, particularly if these situations had emotional significance. Although such effects have not received systematic study, their ubiquity and power is without question. In these circumstances, emotional response is dominated by the idiosyncratic emotional tone of the previous context, and, unless such contexts are widely shared in a culture (e.g. organ music connotes weddings and funerals) the responses they engender will be idiosyncratic. ~specific to individual or situation

12.3.3 Within-person variation

There is a considerable literature on liking and preference which suggests that familiarity with a piece of music affects these variables according to an inverted-U function (e.g. Hargreaves, 1984). When a complex piece is totally unfamiliar response will be low. As it becomes known, liking increases. When overfamiliar it becomes boring and liking decreases again.

On the other hand, many musicians report being emotionally moved by music which is very familiar to them. This could be a function of the very high complexity of the particular pieces for which this is true. It might take an inconceivably large number of exposures to move from the left to the right of the U-curve. Another intriguing suggestion (Jackendoff, 1992) is that some aspects of music processing are modular in the sense developed by Fodor (1983), and, as a consequence, denied full access to conscious memory. 'However well one knows a piece, then, expectation, suspense, satisfaction, and surprise can still occur within the processor. In essence, the processor is always hearing the piece for the first time—and that is why affect remains intact.'

What many discussions of emotional response to music seem to overlook is the dependency of this response on factors which have little to do with the music itself, and much to do with participants' own decisions and attitudes. Listeners can engage greater or lesser degrees of attention and concentration on a piece of music. They can choose different aspects of the music as a focus for their emotional attention. For instance, I can focus on a music event as structure, and experience an emotion commensurate with the interplay of tension and release, form and dynamic within the music. I can focus on the same event as the action of an agent or group of agents, and feel emotions such as admiration, in respect of the skill of the performer, for instance. Again, I can focus on the event as sound, and feel emotions relevant to the purity or sonority of a particular timbre. I can focus on the music as cultural symbol, and feel emotions relevant to group membership, such as patriotism. Because music is multidimensional and multifunctional, there is no one way to listen to a piece of music, and no one emotion appropriate to it. A recent study probing the variety of emotional responses to a single piece of music identified 13 discrete categories of antecedents of such responses, each of which could trigger the whole range of available emotions, but in response to different attributes of the situation (Waterman, 1996).

12.4 Methodological issues

12.4.1 Measurement context

Emotions by their nature are immediate and evanescent: they do not survive long after the triggering event. Measurement in relation to music would therefore seem to demand taking measurements during music listening or performing itself. Some studies have done this (Madsen *et al.* 1993; Waterman, 1996) but, where measurement requires the conscious deliberation of participants in the choice of a response, such experiments are open to the criticism that the focus of emotional response will be on the task rather than the music, so that the task destroys the very thing it is trying to measure. This may possibly be overcome by very simple or well-practised response modes.

Other studies have attempted to preserve the integrity of the musical experience by collecting retrospective data. Such data can be immediate, as when participants are asked to report on their experiences directly a musical passage has finished (Hevner, 1936; Gregory and Varney, 1996), or they can be delayed, as when people are asked to report on typical responses to pieces they hear quite often (Sloboda, 1991). This kind of study is open to the criticism that memory loss and other kinds of bias can be introduced. To address such criticisms requires careful choice of the type of data collected.

12.4.2 Measurement content

One possible form of data is verbal commentary describing the actual emotion felt or perceived. To avoid the problems and ambiguities associated with free verbal description, the majority of researchers have asked participants to choose their responses from predetermined word-lists or bipolar dimensions (e.g. Hevner, 1936; Gregory and Varney, 1996). One problem with such a method is that it is ambiguous as to whether the respondent has actually felt the emotion concerned, or simply recognized the music as possessing that character.

Three other alternatives have been investigated. One is the use of a non-verbal response device, such as a pad to squeeze (Clynes, 1977; de Vries, 1991; Waterman, 1996), or a pointer to move (Madsen *et al.* 1993). In this way, intensity of some experienced dimension is indicated by the participant. It is still not entirely clear whether this response is representing feeling or judgement. A second alternative is the use of direct physiological measures (Collins, 1988). Unfortunately, very little of such work has been published, and it seems quite difficult to establish clear correlations between the nature and intensity of physiological response and the nature and intensity of an emotional experience. A third alternative is the use of self-report on physiological manifestations of strong emotion, such as crying or 'shivers down the spine' (Goldstein, 1980; Sloboda, 1991). These universal, stereotypical, and highly memorable occurrences seem the closest we can get to tapping the emotional experience itself.

12.5 How are musical events and emotions linked?

12.5.1 Gross characteristics

A significant number of studies have collected listener responses across a wide variety of contrasting musical stimuli, predominantly Western and classical (Rigg, 1964; Wedin, 1972; Gabrielsson and Juslin, 1996). The response have usually been verbal judgements of character using predetermined lists or bipolar scales. These studies yield some unsurprising correlations between certain gross characteristics and certain emotions (see Table 12.1). Performers have been shown to make use of similar characteristics under their control to change the emotional character of their performance (Gabrielsson and Juslin, 1996).

12.5.2 Internal structural characteristics

Within a prevailing mood or emotional character, determined by quite general characteristics of a musical passage, individual events seem to carry or heighten the specific emotional character or intensity of a piece of music. The music theorist Deryck Cooke (1959) argued that certain tonal intervals, and melodic sequences constructed from these intervals, carried very specific emotional content. He based his proposal on analysis of a very large body of Western vocal music, showing that particular tonal sequences repeatedly accompany words depicting particular types of emotion. Unfortunately, only one small-scale psychological study (Gabriel, 1978) has ever attempted to verify the theory with experimental data. Although the study failed to find the predicted effects, this could have been because of methodological weaknesses in the study (Sloboda, 1985).

A different theoretical approach to the issue of emotion was introduced by the music theorist Leonard B. Meyer (1956). This was based on the psychological insight that emotions in general are normally experienced due to violations of expectancy (surprises) of some kind. In music, such expectations are built up through the patterning of melodic, rhythmic, harmonic and other structural elements. Sometimes violations of expectancy are quite crude (e.g. sudden changes of key or dynamic). On other occasions they are

Table 12.1 Examples of emotion–music links (after Gabrielsson and Juslin, 1996)

Emotion	Musical characteristics
Serious, solemn	Slow, low-pitched, regular rhythms, low dissonance
Sad	Slow, low-pitched, minor mode, high dissonance
Happy	Fast, high-pitched, major mode, low dissonance
Exciting	Fast, loud, high dissonance

Table 12.2 Examples of thrill-structure links (after Sloboda, 1991)

Thrill type	Structural characteristics
Tears	Appogiatura or suspension melodic or harmonic sequences harmonic movement descending through circle of 5ths
Shivers	Enharmonic change or sudden key-shift sudden dynamic or textural change
Heart	Repeated syncopation prominent event occurring earlier than expected

more subtle, and not necessarily consciously noticed by the listener. Meyer was somewhat pessimistic about the possibility of empirically verifying his proposals, for many of the reasons outlined in Sections 12.3 and 12.4 above.

I have argued (Sloboda, 1991) that the retrospective elicitation of information about the nature and musical location of 'thrills' provides a good chance of generating data relevant to isolating structural determinants of emotional response. In a study where music-lovers were asked to identify known pieces of music that reliably provoked 'thrills', a significant minority were able to identify the thrill-producing segment to within a single phrase. Three main types of thrill were reported: tears (crying, lump in throat); shivers (goose flesh, skin sensations); and heart (racing heart, sinking stomach and other visceral sensations). Table 12.2 shows the main musical features associated with each of these types of thrill.

A recent study has shown that thrills may be elicited during *in vivo* experiments with large numbers of listeners in the same room, and that these responses tend to occur at the same points in the music, although no formal analysis of musical structure at these points was reported (Panksepp, 1995).

The discovered structure–thrill link is somewhat enigmatic. Although each structural device relies for its effect on creation and violation of expectancy, our understanding of these responses in the context of non-musical stimuli is not advanced enough for intelligent analogising in the realm of music. I finish by raising a couple of questions which must be answered if we are to know that we are making real scientific progress in this area:

1. What characteristics of the musical situation make it possible for participants to experience most emotions (including crying) as positive and desirable?
2. What characteristics of musical performances (acoustic, expressive, timbral, social) make different renditions of the same musical work so different in emotional power?

3. What mechanisms allow someone to be emotionally moved by imagining themselves to be hearing a performance of a known piece of music, in the absence of any actual acoustic stimulation?

References

Brodsky, W. (1995) Career Stress and Performance Anxiety in Professional Orchestra Musicians: a Study of Individual Differences and their Impact on Therapeutic Outcomes. PhD Thesis, University of Keele, Staffordshire, UK.

Clynes, M. (1977) *Sentics: the Touch of Emotions*. New York, Doubleday.

Collins, S. C. (1988) Subjective and autonomic responses to western classical music. Unpublished PhD Thesis, University of Manchester, UK.

Cooke, D. (1959) *The Language of Music*. Oxford, Oxford University Press.

de Vries, B. (1991) Assessment of the affective response to music with Clyne's Sentograph. *Psychology of Music*, **19**(1), 46–64.

Fodor, J. A. (1983) *Modularity and the Mind*. Cambridge, MA, MIT Press.

Frey, W. H. (1985) *Crying: The Mystery of Tears*. Minneapolis, Minnesota, Winston Press.

Frijda, N. (1986) *The Emotions*. Cambridge, UK, Cambridge University Press.

Gabriel, C. (1978) An experimental study of Deryck Cooke's theory of music and meaning. *Psychology of Music*, **6**, 13–20.

Gabrielsson, A. and Lindstrom, S. (1993) On strong experiences of music. *Musikpsychologie, Jarbuch der Deutschen Gesellschaft fur Musikpsychologie*, **10**, 114–125.

Gabrielsson, A. and Juslin, P. (1996) Emotional expression in music performance. *Psychology of Music*, **24**(1), 68–91.

Gardner, H. (1973) Children's sensitivity to musical styles. *Merrill-Palmer Quarterly of Behavioral Development*, **19**, 67–77.

Goldstein, A. (1980) Thrills in response to music and other stimuli. *Physiological Psychology*, **8**, 126–129.

Gregory, A. H. and Varney, N. (1996) Cross-cultural comparisons in the affective response to music. *Psychology of Music*, **24**(1), 47–52.

Hargreaves, D. J. (1984) The effects of repetition on liking for music. *Journal of Research in Music Education*, **32**, 35–47.

Hevner, K. (1936) Experimental studies of the elements of expression in music. *American Journal of Psychology*, **48**, 248–268.

Jackendoff, R. (1992) Musical processing and musical affect. In: M. R. Jones and S. Holleran (Eds.) *Cognitive Bases of Musical Communication*. Washington DC, American Psychological Association, pp. 51–68.

Madsen, C. K., Byrnes, S. R., Capperella-Sheldon, D. A., and Brittin, R. V. (1993) Aesthetic responses to music: musicians versus non-musicians. *Journal of Music Therapy*, **30**, 174–191.

Meyer, L. B. (1956) *Emotion and Meaning in Music.* Chicago, University of Chicago Press.

Ortony, A. and Turner, T. J. (1990) What's basic about basic emotions? *Psychological Review*, **97**, 315–331.

Panksepp, J. (1995) The emotional sources of 'chills' induced by music. *Music Perception*, **13**, 171–208.

Pinchot Kastner, M. and Crowder, R. G. (1990) Perception of the major/minor distinction: IV. emotional connotations in young children. *Music Perception*, **8**(2), 189–202.

Rigg, M. G. (1964) The mood effects of music: a comparison of data from earlier investigations. *Journal of Psychology*, **58**, 427–438.

Sloboda, J. A. (1985) *The Musical Mind: the Cognitive Psychology of Music.* Oxford, Oxford University Press.

Sloboda, J. A. (1989a) Music as a language. In F. Wilson and F. Roehmann (Eds.) *Music and Child Development*, St Louis, Missouri, MMB Inc., pp. 8–43.

Sloboda, J. A. (1989b) Music psychology and the composer. In: S. Nielzen and O. Olsson (Eds.) *Structure and Perception of Electroacoustic Sound and Music.* Amsterdam. Elsevier, pp. 3–12.

Sloboda, J. A. (1991) Music structure and emotional response: some empirical findings. *Psychology of Music*, **19**, 110–120.

Sloboda, J. A. (1992) Empirical studies of emotional response to music. In: M. R. Jones and S. Holleran (Eds.) *Cognitive Bases of Musical Communication.* Washington DC, American Psychological Association, pp. 3–50.

Waterman, M. (1996) Emotional responses to music: implicit and explicit effects in listeners and performers. *Psychology of Music*, **24**(1), 53–67.

Wedin, L. (1972) A multi-dimensional study of perceptual-emotional qualities in music. *Scandinavian Journal of Psychology*, **13**, 1–17.

CHAPTER 13

MUSICAL PERFORMANCE AND EMOTION: ISSUES AND DEVELOPMENTS

13.1 Emotional response to music is dynamic

There now exists substantial scientific confirmation for two commonplace observations about the experience of listening to music. The first of these observations is that the intensity of emotional response to a piece of music often rises and falls as the music unfolds. Musical discourse, both formal and informal, talks of climaxes and points of repose, tension and relaxation. In other words there are peaks, where intense emotions (or other affective sensations) are prone to be experienced, and troughs, where the intensity is weak. These peaks and troughs occur at similar moments in the music across different people within a culture, and are repeated in individual hearings separated by as much as one year (Waterman, 1996). Peaks appear to be associated with particular structural features of the music (Sloboda, 1991), and often are accompanied by physical manifestations of emotion such as weeping, pilo-erection, heart-rate changes, etc.

13.2 Performers contribute to emotional power

The second observation is that the nature of the specific performance contributes significantly to the quality of the affective experience. Again, musical discourse abounds with comparisons between different interpretations of the same composition. Music critics earn their living by describing the differences in their reactions to different performances, and attempting to convince readers that their characterizations of one performance as 'thrilling' and another as 'dull' are apt and perceptive. Two converging lines of evidence are pertinent to this phenomenon. On the one hand, listeners within a culture show agreement when asked to characterize complete professional performances along bipolar dimensions such as 'powerful–weak', 'masculine–feminine', 'expressive–inexpressive', and the values of these dimensions correlate to objective features of the performance such as the timing profile of individual notes or beats (e.g. Repp, 1990). On the other hand, when performers are asked to play the same music with different expressive character (happy, sad, angry, expressive, deadpan), their performances show objective differences in expressive microstructure, and listeners are able to assign the intended character to each performance with greater than chance accuracy (Gabrielsson and Juslin, 1996; Kendall and Carterette, 1990). These findings show that, at least in some respects, judgments about performance qualities have some inter-rater reliability, and are not entirely a matter of idiosyncratic taste or whim.

So, there is absolutely no doubt that listeners experience greater or lesser levels of emotional intensity as a result of what composers and performers do. The focus of this paper is on *how* these effects are brought about.

13.3 Intensity matters more than content

I need to make a number of clarifications or qualifying remarks. Firstly, in this paper I am not very much interested in *what* emotion is present, detected, or felt. My interest is in the mechanisms whereby the intensity of any emotion may be brought to a peak. Indeed, I do not even want to make strong claims for music's capacity to embody, express, communicate or induce specific emotions (such as happiness, anger, disappointment, etc.). Roughly speaking I take the position that there is a range of characteristics which an emotion may contain. The more of these characteristics are present in a psychological state the more 'emotion-like' it becomes, but there is no clear cut-off between emotions, feelings, states of arousal, etc. Our interactions with music certainly take us into the territory or domain where to talk of emotions being present is legitimate. In everyday contexts I think emotions can be identified and discussed with precision because they generally involve an event, often enacted by human agents, accompanied by biologically pre-programmed gestures and facial expressions, which has social and personal consequences.

Our identification of, for instance, anger, is aided by the fact that A has acted towards B in a way that has violated B's dignity, rights, or prospects; B is showing signs of emotional arousal, is enacting certain bodily movements and facial gestures, and is verbally expressing that she is aware that A's act has damaged her in some ways. If any one of the cues is missing, it is still possible to make an emotional attribution. The more cues are missing, the more tenuous the identification becomes. Music (at least the 'pure' instrumental music which has dominated high art for the last 200 years) is of its nature impoverished in cues. Music does not directly describe or depict agents with purposes who enact behaviours with social consequences. In this respect it is unlike other emotion-bearing art forms, such as drama, literature, even dance. It does, however, suggest or evoke varying degrees of energy, tension, and arousal. It can suggest or resemble certain types of human gestures and actions. Given shared experience and understandings, it is easy to see how a group of people might be able to extrapolate specific emotions from such cues. It is equally easy to see how there is room for ambiguity and imprecision. Very often we feel that there is an emotion present, we know it is of one general type rather than of another, but we cannot quite tie it down. In such a state of ambiguity and cue-impoverishment we may well expect the profound and semi-mystical experiences that music seems to engender. Our own subconscious desires, memories, and preoccupations rise to flesh out the emotional contours that the music suggests. The so-called 'power' of music may very well be in its emotional cue-impoverishment. It is a kind of emotional Rorschach blob.

13.4 Music blurs the boundary between feeling and judgment

My second qualification is that I am not very concerned with the distinction between recognition of emotion (as somehow inhering in the music) and the experience of emotion within the listener. These are, of course, rather distinct psychological states. Knowing that someone else is angry is not the same as being angry oneself. But again, I think the distinction has much more force in the everyday world of human interaction than it does in the case of music. If you are angry, and I detect your anger, then my own emotional reaction will be a function of my own role in the social drama that is being enacted. If you are angry with *me*, I may well feel scared, or defensive. If you are angry with someone else, then my own feelings may be determined by my relationship to both you and the person you are angry with, as well as my value system. I may feel anger too in the case where I see the injustice as serious, and value your welfare. I may, on the other hand, feel pity or even amusement, if I feel that the event about which you are angry is trivial. The precise logic of the interacting set of beliefs, actions, intentions, and interpretations will almost totally determine my own emotions. In music, most elements of this logic are uncoupled. If I detect some piece of music as containing elements appropriate to anger, then there is a sense in which I am pretty free to ascribe that anger where I will. I may ascribe it to the composer, or to the performer, to myself, to God. None of these ascriptions need bring me up against any of the immediate constraints or contradictions provided by a real-life event in which my own interests and relationships figure. A possible hypothesis is that people are likely to ascribe the emotion they detect within the music to *themselves* at those points where their general level of music-entrained arousal is highest, and other sources of specific emotion are not obtruding or interfering at the same moment.

13.5 Intrinsic versus extrinsic sources of emotion

Why do we need to consider other sources of emotion? Consider the case of a performance of a piece I know well which contains obvious technical shortcomings. I might well become irritated with the performance. But it is not the music as music which is causing the irritation but the actions of the performer as social agent *reflected in* the performance, not arising from the specifically musical intentions of either composer or performer. For instance, at a professional concert I may resent having my time and money wasted by someone who appears not to respect his audience enough to prepare well. Given the existence of this emotion, I may not have the capacity or inclination to ascribe any of my emotion to the musical content, even if my level of emotional arousal is rising or falling as a consequence of the specifically musical contour. I may just feel myself as more or less irritated!

There is some suggestive evidence that negative non-musical emotions (including anger, fear, humiliation, anxiety) are particularly inconsistent with experiencing music-entrained emotion in oneself (Sloboda, 1990). In general, positive emotions (such as love, being proud of, admiration, etc.) seem to make listeners more able to 'own' or 'identify with' the emotional peaks and troughs in the music. It is as if these states both enhance general emotional arousal, and at the same time lower the threshold for self-ascription of the emotions discovered in the music.

13.6 Emotional peaks ascribable to compositional devices

The contributions made by the research community to addressing this issue have to date been inductive in nature. That is so say, we have measured the contour of emotional responsiveness to pre-composed pieces, chosen either at random or by the participants, and have then tried to discover whether the peaks have anything in common.

A variety of methodologies have been tried. One methodology focuses on the time-limited physical manifestations of emotion such as the feeling of tears welling to one's eyes, pilo-erection, and other phenomena which have variously been called thrills, even skin-orgasms. These have been monitored either retrospectively ('tell me which pieces give you reliable thrills', Sloboda, 1991) or concurrently (Panksepp, 1995). Other researchers have used more internal criteria ('press the button when you feel something' (Waterman, 1996). Yet others have used some kind of continuous measure, such as finger-pressure on a pressure-sensitive pad (DeVries, 1991; Madsen *et al.*, 1993, Krumhansl, 1996).

We probably have too little data yet to make definitive conclusions, but I don't know of clear proof that these methods produce hugely differing results. What the data confirm in a general way is that the emotional system is sensitive to change. We don't feel much emotion to steady state. One possible exception to this is music of such generally high levels of sound energy that it is neurologically arousing in its own right (i.e. very loud or very fast music). There is clear evidence that pieces of music which vary in overall energy tend to have emotional peaks at points of high energy, wherever else they may have peaks.

Another possible exception is provided by musical events whose sound characteristics resemble biologically programmed emotional triggers (such as the sound of a female voice).

13.7 Are there mechanical rules for composing emotional peaks?

In 1991, I published a list of 10 music-structural characteristics that appeared repeatedly in passages which Western listeners cited as reliably provoking 'thrills'. Despite a considerable increase in the amount and quality of work on musical emotion in the intervening years, no one has proposed specific modifications or refinements to this list.

I have conjectured that what all these characteristics have in common is that they cause perturbations of one sort or another in expectations, brought about either in the light of the structure of that specific piece, and/or (more commonly) in the light of general features of the body of tonal music as a whole. For instance, an appogiatura creates a local dissonance that violates a basic expectation that melody notes will be taken from the actual or implied harmony at that point. This dissonance is then resolved in the direction of the expected note. A syncopation provides an accent (point of high energy) earlier than the established and conventional metrical structure would predict. And so on.

The problem with both my list and the conjecture which links its members is that this hugely overdetermines the location of emotional peaks. First, it is trivially easy to find instances of these devices scattered all through each of the pieces that provided the specific examples for my list. If the mere presence of such a device were enough for an emotional peak, then there would hardly be a measure of music which did not contain one. The conjecture is also too inclusive. Almost any change in any parameter could be construed as violating some expectancy or other. On this conjecture, 'Twinkle twinkle, little star' (*Ah vous dirai-je, Maman*) should elicit an emotional peak as it moves from the first two repeated notes to the second two. The expectation is that two repeated notes will be followed by a third.

There are two rather obvious moves that one could take to bring theory into a better relation with reality. First, one could postulate that the degree of unexpectedness matters: the more unexpected the more emotional. Second, one could postulate that the density of devices matters: so that the greater number of these devices present within a measure the greater likelihood of that measure being experienced as a peak. These are plausible ideas, but they would need a lot of work before they could be operationalized in empirical studies to test them. It is hard to see how one might provide appropriate data without an automated procedure for detecting the relevant devices in a large corpus of music. Writing the relevant software would be in itself a major exercise in artificial intelligence since it is hard to see how many of these devices could be captured with simple algorithms.

My intuition is that doing the above work might capture some of the variance in emotionality within a piece but by no means all. At this point I will simply make two further conjectures which seem to resonate with musicians that I respect.

13.8 Structural junctions and asynchrony of levels

Almost all descriptions of music (whether professional or informal) characterize it as made up of sections of differing lengths, differing levels of hierarchical embeddedness, and differing levels of importance within the overall plan of the piece. In sonata form, for instance, the start of the recapitulation of the first theme is a very significant and pivotal moment. We could conceive the listener as attempting to obtain some form of structural map of the piece from the cues available. These cues would by and large be boundary cues, signifying the end (or the impending end) of one section and the start of the next. Compositional devices which perturbed expectations at such boundary or junction points should be far more emotionally arousing than similar devices at other points, simply because they are much more crucial to helping or hindering the process of establishing the structural map.

Secondly, emotionally and aesthetically satisfying works of music have a sense of unity and rightness about them. Not any violation of expectancy will cause musically relevant emotion. One could simply stop a piece before the final cadence. That would be surprising, but not musical. Because music is multidimensional and multi-levelled, a device which breaks expectancies on one dimension or one level can confirm expectancies on another. Our aesthetic reaction to such a device is 'how unexpected, but how beautiful, and how right'. A simple example of what I mean is given by the opening melodic phrase of the Albinoni *Adagio for strings* (D C B<flat> A G G F#). On one level of description there is a series of appogiaturas creating and then resolving a dissonance through each successive note. On another level of description the whole sequence conforms to a smooth descending scalar motion, each next note expected in the light of what went before as a single scale step lower than its predecessor. This is a very simple example, but much of the art of professional music analysis is to uncover more complex multiple relationships within works of interest. And this is a task which must be left to analysts. Psychologists have no credible alternative route at this stage of development of the field.

13.9 The problem of experimental control

There is a fundamental scientific problem that besets this research area. Any real piece of music has multiple characteristics at any point. Where we gain our data of emotional response from such pieces, we can never be sure that we are able to fully separate the potentially contributory dimensions of the sound, even if we were able to list them all. Suitable controls may not exist within the body of composed music (for instance where two dimensions of sound are significantly correlated with one another). Yet we cannot hope to easily elicit valid judgments of emotionality from listeners with experimenter-designed atomistic fragments designed to fit some factorial experimental design. Early naive attempts to do this (e.g. Gabriel, 1978) were a complete failure for reasons which are now pretty obvious. Emotions in music are sustained by the rich set of cultural, historical, structural, and situational cues which a properly embedded musical event can elicit. These cues provide a set of enabling conditions for the ups and downs of moment-by-moment emotion. Take these broader cues away and the whole emotional enterprise collapses.

13.10 The performer's contribution: faithfulness to the composers' intentions?

What it is that a performer or interpreter of a notated composition adds to the notation in order to create a compelling experience for a listener?

One suggestion concerning the function of interpretative variation is that it is intended to reinforce and make more apparent to a listener a structural feature which the performer has reason to believe is intrinsically important. Very often, at least in the classical 'notated' canon, the score (or rather, an culturally accepted way of reading the score) determines some of the important structural features, through metrical and phrase marks, notated accents and dynamic marks. So, for instance, pianists have been shown to perform melodies admitting of two valid metrical interpretations in such a way as to communicate the actual notated metre to listeners. This explanation of performance is consistent with the performance tradition which talks of a performance's purpose as to be 'faithful to the composer's intentions'. In this tradition the key interpretative process is the detailed study of the score, accompanied (if the composer is no longer alive) by consultation of historical commentaries, and other markers of 'authenticity'. This perspective allows a position from which judgments of value may be made. One performance is more compelling than another because it emphasizes, rather than obscures, a key structural phenomenon that prior score analysis reveals.

13.11 Faithfulness to convention

There are, however, two distinct types of structural phenomenon within most music, which may engage a listener. The first might be called the *conventional*. This includes that set of phenomena which characterize the music of a whole period or genre. For instance, it is normal for Western melodies to be constructed out of bars or measures of equal duration, linked together into superordinate units, phrases, which normally contain $2n$ measures, where n is an integer not greater than 4. Compositional practices, such as rhythmic repetition, longer than average note durations, etc. are deployed to mark significant structural units and the boundaries between them. There also exist a whole set of conventional performance practices which emphasize phrase structure (e.g. slowing at phrase ends and speeding in phrase middles). Listeners within a culture are so accustomed to these conventions that they find it hard to explicitly notice small performance perturbations in line with the conventions, as Repp (1998) has shown.

13.12 Faithfulness to the dialectical structure

The second kind of structural phenomenon might be called *dialectical*, in that listeners' conventional expectations are challenged or thwarted in some way. These expectations have sometimes been called *schematic* because they derive from schemas that have been built up through extensive exposure to a wide range of music, rather than the *veridical* representation of any single musical object. A basic schema derives from the diatonic scale, and the harmonic relations between its members. Schematic perception 'expects' two consecutive members of a scale to be followed by the next consecutive member in ascending or descending order. A skip or change of melodic direction is thus something that challenges structural expectations at a very basic level. Such dialectical features of compositions are exactly those that we have already found evidence stimulate more intense emotional experiences.

This distinction between conventional and dialectical structure means that performers can 'emphasize' structure in two quite different ways. By emphasizing the conventional structure, the performer can 'feed' schematic expectations. By emphasizing the dialectical structure, the performer can heighten the experience of the unexpected. A simple example of this might be to slightly delay the onset of an enharmonic change. The surprise of the unexpected harmony is heightened by its occurring at a slightly unexpected time. Being 'faithful to the score' does not, therefore, mean giving the listener no surprises. The surprises are, however, precisely those which the performer believes the composer intended the listener to experience.

13.13 Performance as expression of individuality

Alongside, and in some ways in contradistinction to the notion of performer as faithful carrier of the composer's message, is the notion of performer as creator in his or her own right. This tradition of performance lays on the performer the duty to come up with something new, an interpretation which allows us to see the composition in a different light, to make manifest aspects of the music which are normally latent. The commercial realities of performance often press performers in this direction. Why should someone pay money to listen to a performance which is not distinctively different from the one they heard the other day (whether in live performance, or on a recording)? Repp (1997) has provided conclusive documentation of the reality of this pressure towards individuality. In a series of analyses of solo piano performances, some from commercially available professional recordings and some from competent amateurs, he was able to show that amateurs conform more closely to an average interpretation than do professionals. Some professionals are, however, very close to the average, so we can rule out the notion that the average performance is in some sense the result of lack of skill or appropriate musicality. We could see such professionals as operating on 'faithfulness to the score' as their interpretative philosophy. On the other hand, the most extreme performances, as measured on a variety of dimensions, including speed, exaggeration, etc. are almost always those of 'world class' professionals. Typically, many of these performers do things which are not obviously prescribed by the score. Yet, in order to be received as a legitimate performance of the work in question, their interpretative decision must in some way be able to be seen as 'fitting' the music. Not every exaggeration will be acceptable.

13.14 Virtuosity as a boundary case

A rather interesting example of exaggeration which might be emotionally compelling in and of itself, is one where the virtuosity of the performance is, in itself, a source of emotion. I can recall numerous occasions of high emotion brought about by the way that a performer, or group of performers, executes a particularly difficult passage with exceptional accuracy or panache. For instance, we could consider a performance of Chopin's Prelude Op 26 no 16 in B flat minor that was given by Krystian Zimmerman at the finals of the 9th International Chopin Competition in 1975 (from *Frederyk Chopin: International Chopin Piano Competitions Vol. 4.* Polskie Nagrania, 1991, CK 1015). At the time he was 19 years of age. This, and other performances, won him the prize.

The virtuosity in this performance is the predominant aspect of it—it is the thing that anyone who knows anything about piano playing cannot ignore! As I listen to this I can detect a variety of conflicting strands to my emotion. One of these is a kind of stylistic distaste—a sense that Chopin ought not in general to be played this way! Another, much stronger emotion is a complicated and multi-levelled identification with the Polish character (I am half-Polish myself). At a basic level there is just shared pride in the identity, particularly its musical history and passions (this is, after all, a Polish performer, winning a Polish competition with the work of Poland's greatest composer). One level further in there is a sense that this performance reflects something of the Polish character itself—strong, impetuous, passionate, even intemperate. Within its historical context the performance could be further interpreted as an expression of the outraged defiance of an oppressed people at the height of the dead hand of Moscow's cold-war rule of that country, a defiance which was shortly to take shape in the Solidarity movement. Everything I have said so far informs and infects my emotional state for the whole 54 seconds of the performance, from its shattering first few chords to the abrupt final cadence. Then there are further feelings which come and go at particular points in the music. For me, the sections in parallel octaves have incredible emotional power. This is because I know, as a pianist, that the coordination required to bring these off effectively is of an order of magnitude greater than that required to accompany a right-hand line with left-hand chords. This is especially so in the lower registers of the piano where the acoustic interference between notes is so much greater, and therefore requires added precision. When you think he cannot possibly play any faster, there is an accelerando towards the end. This together with a section where the performer thumps the left-hand chords to the point where they become ugly and overpowering, makes me feel that the performer is almost trying to pound the piano and the piece into total destruction. I sometimes feel pummelled and pounded myself as if I was witnessing or being part of an assault taking place. According to one's reading of the social situation, the assault can take on a symbolic significance. It could represent a perception of how the communist regime was undermining Poland's national heritage; demonstrating through the semi-destruction of Chopin what was being done to Poland as a whole. It could simply be an arrogant young pianist assaulting the prejudices of a rigid music establishment.

13.15 Art versus spectacle

The question for this presentation is whether the fact that more or less virtuosity can be detected at various points, apparently leading to more or less emotion, is in itself a case for saying that such emotions are ascribable to the music. My sketch of the Zimmerman performance is designed to suggest that there is no simple or universal answer to that question. In certain cultural and artistic contexts, virtuosity becomes a salient aesthetic variable which is at the intentional service of the artist. But it will be the specifics of the piece, the historical and cultural context of both performer and listener, and the precise variations in virtuosity, which will determine whether or not we put virtuosity on one side or other of the divide we are discussing. In this case I am inclined to ascribe the emotion brought about by virtuosic accelerando as a music-relevant emotion—being a part of the headlong rush towards the untimely and brutal demise of the piece. On the other hand, the particular thrill I receive from the bass parallel octaves is a consequence of my pianistic experience with modern grand pianos (which might be unlike the piano used by either Zimmerman or Chopin) and sits pretty much outside any musical considerations. In the former case virtuosity is at the service of structure, and contributes to artistry. In the latter case virtuosity floats free of structure, and contributes only to spectacle (which is a legitimate source of emotion but has nothing to do with music as such, even though some music may, as it happens, be spectacular).

I have indulged in this rather personal analysis primarily to show just how complex and multi-layered are the elements of emotion to any piece of music. Even something as apparently straightforward as virtuosity is actually a deeply socially embedded judgment, sensitive to one's beliefs about the context, the level of skill displayed, and its aesthetic appropriateness. Of course psychology must take isolated fragments of this picture in order to make rigorous scientific progress, but we have constantly to relate our discrete findings back to the full richness of emotional and aesthetic experience if we are to retain ecological generality.

13.16 Mapping relationships between performance characteristics and listener response

We (Sloboda *et al.* 1997) have described a preliminary attempt to characterize, for a single short piece of romantic piano music, the nature of the relationship between performer decisions and listener's judgments of emotionality.

In order to systematically explore relationships between moment-to-moment variations in a musical sequence and corresponding variations in listener response, a means is required of assessing listener response concurrently with the musical stimulation. Our understanding of the relationship between physiological measures and emotional impact is not yet very detailed. However, several investigators have successfully used a method whereby listeners operate a continuously variable manual control during music listening in order to indicate the degree of some quality of the music as it unfolds over time (e.g. Krumhansl, 1996). The functions so obtained appear to be reliable, both within and between individuals.

The main purpose of our study was to provide continuous ratings of emotionality for a range of performances of the same piece of music, in order to determine (1) that there is enough agreement between different listeners for reliable differences between the emotionality functions of different performances to be established, and (2) whether there are reliable correlates of emotionality within performances: whether arising from conventional or dialectic structures, or performer's creative departures from such structures. Results showed that listeners showed significant agreement about which performances (and which portions of them) were most emotionally powerful.

Our means of isolating emotionally interesting segments of individual performances was as follows:

- 27 listeners heard each performance, and a mean emotionality trace for that performance was generated on the basis of the average of all 27 ratings at each point (*individual trace*).
- A grand mean trace of all 20 performances was derived by averaging the mean traces for the individual performances (*average trace*).
- Three independent raters identified locations where the individual traces substantially diverged in slope from the average trace over at least an entire measure of the music (i.e. one trace went up where the other trace stayed level or went down). 24 such locations were discovered.
- We took the 10 largest divergences, and undertook analysis of the MIDI files generated by performances at these points. Rather than create an artificial average performance, we used the individual performance that yielded an emotionality trace that was closest to the average, and compared different individual performances to that.
- We examined the MIDI files for up to two measures prior to the start of the emotionality divergence, on the grounds that emotional responses are often integrative and require time to 'come on line'.
- We looked at loudness, inter-onset-interval, and left–right onset asynchronies, and compared their values in the key segments both to what that performer did immediately before, and also to what the emotionally average performer did at that point.

In 9 out of 10 cases we found clear evidence of a change or contrast in at least one of these parameters that could unambiguously be linked to the change in emotionality.

In cases where a rise in emotionality was involved, the performance changes tended to be within one measure either side of a phrase boundary, offering some support for the notion that points of structural importance are key locations for emotion-enhancing performance variations. Within these, some clear examples of dialectic devices were evident—for instance, performers using conventional performance markers for phrase boundaries ahead of the phrase boundary.

Detailed analysis of the MIDI outputs of the performances demonstrated that high-emotion performances mostly demonstrated 'dialectical' rather than 'conventional' expressive gestures, going against genre-specific expectations for locations of timing or dynamic extremes. The question of whether the particular dialectical devices were faithful to the composer's intentions is a difficult one. It may be an unanswerable one for conceptual as much as historical reasons (i.e. the composer may not have a specific performance in mind, and may recognize in a performance a legitimate aspect of his work which he had not explicitly designed to be emphasized). In this particular piece, all we can say is that several of the emotion-bearing performance devices were not related to obvious dialectical aspects of the composed structure, but creative additions to this dialectic by the performer.

13.17 Do performers intend to communicate emotion?

There is much talk of music as being a medium for emotional communication. Although we can undoubtedly feel emotion in music, can we really say that there is emotional communication going on? For communication to happen, we would seem to require that the communicator intended something, and there is some evidence that the intended message was received by the audience. For the communicator to know that communication has been successful, he or she requires some feedback, direct or indirect, from the audience.

I have nothing at this point to say on how composers' emotional intentions might be realized or studied, but it is rather easier to make some preliminary remarks about performers. After all, they are here to speak. Composers are often unavailable.

As a follow-up to Sloboda *et al.*'s (1997) study, we interviewed each pianist about their communicative intentions in the specific performances we recorded. We found that pianists agreed in broad terms about what emotion the specific piece designated. This agreement could be a complex function of (1) their own unmediated response to hearing a person perform it, who could be themselves, (2) their knowledge of the discourse surrounding this piece in the musical community (texts, opinions of teachers, etc.). Their comments, however, focused around the notion of the music 'speaking directly' to them, either through their own interaction with the score in rehearsal, or, in some cases, through influential public performances by other pianists, which showed them something important about the piece.

Although pianists agreed about the overall character of the work, they disagreed, sometimes quite extremely, concerning the emotional microstructure of the piece. Does the second phrase have a different emotional character to the first, and if so what is it? Here pianists had quite different things to say. They were quite ambiguous about the extent to which they sought or valued audience response. Many of them made quite strong statements rejecting the idea that what an audience feels is of any concern to them at all. A common tactic for performers is to use their own emotional reactions to their performance as the yardstick of effective performance. Since this creates a closed loop which excludes the audience altogether, one might question whether the concept of emotional *communication* is valid at all in many music performance contexts.

What allows us as scientists to break out of that loop is the measuring of listener emotional response against explicit performance intentions (even though performers are habitually unable or unwilling to do that). In our study, we asked each performer to give an account of the major interpretative decisions made, immediately after their performance. Even though there was no pressure on them to be systematic or exhaustive, such that the average number of expressive intentions mentioned was only 5, six of the 10 locations identified above as leading to major shifts in emotionality were explicitly referred to by the performers.

13.18 Summary

It is a commonly held folk belief that the emotional power and freshness of music performance is in its intuitive spontaneity, which cannot be captured in words or specific moments consciously planned by performers and consciously identified by listeners. The work which I have outlined suggests the trail from performance intention to listener response may be more transparent than the folk belief would hold. Musicians study musical texts, experiment with different interpretative devices, and make conscious decisions to incorporate specific devices (based on performance parameter contrasts), which can be described and accounted for at some level of verbal specificity. These devices drive listeners' responses, which, in the cases we examined, lead to divergences in rated emotionality at, or immediately after the location of the devices. None of this devalues the performer's art, because it is the precise nature and location of these contrasts, chosen with an expert knowledge of piece and genre, neither overstated nor so tiny as to be imperceptible, which determines whether the listener's emotions remain tied to and focused on the unfolding musical structure, or whether they jump out of the frame because the performance is too boring, too exaggerated, or in some other way inappropriate to the work and the context. We may know something about what makes a performance emotional. We know almost nothing about what makes it count as a contribution towards art!

References

DeVries, B. (1991) Assessment of the affective response to music with Clynes' Sentograph. *Psychology of Music*, **19.1**, 46–64.

Gabriel, C. (1978) An experimental study of Deryck Cooke's theory of music and meaning. *Psychology of Music*, **6**, 13–20.

Gabrielsson, A. and Juslin, P. (1996) Emotional expression in music performance. *Psychology of Music*, **24.1**, 68–91.

Kendall, R. A. and Carterette, E. C. (1990) The communication of musical expression. *Music Perception*, **8**, 129–164.

Krumhansl, C. L. (1996) A perceptual analysis of Mozart's Piano Sonata K. 282: segmentation, tension, and musical ideas. *Music Perception*, **13.3**, 401–432.

Madsen, C. K., Byrnes, S. R., Capperella-Sheldon, D. A., and Brittin, R. V. (1993) Aesthetic responses to music: musicians versus non-musicians. *Journal of Music Therapy*, **30**, 174–191.

Panksepp, J. (1995) The emotional sources of 'chills' induced by music. *Music Perception*, **13.2**, 171–208.

Repp, B. (1990) Patterns of expressive timing in performances of a Beethoven Minuet by nineteen famous pianists. *Journal of the Acoustical Society of America*, **88**, 622–641.

Repp, B. (1997) The aesthetic quality of a quantitatively average music performance: two preliminary experiments. *Music Perception*, **14.4**, 419–444.

Repp, B. (1998) The detectability of local deviations from a typical expressive timing patters. *Music Perception*, **15.3**, 265–290.

Sloboda, J. A. (1990) Music as a language. In F. Wilson and F. Roehmann (Eds.), *Music and child development*. St. Louis, Miss.: MMB Music Inc.

Sloboda, J. A. (1991) Music structure and emotional response: some empirical findings. *Psychology of Music*, **19**, 110–120.

Sloboda, J. A., Lehmann, A. C., and Parncutt, R. (1997) Perceiving intended emotion in concert-standard performances of Chopin's Prelude No. 4 in e-minor. In A. Gabrielsson (Ed.) *Proceedings of the 3rd ESCOM Conference*. Uppsala: Department of Psychology.

Waterman, M. (1996) Emotional responses to music: implicit and explicit effects in listeners and performers. *Psychology of Music*, **24.1**, 53–67.

TALENT AND SKILL DEVELOPMENT

CHAPTER 14

MUSICAL EXPERTISE

This chapter treats six connected issues having to do with musical expertise. Section 14.1 examines the difficulties associated with characterizing expertise in a way that offers a genuine foothold for cognitive psychology, and I suggest that expertise may not, in fact, be 'special' in any cognitively interesting sense. Section 14.2 goes on to review some experimental studies of music, which suggest that most members of a culture possess tacit musical expertise, expressed in their ability to use high-level structural information in carrying out a variety of perceptual tasks. This expertise seems to be acquired through casual exposure to the musical forms and activities of the culture. Section 14.3 provides two detailed examples of exceptional musical expertise (a musical savant and a jazz musician) that apparently developed in the absence of formal instruction, suggesting that normal and 'exceptional' expertise may be parts of a single continuum. The evidence presented in section 14.4 suggests that a major difference between musical expertise and many other forms of expertise is that musical expertise requires an apprehension of a structure–emotion mapping. Without this, the ability to perform with 'expression' cannot be acquired. Section 14.5 outlines some evidence to suggest that these structure–emotion links become firmly established during middle childhood, under certain conditions, and that these conditions are predictive of future development of musical expertise. Finally, section 14.6 reviews some research efforts that are attempts to clarify the precise nature of the structure–emotion link and are showing that definite types of structures seem to mediate distinct emotions.

14.1 What is expertise?

In beginning to think about how a psychologist who deals with music could contribute in a specific way to a volume on expertise, it became clear to me that most of the recently published work on musical competence has made little attempt to define or characterize musical expertise. What we have, instead, is a varied collection of empirical studies on single aspects of what some musicians do. The topics of such studies range from pitch memory (Ward and Burns, 1982), through synchronization in performance (Rasch, 1988), to planning a composition (Davidson and Welsh, 1988), and it is not immediately clear that such accomplishments have anything in common other than the fact that they are different aspects of handling the organized sounds our various societies label as music.

That observation led back to a logically prior question: Is there anything that all examples of expertise *in general* should or might have in common? More precisely, is there anything about the *internal* psychological structures of certain accomplishments that marks them out as examples of expertise? It is important to remember that when someone is declared an expert, that is a social act that may or may not correspond to an intrinsic characteristic of the person so designated.

One possible definition of an expert is 'someone who performs a task significantly better (by some specified criterion) than the majority of people'. According to this definition, Chase and Ericsson's (1981) digit memorizer SF is an expert. If, however, digit-span recall became a popular hobby, then he might well be overtaken by sufficient numbers of people so that he would cease to be considered an expert. Such a relativistic attribution of expertise clearly would preclude the possibility of any *cognitive* account of expertise, because the cognitive apparatus that earned SF expert status would remain precisely the same after SF was no longer labeled an expert. It does, however, seem to me that exactly such a relativistic conception underlies much common talk of expertise, and to a certain extent determines the agendas of 'expertise' research.

For cognitive psychology to have an authentic foothold, we have to find a characterization of expertise that will allow any number of people (up to and including all) to be expert in a particular area. For instance, many would, I think, agree that the vast majority of people are expert speakers of their native languages. I shall later suggest that the majority of our population possess particular types of musical expertise. A possible definition with this outcome might relate to the reliable attainment of specific goals within a specific domain. So, for instance, one is an expert diner if one can get a wide variety of foodstuffs from plate to mouth without spilling anything.

An apparent problem with this definition, however, is that there is no lower limit to the simplicity or specificity of the task to which one can apply it. For instance, this definition would allow each of us to be expert at pronouncing his or her own name or at folding his or her arms. It may seem that we need more than goal attainment to attribute expertise. For instance, one may want to say that an expert is someone who can make an appropriate response to a situation that contains a degree of unpredictability. So the expert bridge player is one who can work out the play most likely to win with a hand that the player has never seen before; the expert doctor is one who can provide an appropriate diagnosis when faced with a configuration of symptoms never before encountered. In this way we might be able to carve out precisely the set of activities in which the contributors to this book have been interested.

On further examination, however, it is not as easy to apply this distinction as it might first appear. Pronouncing one's own name can also be seen as an act requiring the handling of unpredictability. It is an act that is occasioned by cues (external or internal) that can vary. One must be able to retrieve and execute the required motor program regardless of the immediate mental context. The complexity of these apparently simple acts is soon revealed when one attempts to construct machines that can do the same tasks, as the discipline of artificial intelligence has amply documented (e.g. visual recognition [Marr, 1982]).

It is difficult for me to escape the conclusion that we should abandon the idea that expertise is something special and rare (from a cognitive or biological point of view) and move toward the view that the human organism is in its essence expert. The neonatal brain is already an expert system. 'Becoming expert' in socially defined ways is the process of connecting 'intrinsic' expertise to the outside world so that it becomes manifest in particular types of behaviors in particular types of situations. I believe that Fodor (1975), from another point of view, was articulating a similar proposal: To broadly paraphrase Fodor, 'You can't learn anything you don't already know'.

To look at expertise in this way may require reversal of some of our perspectives on familiar situations. For instance, when considering Chase and Ericsson's (1981) study of SF, it is easy to allow one's focus of attention to fall on the two hundred hours of practice that moved him from average to the world's best, implicitly equating the acquisition of the expertise with the work that went on in the practice period under observation. The perspective to which I am increasingly drawn suggests that we focus our attention instead on what SF brought to the experimental situation. SF's intimate knowledge of running times was, from this perspective, the principal manifestation of expertise that 'bootstrapped' the digit-span task, and it seems to me that the most interesting psychological considerations are how and why that knowledge came to be applied to the task in hand when it did. What determined that it would be applied after about fifteen hours of practice rather than instantaneously or not at all? A plausible answer to that question may well be 'chance' (e.g. a particular sequence of numbers that strongly reminded SF of a well-known running time).

In other words, the broad answer to the question of how SF became expert at the digit-span task is that he was able to increment his expertise by approximately 0.01 percent in a situation in which he was already expert at a number of things, including running times, that supplied the other 99.99 percent of what was needed. And each of those preceding areas of expertise was likewise resting on other forms of expertise in the same relationship in a constant, unbroken sequence back to birth and beyond. What made SF 'exceptional' in conventional terms was no more than a unique set of life experiences. In the sections that follow, I pursue some implications of this way of looking at expertise as applied to music.

14.2 Acquiring musical skill

One of the principal reasons for studying expertise is practical. Given that it would be socially desirable for certain manifestations of expertise to be more widespread than they are, we want to know what we can do to assist people to acquire them. The issue becomes acute in relation to formal education, where the general perception is that we set up environments that are supposed to encourage expertise, but that many individuals still do not achieve levels that we know to be possible (whether it be learning a foreign language, a musical instrument, or physics skill). We want to be able to tell teachers that there are principled things that they can do to increase the frequency of those 0.01 percent increments in learning.

Music is no exception to this, and music teachers are continually inquiring of psychologists how psychological insights can inform their work. It is their perception that musical expertise is taught and acquired with great difficulty. They speak of 'tone-deaf' children (usually children unable to sing in tune); they speak of the difficulty of teaching sight-reading, of teaching rhythm, of teaching good intonation on a string instrument, and so on.

My early research on the skill of sight-reading has been summarized elsewhere (Sloboda, 1984). That research was carried out under the influence of the previously published work of Chase and Simon (1973) on chess perception. Their research showed that, like playing chess, reading of music depended on an ability to pick up various sorts of patterns in the stimulus. For instance, good sight-readers were found to be much more prone than poor sight-readers to a sort of 'proofreader's error' (Sloboda, 1976a) whereby notational mistakes out of character with the genre were automatically corrected back to what the genre would have predicted. Their ability to use music structure to 'chunk' notes could account for their superior short-term memory for notation (Halpern and Bower, 1982; Sloboda, 1976b).

Encouraging as it was to find results for music that so clearly paralleled Chase's findings, I became progressively more disheartened as I talked about those results to groups of teachers. The question they all asked was of what prescriptions I would draw from my results for the teaching of sight-reading, and after some hand waving I really had to admit that there were no prescriptions that I could draw at that time. I did not know how one could teach children to 'see' structures.

Since then I have come to realize that in order to 'see' musically signifi-cant structures, one first must be able to 'hear' those structures, and I have learned from reading some excellent recent research that the process of coming to 'hear' musical structure is a process that occurs quite naturally for the majority of children as a function of normal enculturation. For instance, Zenatti (1969) showed that children at age 7 show a distinct memory advantage for sequences conforming to rules of normal tonal progression, as compared with atonal sequences. This advantage is not shared by children of age 5. Similar results were obtained from studying children's songs (Dowling, 1982, 1988; Gardner, Davidson, and McKernon, 1981). There is a definite age progression from tonal inconsistency and instability toward conformity to the norms of the tonal culture.

An experiment I conducted earlier (Sloboda, 1985a) showed that the pro-gressing of the ability to discriminate between 'legal' and 'illegal' sequences did not seem to depend on children's receiving any sort of formal music instruction. Almost no children at age 5 made meaningful discriminations, whereas almost all 11-year-olds made discriminations in accordance with those of adults (and music harmony textbooks). The children who were receiving formal music lessons did not fare better than other children.

Although many experiments with adults have shown cognitive differences between musicians and nonmusicians, some studies have shown little differ-ence. For instance, Deliège and El Ahmahdi (1990) showed that musicians and nonmusicians were remarkably similar in the segmentations they sug-gested for an atonal piece. That may have been partly attributable to the relative unfamiliarity of the genre to both groups. More strikingly, Bigand (1990) showed that nonmusicians had an ability similar to that of musicians to classify superficially different conventional tonal melodies into groups containing underlying structural similarities. Studies of memory recall for melodies (Sloboda and Parker, 1985) have shown that musicians and non-musicians have similar abilities to preserve higher-order structure at the expense of note-to-note detail.

The research literature, therefore, leads to the conclusion that human beings pick up quite high-level implicit (or tacit) knowledge about some major structural features of the music of their culture. They gradually improve their ability to do this over the first ten or more years of life and preserve this ability into adulthood. We may presume that this is achieved through informal engagement in the everyday musical activities that abound in almost all human cultures (e.g. nursery rhymes, hymns, dances, popular songs, playground games). In our own culture these forms are, of course, massively reinforced through the broadcast media.

In this way, almost every member of a culture is a musical expert, but the expertise is usually hidden and tacit. It may not exhibit itself in abilities to sing or play. It is, however, manifested in a variety of perceptual and memory tasks. Nearly all of us can identify some kinds of 'wrong notes' when we hear them, even though we cannot always say why the notes are 'wrong'.

Tacit expertise depends, in part, on being in a culture in which one is exposed to products in the specified domain without the necessity for active engagement. This allows the dissociation between receptive expertise and productive expertise. Such a dissociation would not normally occur in chess, or bridge, or physics, because the only way one normally gets exposure to the relevant structures is by *doing* the activity.

It is not the purpose of this essay to give an account of the various developments in understanding what it is that people know when they know about music structure. Suffice it to say that it seems necessary to postulate mechanisms for representing music that are multidimensional and hierarchical. This means that music can be characterized by points of greater or lesser prominence or distance from one another and that various dimensions may be in synchrony or in opposition. This gives rise to complex patterns of tension and resolution at different hierarchical levels. Some of the most influential characterizations of musical representation have been offered by Lerdahl and Jackendoff (1983), Krumhansl (1990), and Meyer (1973).

More pertinent for our current purposes is the observation that at least some of these structures seem capable of being represented in a connectionist network (Bharucha, 1987). A connectionist model of the brain shows one way in which it might be possible for knowledge of complex structures to be built up simply as a result of frequent exposure to relevant examples. Such an activity seems to be an essential requirement of any mechanism that acquires expertise from environments that are not engineered to be instructional (i.e. most environments).

14.3 Acquisition of musical expertise in noninstructional settings

Musical expertise, in the foregoing sense, is possessed by the majority of untutored members of any culture. This is not, however, what most people mean when they refer to musical expertise; they mean overt skills of performance or composition. Surely these cannot be acquired other than through formal instruction. It is certain that such skills are acquired mainly through instruction, at least in our culture, but there is some evidence that such instruction is not necessary. Several cases of overt expertise have apparently arisen without any formal tuition or intervention by other experts. An examination of these cases is particularly important if we are to isolate the general conditions for the acquisition of expertise.

14.3.1 Musical prodigies and savants

There have been several documented cases of children who showed exceptional precocity at various musical skills. Some of them, such as Mozart, went on to become exceptional adults. Others did not sustain their exceptionality into adult life (see Bamberger, 1986, for a cognitive account of adolescent 'burnout' among musical prodigies). One of the fullest accounts of a child musical prodigy was given by Revesz (1925), who made an intensive study of the young Hungarian prodigy Erwin Nyherigazy (EN). Although EN had a great deal of formal tuition and support from professional musicians from an early age, he soon surpassed his teachers in his ability to commit tonal piano music to memory on one or two exposures.

There is another group of prodigies who, by and large, do not receive formal instruction: the so-called idiots savants (see Treffert, 1988, for a recent review). The savant is a person of generally low IQ, usually male, and often autistic, who has developed a skill in one defined area to a level quite exceptional compared with the general population. Although such cases have been reported in the literature for many years, the reports have mostly been only anecdotal and impressionistic contributions to the psychiatric literature. Only in the past decade have systematic investigations of musical savants been reported in the cognitive literature (e.g. Miller, 1987).

One of these studies concerned the autistic savant NP (Sloboda, Hermelin, and O'Connor, 1985). At the time of detailed study, NP was in his early twenties, and we were able to document his ability to recall a tonal piano movement almost perfectly twelve minutes after first hearing it. Two features of the study were particularly noteworthy: (1) His ability did not extend to a simple atonal piece, and (2) the few errors in his recall of the tonal piece were largely in conformity with the rules of the genre. We concluded that NP's recall ability was predicated on his ability to code and store tonal music in terms of its structural features. In that respect, NP's ability was every bit as 'intelligent' as the memory performance of chess masters. Other studies of musical savants (Hermelin, O'Connor, and

Lee, 1987; Miller, 1987; Treffert, 1988) have confirmed the importance of structural knowledge in supporting their skills.

Because NP was still relatively young when studied, it was possible to talk to people who knew him at different points in his life and observed his ability develop. It seems that NP's early life was one of considerable cultural deprivation. As far as we know, he had few, if any, opportunities to interact with musical instruments and was not encouraged to sing or to engage with music. His precocity was first noticed at about the age of 6 years, when he spontaneously reproduced at the piano a song that a staff member at his day-care center had just played. From the point on, he was given many opportunities and encouragements to interact with music and musical instruments, although nothing approaching 'instruction' was ever possible with this profoundly nonverbal individual. Even now his 'lessons' consist of a pianist playing pieces that NP then reproduces. A tape recording of his accomplishments at the age of 8 years shows memory and performance skills that were impressive for an autistic child, though by no means as polished and outstanding as his current performances.

How did NP's skill compare with 'normal' skill at the various stages of his life? At age 6 or 7, it was not clear that his memorization abilities were abnormally good. Most untutored children of that age are capable of memorizing short songs, and many can succeed in picking them out on a piano by a process of trial and error. What distinguished NP at that age was his ability to map his internal knowledge of songs directly and without error onto the piano keyboard and to choose appropriate fingering patterns. His performances of tonal music have always been characterized by an absence of hesitation or experimentation, no doubt assisted by his possession of absolute pitch. We have no information that would help us to explain how NP acquired his knowledge without having had any known opportunity to practice before the age of 6.

For the period of his early twenties, the comparison with normals showed a somewhat different pattern. His technical accomplishments were then not unusual. Many reasonably proficient pianists can choose appropriate fingerings for musical passages immediately and automatically. What made NP quite unusual was the *length* of the musical material he could commit to accurate memory after a single hearing. This is a skill shared by few adults at any level of musical expertise, although there are adult musicians of my acquaintance who claim that they could do what NP does when they were age 12 or 13. They no longer can do it, because it has not seemed interesting or worthwhile for them to practice and maintain that particular skill.

We may ask what conditions seem to be associated with the acquisition of the expertise of NP and other savants. The first common factor seems to be a high degree of intrinsic motivation for engagement with a single activity sustained over many years. Such motivation usually has a strong obsessional component, in that given freedom, the savant will spend all available time on the activity, without ever tiring of it.

The second factor is an environment that provides frequent opportunities for the practice of the skill in question. In the case of a musical savant, this may include the provision of regular access to instruments, broadcast media, and musical events. It is possible to suppose that whatever level of cultural deprivation NP suffered during his earliest years, he at least would have been exposed to music through the broadcast media.

The third factor is, of course, the exceptional amount of time spent in cognitive engagement with the materials and activities relevant to the skill in question (practice). It is difficult to estimate the amount of time NP spent thinking about music when not playing or listening to it, but obvious external involvement probably amounted to four to five hours per day.

The fourth factor, therefore, is the availability of the time and opportunity to 'indulge' the obsession. It may be because fewer societal demands are made on people with low IQs that they are 'allowed', even encouraged, to devote their attentions in this way.

The fifth factor is the complete absence of negative external reinforcement related to attainment or lack of it. There is, therefore, little possibility of a savant's developing self-doubt, fear of failure, or any of the other blocks that inhibit and sometimes prevent normal or exceptional accomplishment.

14.3.2 Jazz musicians

It is probable that many of the world's musical cultures, particularly the informal, nonliterate 'folk' cultures, have been breeding grounds for expertise. Some anthropological work (e.g. Blacking, 1976) suggests that this is true of indigenous Third World cultures. The jazz culture of New Orleans in the early part of this century may not have been greatly different from those other cultures in many respects. Its advantage for us is that jazz rapidly spread from New Orleans to become part of mass culture and contributed an entirely new facet to the face of Western culture. Its leaders became cult heroes, and jazz itself became a subject for intensive academic scrutiny. For these reasons, we have far more detailed biographical information about jazz musicians than about the musicians from all of the world's other nonliterate cultures put together.

It appears that most of the early jazz players were self-taught. Among the self-taught players who became international names were Bix Beiderbecke, Roy Eldridge, and Louis Armstrong. Collier's (1983) study of Armstrong is particularly detailed, and it allows us to look at Armstrong's musical development in some detail as a 'prototype' of untutored expertise.

Armstrong spent most of his early years in a neighborhood known as 'Black Storeyville', an area designated for black prostitution. One of the features of that neighborhood was the continual live music, performed by dance bands and 'tonk' bands, which often would play on the street to attract custom. Having little knowledge of the world outside, Armstrong had little more than pimps and musicians as male role models. His father had abandoned his mother before he was born. His childhood was one of extreme poverty and deprivation, and from the age of 7 years he had to work, steal, and hustle to make money for his mother and himself. At the age of 8 or 9 years he formed a vocal quartet with some other boys in order to pick up pennies on street corners. The group lasted two or three years and probably practiced and performed in public two or three times per week. That provided several hundred hours of improvised part singing, which as Collier observed, 'would have constituted a substantial course in ear training—far more than most conservatory instrumentalists get today'.

At the age of 13 or 14 years, Armstrong was involved in an incident with a gun and was, as a result, sent to the Colored Waif's Home (known as the Jones Home). There the boys were taught reading, writing, and arithmetic, with gardening as a sideline. The home had a band that played once a week around the city. After six months in the home, Armstrong was allowed to join the band, first playing tambourine, then drums, then alto horn. It is clear from contemporary accounts that many of the bands playing in the streets of New Orleans were fairly informal groups with an 'anything goes' attitude. It was quite easy for a novice to join in the general noise, just playing the notes he knew, and his mistakes and split notes would pass without comment. Armstrong quickly learned how to get sounds out of the horn, and his vocal experience made it easy for him to work out appropriate parts to the songs the band played. His talent was noticed, and he was promoted to bugle player. He gradually improved to become the band's leader, but he left the home and the band after two years, at age 16. Nothing he experienced in the home would merit the term 'formal teaching'.

Armstrong found casual work driving a coal cart, which occupied his days, but during the evenings he began playing jazz in the blues bands of the tonks. He did not at that stage own a cornet, and so it was impossible for him to practice. He simply went around to the various bands asking cornetists to let him sit in for a few numbers. Blues music provided a good vehicle for gaining jazz expertise. Blues songs featured slow tempos in two or three of the easiest keys. The set melodies were of the simplest sort; in many cases there was no set melody at all, and the cornetist would string phrases together from a small repertoire of stock figures.

At age 17, Armstrong acquired his first cornet and began to practice and work regularly at one of the tonks. The work paid little, and so he kept his coal job during the day. At some point in that period Armstrong met Joe Oliver, acknowledged as the best cornetist in New Orleans. Armstrong began hanging around the places where Oliver played, running errands, carrying his case, and eventually sitting in for him. Oliver became Armstrong's sponsor and to some extent his teacher. According to Collier, however, Oliver did not influence Armstrong's style and probably did little more than show Armstrong some new tunes and possibly a few alternative fingerings.

By age 19, Armstrong was finding employment on local riverboat excursions. Then, for three summers running, he made long trips, playing every day. For the first time in his life music had become his predominant activity. The band played seven nights per week, doing fourteen numbers and encores each night. They rehearsed two afternoons per week, and the repertoire changed every two weeks. It was only after joining the riverboats that Armstrong learned how to read music and had to acquire the discipline of playing what was written rather than what he felt like playing. When he left the riverboats at age 23, he was an established professional musician.

If Armstrong's early life was a prototype for untutored acquisition of expertise, which of its features might we highlight for future corroboration? One obvious feature was the casual immersion in a rich musical environment with many opportunities to listen and observe. A second feature was the early systematic exploration of a performance medium (in his case, voice). Third, as far as we can judge, his early experiences allowed a great deal of freedom to explore and experiment without negative consequences. A fourth feature was a lack of distinction between 'practice' and 'performance'. The learning took place on the job. A fifth feature was an enduring motivation to engage in music—in Armstrong's case, a complex mix of internal and external motivations, but arguably with internal motivations dominating. A sixth feature was a graded series of opportunities and challenges available or sought out as the expertise developed.

In many ways, this list of features fits the case of a savant such as NP. The principal differences in the two examples cited here relate to motivation and challenge. NP's motivation did not have a significant external component, and partly for that reason it is not clear that his challenges either arose or were grasped with the same frequency as those of Armstrong. It is easy to imagine NP remaining on a performance plateau. Armstrong went on growing and changing throughout his life.

What these case studies show is that high levels of expertise are achievable without instruction. This does not, of course, mean that instruction is useless. By providing a structured progression of information and challenges for a learner, geared precisely to the learner's capacities at a given time, a teacher may be able to accelerate a learner's progress. Not every person has the opportunity to extract the relevant experiences from the 'natural' environment that Armstrong had. A formal instructional environment can engineer the conditions for such extraction. The danger of all such environments is that goals and standards are imposed on the learner, rather than being chosen. The consequence can be to inhibit intrinsic motivation and originality (Amabile, 1983). If external constraints are extreme, it may even be that the ability to enjoy music will be destroyed.

In this connection, one other difference between NP and Armstrong has not been brought out thus far. One of the most striking aspects of NP's musical life was its lack of affect. All pieces in his repertoire were played in a 'wooden', unexpressive manner. Although his immediate reproduction showed some of the expressive features of the model, within twenty-four hours all expressive variation was 'washed out', leaving a rigid metronomical husk. It was as if NP had no means of understanding (and thus relating to the structure of) the small variations in timing, loudness, and timbre that are the lifeblood of musical performances. From the earliest recording we have of Armstrong's music, in contrast, we find a richly expressive, flexible performance that bends tone and time in ways that have strong impact on many listeners. Armstrong is not hailed as the king of jazz for his technique, impressive as it was. There are others who match or surpass him in technique. He is revered for the life he could breathe into the simplest material.

NP was one of a rather small number of people who appear to gain complete satisfaction from relating to music as pure structure or syntax. What brings the vast majority of us to music, and keeps us with it, is something additional: its power to mediate a vast range of emotionally toned states, ranging from the subtle to the overwhelming. Because modern systematic studies of music have approached it with the tools of cognitive science and linguistics, the emotional aspect of music has been virtually overlooked, and naive readers of modern research studies might be forgiven for thinking that music is simply another kind of complex structure to be apprehended, like chess or physics.

I know that those who are expert in chess or physics say that there is beauty and emotion in those activities too, but there is a sense in which such things are not central to the skill. One can write a perfectly effective computer program for chess that will not need any information about how particular chess positions or games will affect the emotions of certain human players. I think there is a strong case for saying that a computer could never adequately simulate Louis Armstrong without some implementation of a theory of the emotions.

14.4 Expression and emotion as foundational aspects of musical expertise

Those approaching music with the prejudices and preoccupations of experimental psychology have been wary of examining the emotional aspect, for methodological and conceptual reasons. Rather than examine these reasons in detail, I should like to point to some recent investigations that seem to have 'opened doors' into this area.

The advent of the microcomputer and microtechnology has, for the first time, made possible easy and accurate transfer of detailed performance information into computers for sophisticated analysis. The past decade has seen a number of studies (Clarke, 1985; Gabrielsson, 1983; Shaffer, 1981; Sloboda, 1983; Sundberg, 1988; Todd, 1985) that have measured minute expressive variations in performance loudness and timing. These studies have shown several things: (1) A given player can consistently repeat given variations on successive performances; (2) these perturbations are not random but, rather, are intentional, and performers can alter them to a greater or lesser extent at will; (3) many of these perturbations are rule-governed and relate to the formal structure of the music in systematic ways.

My own studies (Sloboda, 1983, 1985b), for instance, have shown that timing deformations are organized around the strong metrical beats of tonal melodies in a way that makes the metrical structure clearer for listeners than it is when such deformations are not present. Although we do not yet have the evidence, this line of research suggests that all effective expression may be systematic and rule-governed in this way, helping to highlight musical structures in a way that makes their emotion-bearing content more manifest to listeners.

The other line of contemporary thinking that converges with the experimental work on expression is the music-theory work of such writers as Leonard Meyer (Meyer, 1956, 1973) and Fred Lerdahl (1988a, 1988b; Lerdahl and Jackendoff, 1983). Meyer has convincingly argued that emotion in music arises out of the complex, often subliminal web of expectations and violations of expectations that musical structures unfold over time (Narmour, 1977). Lerdahl (1988b) takes this a step farther by suggesting that only structures that have certain formal properties (such as discreteness and hierarchical organization) can be directly detected by listeners (Balzano,

1980; Shepard, 1982). Only such structures will be effective in creating the types of tensions and resolutions that can support the emotional activities and responses peculiar to music. Lerdahl has particularly enraged certain sections of the avant-garde music community by claiming that traditional tonal music satisfies his criteria, whereas such forms as serial music do not. This could be used as an explanation of why tonality has been able to resist all attempts to oust it from center stage in music and why many avant-garde genres have but limited appeal. The general thrust of all this thinking about music gets independent support from cognitive theorists (e.g. Ortony, Clore, and Collins, 1988) who characterize the cognitive substrate of all emotion in terms of the violations of various classes of expectations.

These strands of work lead toward the following set of working hypotheses about the vast central bulk of the world's music:

1. One major function of music is to suggest or mediate a range of emotional responses.

2. Common musical structures have particular perceptible properties that support the patterns of expectation underlying such emotions.

3. Expression in musical performance has the effect of making these structural features more prominent, and thus of heightening the emotional response.

14.5 The roots of musical expertise

At the beginning of this chapter, I asked whether all aspects of musical expertise have anything in common. By a rather circuitous route I now come to a proposed answer, which is that they involve apprehension and use of the structure–emotion link. At whatever level, and for whatever activity, what makes the behavior *musically*, as opposed to technically or perceptually, expert is its manifestation of this link. I take it as axiomatic that emotions do not have to be learned (although they may be refined and differentiated through experience). They are part of the 'expert system' with which we are born. So what must be learned is how to apprehend those features of musical structures that can be mapped onto and therefore evoke our existing emotions.

Hevner's (1936) pioneering work showed that adult members of a culture generally agree on the emotional characterization of a passage of music, in that they tend to select similar adjectives to describe it (e.g. majestic, gloomy, playful). Gardner (1973) has shown that this ability develops through childhood, with younger children able to use only rather crude descriptions (such as 'loud' or 'jumpy'). It is, of course, possible that particular kinds of music have come to acquire conventional meanings by routes that do not involve the listener's own emotions. Laboratory studies of people's abilities to *describe* music do not show how these abilities were acquired.

Direct observational studies of children's emotional responses to music have been rare. Moog's (1976) studies showed that preverbal infants could demonstrate quite strong expressions of delight or fear on hearing music. The available evidence suggests that tone quality is the aspect of music that elicits the strongest early reactions. Smooth, treble-register sounds seem to elicit the strongest reactions of attention and pleasure. Most children below the age of 5 years seem not to be particularly interested in unpitched rhythms and seem not to differentiate emotionally between music played in conventional harmony and that played dissonantly.

As children grow older, it is less easy to record emotional responses by direct observation. Socialization leads to significant suppression of direct emotional expression. An alternative approach that I have been pursuing (Sloboda, 1989) is to ask adults to recall musical experiences from the first ten years of life. The literature on autobiographical memory (Brown and Kulik, 1977; Rubin and Kozin, 1984) suggests that experiences connected with significant emotion may be particularly retrievable. The method also has the advantage of tapping musical experience in a range of naturalistic contexts, rather than in restricted experimental contexts. In addition to asking these adults for information about childhood events and their contexts, I also ask them if those experiences had any particular significance for them. Information about the involvement of music in their lives, including formal music tuition, is also collected.

The findings from these studies indicate that most subjects seem to be capable of producing at least one memory. Some people readily recalled as many as ten different events. No event was recalled from an age earlier than 3 years, but from 4 to 10 years the age spread was fairly even. Analysis of the words used by adults to describe the character of their experiences (both of the music itself and of their reaction to it) showed an interesting age progression. Memories from around age 5 tended to characterize music in rather neutral descriptive terms (e.g. 'fast', 'loud', 'simple'), and the responses to it in terms of general positive enjoyment (e.g. 'love', 'like', 'enjoy', 'excited', 'happy'). Looking back to age 8, subjects characterized music in terms of its affective or sensual characteristics (e.g. 'beautiful', 'liquid', 'funny'), and the responses to it were recalled in terms of wonder or surprise (e.g. 'enthralled', 'incredulous', 'astounded', 'overwhelmed', 'awe-struck'). Finally, harking back to around age 9, some memories contained strong feelings of sadness (e.g. 'melancholy', 'sad', 'apprehensive').

It is of particular significance that the ability to respond to music in terms of wonder arises at about the age when children can be shown to distinguish reliably between tonal and atonal music. This strongly suggests that the particular violations of expectations that mediate some of the more 'advanced' emotional responses to music require the ability to represent music in terms of the structural categories of tonal music. It is also significant that the progression of responsivity seems to owe nothing to explicit formal instruction. The majority of the experiences reported *preceded* the onset of formal musical training, and in several cases such an experience spurred the child to seek instruction. Learning the structure–emotion link seems to proceed in the absence of formal instruction.

Some of the memories reported clearly had the status of what some people call 'peak experiences'—unusual and deeply rewarding experiences of a complex emotional/intellectual character. The research showed that people who have had such peak experiences were more likely than others to pursue involvement with music for the rest of their life. The experiences provided a strong source of internal motivation to engage with music in a systematic way (arguably in part to increase the likelihood of replicating the experiences). Educators wishing to raise the general level of musical skill might well be advised to consider how they can help increase the frequency of such experiences in the population, because it is clear that not every child has them.

The memory research provided some interesting clues on this latter point as well. It was discovered that almost none of those peak experiences had occurred in situations of external constraint or anxiety. The most likely environment for a peak experience was at home, on one's own or with friends and family, and while listening to music. The least promising environment was at school, with teachers, while performing. The individual stories graphically revealed the kinds of anxieties and humiliations many children were made to suffer in relation to music by insensitive adults or through insensitive educational practices. These acted as strong disincentives to further engagement with music and seemed to block the possibility of making links between emotions and the intrinsic characteristics of music.

A similar lesson emerges from a recent study of leading American concert pianists by Sosniak (1989). None of those in her sample showed exceptional promise as a child, but in every case their early lessons were associated with fun and exploration, rather than with practical achievement. It seems that, at least for the crucial early stages of musical development, there is no special strategy we should recommend to educators, other than to stop worrying about particular apparent skill deficiencies and concentrate on not getting in the way of children's enjoyment and exploration of music. In such contexts, children become natural experts who spontaneously seek what they require to bring their expertise to bear on particular practical accomplishments.

14.6 Musical structure and emotion

The final question I wish to raise in this chapter concerns the precise nature of the structure–emotion link: What structures elicit what emotions, and why? Although musicologists have long debated this point (e.g. Cooke, 1959; Meyer, 1956), there have been remarkably few attempts to collect empirical data on it. A few physiological studies (e.g. Goldstein, 1980; Nakamura, 1984) have shown that reliable changes in such indices as heart rate and skin conductance can be shown as people listen to specific pieces of music. But such studies generally have not involved subjecting the music itself to detailed structural analysis. A particular characteristic of emotional responses to music is that they often change in nature and intensity over the duration of a piece and are linked to specific events (rather than being a general 'wash' of a particular mood). In this respect, they are similar in nature to emotional responses to drama or fiction. To my knowledge, no published studies provide data on the specific points in musical compositions at which intense or peak emotional experiences take place. One problem is that it is difficult to get intersubjective agreement on how to characterize these experiences. Some of my own recent research entails an attempt to circumvent this problem by asking people to report (retrospectively, at this stage) on the locations in musical compositions at which they reliably experience direct physical manifestations of emotion (e.g. tears, shivers). A significant minority of subjects have been willing and able to do this and have provided a corpus of some 165 'moments' of reliable emotional response. Full details of this study are reported in Sloboda (1991). An analysis of the subset comprising classical instrumental excerpts has revealed three clusters of structural features associated with three different types of responses. These are summarized in Table 14.1.

This pattern requires confirmation with other types of music and also by direct observation in experimental situations. If confirmed, it will show that many of the emotional responses to music require that the listener, at some level, represent high-level structure. For instance, one cannot define 'melodic appoggiatura' apart from a description of music in terms of strong and weak beats within a metrical structure and of discord and resolution within a tonal framework. This is one reason we find it difficult to respond

Table 14.1 Emotion and musical structure

Emotional response	Associated structural features
Tears or lump in throat	Melodic appoggiatura
	Melodic or harmonic sequence
	Harmonic or melodic acceleration to cadence
Shivers down spine or goose pimples	Enharmonic change
	Delay of final cadence
	New or unprepared harmony
	Sudden dynamic or textural change
	Descending circle of 5ths in harmony
Racing heart and 'pit of stomach' sensations	Harmonic or melodic acceleration
	Sudden dynamic or textural change
	Repeated syncopation
	Prominent event arriving earlier than expected

emotionally to the music of other cultures as do the members of those cultures. We have not yet assimilated the means of representing their musical structures that would allow the appropriate structure–emotion links to be activated.

We have many interesting and important questions to explore, such as why these particular structures mediate these particular emotions in the way that they do. Research, however, has begun to clarify a major strand in musical expertise that distinguishes it starkly from the other forms of expertise represented in this volume. It suggests that the central conditions for acquisition of musical expertise are as follows:

1 Existence in a musical culture of forms that have perceptible structures of certain kinds (as specified by Lerdahl and others)

2 Frequent informal exposure to examples of these forms over a lifetime

3 Existence of a normal range of human emotional responses

4 Opportunity to experience these emotions mediated through perceived musical structures, which in itself requires

5 Opportunity to experience music in contexts free of externally imposed constraints or negative reinforcements

If we can ensure these conditions, then the problems associated with bringing individuals to levels of achievement we would currently regard as exceptional may turn out to be trivial.

References

Amabile, T. M. (1983) *The social psychology of creativity.* New York: Springer-Verlag.

Balzano, G. J. (1980) The group-theoretic description of twelvefold and micro-tonal pitch systems. *Computer Music Journal,* **4**, 66–84.

Bamberger, J. (1986) Cognitive issues in the development of musically gifted children. In R. J. Stemberg and J. E. Davidson (Eds.), *Conceptions of giftedness* (pp. 388– 416). Cambridge University Press.

Bharucha, J. J. (1987) Music cognition and perceptual facilitation: A connectionist framework. *Music Perception,* **5**, 1–30.

Bigand, E. (1990) Abstraction of two forms of underlying structure in a tonal melody. *Psychology of Music,* **19**, 45–59.

Blacking, J. (1976) *How musical is man?* London: Faber.

Brown, R. and Kulik, J. (1977) Flashbulb memories. *Cognition,* **5**, 73–99.

Chase, W. G. and Ericsson, K. A. (1981) Skilled memory. In J. R. Anderson (Ed.), *Cognitive skills and their acquisition* (pp. 141–189). Hillsdale, NJ: Erlbaum.

Chase, W. G. and Simon, H. A. (1973) The mind's eye in chess. In W. G. Chase (Ed.), *Visual information processing* (pp. 215–281). New York: Academic Press.

Clarke, E. F. (1985) Structure and expression in rhythmic performance. In P. Howell, I. Cross, and R. West (Eds.), *Musical structure and cognition* (pp. 209–236). London: Academic Press.

Collier, J. L. (1983) *Louis Armstrong: An American genius.* New York: Oxford University Press.

Cooke, D. (1959) *The language of music.* London: Oxford University Press.

Davidson, L. and Welsh, P. (1988) From collections to structure: The developmental path of tonal thinking. In J. A. Sloboda (Ed.), *Generative processes in music: The psychology of performance, improvisation and composition* (pp. 260–285). London: Oxford University Press.

Deliège, I. and El Ahmahdi, A. (1990) Mechanisms of cue extraction in musical groupings: A study of perception, on *Sequenza VI* for viola solo by Luciano Berio. *Psychology of Music,* **19**, 18–44.

Dowling, W. J. (1982) Melodic information processing and its development. In D. Deutsch (Ed.), *The psychology of music* (pp. 413–430). New York: Academic Press.

Dowling, W. J. (1988) Tonal structure and children's early learning of music. In J. A. Sloboda (Ed.), *Generative processes in music: The psychology of performance, improvisation and composition* (pp. 113–128). London: Oxford University Press.

Foder, J. A. (1975) *The language of thought.* Hassocks, Sussex: Harvester Press.

Gabrielsson, A. (1988) Timing in music performance and its relation to music experience. In J. A. Sloboda (Ed.), *Generative processes in music: The psychology of performance, improvisation and composition* (pp. 27–51). London: Oxford University Press.

Gardner, H. (1973) Children's sensitivity to musical styles. *Merrill-Palmer Quarterly of Behavioral Development*, **19**, 67–77.

Gardner, H., Davidson, L., and McKernon, P. (1981) The acquisition of song: A developmental approach. In *Documentary report of the Ann Arbor Symposium*. Music Educators' National Conference, Reston, VA.

Goldstein, A. (1980) Thrills in response to music and other stimuli. *Physiological Psychology*, **8**, 126–129.

Halpern, A. R. and Bower, G. H. (1982) Musical expertise and melodic structure in memory for musical notation. *American Journal of Psychology*, **95**, 31–50.

Hermelin, B., O'Connor, N., and Lee, S. (1987) Musical inventiveness of five idiots-savants. *Psychological Medicine*, **17**, 79–90.

Hevner, K. (1936) Experimental studies of the elements of expression in music. *American Journal of Psychology*, **48**, 246–268.

Krumhansl, C. (1990) *Tonal structures and music cognition.* New York: Oxford University Press.

Lerdahl, F. (1988a). Tonal pitch space. *Music Perception*, **5**, 315–350.

Lerdahl, F. (1988b). Cognitive constraints on compositional systems. In J. A. Sloboda (Ed.), *Generative processes in music: The psychology of performance, improvisation and composition* (pp. 231–259). London: Oxford University Press.

Lerdahl, F. and Jackendoff, R. (1983) *A generative theory of tonal music.* Cambridge, MA: MIT Press.

Marr, D. A. (1982) *Vision.* San Francisco: Freeman.

Meyer, L. B. (1956) *Emotion and meaning in music.* Chicago: University of Chicago Press.

Meyer, L. B. (1973) *Explaining music.* Berkeley: University of California Press.

Miller, L. K. (1987) Sensitivity to tonal structure in a developmentally disabled musical savant. *Psychology of Music*, **15**, 76–89.

Moog, H. (1976) *The musical experience of the preschool child* (C. Clarke, Trans.). London: Schott.

Nakamura, H. (1984) Effects of musical emotionality upon GSR and respiration rate: The relationship between verbal reports and physiological responses. *Japanese Journal of Psychology*, **55**, 47–50.

Narmour, E. (1977) *Beyond Schenkerism: The need for alternatives in music analysis.* Chicago: University of Chicago Press.

Ortony, A., Clore, G. L., and Collins, A. (1988) *The cognitive structure of the emotions.* Cambridge: Cambridge University Press.

Rasch, R. A. (1988) Timing and synchronization in ensemble performance. In J. A. Sloboda (Ed.), *Generative processes in music: The psychology of performance, improvisation and composition* (pp. 70–90). London: Oxford University Press.

Revesz, G. (1925) *The psychology of a musical prodigy.* London: Kegan Paul, Trench, and Trubner.

Rubin, D. C. and Kozin, M. (1984) Vivid memories. *Cognition*, **16**, 81–95.

Shaffer, L. H. (1981) Performance of Chopin, Bach, and Bartok: Studies in motor programming. *Cognitive Psychology*, **13**, 326–376.

Shepard, R. N. (1982) Structural representations of musical pitch. In D. Deutsch (Ed.), *The psychology of music* (pp. 344–390). New York: Academic Press.

Sloboda. J. A. (1976a) The effect of item position on the likelihood of identification by inference in prose reading and music reading. *Canadian Journal of Psychology*, **30**, 228–236.

Sloboda, J. A. (1976b) Phrase units as determinants of visual processing in music reading. *British Journal of Psychology*, **68**, 117–124.

Sloboda, J. A. (1983) The communication of musical metre in piano performance. *Quarterly Journal of Experimental Psychology*, **A35**, 377–396.

Sloboda, J. A. (1984) Experimental studies of music reading: A review. *Music Perception*, **2**, 222–236.

Sloboda, J. A. (1985a) *The musical mind: The cognitive psychology of music.* London: Oxford University Press.

Sloboda, J. A. (1985b) Expressive skill in two pianists: Style and effectiveness in music performance. *Canadian Journal of Psychology*, **39**, 273–293.

Sloboda, J. A. (1989) Music as a language. In F. Wilson and F. Roehmann (Eds.), *Music and child development: Proceedings of the 1987 Biology of Music Making Conference* (pp. 28–43). St. Louis: MMB Music.

Sloboda, J. A. (1991) Music structure and emotional response: Some empirical findings. *Psychology of Music*, **19**(2).

Sloboda, J. A., Hermelin, B., and O'Connor, N. (1985) An exceptional musical memory. *Music Perception*, **3**, 155–170.

Sloboda, J. A. and Parker, D. H. H. (1985) Immediate recall of melodies. In P. Howell, I. Cross, and R. West (Eds.), *Musical structure and cognition* (pp. 143– 167). London: Academic Press.

Sosniak, L. (1989) From tyro to virtuoso: A long-term commitment to learning. In F. Wilson and E Roehmann (Eds.), *Music and child development: Proceedings of the 1987 Biology of Music Making Conference* (pp. 274–290). St. Louis: MMB Music.

Sundberg, J. (1988) Computer synthesis of musical performance. In J. A. Sloboda (Ed.), *Generative processes in music: The psychology of performance, improvisation and composition* (pp. 52–59). London: Oxford University Press.

Todd, N. (1985) A model of expressive timing in tonal music. *Music Perception*, **3**, 33–58.

Treffert, D. A. (1988) The idiot savant: A review of the syndrome. *American Journal of Psychiatry*, **145**, 563–572.

Ward, W. D. and Burns, E. M. (1982) Absolute pitch. In D. Deutsch (Ed.), *The psychology of music* (pp. 431–452). New York: Academic Press.

Zenatti, A. (1969) *Le développement génétique de la perception musicale.* Monographies Français Psychologiques No. 17.

CHAPTER 15

MUSICAL ABILITY

15.1 What is musical ability?

The use of the term 'musical ability' may already seem to presuppose too much. Such a term suggests that there is some common factor, or set of factors, underlying all accomplishments in the sphere of music. How does this square with the fact that there are singers who cannot read music, pianists who cannot sing in tune, performers who cannot compose, and music critics who can neither play an instrument nor compose? Do all such people possess some common attribute in virtue of which they can be said to be musically able? Those who have applied the concepts and methods of contemporary cognitive psychology to music would answer 'yes' to this question. They would say that musical ability is a particular sort of acquired cognitive expertise, entailing at its core the ability to *make sense* of musical sequences, through the mental operations that are performed on sounds (whether real or imagined). The term 'make sense' is somewhat analogical. Musical idioms are not languages, and do not have referential meaning in the way that languages such as English do. They do, however, have complex multi-levelled structural features which resemble syntax or grammar (Lerdahl and Jackendoff 1983).

How do we know if and when a person is 'making sense' of some music? There are a number of ways in which psychologists have operationalized this ability. First, people who are 'making sense' of music should be able to remember music which conforms to a cultural 'language' better than music which does not. There are many demonstrations that this is so, even in fairly young children (e.g. Deutsch 1980, Zenatti 1969). This exactly parallels findings in other domains such as chess. Chess players recall meaningful (i.e. game-plausible) boards better than random boards (Chase and Simon 1973). Second, people who make sense of music tend to make plausible substitutions when asked to recall music they have just heard (Sloboda and Parker 1985, Sloboda *et al.* 1985, Oura and Hatano 1988). This is similar to the well-established finding that people rarely remember verbal information word-for-word, but reconstruct in their own words something that *means* the same as what they heard. This kind of finding suggests that people generally store something more abstract than the actual words or notes.

A third criterion for making sense of music is the ability to correctly judge whether or not given sequences are acceptable according to cultural rules. There is strong evidence that most children can reject blatant violations, such as discords, by the age of seven, and more subtle ones, such as unfinished cadences, by the age of ten (Sloboda 1985). A final criterion is the ability to correctly identify the consensual mood or emotion of a musical passage. Again, we have rather strong evidence that the broad parameters of this ability are in place for most children by the age of five (Pinchot-Kastner and Crowder 1990).

Although people vary quite widely in the level of sophistication to which they have developed their ability to make sense of music, the available evidence points to the conclusion that the vast majority of the population have acquired a common receptive musical ability, clearly evident through experimental demonstration, by the end of the first decade of life, *regardless of accomplishment in any particular sphere of musical performance, and regardless of having been in receipt of any formal musical education or training.*

15.2 How is musical ability acquired?

What features of music and the human mental apparatus make this widespread ability possible? There is broad agreement between music theorists and psychologists (e.g. Bregman 1990, Deutsch 1992, Huron 1991, Lerdahl 1988, Meyer 1956, Narmour 1990) that the most prevalent musical idioms have structural and mathematical properties that make them easily analysable by universal pre-cultural mechanisms of auditory perceptual grouping. Connectionist models of learning applied to music (e.g. Bharucha 1987, Gjerdingen 1990) demonstrate one way in which complex mental representations might be built up from such simple groupings on the basis of repeated exposure to a variety of musical examples sharing similar structures. There is also the beginnings of an understanding of how the confirmation and violation of expectations built up within such a system may lead to the experience of music-induced emotion and mood (Jackendoff 1991, Narmour 1991, Sloboda 1991). We may, therefore, make the strong conjecture that exposure through enculturation to certain types of music can be a sufficient condition for the development of musical ability. What remains to be explained is why individuals develop at different rates and to different levels.

Cognitive psychologists who study expertise in general have come to a simple but far-reaching general solution to the problem of individual differences, which may be summed up in the old proverb 'practice makes perfect'. More precisely, level of expertise seems to be a monotonic function of the duration of relevant cognitive activity. Most computer-based models of expert systems, including connectionist models, function according to this principle, because the relevant learning takes place through the processing of a large number of examples. The more examples processed, the more elaborate are the knowledge structures. If exposure to music is at least *one* of the preconditions for relevant cognitive activity, it is clear that different developmental trajectories may start very early indeed. For example, pregnant mothers who sing may provide their fetus with a particularly rich early database. Lest it be thought that the neonatal brain does not have the capacity to analyse and store music, I should point to recent evidence that infants exposed to particular pieces of music before birth show distinct preferences for those same pieces after birth (Hepper 1991).

Perhaps, however, the most common way by which young people come to increase their degree of cognitive involvement with music is by starting to perform it, through singing, or by learning a musical instrument. Such involvement forces cognitive engagement in a way that mere exposure may not. For most observers, it is the ability of people to perform well which constitutes the evidence on which we judge their musical ability.

We need, however, to be quite clear that there are several distinct abilities involved in performing a musical instrument, and only some of them are 'musical' in the sense I have been discussing. The other abilities are what I would call 'technical'. For example, a pianist may be able to play a difficult passage very quickly, very evenly, and very accurately. This will be possible because of very highly developed control systems for execution of hand and finger movements. The development of such systems to high levels will have required much practice, and they are manifestations of expertise. It is, however, possible that a person could learn to play a piece of music 'technically' without having 'understood' it musically at all. Such a technically perfect performance could equally well be generated by mechanical means.

15.3 Expressive performance

It is well established that notationally perfect performances of music are experienced by most listeners as dull, mechanical and uninteresting. What makes any performance musically interesting are the slight fluctuations in duration, loudness, pitch and timbre which together constitute expressive performance. Such fluctuations are what distinguishes one performance from another, and their importance is what keeps professional performers in business. Were it not for this, we could get computers to generate once-and-for-all perfect performances of musical works, and close most of our symphony halls and conservatories!

Recent research has made it increasingly clear that the existence of expressive performance is the best evidence we can obtain that musicians *understand* the music they are playing. This is because expressive variations are by no means random or idiosyncratic. A wide range of studies (e.g. Clarke 1988, Gabrielsson 1988, Shaffer 1981, Sloboda 1983) has shown that microvariations are highly systematic, both within the same performer and across different performers. Many of such variations are designed to make important structural features of the music more prominent to the listener. Their systematicity therefore depends upon the performer having understood what *are* the important structures. The best test that this understanding is deeply rooted in a performer is to ask that performer to sight-read some music he or she has never seen before. If a performer can apply appropriate expression in such a situation, then his or her understanding must be fully internalized. Evidence of such ability does indeed exist (Sloboda 1983), and it is often so deeply internalized that performers are not fully aware of the details of their own expressive repertoires; they have become intuitive and semi-automatic. This should not surprise us, because it is another well-documented characteristic of all cognitive expertise. Many people mistakenly assume that intuitive behaviour must be innate. This is a major fallacy. Any well-practised habit eventually becomes automatic.

It may seem at first sight that the statement that expression is systematic conflicts with the existence of interesting differences between performers. The contradiction is, however, more apparent than real. Performers differ from one another not so much in the nature of expressive devices used, but in their distribution and intensity. So, for example, one performer may achieve by subtle dynamic fluctuations what another achieves by temporal fluctuations. Such differences between performers, or between the same performer at different times, can be characterized as differences in expressive 'style' (Sloboda 1985).

15.4 Developing expressive skills alongside technical skills

Because high level musical performance has this dual technical–expressive aspect, the conditions for the development of expert performers must allow development on both fronts. This is quite difficult to achieve.

There are many music professionals who are technically adept but lack a high level of expressive skill. There are also many non-professionals who have a high level of expressive insight, but cannot realize their expressive intentions in music of any technical complexity. The master performer is that relatively rare person who has managed to develop both technical and expressive skills to a high level in tandem. How is it done?

We now have evidence from a number of biographically based research studies (Ericsson *et al.* 1993, Sloboda and Howe 1991, Sosniak 1985) that confirms that music is no exception to the general rule that 'practice makes perfect'. The study of Ericsson *et al.* shows that student violinists rated as excellent by their professors have, by the age of 21, accumulated on average around twice as many hours of practice over the lifespan (10 000 hours) as more average players (5000 hours). Sosniak, in a study of 24 top pianists in the USA, showed that none of them showed particular signs of exceptional ability at the outset of training. Exceptionality was something which developed gradually through the early years of formal training. Indeed, the notion that very early achievement is the normal precursor of adult excellence finds very little support in the documented research literature. The child prodigy may be the exception rather than the norm.

It is not very easy for a young person to accumulate 10 000 hours of practice between starting an instrument (typically around the age of six or seven at the earliest) and the age of 21. To get some idea of the workload that figure implies, one can calculate that the accumulation of 10 000 hours of practice would require two hours every day of the year for 14 years. In reality, the typical 'expert' practice pattern begins with 15–30 minutes per day, and increases to 4–6 hours per day by the age of 21. Practice activities are not always inherently rewarding to young children, and we (Sloboda and Howe 1991) found that most children in a sample of students at a specialist music school had not always enjoyed practice as young children. They often required parental support, even direct supervision, to accomplish regular practice.

Indeed, the quality of the child's relationship with significant adults, both parents and teachers, appeared crucial in predicting long-term involvement with musical performance. The parents in our sample (Sloboda and Howe 1991) were characterized by a very high level of involvement in their children's musical life. In addition, students tended to remember their first teachers, not so much for their technical adeptness as for the fact that they made lessons fun. They communicated both their love of music and their liking for their pupil. Personal warmth seemed an important characteristic. Critical, confrontational or achievement-oriented approaches seemed not to be successful, at least in the early stages of learning.

We (Sloboda and Howe 1991) also found some surprising differences between the best and the average students in our sample. It turned out that the best students had done *less* formal practice in their early years than had the average students, and that their parents were less accomplished musically than the parents of the average children. The rich qualitative data obtained from interviews with these students strongly suggests a social–motivational explanation for these findings. Children whose parents were not musically accomplished tended to receive a high level of praise and admiration from their families for objectively rather modest achievements. This, in its turn, encouraged the children to develop a strong sense of themselves as special, as the 'musician' in the family. Musical parents tended to have higher standards, which were reflected in a more rigid, achievement-oriented, family environment, with much less admiration for modest achievements.

There is some indication that the best students did not spend less time on musical activity than their less able peers, but that they simply spent less time on formal task-oriented practice and more time on free exploration of the musical medium (improvisation, and other activities often perjoratively described by both children and parents as 'messing about'). I can certainly remember from my own childhood that I would despatch my lesson tasks in 10 minutes or so, and then spend hours 'tinkering' on my own projects, with the forbearance of my long-suffering parents, who none the less were often driven to enquire 'what *is* that strange noise you are making: are you sure it is part of your practice?'

These initially unexpected results now make a lot of sense to me. One may suppose that, by and large, formal task-oriented practice encourages the development of technical rather than expressive skills, whereas exploratory and improvisatory activities encourage the individual's expressive development. Successful musicians are those who have been able to achieve a proper balance between these two types of activity.

There is a considerable body of evidence, much of it anecdotal, but some experimental (e.g. Sloboda 1989), that there are two types of motivation to engage with music. One motivation is what one might call 'intrinsic'. It develops from intense pleasurable experiences with music (of a sensual, aesthetic or emotional kind) which lead to a deep personal commitment to music. The other motivation is what one might call 'extrinsic', and is concerned with achievement. Here, the focus is not so much on the music itself as on achieving certain goals (e.g. approval of parents, identification with role models, winning competitions). Clearly, any one individual will have a mixture of the two types of motivation. There is some evidence, however, that a too early emphasis on achievement can inhibit intrinsic motivation. In simple terms, children become so concerned about what others may be thinking of their performance that they have little attention left to allow the potential of the music to engage their aesthetic and emotional sensibilities deeply. All music becomes a source of anxiety.

Research on people's experiences with music in school (Sloboda 1989) shows that many remember their earliest encounters with music as ones of anxiety or humiliation which left them with the sense that they were not musically able. Those people who survived such environments were often those who had already experienced music as intensely pleasurable in some other context.

It seems that our society—particularly our system of formal education—is set up to produce a large number of musical 'walking wounded'. What may be needed to remedy that is the rehabilitation of the notion that, in the sphere of music if nowhere else, deep emotional experiences and sensual enjoyment are as important and valid as hard work and technical achievement. One of the reasons why music seems to be seen by many children as an essentially female activity may be the strong male conditioning against emotional display, which is fully present by the age of six or seven in most cultures. One of the unexpected findings of our study was the huge sense of relief and safety felt by some boys when they were able to get to a specialist music school where music was at last seen as a quite normal activity for boys (Howe and Sloboda 1991).

Finally, there is considerable evidence that children are aware of the associations of different types of music with social group identity. Schools often present children with the notion that classical music is superior to the popular and folk idioms with which they more naturally identify. Children can reject classical music as too highbrow and also become intimidated by the apparent requirement to step outside what seems comfortable and familiar before they can produce 'acceptable' music. Most of us are aware of the child who presents as incompetent in a singing class, but can be found the same day in the school bus joining in an informal sing-along session with competence and enthusiasm. There are strong social pressures from peers to conform to the norm and hide a potential liking for music which is 'different' (Finnas 1987). This means that teachers need to introduce music through, rather than in opposition to, the cultural musical norms of their students.

References

Bharucha, J. J. (1987) Music cognition and perceptual facilitation: a connectionist framework. *Music Perception,* **5**, 1–30.

Bregman, A. S. (1990) *Auditory scene analysis: the perceptual organisation of sound.* MIT Press, Cambridge, M. A.

Chase, W. G. and Simon H. A. (1973) Perception in chess. *Cognitive Psychology,* **4**, 55–81.

Clarke, E. F. (1988) Generative principles in music performance. In: Sloboda J. A. (ed) *Generative processes in music: the psychology of performance, improvisation, and composition.* Oxford University Press, Oxford, pp. 1–26.

Deutsch, D. (1980) The processing of structured and unstructured tonal sequences. *Perception and Psychophysics,* **23**, 215–218.

Deutsch, D. (1982) Grouping mechanisms in music. In: Deutsch, D. (ed) *The psychology of music.* Academic Press, New York, pp. 99–134.

Ericsson, K. A., Krampe, R. Th., and Tesch-Römer, C (1993) The role of deliberate practice in the acquisition of expert performance. *Psychological Review,* **100**, 363–406.

Finnas, L. (1987) Do young people misjudge each other's musical tastes? *Psychology of Music,* **15**, 152–166.

Gabrielsson, A. (1988) Timing in music performance and its relations to music experience. In: Sloboda J. A. (ed) *Generative processes in music: the psychology of performance, improvisation, and composition.* Oxford University Press, Oxford, pp. 27–51.

Gjerdingen, R. O. (1990) Categorization of musical patterns by self-organizing neuronlike networks. *Music Perception,* **7**, 339–369.

Hepper, P. G. (1991) An examination of foetal learning before and after birth. *Irish Journal of Psychology,* **12**, 95–107.

Howe, M. J. A. and Sloboda, J. A. (1991) Problems experienced by young musicians as a result of the failure of other children to value musical accomplishments. *Gifted Education,* **8**, 102–111.

Huron, D. (1991) The avoidance of part-crossing in polyphonic music: perceptual evidence and musical practice. *Music Perception,* **9**, 93–104.

Jackendoff, R (1991) Musical parsing and musical affect. *Music Perception,* **9**, 199–230.

Lerdahl, F (1988) Cognitive constraints on compositional systems. In: Sloboda J. A. (Ed.) *Generative processes in music: the psychology of performance, improvisation, and composition.* Oxford University Press, Oxford, pp. 231–259.

Lerdahl, F. and Jackendoff, R. (1983) *A generative theory of tonal music.* MIT Press, Cambridge, MA.

Meyer, L. B. (1956) *Emotion and meaning in music.* University of Chicago Press, Chicago, IL.

Narmour, E. (1990) *The analysis and cognition of basic melodic structures: the implication– realisation model.* University of Chicago Press, Chicago, IL.

Narmour, E. (1991) The top-down and bottom-up systems of musical implication: building on Meyer's theory of emotional syntax. *Music Perception,* **9**, 1–26.

Oura, Y. and Hatano, G (1988) Memory for melodies among subjects differing in age and experience in music. *Psychology of Music,* **16**, 91–109.

Pinchot-Kastner, M. and Crowder, R. G. (1990) Perception of the major/minor distinction: IV. Emotional connotations in young children. *Music Perception,* **8**, 189–202.

Shaffer, L. H. (1981) Performances of Chopin, Bach, and Bartok: studies in motor programming. *Cognitive Psychology,* **13**, 326–376.

Sloboda, J. A. (1983) The communication of musical metre in piano performance. *Quarterly Journal of Experimental Psychology. A, Human Experimental Psychology,* **35**, 377–396.

Sloboda, J. A. (1985) Expressive skill in two pianists: style and effectiveness in music performance. *Canadian Journal of Psychology,* **39**, 273–293.

Sloboda, J. A. (1989) Music as a language. In: Wilson, F., Roehmann F (eds) *Music and child development.* MMB Music, Saint Louis, MO, pp. 28–43.

Sloboda, J. A. (1991) Music structure and emotional response: some empirical findings. *Psychology of Music,* **19**, 110–120.

Sloboda, J. A. and Howe, M. J. A. (1991) Biographical precursors of musical excellence: an interview study. *Psychology of Music,* **19**, 3–21.

Sloboda, J. A. and Parker, D. H. H. (1985) Immediate recall of melodies. In: Howell, F., Cross, I., West R (eds) *Musical structure and cognition.* Academic Press, London, pp. 143–167.

Sloboda, J. A., Hermelin, B., and O'Connor N. (1985) An exceptional musical memory. *Music Perception,* **3**, 155–170.

Sosniak, L. A. (1985) Learning to be a concert pianist. In: Bloom B. S. (ed) *Developing talent in young people.* Ballantine Books, New York, pp. 143–167.

Zenatti, A. (1969) *Le développement génétique de la perception musicale.* Monographies Français Psychologique No. 17.

CHAPTER 16

THE ACQUISITION OF MUSICAL PERFORMANCE EXPERTISE: DECONSTRUCTING THE 'TALENT' ACCOUNT OF INDIVIDUAL DIFFERENCES IN MUSICAL EXPRESSIVITY

16.1 The curious case of 'musical talent'

Considering how widespread a phenomenon music is within our society and the fact that listening to music is an important part of so many people's daily lives, it is something of an enigma that so few people develop any significant level of music performance ability. Not only do many people never attempt to learn an instrument, but the majority of those who undertake some form of structured learning activity abandon their efforts within a few years.

In countries such as the United States and the United Kingdom, almost every child in school receives classroom music instruction from an early age. Yet the general level of musical achievement in the school-age population is surely well below that of many other skills addressed by the school curriculum.

An apparently almost irresistible popular line of explanation for this general lack of musical accomplishment in the population is the invocation of the presence or absence of 'musical talent'. Sloboda, Davidson, and Howe (1994) proposed the existence of a folk psychology of talent, which postulates substantial innately determined differences between individuals in their capacity for musical accomplishment. According to the folk psychology account, few people become expert musical performers because few people have the necessary talent. This folk psychology is evident in the structures and rhetoric of the music conservatoire (see, e.g., Kingsbury, 1988), and also in the beliefs of people involved in schools. For instance, O'Neill (1994) demonstrated that schoolchildren as young as 8 years old are already more likely to believe that music ability cannot be improved by effort than sporting skill. A recent survey by Davis (1994) shows that more than 75% of a sample comprised mainly of educational professionals believed that composing, singing, and playing concert instruments required a special gift or natural talent. Other activities, such as playing chess, performing surgery, and writing nonfiction, were seen as requiring talent by less than 40% of the sample, as, curiously, was orchestral conducting!

Although not wishing (or being in a position) to deny that inherited differences between individuals may play some role in determining to what extent musical skills are acquired, one major purpose of this chapter is to marshal evidence and arguments for an alternative view to the prevalent folk psychology. This alternative view holds the capacity for musical accomplishment of one sort or another to be a species-defining characteristic (along with the capacity to learn a language, develop motor skills, etc.). As with these other skills, musical development may be impeded by inherited deficiencies, but such deficiencies only cause major problems in a relatively small minority of cases. Most humans are 'primed' to become musicians. Therefore, for an account of why they fail to develop significant levels of performance skill, we need to look elsewhere than lack of supposed talent.

In reviewing the state of this debate, I summarize some material and go over arguments already published elsewhere. The specific issue that I want to address in greater detail in this chapter is the distinction between technical and expressive aspects of musical performance. Those who are prepared to concede that talent might not be the best explanation of technical development are much more reluctant to concede on the issue of expressivity. Expressive musicianship is widely considered to be intuitive, spontaneous, unteachable to those who do not display it, and a prime manifestation of talent. If we can rescue expressivity from the folk psychology of talent, then the rest of musical expertise comes with it rather easily.

16.2 What can we know about inheritance of musical ability?

The usual source of evidence on heritability of psychological characteristics is, of course, the literature on twin studies. The methodological and theoretical traps of this literature are well known, particularly in the context of IQ studies, and it is outside my concerns or expertise to rehearse the arguments here. There are two points to make with respect to music. First, there exists no generally accepted psychometric measure of musical ability that has the validity and reliability of standard measures of intelligence. There are no widely accepted 'MQ' tests. Second, even if all the difficulties with twin studies are set aside, such studies seem to conclude that differences in musical ability are considerably less dependent on inherited factors than are differences in IQ (Coon and Carey, 1989).

Plomin and Thompson (1993) recently offered the hope of a means of transcending the inherent difficulties of twin studies by a new technique of *allelic association,* which allows direct comparison of genetic material between large numbers of unrelated individuals varying on some known psychological property such as IQ. This technique uses analysis of genetic material found in human blood cells. Hints that genetic correlates of high IQ have been established by this group have, however, yet to be substantiated in print, and the technique is too new to have been properly evaluated, let alone applied to music or other skill domains.

A different source of evidence concerning genetic foundations of musicality comes from direct research on the capacities of human infants pre- and postterm. Research on prenatal capacities (see Hepper, 1991; Lecanuet, 1995) and postnatal musical cognition (see Papousek, 1995; Trehub, 1990) suggests that the vast majority of human infants have rather similar, and surprisingly sophisticated, means of handling musical stimuli. These universal capacities lead to an astonishing flowering (from the sixth month on) of spontaneous premusical generativity. All but the most severely learning-disabled children display a rich vocabulary of pitch- and rhythm-modulated utterances. As in the case of language, these utterances can be shown to pass through a number of stages that can well be described in terms of different systems of underlying grammatical rules that succeed one another in an orderly way (Imberty, 1995).

Although individual differences in infant functioning are remarkably difficult to research, for methodological and practical reasons (see Colombo, 1993), it would seem that developmental research has shown that the average human infant displays musical capacities as early, if not earlier, than linguistic capacities, and in a far more developed and overt form than any capacities that might be supposed to underlie other skills such as mathematical, artistic, or athletic skills. Nothing in this literature prepares us for the dismal musical outcomes observed in our culture in late childhood and adulthood.

It would be impossible for me to address the issues of musical expertise without recurrent reference to the most recent large-scale study in which I have been involved, with colleagues Michael Howe, Jane Davidson, and Derek Moore (Davidson, Sloboda, and Howe, 1994; Howe, Davidson, Moore, and Sloboda, 1995; Sloboda and Davidson, 1995; Sloboda, Davidson, Howe, and Moore, 1996; Sloboda, Davidson, Moore, and Howe, 1994). This study, named the Leverhulme Project in honor of its funding source, the Leverhulme Trust, obtained a wide variety of information, mostly biographical, on 257 young people in England. They were selected to represent a range of current performance achievement on musical instruments, from the outstandingly able through to the modal 'tried an instrument but gave it up'. Individuals at different levels of accomplishment were roughly matched for age, gender, instrument, and socioeconomic class. We established five major ability groups, whose rank ordering was validated by differences in objective performance measures (musical examinations set by a national UK examining body). Group 1 comprised 119 students of a specialist music school, where entry is by competitive audition. This group represents the highest ability level. Graduates of the school regularly win national performance competitions, and typically go on to conservatory study and careers as professional performers. Groups 2, 3, and 4 comprised current players of musical instruments, classified in terms of their levels of aspiration for excellence in musical performance. The members of Group 2 had failed the entry audition to the specialist school. The members of Group 3 had inquired about but had failed to apply for entry to the specialist school. The members of Group 4 were current 'players for pleasure' in an ordinary state school, undistinguished in its general level of musical education. Group 5 comprised pupils of the same school as Group 4, who had begun to learn an instrument, but had given up study after a period of 6 months or more. Each participant was interviewed, and answers cross-checked for reliability in individual interviews with a parent of each participant.

It is very important for later steps in the argument to note that all these young people were learning musical instruments in what might be described as the 'classical conservatoire culture', where emphasis is on reproduction of musical artworks within the formal classical tradition, represented by composers such as Mozart, Beethoven, Rachmaninov, and Stravinsky. The characteristics of this tradition are (a) concern with accurate and faithful reproduction of a printed score, rather than with improvisation or composition; (b) the existence of a central repertoire of extreme technical difficulty; (c) definitions of mastery in terms of ability to perform items from a rather small common core set of compositions within a culture; and (d) explicit or implicit competitive events in which performers are compared with one another by expert judges on their ability to perform identical or closely similar pieces, such judgments forming an important element in decisions about progression and reward within the culture. Other musical cultures exist, such as jazz, pop, or folk cultures, which have very different characteristics. It should not be supposed that findings from studies of conservatoire culture musicians can be straightforwardly applied to other forms of musical activity.

It has often been supposed that individual differences in musical accomplishment are prefigured by individual differences in early signs of musicality. Building on accounts of one or two legendary 'geniuses' such as Mozart, and other accounts of child prodigies (e.g. Revesz, 1925/1970), commentators have often assumed that individuals displaying unusually high ability in adolescence or later must have always been unusual. We attempted to test this claim in the Leverhulme Project by asking detailed and specific questions of the parents of all participants concerning the age of occurrence of particular early manifestations of musical ability, such as the first age at which the child could reproduce by singing a recognizable tune from the culture.

The results were clear (Howe *et al.*, 1995). Similarities between the five groups far outweighed the differences, which were nonexistent on many measures, and when present did not always favor the highest ability group. The difference most favorable to the 'talent' account was a 6-month average advantage for Group 1 in singing a recognizable tune (18 months of age, as opposed to 24 months for the other groups). However, this group showed earlier parent-initiated musical activity, too, and so the result may be a consequence of differential parental behavior. We have considerable evidence from other parts of our study that the parents of the highest achieving group showed unique behavioral characteristics. Although there are obvious interpretational difficulties with retrospective studies, this study lends little credence to the notion of large individual differences in early musicality that prefigure later achievement. The results are entirely consistent with the data obtained by direct study of very young children. Most children show a variety of overt musical behaviors at an early age, and few stray far from established norms.

16.3 The role of practice

Ericsson, Krampe, and Tesch-Römer (1993) provided compelling evidence for a conclusion of some generality with respect to acquisition of expertise. Their conclusion is that level of expertise is a direct function of the amount of effortful formal practice of that skill undertaken by an individual. Their own work on student and professional instrumental players has shown that the highest achieving individuals consistently undertook around twice as much daily practice as moderate achievers, over long periods of childhood, adolescence, and early adulthood. Similar findings have been obtained in other domains such as chess and sport.

The Ericsson position offers a strong challenge to the folk psychology of talent, which, in the case of music and many other skills, assumes that high-achieving individuals acquire their outstanding skill with the same or even less practice than others.

The Leverhulme Project has provided data that fully confirm and strengthen the practice hypothesis (Sloboda et al., 1994, 1996). All participants were asked to provide estimates of average daily formal practice for each year of life since beginning to learn an instrument, with formal practice defined as activities directly related to tasks set by the instrumental teacher in the previous lesson. A subset of the sample also kept a detailed record of practice activities over a 42-week period.

The two main subcomponents of such practice were named as scales and pieces. *Scales* is a shorthand designation for work on scales, arpeggios, and other technical exercises without musical interest or merit in their own right, but designed to provide exhaustive and repetitive opportunities for mastery of technical aspects of playing. *Pieces* designates work on items from the musical repertoire toward the end goal of polished performance.

The relationship between practice and achievement level was strongly confirmed, and extended across the entire sample. Members of Group 1 were, even by the age of 12, practicing an astonishing 800% more than the members of Group 5 (2 hours a day, as compared to 15 minutes a day). The intermediate groups fell between these extremes in exact order of achievement. The practice–achievement relationship does not, therefore, break down at low levels of achievement. We found no individuals in our sample who practiced as much as 2 hours per day yet failed to achieve high levels of skill! Such cases would surely be predicted in considerable numbers were the folk psychology view correct.

A chance feature of the UK instrumental education system allowed us to be even more definitive about the practice–achievement relationship than Ericsson et al. (1993). The vast majority of children learning instruments in the UK are entered by their teachers into a national system of graded instrumental examinations, which are set and examined by a nationally constituted panel of trained assessors, whose purpose is to provide equivalent measurements across the country. There is a preliminary grade, and eight main grades, which, as a very rough guide, might each represent a year's additional work on an instrument. The pedagogic practices of many teachers are totally determined by the requirements of these grade examination syllabi.

Every child in our sample had entered for these examinations, and we were able to ascertain at what age each grade level had been reached. This allowed, for each group, the calculation of the average number of hours of formal practice required to achieve each grade. This amount proved to be not significantly different between groups. The relationship between grade level and practice for the whole sample is shown in Figure 16.1. This indicates, for instance, that, regardless of ultimate achievement level, it takes an average of 1200 hours of formal practice in total to achieve Grade 5 standard (or 300 hours to get there from Grade 4). The reason that Group 1 members achieve grade exam successes earlier than other groups seems entirely due to accumulation of the requisite amount of practice more quickly. There is absolutely no evidence of a 'fast track' for high achievers. Indeed, there is a nonsignificant trend for high achievers to practice more than low achievers to reach a particular grade.

Of course, as one might expect, there is a fairly high degree of within-group variance in amounts of practice undertaken to achieve a given grade.

One can suppose differences in instrument, practice strategy, teaching efficiency, concentration, and other factors to account for this (see Lehmann, 1997 for an elaboration of this argument). There might even be some contribution from inherited differences. The important thing for this discussion is that this variability is present at all levels of achievement, and therefore is not constitutive of achievement, as the folk psychology account would demand.

Several studies of expertise have been criticized for not including a 'dropout' group. Group 5 of this study comprises such a dropout group. The fact that this group shows exactly the same relationship between practice

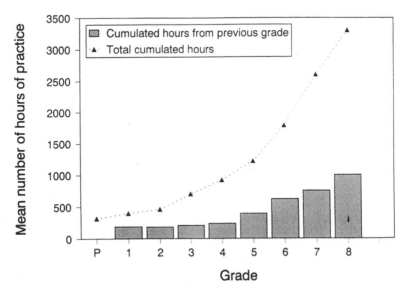

Figure 16.1 Relationship of cumulated hours of practice to grade achievement for young instrumentalists. Data are means for 257 instrumentalists in five ability groups. There are no significant differences between groups at any grade level.

and achievement as any other group suggests that putative differences between persisters and dropouts (in terms of 'talent', self-beliefs, and motivation) influence only the duration of practice activities, and not the effectiveness of those activities once undertaken, in improving skill.

The Leverhulme study also provided some data that helped explain why the groups differed so much in the amount of daily practice they were capable of (Davidson, Howe, Moore, and Sloboda, 1996; Davidson *et al.*, 1994). At the outset of instrumental study, groups were broadly equivalent on a crude measure of practice motivation. All reported having periods when motivation to practice was low, and when they probably would not have practiced at all without parental intervention. They displayed little of the 'rage to master' reported in the case of some precocious young artists. Two things marked the higher achieving children. First, the nature and level of early parental involvement was significantly different. Parents of Group 1 students were more likely to attend instrumental lessons with their children, obtain detailed feedback and instructions from teachers, and actively supervise daily practice on a moment-to-moment basis, often at some considerable cost to their own schedule. For instance, one family with three high-achieving siblings adopted a daily routine in which the father would supervise the individual practice of each child in 30-minute intervals from 6.00 a.m. until 7.30 a.m. prior to the family dispersing to school and work. Parents of low-achieving children were less likely to have meaningful contact with the teacher, and were likely to confine their domestic interventions to telling children to 'go and do your practice', without any direct involvement in it. In sum, therefore, it seems that abnormally high levels of early practice are sustained by abnormal levels of social and cognitive support, mainly from parents.

The second feature of the higher achieving children was a gradual age-related move toward self-motivation for practice as adolescence progressed. These individuals appeared to be finding their own motivations for practice, although the study did not systematically probe what these were. Arguably, those who make faster progress get to work on more interesting and complex music, obtain greater mastery, perceive themselves as successful, and identify with teachers or other high-level performers as role models. All of these factors have been experimentally demonstrated in other domains to have strong effects on motivation (e.g. Amabile, 1983; Dweck, 1986), and we found examples of all of these factors in the informal comments of the interviewees.

The diary study showed, however, that even among the highest achieving groups, there were large fluctuations in daily practice duration as a function of external circumstances. These individuals practiced most before important concerts, and least during school vacation. Despite these fluctuations, however, Group 1 still demonstrated the most week-to-week stability in practice duration, and confirmed Ericsson *et al.*'s (1993) finding that high-achieving individuals tend to do more of their practice in the morning. In our sample this effect was particularly strong for scales practice. High-achieving young people tend to concentrate the more grueling repetitive technical practice at the time of day when they are physically and cognitively at their peak.

16.4 Technical versus expressive aspects of music performance

Advanced music performance requires high levels of technical skill. This is not only because much core repertoire requires extremely rapid movements, but also because very small differences in the positioning or timing of movements can make huge differences in the perceptual qualities of the sound. For instance, accurate tuning in violin playing can be disrupted by positioning deviations of fingers on the string of less than 1 millimeter. The technical difficulty of classical instrumental performance is recognized by the long-standing tradition of manuals, tutors, and exercises designed solely to address technical problems through highly systematic and repetitive practice. The sequences that are used for such purposes often have little or no aesthetic interest. From the very outset of instrumental learning, most teachers encourage their pupils to devote the first part of any practice period to technical exercises, before going on to work at repertoire. The teaching of technique is commonly based on some set of theoretical assumptions about optimal posture, muscle tension, transitions between different positions, and so on. These assumptions have general components that resemble those found in the pedagogy of other skills. For instance, many musical theories make general assumptions about the desirability of economies in both effort and movement, which resemble assumptions behind sporting or athletic technique. Most of the theories, however, devote the bulk of their efforts toward the peculiar problems of the interface between the human body and the particular instrument.

Because the shape, size, and sound-producing mechanisms of musical instruments are so different from one another, there is very little in common between, say, violin technique and piano technique. Perhaps even more important, musical instruments require, by and large, bodily movements of a type not common in other domains of human activity. These almost always involve small but precisely timed and located finger movements that show high degrees of independence from one another. A very fundamental issue in nearly all instrumental performance is the move toward complete independence of fingers and hands one from another. The nonmusical skill with the most similar set of requirements is typing, but even there, the level of specificity of finger movement speed and timing is of a much lower order. By and large it does not matter when a key is depressed, so long as the sequence of keys is in the correct order. Furthermore, typing rarely involves the simultaneous depression of two or more fingers. Skills such as piano playing require this routinely.

For all these reasons, we can predict that the acquisition of high levels of technical competence on an instrument will take a long time and will require much practice specifically tailored to the requirements of each instrument. People have, in effect, to learn a whole new set of motor programs for each different instrument. There are few previously learned skills that the learner can build on. We may suppose that if there is any transfer of training between different instruments it reflects either their physical similarity (e.g. piano and harpsichord, violin and viola) or other nonmotor skills (e.g. the ability to read music) that both instruments require.

It has long been recognized by musicians, and more recently confirmed by psychological research (Clarke, 1988; Gabrielsson, 1988; Shaffer, 1981; Sloboda, 1983) that mere technical prowess does not make an effective musical performer. Playing the notes as written with speed and fluency is the starting point for artistic excellence, not the finish.

High-level performers add value to the score by a range of expressive devices that affect the microstructure of timing, loudness, timbre, and other elements, resulting in notes that are equal in the notation being performed unequally in some respect. We know a number of things for certain about expressive performance:

1 The deviations from exactitude are intentional. That is, they are not unintentional by-products of technical deficiencies, or products of random noise in the motor system. We know this because a performer can (a) reproduce the same deviations on occasions that may be widely separated in time (Shaffer, 1984), and (b) produce a different expressive profile in response to changes in task demand (Palmer, 1989; Sloboda, 1983).

2 The deviations are, in part, applied without conscious awareness. Performers asked to produce expressionless 'deadpan' performances are normally incapable of doing this. Reduced features of expressive performances are still present (e.g. Gabrielsson, 1974, 1988). Even when

performers know they are being deliberately expressive, they do not have full conscious awareness of every detail of their performance.

3 The deviations are systematic. That is to say, a given performer applies the same type of deviation at analogous points in a musical structure, and performers within a culture tend to use the same types of expressive devices.

4 The deviations are constrained by the structure of the music. This means that expression takes account of structure, and in some situations is intended to reinforce the structure by making it more manifest or salient to a listener. Musicians can have rational debates about the relative merits of different ways of playing the same piece, because it is not the case that 'anything goes' in expression.

5 The deviations are unique in some respects to a given performer. At first glance this seems to contradict the third point already given. However, even if two performers use exactly the same set of expressive devices, they can still sound quite different from one another because of their differences in frequency of use of the various devices, the distribution of magnitudes of deviations, and other 'free' parameters. Hence, each performer has a distinct performing style that is recognizable to connoisseurs (Sloboda, 1985).

6 The deviations are detectable by listeners, and assist their processes of forming representations of the music. For instance, where the music is metrically ambiguous, expert performance disambiguates the meter (Sloboda, 1983).

7 Expressive skill develops over long timespans. Commentators on internationally known performers often trace significant changes in expressive character of recorded performances over a lifespan. It is generally held that 'mature' interpretations are unlikely to be achieved within the first 10 years of performing an instrument. Where the issue has been studied experimentally, it has been found that performers with several decades of performing experience show distinct superiority in the consistency and effectiveness of expression, as compared to performers with only one decade of performing experience (Sloboda, 1983).

Expressive performance, unlike technical performance, is not systematically taught or acquired through the use of manuals or sets of exercises. We can observe two processes at work in the acquisition of expression. First is the use of expressive models. A teacher will play something and ask the student to imitate the expression. In later stages of development, performers avidly seek out the performances of other musicians for purposes of analysis and comparison. The second process is the encouragement of the development of an individual's own expressive style. An individual is invited to generate alternative expressive solutions and exercise some independent judgment in deciding among them.

16.5 Deconstructing the talent account of expression

When conversing with music professionals, particularly those who teach, a very common experience recounted by these professionals is the existence of young musicians who seem to be 'primed' to make unusually rapid progress in the acquisition of expressive performance when compared with the norm. This unusual rapidity can be observed in both imitation and generativity. So, on the one hand, there appear to be individuals who are capable of imitating expressive models with unusual accuracy or rapidity; and on the other, there appear to be individuals who spontaneously generate appropriate expressive variations in the absence of an immediate model. To a great extent, it is such observations that support the notion of a small group of talented individuals, separated from the norm.

16.5.1 Imitative expression

For the purposes of the argument, assume that these observations by teachers are reliable, accurate, and free from the kinds of biases that can so easily infect judgments of this sort. Let us first of all take the case of imitation. There is, of course, a limiting condition that must pertain if the listener is to detect an intended imitation of expression; that is, that the performance as a whole must be technically more stable than the parameters of the expressive device being detected. To take a concrete example, let us suppose that the device to be imitated is an expressive lengthening of 25% over and above the notated duration of a given note in a phrase. In this case, in order for the lengthening to be detected the average variability in note lengths over the passage as a whole must be no greater than, say, 10% (psychophysical considerations would determine the exact ratio required). If technical stability is not achieved, then we have the possibility that an individual is able to form a representation of a heard expressive device, generate a performance intention in which this device is present, and thus intended for performance, but fail to translate the intention into an adequate motor program. This has the consequence that some differences between individuals in supposed observed expressive ability are actually technical differences. Technical difficulties can be caused by many things, one of them, of course, being lack of practice. However, there are other factors at play in any individual instance. For instance, an overanxious child might well suffer technical disruption more easily than a confident child. A child who knows the piece being played, or knows pieces like it, might be able to form a representation of the notes it contains more rapidly and efficiently. Many of these factors will lead to fairly stable and reliable differences between individuals in their ability to 'deliver' expressive imitation, at least in the short term, but they have nothing to do with differences in expressive ability, *per se*. It may not be possible for an individual informal observer to distinguish these cases of production deficiency from true differences in expressivity. Only controlled formal quasi-experimental observation may have the necessary discriminatory power.

Let us assume, however, that there is a residue of cases that do not fall foul of these problems. These cases would be individuals of equal technical capacity, in general, and in respect to the piece presented in this situation, who nevertheless show significant differences in capacity to imitate the expressive deviations being demonstrated. What account might we give of these differences that did not rely on talent?

My proposal is based on how individuals might solve the problem of storing the large amount of analog information that appears to be involved in remembering expressive details. There is a great deal of evidence that musical memory, like any other kind of memory, requires categorical structural representation that reduces the information load to manageable proportions. Most tonal music solves the problem by allowing that all musical inputs are reducible to a canonical form in which, for instance, all pitches are subsumed into one of a small number of categories (5–12 per octave according to specific genre), and all durations are likewise subsumed (usually equal subdivisions of a primary beat, 2, 4, 8, 3, and 6 being the most common). To have represented a piece of music tonally means to have extracted these categories from a much richer surface. Expressive deviations are contained in that part of the input that the categorization process must ignore, so representing it means recovering some of it before it is lost. This recovery cannot be a simple list of all the analog information present, because humans do not have the capacity to store such information, which would resemble the output from a performance to a MIDI file, containing the precise duration, loudness, and timbral qualities of every successive note.

We need to translate the expressive information into something more abstract before it can be stored. This abstract representation has two requirements: (a) it must link otherwise apparently arbitrary changes in timing, loudness, and other characteristics of successive notes one to another through some function or formula that can then be run in reverse during performance to regenerate something approximating the original pattern of deviations; and (b) it must mark the starting and end positions of a particular function or formula in the canonical representation of pitch time categories within the tonal representation of the piece. To put this in more everyday musical language, the expressive device must have a shape that has a definite location in the musical structure. We store the shape and its location rather than the analog data. Change the shape or change the location of the shape and you have a different expressive outcome.

My contention is that what bootstraps the process of representing expressive devices in music is the existence of extra-musical functions and formulas that act as ready-made templates onto which musical expression can be mapped. The individual who presents as 'talented' with respect to expressive imitation is the individual who has (a) acquired an appropriate repertoire of extra-musical templates, and (b) has made the appropriate connections between domains that allows them to be applied 'by analogy' to music.

These templates arise from a number of domains, the most plausible being those of bodily and physical motion, gesture, speech and vocal intonation, and expressions of emotion. Such linkage has been suggested by a number of studies (e.g. Clynes, 1983, 1986; Repp, 1992, 1993; Todd, 1992). There are a number of factors that can account for individual differences in the facility of this linkage:

1 Differences in nonmusical expressivity. Most theories of emotional expression (see Frijda, 1986, for instance) seem to accept that the fundamental forms of such expression are universal, innate, and species defining. What determines individual differences are cultural and social factors, concerned with repression of spontaneous expression and replacement with stylized variants. Some of these factors may be rather specific (e.g. a family environment in which emotional expression is discouraged). Others may be more general. For instance, Sloboda (1991a) provided evidence for the assertion that many children experience performance-related anxiety in music education settings, which overrides any possibility of attending to and representing the expressive characteristics of the music itself. O'Neill and Boulton (1996) and others (Abeles and Porter, 1978; Delzell and Lepplar, 1992) have demonstrated how gender-role stereotypes play a major role in determining what kind of musical engagement is thought to be appropriate by boys and girls. These stereotypes will impact on the kind of expressive or emotional awareness that children will be prepared to bring to music.

2 Differences in the ability to identify and retain the musical location of features requiring expressive treatment. Expressive gestures in music typically have a focus, even if they are spread over a number of notes. So, for instance, a particular note may be expressively marked by a increase in volume prior to it, and a decrease in volume after it. How is someone to remember where the focus of an expressive device is? In the light of the characteristics of expert expressive performance described earlier, it is probable that events are marked for expressive treatment in virtue of their structural characteristics. Therefore, a particular note is the focus for expressive treatment because it is harmonically, rhythmically, and thematically important. The ability to locate an expressive device will therefore be affected by the extent to which those structures are encoded in the person's representation. This will be affected by the degree of experience with that particular genre of music.

3 Differences in the degree of awareness of, and elaboration of, the cross-domain analogy. It is relatively well accepted that analogies need to be noticed before they can be incorporated in cognitive strategies, and that the initial noticing of the analogy may happen quite suddenly. For instance, in Chase and Ericsson's (1981) seminal study on Falloon's digit span, they report that on Day 4 of trials he had reached an asymptote of performance, whereas on Day 5, after discovery of the 'running times' analogy, he was able to dramatically increase his span. We may speculate that what caused the analogy to be noticed was some number sequence that triggered a particularly strong association to a running time that was highly salient for this subject. For another runner, it might have been a quite different number that triggered the analogy, and this may have happened sooner, later, or never. In the case of music, we can suppose that the expressive analogy is bootstrapped by the experience of an expressive gesture that evokes a strong association to a salient nonmusical gesture for that individual.

4 Differences in the degree of monitoring of one's own performance for intended expressive outcomes. There is quite clear evidence available that so-called tone deafness is nothing of the sort. Individuals identified as tone-deaf are unable to match a heard pitch by singing. This is not, however, due to any deficit in pitch perception or memory, which is just as acute as the average correct singer. Rather, it is due to an inability to monitor one's own vocal output and make appropriate adjustments. By providing enhanced feedback, for instance, computer-generated visual representation of one's own sung pitch as compared to a standard, it is possible to teach individuals to adjust their vocal pitch, and, eventually,

to do so without the visual feedback (Welch, Howard, and Rush, 1989). This is essentially the same technique that is used in biofeedback to teach people to control their own heart rate or skin conductance. In relation to expressive performance, it is commonplace for teachers to observe that their pupils do not monitor the expressive outcomes of their own performances. Rather, they seem to be monitoring their expressive intentions, and take the intention for the deed. Such a situation occurs when, for instance, a teacher asks a pupil to copy a dynamic shape (getting louder then getting softer), the pupil does something, the teacher says she cannot hear any difference, but the pupil believes that he did play louder and then softer. Such scenarios can easily lead to incorrect attributions ('the child is inexpressive'), which may not encourage the teacher to seek ways of helping the pupil monitor their own performance more appropriately.

5 Differences in degree of emotional response to the expressive device. There is considerable suggestive evidence (see Sloboda, 1991a) that the ability of individuals to experience music-generated emotional response is a function of the degree to which their emotional response is not captured by factors extrinsic to the music. Thus, where the context of music is a source of threat or anxiety, the emotional response to the situation is determined by sell-related emotions (self-esteem, self-preservation, group conformity) in a way that seems to block the kind of relaxed attentiveness that is a precondition for strong aesthetically based responses to music. Such emotional blocks act as overarching factors that reduce the likelihood of noticing and internalizing the analogy between musical and nonmusical expression. In some individuals, the blocks seem to have become chronic, and independent of actual external context. Music itself triggers anxiety, by association (e.g. 'Whenever I hear music I remember the humiliation of being told by my teacher that I was singing out of tune').

There are no doubt other factors that could be adduced to account for individual differences. The demonstration of their existence is a task for future empirical research, but each of them is a specific causal hypothesis in which considerations of supposed talent or its absence are really of not much help in moving toward a better understanding of individual differences.

16.5.2 Generative expression

Almost all that one can say about imitation can also be said about individual differences in expressive generation, but there are some additional sources of variance. First, we need to be clear that there are two different types of generativity One (Type 1) is closely related to imitation in that the sequence of notes is prescribed—and an expressive contour must be fitted to this pre-existent sequence. The other (Type 2) is rather different, and relates to improvisatory mode, where the notes are chosen by the performer along with their expression. This latter kind of expressivity almost never occurs in the conservatoire culture.

Type 1 generativity requires the recognition that a certain musical sequence admits of expressive treatment in the absence of the immediate presentation of a specific expressive model for that sequence. A clear example of generative expression is in the case where an individual sight-reads from an unedited score, or where an individual imitates an inexpressive model, or incorporates different expression from that offered. It is highly likely that another kind of analogical thinking is needed here. The logic would run something like this: The present sequence is similar in musical structure or form to a sequence experienced in another context; in that other context such-and-such an expressive tactic seemed to work well; therefore let us try it here. Another way of expressing this logic within musical discourse is to say that there are expressive conventions within a musical culture, and that these conventions may be learned more or less thoroughly. Nothing in this requires that a performer be able to consciously articulate the known convention. It may be entirely embodied within a non-verbal performance 'habit' or 'production rule', to use a more theoretically fashionable term.

Individual differences in expressive generativity may, in this case, be linked to individual differences in the opportunities that an individual has had to learn these conventions. This will be partly a matter of exposure to appropriately expressive performances of others, but also of factors such as the five adduced earlier with respect to imitative performance.

Type 2 generativity has a rather different etiology. The developmental literature shows that expressive improvisation is the norm in infants and young children. In the vocal play of young children, expressive gesture is almost the guiding force of vocalizations. Infants sigh, chortle, coo, and make other directly recognizable emotional signals, then they embellish these with pitch and temporal patterning. They also sing while engaged in physical activity, and so naturally coordinate their vocalizations with their bodily movements. What then seems to happen in midchildhood is that the formal characteristics of music separate out from the expressive. Children become very concerned with imitating recognizable tunes of their culture, and at the same time, are learning the control of emotional expression as part of socialization. By the early school years, at least in our own culture, improvisation (except where cherished and nurtured by perceptive adults) has all but dried up. Group singing and group instrumental playing, at the early stages of education, encourage this process of suppression of individual expression in favor of subordination to the group. Regrafting of expression within the elaborated formal musical structures of midchild-hood represents a formidable challenge for many children. It requires going directly against the mainstream of cultural separation and repression. I believe that children require very clear enabling conditions for that to happen. We learn from music therapists that emotionally repressed individuals can discover strong and intuitive emotional expressivity within themselves when offered a music performance medium in which they come realize there are no preordained standards of correctness. Typical music therapy, at least within the UK, will not offer models that are part of the standard conservatoire culture, but might, for instance, offer an individual a large array of percussion instruments, and encourage significant bodily and sonic exploration. In such a context, for instance, anger maybe gesturally expressed in a very direct way through the force with which an instrument is struck. Children may need an opportunity of a similar sort to be expressive. It is extremely significant to me that so many teachers and parents tell stories of children who appear 'unmusical' (or at least unremarkable) in standard music lessons, but then are found engaging in highly expressive and creative forms of musical behavior outside the formal classroom culture, be it involvement in playground games involving singing, or in the formation of peer-organized groups, using popular forms such as pop, jazz, or folk. This seems to me to suggest key contexts in which the individual senses 'permission' to be expressive. For many young people, the conservatoire culture does not provide such permission, and we may need to discover more precisely how those few that do flourish expressively within that culture are protected from the normal inhibitory processes. They are the ones who can, to some extent at any rate, feed on the well-springs of their own primal musical expressive generativity.

16.6 Concluding remarks

I realize that many of the comments I have made in this chapter are somewhat speculative. I believe it is appropriate in a conference of this sort to go out on a limb, and push a particular line of argument for all it is worth. I do not wish any of the arguments I put forward to be taken as conclusive, but rather suggestive. In many cases the evidence for particular kinds of processes needs to be gathered. In other cases, weaknesses in the argument need to be exposed. I hope that other participants will be merciless in this respect. We need to find the holes in each other's positions in the pursuit of scientific clarity.

What I have hoped to do is sketch out the framework of a position in which talent is not so much disproved as dissolved into a whole set of complex interacting factors and causes, each of which has its own logic and determining conditions. It is the intricacy and complexity of musical growth and development that makes for fascination and scientific discovery, not some ultimately arid dispute between oversimplistic extremes.

To summarize the steps in my argument:

1 Music seems to be biologically constitutive of early human functioning.

2 Music education in Western cultures produces a dismal yield of achievement.

3 Heritability estimates, where available, are low.

4 Technical expertise within the conservatoire culture requires practice levels far in excess of cultural norms because of its unique properties with respect to particular instruments and the specific requirements of that culture to master a technically demanding canon.

5 Such practice is sustained by external motivators in the early years, but by increasing development of internal sources through development.

6 Expressive expertise has rationality and develops through practice.

7 Significant individual differences in expression are noticed by teachers at early stages in instrumental learning.

8 Unlike technique, expression has characteristics that are similar to extra-musical activities (bodily and emotional gestures).

9 This creates opportunities for learning by analogy.

10 A whole range of plausible factors can influence the ease of uptake of this analogy.

11 The articulation and investigation of these factors constitutes a progressive agenda for the scientific study of musical skill.

References

Abeles, H. F. and Porter, S. Y. (1978) Sex-stereotyping of musical instruments. *Journal of Research in Music Education*, **26**, 65–75.

Amabile, T. M. (1983) *The social psychology of creativity*. New York: Springer Verlag.

Chase, W. G. and Ericsson, K. A. (1981) Skilled memory. In J. R. Anderson (Ed.), *Cognitive skills and their acquisition* (pp. 141–189). Hillsdale, NJ: Lawrence Erlbaum Associates.

Clarke, E. F. (1988) Generative principles in music performance. In J. A. Sloboda (Ed.), *Generative processes in music: The psychology of performance, improvisation, and composition* (pp. 1–26). London: Oxford University Press.

Clynes, M. (1983) Expressive microstructure in music, linked to living qualities. In J. Sundberg (Ed.), *Studies of music performance* (pp. 76–181). Stockholm: Royal Swedish Academy of Music.

Clynes, M. (1986) Music beyond the score. *Communication and Cognition,* **19,** 169–194.

Colombo, J. (1993) *Infant cognition: Predicting later intellectual functioning.* Newbury Park, CA: Sage.

Coon, H. and Carey, G. (1989) Genetic and environmental determinants of musical ability in twins. *Behavior Genetics,* **19,** 183–193.

Davidson, J. W., Sloboda, J. A., and Howe, M. J. A. (1994) The role of family and teachers in the success and failure of music learners. *Proceedings of the Third International Conference for Music Perception and Cognition* (pp. 359–360). University of Liège, Belgium: URPM.

Davidson, J. W., Howe, M. J. A., Moore, D. G., and Sloboda, J. A. (1996) The role of parental influences in the development of musical performance. *British Journal of Developmental Psychology,* **14,** 399–412.

Davis, M. (1994) Folk music psychology. *The Psychologist,* **7**(12), 537.

Deizell, J. K. and Lepplar, D. A. (1992) Gender association of musical instruments and preferences of fourth-grade students for selected instruments. *Journal of Research in Music Education,* **40,** 93–103.

Dweck, C. S. (1986) Motivational processes affecting learning. *American Psychologist,* **41**(10), 1040–1048.

Ericsson, K. A., Krampe, R., and Tesch-Romer, C. (1993) The rule of deliberate practice in the acquisition of expert performance. *Psychological Review,* **100,** 363–406.

Frijda, N. H. (1986) *The emotions.* Cambridge, UK: Cambridge University Press.

Gabrielsson, A. (1974) Performance of rhythm patterns. *Scandinavian Journal of Psychology,* **15,** 63–72.

Gabrielsson, A. (1988) Tuning in music performance and its relation to musical experience. In J. A. Sloboda (Ed.), *Generative processes in music: The psychology of performance, improvisation, and composition* (pp. 27–51). London: Oxford University Press.

Hepper, P. G. (1991) An examination of fetal learning before and after birth. *Irish journal of Psychology,* **12,** 95–107.

Howe, M. J. A., Davidson, J. W., Moore, D. G., and Sloboda, J. A. (1995) Are there early childhood signs of musical ability? *Psychology of Music,* **23**(2), 162–176.

Imberty, M. (1995) Linguistic and musical development in pre-school and school age children. In I. Deliège andJ. A. Sloboda (Eds.), *Musical beginnings: The origins and development of musical competence* (pp. 191–213). London: Oxford University Press.

Kingsbury, H. (1988) *Music, talent, and performance: A conservatory cultural system.* Philadelphia: Temple University Press.

Lecanuet, J. P. (1995) Prenatal auditory experience. In I. Deliège and J. A. Sloboda (Eds.), *Musical beginnings: The origins and development of musical competence* (pp. 5–54). London: Oxford University Press.

Lehmann, A. C. (1997) Acquisition of expertise in music: Efficiency of deliberate practice as a mediating variable in accounting for sub-expert performance. In I. Deliège and J. A. Sloboda (Eds.), *Perception and cognition of music.* Mahwah, NJ; Lawrence Erlbaum Associates.

O'Neill, S. (1994) Factors influencing children's motivation and achievement during the first year of instrumental music tuition. Paper presented at the Third International Conference on Music Perception and Cognition, Univerity of Liège, Belgium, July 1994.

O'Neill, S. and Boulton, M. (1996) Boys' and girls' preferences for musical instruments: A function of gender? *Psychology of Music,* **24.2**, 171–183.

Palmer, C. (1989) Mapping musical thought to musical performance. *Journal of Experimental Psychology: Human Perception and Performance,* **15**, 331–346.

Papousek, H. (1995) Musicality and infancy research. In I. Deliège and J. A. Sloboda (Eds.), *Musical beginnings: The origins and development of musical competence* (pp. 37–55). London: Oxford University Press.

Plomin, R. and Thompson, L. A. (1993) Genetics and high cognitive ability in G. Bock and K. Ackrill, (Eds.), *The origins of high ability: Proceedings of Ciba Symposium 178* (pp. 67–84). London: Wiley.

Repp, B. H. (1992) A constraint on the expressive timing of a melodic gesture: Evidence from performance and aesthetic judgment. *Music Perception,* **10**, 221–242.

Repp, B. H. (1993) Music as motion: A synopsis of Alexander Truslit's (1938) *Gestaltung und Bewegung in der Musik. Psychology of Music,* **21**, 48–72.

Revesz, C. (1970) *The psychology of a musical prodigy.* Freeport, NY: Books for Libraries Press. (Original work published 1925).

Shaffer, L. H. (1981) Performance of Chopin, Bach, and Bartok: Studies in motor programming. *Cognitive Psychology,* **13**, 326–376.

Shaffer, L. H. (1984) Timing in solo and duet piano performances. *Quarterly journal of Experimental Psychology,* **36A**, 577–595.

Sloboda, J. A. (1983) The communication of musical metre in piano performance. *Quarterly Journal of Experimental Psychology,* **35A**, 377–396.

Sloboda, J. A. (1985) Expressive skill in two pianists: Metrical communication in real and simulated performances. *Canadian Journal of Psychology,* **39**(2), 273–293.

Sloboda, J. A. (1991a) Music as a language. In F. Wilson and F. Roehmann (Eds.), *Music and child development* (pp. 28–43). St. Louis, MO: MMB Music.

Sloboda, J. A. (1991b) Musical expertise. In K. A. Ericsson and J. Smith (Eds.), *Toward a general theory of expertise: Prospects and limits* (pp. 153–171). New York: Cambridge University Press.

Sloboda, J. A. and Davidson, J. W. (1995) The young performing musician. In I. Deliège and J. A. Sloboda (Eds.), *The origins and development of musical competence* (pp. 171–190). London: Oxford University Press.

Sloboda, J., Davidson, J., and Howe, M. J. A. (1994) Is everyone musical? *The Psychologist*, **7**(8), 349–354.

Sloboda, J. A., Davidson, J. W., Howe, M. J. A., and Moore, D. C. (1996) The role of practice in the development of performing musicians. *British Journal of Psychology*, **87**, 287–309.

Sloboda, J. A., Davidson, J. W., Moore, D. C., and Howe, M. J. A. (1994) Formal practice as a predictor of success or failure in instrumental learning. In *Proceedings of the Third International Conference for Music Perception and Cognition* (pp. 125–126). University of Liège, Belgium: URFM.

Todd, N. P.M. (1992) The dynamics of dynamics: A model of musical expression. *Journal of the Acoustical Society of America*, **91**, 3540–3550.

Trehub, S. E. (1990) The perception of musical patterns by human infants: The provision of similar patterns by their parents. In M. A. Berkeley and W. C. Stebbins (Eds.), *Comparative perception: Vol. 1. Basic mechanisms* (pp. 429–59). New York: Wiley.

Welch, C. F., Howard, D. M., and Rush, C. (1989) Real-time visual feedback in the development of vocal pitch accuracy in singing. *Psychology of Music*, **17**, 146–157.

CHAPTER 17

ARE SOME CHILDREN MORE GIFTED FOR MUSIC THAN OTHERS?

17.1 Is 'talent' the best account of individual differences?

Imagine a common situation, in which a teacher gives a simple musical task to two 5-year-old children (for instance to reproduce a heard melody by singing it). Child A listens to the melody once, and then delivers a lively and accurate reproduction of it. Child B listens to the melody several times, but can only deliver a hesitant and inaccurate response. This pattern is repeated in a range of different tests. Clearly, the level of musical accomplishment of these two children is very different. How are we to explain such a difference?

It is very common for observers to invoke the notion of 'talent' or 'gift' at this point. Child A is said to musically gifted, whereas child B is not. Child A may be supposed to have a 'natural aptitude' for music, and 'inborn ability' to handle sounds. This is usually connected to the notion that such capacities are fixed and immutable. These kinds of lay explanations can then lead to prescriptions for action. For instance it may be concluded that child A will be able to profit from music instruction whereas child B will not.

It is really important to grasp that there is absolutely nothing within the performances of these two children which logically invokes explanations in term of 'talent', even if neither child has engaged in formal musical activities up to that point. The observed outcome is entirely consistent with a different explanation, in which we assume that the two children are equally 'talented', that is, they have exactly equal innate potential or aptitude for musical activity. The differences in their performances may be entirely due to differences in the knowledge-handling structures and strategies for dealing with music that they have acquired prior to testing.

Evidence for inheritance of differences in specific intellectual and mental characteristics is, in fact, very hard to find. There are clearly some specific genetic disorders which result in gross deficiencies in mental operation over a wide range of tasks. In some cases, it has been possible to identify a single gene or a small number of genes which are responsible for the disorder (e.g. Huntingdon's disease). Researchers have not yet discovered any single genes which appear to accompany exceptionally high levels of ability. It is generally believed that the neurological underpinning for complex psychological abilities is multi-genetic, that is, the result of the action of many different genes. Although some researchers (e.g. Plomin and Thompson, 1993) are confident that new genetic techniques will eventually isolate individual genes associated with high IQ, no such genes have been discovered to date.

On the other hand there is a large and growing body of evidence from a number of sources (see Storfer, 1990 for a comprehensive review) that differences in early childhood experience can have a profound effect on later cognitive functioning. These early experiences can begin before birth, because the fetal hearing system achieves some degree of maturity during the second trimester. Indeed, research by Hepper (1991) shows that specific pieces of music, played to prenatal infants through loudspeakers placed on the mother's stomach, were then subsequently recognized by the infants when played to them after birth (as evidenced by changes in their attentiveness to these pieces as compared with novel pieces). Such learning can, of course, take place naturally. Sounds at above 80 dB sound pressure level are normally audible within the uterus. If pregnant mothers sing or play instruments, then their unborn children may, therefore, be able to hear them. Loud music in the immediate environment of the mother may also be heard clearly.

Most learning experiences, however, occur after birth. In our own studies of the early lives of young musicians (Sloboda and Howe, 1991; Howe and Sloboda, 1991a; Howe et al., 1995) we have found that many, but not all, of the parents sang to their children (particularly at sleep time) every day from birth. Many also engaged in song games, encouraging children to dance and sing to music, and other kinds of informal home activities. Because these are seen by many parents as 'ordinary' activities, their importance as learning opportunities can be seriously underestimated (Papousek, 1982).

Although research on the long-term effects of early musical stimulation has not been carried out, there is good evidence for language stimulation (Whitehurst et al., 1988; Fowler, 1990). In one study, parents were asked to engage with their one- and two-year-old children in simple structured interactive language games for a few minutes each day over a period of a few months. These games included such things as naming objects and then asking the child to repeat the name. Many parents do these activities as a matter of course, and are surprised to learn that other parents almost never do these things regularly with their children. The study found that parents who did these games with their children secured substantial and long-lasting gains in the language competence of their children.

The conclusion from these studies is that very young children can receive extremely different levels of exposure to and engagement with music simply as a result of the informal musical activities of their immediate family members. By the time they start school, these differences can lead to wide disparities in ability to do a variety of musical tasks.

So far the discussion has treated young children as passive recipients of differing amounts of musical stimulation. But, of course, children are active participants in their own learning. As a result of pleasurable associations, or experiences of mastery (e.g. Renninger and Wozniak, 1985), some children will begin to seek out musical stimulation and activity in preference to other kinds of activity. They will ask for music games to be begun or continued. They will engage in spontaneous singing or dancing activities. They will ask for certain songs or records to be played over and over again. In this way, a child becomes to be seen by those around him/her as particularly sensitive to and involved in music, and therefore be considered to have a 'music oriented' personality.

Although some people like to think that a particular preference for musical sounds might be inborn in some infants, I think this is unlikely. An orientation towards sound is likely to be a universal feature of human beings when one considers its importance in early life (see, for instance, Fassbender, 1993). It seems to me much more likely that early preferences develop as a result of positive or negative experiences which incline the individual to engage or disengage from certain types of activity. These factors are essentially emotional or motivational, and I will return to discuss them in more detail in a later section. It is particularly important to realize that these positive or negative experiences can be private and unnoticed (by others). Parents may be convinced that they treated two siblings in exactly the same way, but because they cannot control every aspect of a child's experience, there is no guarantee that the two children will develop equal levels of musical skill. In fact, intra-family dynamics are often such that differences between siblings within a family can often be very marked indeed (Storfer, 1990). There is no greater fallacy than assuming that children in the same family have had the same experiences.

To summarize the argument so far, I hope I have demonstrated that it is generally impossible to conclude, from observing two children differing in musical behaviour, that they differ in musical talent, if by talent one means an inherited or inborn difference in capacity. This is true no matter how early one observes the behaviour, or what kind of behaviour it is one

observes. All 'tests' of musical 'ability' or 'aptitude' measure actual performance, not potential. It is, of course, true that well-designed tests are somewhat predictive of future achievement. But this is because those children
that are already ahead are likely to stay ahead if all other things remain
equal. If Child A knows more than Child B at time 1, and both learn equal
amounts between time 1 and time 2, then Child A will still know more
than Child B at time 2.

This is just one reason why the ascription of differences in talent tends to
become a 'self-fulfilling' prophecy. Another reason concerns the effect that
attributing 'talent' to an individual has on the beliefs and behaviours of that
individual and those that interact with him or her. Dweck and colleagues
(e.g. Dweck, 1986) have shown that children who believe intellectual
capacity to be fixed are less resistant to failure on academic tasks, and will
cease from problem-solving effort when faced with failure (the typical cognition is 'I can't do it' or 'I'm no good at maths', etc.). In contrast, children
who believe that ability can be improved through learning and effort persist
with tasks even when faced by initial failure. There is evidence (Vispoel
and Austin, 1993) that children's beliefs about musical ability have a similar
effect on their willingness to persist in solving difficult classroom musical
tasks.

A detailed investigation of motivational factors affecting musical learning
has been undertaken recently by O'Neill (O'Neill, 1996, 1997, O'Neill and
Sloboda, 1997). In this study, 50 children were tested before starting their
first instrument lesson, and then again after one year. A variety of tests of
musical and intellectual ability were administered prior to instruction. There
was also a test of 'resistance to failure'. In this, children were given a non-
musical task at which they first succeeded, then failed due to experimenter
manipulation. On a third attempt at the task, some children renewed their
efforts and improved their performance, others stopped making an effort
and their performance dropped. The first type of child was described as
having 'mastery orientation', while the second type had 'helpless orientation'. These motivational orientations did very well at predicting instrumental progress after one year. In contrast, the music and intellectual
ability measures did not predict progress at all.

It is also well established (Rosenthal and Jacobson, 1968; Brophy and
Good, 1970) that teachers' beliefs about their students abilities affect their
behaviour towards those children. When a teacher believes a child has
high potential, the teacher is more likely to set the child challenging tasks,
and encourage him/her to succeed. When a teacher believes a child has
low potential, the teacher is more likely to set the child non-challenging
tasks, and give less encouragement for high expectations. Several studies

have shown that one can improve a child's academic performance simply by giving the teacher apparently substantiated (but in fact bogus) information about the child's high academic potential.

Not only, therefore, is the ascription of differences in musical talent usually without empirical foundation or logical justification, it can actually reinforce and increase the very achievement differences upon which the original ascription was made. That being so, the most consistent and educationally sound conclusion to adhere to at the present time is that if there is such a thing as musical talent (interpreted as an inborn capacity for and predisposition towards musical activity), then it exists to equal measure in the vast majority of the population, and in no way accounts for the very wide range of adult musical accomplishment that exists in the populations of industrialized societies such as ours.

This conclusion is, I have to admit, not accepted by all researchers in the field. Debate continues to flourish, and readers interested in assessing alternative positions are referred to the sets of published commentaries on two target articles which elaborate the broad position taken here (Sloboda *et al.*, 1994; Howe *et al.*, 1998). A forceful defence of 'talent' may be found in Winner (1996).

With our conclusion in mind we can turn to a question which I believe to be much more profitable. That is, what are the psychological mechanisms that underlie musical achievements? Such psychological mechanisms taken together constitute the 'ability' of a person. I am much happier with the term 'ability' than I am with the term 'talent'. To label someone as able does not seem to me to involve any assumptions about the origins of that ability. When we understand something of the nature of musical ability we will be in a much better position to explain, predict, and bring it about (Sloboda, 1996).

17.2 The nature of musical ability

Although the term 'musical ability' is somewhat less laden with interpretation than the term 'talent', it may still presuppose too much. It suggests, for instance, that there is some common factor, or set of factors, underlying all accomplishments in the sphere of music. How does this square with the fact is that there are singers who cannot read music, pianists who cannot sing in tune, performers who cannot compose, and music critics who can neither play an instrument nor compose? Do all such people possess some common attribute in virtue of which they can be said to be musically able?

Much contemporary research on music supports the notion that there is indeed such a common attribute, which is the ability to *make sense* of musical sequences, through the mental operations that are performed on sounds (whether real or imagined). The term 'make sense' is something of an analogy. Musical idioms are not languages in the sense that they do not refer to states of affairs in the world in the way that languages like English do. They do, however, share with languages structures which resemble syntax or grammar (Lerdahl and Jackendoff, 1983). Musical ability entails the ability to detect and use these structures in the mental manipulation of music. Another term that is sometimes used for the process of making sense of music is 'audiation'.

How do we know if and when a person is 'making sense' of some music? There are a number of ways in which psychologists have operationalized this ability. First, people who are 'making sense' of music should be able to remember music which conforms to a cultural 'grammar' (e.g. diatonic tonality) better than music which does not. There are many demonstrations that this is so, and that fairly young children already show such an advantage (e.g. Zenatti, 1969; Deutsch, 1980). Similar things have been found for other skills such as chess. For instance, chess players recall meaningful (i.e. game plausible) boards better than random boards (Chase and Simon, 1973). Second, people who 'make sense' of music tend to make grammatically plausible substitutions when asked to recall music they have just heard (Sloboda and Parker, 1985; Sloboda *et al.*, 1985; Oura and Hatano, 1988). This is similar to the well-established finding that people rarely remember verbal information word-for-word, but reconstruct in their own words something that *means* the same as what they heard. This kind of finding suggests that people generally store something more abstract than the actual words or notes.

A third criterion for 'making sense' of music, is the ability to correctly judge whether or not given sequences are acceptable according to cultural rules. There is strong evidence that most children can reject blatant violations, such as discords, by the age of seven, and more subtle ones, such as unfinished cadences, by the age of ten (Sloboda, 1985). A final criterion is the ability to correctly identify the consensual mood or emotion of a musical passage. Again, we have rather strong evidence that the broad parameters of this ability are in place for most children by the age of five (Pinchot-Kastner and Crowder, 1990; Terwogt and Van Grinsven, 1991).

Although people vary quite widely in the level of sophistication to which they have developed their ability to make sense of music, the available evidence points to the conclusion that the vast majority of the population have acquired a common ability to make sense of music, clearly evident through experimental demonstrations such as the ones described above, by the age of 10, regardless of accomplishment in any particular sphere of musical performance, and regardless of having been in receipt of any formal musical education or training.

This is quite an important conclusion to bear in mind, because most people think of specific performance skills, like being able to sing or play the piano, as being the principal signs of ability. These are the kinds of skills that tend to be most often addressed, noticed, and assessed in formal education. My point is that these specific visible performance skills usually rest on previously acquired but 'hidden' receptive skills. If we return to the two hypothetical children discussed in the opening section of this chapter, we can see that it is quite possible that both children are equally 'able' (same level of ability to 'make sense' of the music) but perform differently because child A has had specific singing-related experiences which child B has not had. In this case, appropriate singing experience should help child B catch up with child A. On the other hand, child B may do less well than child A because she has not acquired the 'ability' (cognitive procedures) necessary to make sense of the music. In this case, specific singing experience may not allow child B to catch up with child A, because the deficit is at a more fundamental level. I believe that it may sometimes be this latter case that persuades teachers and parents that there are differences in 'talent' between two children. The argument of this section is that these differences should more properly be seen as differences of ability, susceptible to reduction or removal by appropriate learning. It is simply that the kind of learning required in the two cases is different.

All of the preceding argument does not mean, of course, that no genetic factors are ever important in the growth of musical ability and achievement. Operatic singers require certain vocal tract characteristics which affect resonance and quality. Much piano repertoire demands a large hand span. Sometimes children who have good voices may be labelled as 'gifted' even when their musical ability is not high. This may lead to the kinds of life experiences which eventually produce high levels of musical ability. But having a good voice is not, in itself, any indication of musical ability, any more than possessing a Stradivarius will of itself turn an indifferent violinist into a good one.

17.3 The acquisition of musical ability

What features of music and the human mental apparatus make it possible for most people to acquire a basic level of musical receptive ability without formal training? There is broad agreement between music theorists and psychologists (e.g. Meyer, 1956; Deutsch, 1982; Lerdahl, 1988; Bregman, 1990; Narmour, 1990; Huron, 1991) that the most prevalent musical idioms have structural and mathematical properties that are easily picked up by basic perceptual mechanisms that are built in to the 'hard-wiring' of the brain. These properties include repetition and grouping according to pitch or duration. Contemporary theories of learning applied to music (e.g. the 'connectionist' models of Bharucha, 1987 and Gjerdingen, 1990) have demonstrated how quite complex mental representations may be built up from such basic processes as a result simply of repeated exposure to a variety of musical examples sharing similar structures. These representations will include knowledge of what we would describe as scale or tonality, such that pairs of sequences like C–D–E–F–G and F–G–A–B–C will be detected by the system as 'the same' (i.e. both scale sequences in the key of C-major) even though their intervallic and physical characteristics are different. The sophistication of the patterns that the system can match in some way will be a direct function of the number and range of musical examples to which it has been exposed. In human terms this could come about by precisely the differing levels of childhood experiences discussed in Section 17.1. The more sophisticated the system, the better 'sense' it makes of a wider range of musical material. Through learning of this sort, a basic and universal system is transformed into a culturally tailored system that reflects and responds best to the music in the surrounding environment of the individual. This allows us to understand why it is that people find it hard to make initial sense of music from other cultures. For instance, most Westerners find it hard to reproduce melodies of Indian or Arabic origin, which are built on different scale systems.

We also have the beginnings of an understanding of how the confirmation and violation of expectations built up within such a system may lead to the experience of emotion and mood to music. Many emotions to music seem to be responses to various kinds of surprise within the harmonic or rhythmic structure (Meyer, 1956; Jackendoff, 1991; Narmour, 1991; Sloboda, 1991a).

17.4 Performance ability

The foregoing discussion should have helped to make it clear that there are several distinct abilities involved in performing a musical instrument, and only some of them are 'musical' in the sense we have been discussing. The other abilities are what I would call 'technical'. For instance, a pianist may be able to play a difficult passage very quickly, very evenly, and very accurately. This will be possible because of very highly developed control systems for execution of hand and finger movements. Such systems will have required much practice to develop to high levels, and are manifestations of expertise. It is, however, possible that a person could learn to play a piece of music 'technically' without having 'understood it' musically at all. Such a 'technically perfect' performance is one that could equally well be generated by mechanical means.

It is well-established that notationally 'perfect' performances of music are experienced by most listeners as dull, mechanical and uninteresting. What makes any performance musically interesting are the slight fluctuations in duration, loudness, pitch, and timbre which together constitute *expressive performance* (see Chapter 9). Such fluctuations are what distinguish one performance from another, and their importance is what keeps professional performers in business. Were it not for this, we could get computers to generate once-and-for-all perfect performances of musical works, and close most of our symphony halls and conservatories!

Recent research has made it increasingly clear that the existence of expressive performance is the best evidence we can obtain that a musician *understands* the music she is playing. This is because expressive variations are by no means random or idiosyncratic. A wide range of studies (e.g. Shaffer, 1981; Sloboda, 1983; Clarke, 1988; Gabrielsson, 1988) has shown that microvariations are highly systematic, both within the same performer and across different performers. Many of such variations are designed to make important structural features of the music more prominent to the listener. Their systematicity therefore depends upon the performer having understood what *are* the important structures. The most convincing evidence that this understanding is deeply rooted in a performer may well be to ask that performer to sight-read some music she has never seen before. If she can apply appropriate expression in such a situation, then her understanding must be fully internalized. In contrast, in a rehearsed performance there always exists the remote possibility that expressive devices have been learned 'by rote' without any real understanding. Evidence of expressively appropriate sight-reading does indeed exist (Sloboda, 1983), and it is very often so deeply internalized that the performer is not fully aware of the details of her own expressive repertoire. It has become intuitive and semi-automatic. This should not surprise us. It is another well-documented characteristic of all cognitive expertise. Many people mistakenly assume that intuitive behaviour must be innate. This is a major fallacy. Any well-practised habit eventually becomes automatic.

It may seem at first sight that the statement that expression is systematic conflicts with the existence of interesting differences between performers. The conflict is, however, more apparent than real. Performers differ from one another, not so much in the nature of expressive devices used, but in their distribution and intensity. So, for instance, one performer may achieve by subtle dynamic fluctuations what another one achieves by temporal fluctuations. Such differences between performers, or between the same performer at different times, can be characterized as differences in expressive 'style' (Sloboda, 1985).

Because high-level musical performance has this dual technical–expressive aspect, the conditions for the development of expert performers must allow development on both fronts. This is quite difficult to achieve. There are many music professionals who are technically adept but lack a high level of expressive skill. There are also many non-professionals who have a high level of expressive insight, but cannot realize their expressive intentions in music of any technical complexity. The master-performer is that relatively rare person who has managed to develop both technical and expressive skills to a high level in tandem. How is it done?

17.5 Making the expert performer

We now have evidence from a number of biographically based research studies (Sosniak, 1985; Sloboda and Howe, 1991; Ericsson *et al.*, 1993; Sloboda *et al.*, 1996) that confirm that music is no exception to the general rule 'practice makes perfect'. The study of Ericsson *et al.* shows that student violinists rated as excellent by their professors have, by the age of 21, accumulated on average around twice as many hours of practice over the lifespan (10 000 hours) as more average players (5000 hours). These data were obtained from a study where violinists were asked to estimate retrospectively the average number of hours per week of practice for each year of their life. For the current year these data were confirmed by practice diaries kept by all participants.

Sosniak, in a study of 24 top US pianists, showed that none of them showed particular signs of exceptional ability at the outset of training. Exceptionality was something which developed gradually through the early years of formal training. Indeed, the notion that very early achievement is the normal precursor of adult excellence finds very little support in the documented research literature. The 'child prodigy' may be the exception rather than the norm.

Sloboda *et al.* (1996) extended the generality of the above findings by obtaining practice data from various categories of young musician, from the highly able to the least able. Their data showed that rate of progress (as measured through objective examination scores) was entirely a function of the number of hours of practice undertaken. A common belief held by teachers and parents is that 'talented' children can achieve a given level of performance after less practice than 'untalented' children. The data from this study firmly refute this idea. Able musicians achieve more because they practise more. For instance, at age 12, the children who were most advanced were practising on average for 120 minutes per day. The children who were least advanced at the same age were achieving average daily practice of only 15 minutes. This represents an 800% difference between the best and worst players. No wonder the able performers did so well!

It is not very easy for a young person to accumulate 10 000 hours of practice between starting an instrument (typically around the age of 6 or 7 at the earliest) and the age of 21. To give some idea of the workload that implies, it would require 2 hours every day of the year for 14 years to accumulate 10 000 hours of practice. In reality, the typical 'expert' practice pattern begins with 15–30 minutes per day, and increases to 4–6 hours per day by the age of 21. Practice activities are not always inherently rewarding to young children, and even the most able young musicians often required parental support, even direct supervision, to accomplish regular practice (Sloboda and Howe, 1991; Davidson *et al.*, 1996).

Indeed, the quality of the child's relationship with significant adults, both parents and teachers, appears crucial in predicting long-term involvement with musical performance. The parents or high achievers are characterized by a very high level of involvement in their children's musical life. In addition, students tend to remember their first teachers, not so much for their technical adeptness, as for the fact that they made lessons fun. They communicated both their love of music and their liking for their pupil. Personal warmth seems an important characteristic. Critical, confrontational, or achievement-oriented approaches, seems not to be successful, at least in the early stages of learning (Davidson *et al.*, 1998).

Of course, sheer amount of practice is a rather crude measure from a psychological point of view. The nature of learning will depend on what is done during practice as well as how much of it is done. Surprisingly, there is little reliable scientific information on how musicians practise (what exists is well summarized by Hallam, 1997). One clear finding is that experienced performers pay more attention to structural matters when practising. Clearly, since expressive performance is closely related to the detailed structure of a composition, practice that shows awareness of structural factors is more likely to lead to the development of an appropriate expressive repertoire.

17.6 Emotion and motivation

There is a considerable body of evidence that there are two types of motivation to engage with music. One motivation is what one might call 'intrinsic'. It develops from intense pleasurable experiences with music (of a sensual, aesthetic, or emotional kind) which lead to a deep personal commitment to music. The other motivation is what one might call 'extrinsic', and is concerned with achievement. Here, the focus is not so much on the music itself as on achieving certain goals (e.g. approval of parents, identification with role models, winning competitions). Clearly any one individual will have a mixture of both types of motivation. There is some evidence, however, that too early an emphasis on achievement can inhibit intrinsic motivation. In simple terms, children become so concerned about what others may be thinking of their performance, that they have little attention left for the potential of the music to engage their aesthetic and emotional sensibilities deeply. All music becomes a source of anxiety.

This conclusion is supported by a study of autobiographical memories (Sloboda, 1990). In this study, musician and non-musician adults were asked to recall events from the first 10 years of life that had any connection at all with music. They were given a number of questions to stimulate recall, such as where the event took place, what event the music was part of, who they were with, and what significance the experience had for them. The 113 'stories' obtained in this way could be classified along two dimensions. One related to the 'internal' significance of the event, that significance which was attributed to the music itself. The other related to the 'external' significance, attributable to the context. In each case the value of the dimension could be positive, neutral, or negative.

Many of the musicians reported deeply felt and intensely positive early experiences to the 'internal' aspect of musical events, which seemed to lift them outside the normal state of awareness. For instance, one young woman reminisced as follows:

> I was seven years old, and sitting in morning assembly in school. The music formed part of the assembly service. I was with my friends Karen, Amelia, Jenny, Allan. The music was a clarinet duet, classical, probably by Mozart. I was astounded at the beauty of the sound. It was liquid, resonant, vibrant. It seemed to send tingles through me. I felt as if it was a significant moment. Listening to this music led to me learning to play first the recorder and then to achieve my ambition of playing the clarinet. Playing the clarinet has altered my life; going on a paper round and saving up to buy my own clarinet; meeting friends in the county band. . . . Whenever I hear clarinets being played I remember the impact of this first experience.

Others, more often the non-musicians, recalled events where the music itself was not remembered as significant in itself, but rather its context, which was often one of anxiety, humiliation, or embarrassment.

Being made to perform in front of other, being criticized, being laughed at, were common experiences. In almost every mixed audience where I report these results, a large proportion of the non-musicians identify just such experiences which they believe turned them away from music and persuaded them that they were not 'musical'. In almost none of these cases was the person able to experience the music as a source of positive significance.

Frequency analyses of the subcomponents of the stories showed three factors which were statistically associated with positive internal experiences:

- the event occurred at home, in church, or at a concert hall, rather than at school
- the event occurred while the child was listening rather than performing
- the child was on his/her own, with family or friends, rather than with a teacher.

In each case, these conditions seem to be connected with lack of expectation of or assessment of the child, but rather a relaxed, non-threatening environment where nothing is being asked of the child. Perhaps such an environment is necessary for music to work its strongest effects on individuals.

These deeply positive 'peak' childhood experiences seem important for the development of musical ability for two reasons. First, these experiences are so pleasurable that children often increase their engagement with music in the hope of repeating them. Second, these experiences seem to be intimately connected to the person's understanding of the musical structures which are crucial to performance expression. Sloboda (1991a) has shown that adult music listeners identify many of their moments of most intense emotional response with quite specific musical structures such as appogiaturas or enharmonic changes. These structures are ones which manipulate listener's expectancies in some way. Unless one has experienced the 'delicious' surprise of an enharmonic change through listening, it is hard to see how one could effectively add the appropriate performance expression to such a change to heighten its effect for listeners (such expression might arguably be a slight slowing which delays and emphasizes the onset of the unexpected chord). Experience must precede performance. Children who are focusing emotional attention on the performance and other extrinsic factors rather than on the music itself may not be able to build the structure–emotion links that are the key to spontaneous expressive playing.

It seems that our society, particularly, our system of formal education, is set up to produce anxiety and self-doubt rather than love of music. What may be needed to remedy that is the rehabilitation of the notion that, in the sphere of music if nowhere else, deep emotional experiences and sensual enjoyment are as important and valid as hard work and technical achievement. One of the reasons why music seems to be seen by many children as an essentially female activity may be the strong male conditioning against emotional display, which is fully present by the age of 6 or 7 in most male cultures. One of the unexpected findings of Sloboda and Howe's study was the huge sense of relief and safety felt particularly by some boys, when they were able to get to a specialist music school where music was at last seen as a quite normal activity for boys, and where they could escape the mockery and misunderstanding of their peers (Howe and Sloboda, 1991b).

If school experiences are such strong inhibitors of musicality for many children, this may go a long way to explain why so few children ever reach high levels of performance ability. Children who succeed may well be the children who had lucky early experiences, supportive rather than undermining musical relationships, and encouragement of musical autonomy and feeling. It is salutary to remember that many excellent musicians received little or no formal training at all (see for example Collier's (1983) detailed description of Louis Armstrong's acquisition of jazz skill, summarized and commented on by Sloboda, 1991b), and that many young people develop considerable expertise as popular musicians with little or no help from their classically trained teachers. There also exist many cultures, especially traditional non-Western cultures, where the spread of musical accomplishment in the population is much more even than it is in modern industrialized cultures. In such cultures, participation in musical activity is often more rooted in the whole everyday life and work of the community, rather than being conceived of as something separate or special (e.g. Blacking, 1976).

Finally, there is considerable evidence that children are very aware of the associations of different types of music with social group identity. Very often schools present children with the notion that classical music is superior to the popular and folk idioms with which they more naturally identify, and with which they have the greatest experience. Children can both reject classical music as 'too highbrow' and also become intimidated by the apparent requirement to step outside what seems comfortable and familiar before they can produce 'acceptable' music. Most teachers are aware of the child who presents as incompetent in singing class, but can be found the same day in the school bus joining in an informal 'sing-along' session with competence and enthusiasm. There are strong social pressures from peers to conform to the norm and hide a potential liking for music which is 'different' (Finnas, 1987). This means that teachers need to introduce music through, rather than in opposition to, the cultural musical norms of their students.

17.7 From able child to able adult

Most of what we have discussed to this point relates to the development of musical ability through childhood into adolescence. Many promising adolescents never, however, reach the highest levels of musical excellence. Some of these are 'happy' drop-outs, individuals who have many other interests and skills and are not prepared to make the level of commitment required for a professional music career. They are content to remain as proficient amateurs. Others drop out as part of the process of developing self-knowledge and autonomy. They realize that their parents' investment in their musical development has always been considerably greater than their own and that they have never really acquired their own individual commitment to music. A third group (described in some detail by Bamberger, 1986) are those who experience a difficult transition from the unreflexive and intuitive modes of musical thinking characteristic of children to the more analytical and self-critical modes of adult thinking where what once seemed easy now appears to 'fall apart' and become problematic.

Among those who continue to higher levels of training, the most success-ful musicians appear to be those with the highest levels of commitment and self-discipline. The best violinists in Ericsson *et al.*'s (1993) study were those who practised regularly every morning at the same time, spent more time in daytime sleeping or 'napping', particularly in the afternoon (arguably needed to recover from the effortful activity of practice) and spent least time on leisure activities.

A study by Manturszewska (1990) suggests that a further precondition of transition to musical maturity is the existence of a deep and significant 'master–student' relationship with a respected older professional, very often the student's instrumental teacher. Even at this relatively late stage the relationship is concerned with more than technical and performance development. It is a relationship of personal involvement which often leads to lifelong friendship. The existence of a older and more well-connected 'mentor' has been observed in many other fields of creative and profes-sional endeavour as a frequent accompaniment to the highest levels of achievement. The development of such relationships seems to depend, in part, on the stability of the student's relationship with his or her own parents (Butler, 1993). Where parents have been over-critical and under-supportive, students tend to be fearful of their teachers and project onto them the role of 'punishing parent' in a way which undermines the possibility of healthy 'mentor' relationships developing.

17.8 Conclusions

I hope that this chapter has provided the basis of possible answers to the kinds of question that lay people often pose to psychologists. Individual differences, even within families, are easily accounted for by individual differences in experience, leading to different motivations and learning outcomes. No family can provide the 'same' environment for two siblings. Indeed the mere fact that one sibling takes up music may incline the other sibling not to.

It is impossible to accurately predict the future musical achievement of a given child from its behaviour at age 5. Much depends on the circumstances in which music is introduced and how parents and teachers handle the musical relationship. Although there may be a statistical correlation between early and later achievement in the population as a whole, this should not be taken as a deterministic causal relationship.

What we can say with some certainty is that there are a set of circumstances which will increase the chances of attainment of high levels of excellence. These are, early and frequent casual exposure to the music of a culture, opportunities to engage with this music in a relaxed enjoyable environment without performance expectations, early positive encouragement from parents and teachers to engage in musical activity but respect for the child's own autonomy and explorations, a balance between technical and expressive activities, an increasing commitment to high levels of time investment in practice, and the eventual commitment to excellence in the context of a supportive and long-lasting 'master–student' relationship.

This picture contradicts three deeply ingrained cultural myths. The first myth is that musical achievement depends upon the pre-existence of a rare inherited quality 'talent'. I have argued instead that it builds on a basic aptitude which is shared by almost all human beings. The second myth is that musical excellence grows from within by solitary effort. The studies summarized here emphasize the social nature of musical development, in which the achievement of one is the result of effort by many. The third myth is that work and pleasure are separate. The evidence I have outlined here suggests that unless one gains and retains deep pleasure in music throughout the years of learning, the pinnacles of expressive performance will always remain out of reach.

References

Bamberger, J. (1986) Cognitive issues in the development of musically gifted children. In R. J. Sternberg and J. E. Davidson (Eds.) *Conceptions of Giftedness*. Cambridge: Cambridge University Press.

Bharucha, J. J. (1987) Music cognition and perceptual facilitation: a connectionist framework. *Music Perception*, **5**, 1–30.

Blacking, J. (1976) *How Musical is Man?* London: Faber.

Bregman, A. S. (1990) *Auditory Scene Analysis: the perceptual organisation of sound*. Cambridge, MA.: MIT Press.

Brophy, J. E. and Good, T. L. (1970) Teachers, communication of differential expectations for children's classroom performance: some behavioural data. *Journal of Educational Psychology*, **61**, 365–74.

Butler, C. (1993) The effects of psychological stress on the success and failure of music conservatoire students. MPhil Thesis: University of Keele, England.

Chase, W. G. and Simon, H. A. (1973) Perception in chess. *Cognitive Psychology*, **4**, 55–81.

Clarke, E. F. (1988) Generative principles in music performance. In J. A. Sloboda (Ed.) *Generative Processes in Music: the psychology of performance, improvisation, and composition*. London: Oxford University Press.

Collier, J. L. (1983) *Louis Armstrong: An American genius*. New York: Oxford University Press.

Davidson, J. W., Howe, M. J. A., Moore, D. G., and Sloboda, J. A. (1996) The role of parental influences in the development of musical ability. *British Journal of Developmental Psychology*, **14**, 399–412.

Davidson, J. W., Sloboda, J. A., Moore, D. G., and Howe, M. J. A. (1998) Characteristics of music teachers and the progress of young instrumentalists. *Journal of Research in Music Education*, **46.1**, 141–160.

Deutsch, D. (1980) The processing of structured and unstructured tonal sequences. *Perception and Psychophysics*, **23**, 215–218.

Deustch, D. (1982) Grouping mechanisms in music. In D. Deutsch (Ed.) *The Psychology of Music*. New York: Academic Press.

Dweck, C. S. (1986) Motivational processes affecting learning. *American Psychologist*, **41**, 1040–1048.

Ericsson, K. A., Krampe, R. T., and Tesch-Romer, C. (1993) The role of deliberate practice in the acquisition of expert performance. *Psychological Review*, **100.3**, 363–406.

Fassbender, C. (1993) *Auditory Grouping and Segregation Processes in Infancy*. Norderstedt: Kaste Verlags.

Finnas, L. (1987) Do young people misjudge each other's musical tastes? *Psychology of Music*, **15**, 152–166.

Fowler, W. (1990) Early stimulation and the development of verbal talents. In M. J. A. Howe (Ed.) *Encouraging the Development of Exceptional Skills and Talents.* Leicester: BPS Books.

Gabrielsson, A. (1988) Timing in music performance and its relations to music experience. In J. A. Sloboda (Ed.) *Generative Processes in Music: the psychology of performance, improvisation, and composition.* London: Oxford University Press.

Gjerdingen, R. O. (1990) Categorization of musical patterns by self-organizing neuronlike networks. *Music Perception, 7,* 339–369.

Hallam, S. (1997) What do we know about practising? Towards a model synthesising the research literature. In H. Jorgensen and A. C. Lehmann (Eds.). *Does Practice Make Perfect? Current theory and research on instrumental and music practice.* Oslo: Norges Musikkhogskole, pp. 53–70.

Hepper, P. G. (1991) An examination of fetal learning before and after birth. *Irish Journal of Psychology, 12,* 95–107.

Howe, M. J. A. and Sloboda, J. A. (1991a) Young musicians' accounts of significant influences in their early lives: 1. the family and the musical background. *British Journal of Music Education, 8,* 39–52.

Howe, M. J. A. and Sloboda, J.A. (1991b) Problems experienced by young musicians as a result of the failure of other children to value musical accomplishments. *Gifted Education, 8,* 102–111.

Howe, M. J., A., Davidson, J. W., Moore, D. G., and Sloboda, J. A. (1995) Are there early childhood signs of musical ability? *Psychology of Music, 23,* 162–176.

Howe, M. J. A., Davidson, J. W., and Sloboda, J. A. (1998) Innate talent: reality or myth? *Behavioural and Brain Sciences, 21.3,* 399–442.

Huron, D. (1991) The avoidance of part-crossing in polyphonic music: perceptual evidence and musical practice. *Music Perception, 9,* 93–104.

Jackendoff, R. (1991) Musical parsing and musical affect. *Music Perception, 9,* 199–230.

Lerdahl, F. (1988) Cognitive constraints on compositional systems. In J. A. Sloboda (Ed.) *Generative Processes in Music: the psychology of performance, improvisation, and composition.* London: Oxford University Press.

Lerdahl, F. and Jackendoff, R. (1983) *A Generative Theory of Tonal Music.* Cambridge, MA: MIT Press.

Manturszewska, M. (1990) A biographical study of the life-span development of professional musicians. *Psychology of Music, 18,* 112–139.

Meyer, L. B. (1956) *Emotion and Meaning in Music.* Chicago: University of Chicago Press.

Narmour, E. (1990) *The Analysis and Cognition of Basic Melodic Structures: the implication-realisation model.* Chicago: University of Chicago Press.

Narmour, E. (1991) The top-down and bottom-up systems of musical implication: building on Meyer's theory of emotional syntax. *Music Perception, 9,* 1–26.

Oura, Y. and Hatano, G. (1988) Memory for melodies among subjects differing in age and experience in music. *Psychology of Music*, **16**, 91–109.

O'Neill, S. A. (1996) Factors influencing children's motivation and achievement during the first year of instrumental music tuition. Unpublished PhD Thesis, Keele University, UK.

O'Neill, S. A. (1997) The role of practice in children's early musical performance achievement. In H. Jorgensen and A. C. Lehmann (Eds.). *Does Practice Make Perfect? Current theory and research on instrumental and music practice*. Oslo: Norges Musikkhogskole, pp. 53–70.

O'Neill, S. A. and Sloboda, J. A. (1997) The effects of failure on children's ability to perform a musical test. *Psychology of Music*, **35.1**, 18–34.

Papousek, M. (1982) The 'mother tongue method' of music education: psychobiological roots in oroverbal parent-infant communication. In J. Dobbs (Ed.). *International Music Education*. ISME Yearbook 1982.

Pinchot-Kastner, M. and Crowder, R.G. (1990) Perception of the major/minor distinction: IV. Emotional connotations in young children. *Music Perception*, **8**, 189–202.

Plomin, R. and Thompson, L. A. (1993) Genetics and high cognitive ability. In K. Ackrill (Ed.) *The Origins and Development of High Ability: Proceedings of Ciba Symposium 178*. London: Wiley.

Renninger, K. A. and Wozniak, R. N. (1985) Effect of interest on attentional shift, recognition and recall in young children. *Developmental Psychology*, **21**, 624–632.

Rosenthal, R. and Jacobsen, L. (1968) *Pygmalion in the Classroom: teacher expectation and pupil's intellectual development*. New York: Holt, Rinehart and Winston.

Shaffer, L. H. (1981) Performances of Chopin, Bach, and Bartok: studies in motor programming. *Cognitive Psychology*, **13**, 326–376.

Sloboda, J. A. (1983) The communication of musical metre in piano performance. *Quarterly Journal of Experimental Psychology*, **35A**, 377–396.

Sloboda, J. A. (1985) Expressive skill in two pianists: style and effectiveness in music performance. *Canadian Journal of Psychology*, **39**, 273–293.

Sloboda, J. A. (1990) Music as a language. In F. Wilson and F. Roehmann (Eds.) *Music and child development*. St. Louis, MI: MMB Inc.

Sloboda, J. A. (1991a) Music structure and emotional response: some empirical findings. *Psychology of Music*, **19**, 110–120.

Sloboda, J. A. (1991b) Musical expertise. In K. A. Ericsson and J. Smith (Eds.) *Toward a General Theory of Expertise: prospects and limits*. New York: Cambridge University Press.

Sloboda, J. A. (1996) The acquisition of musical performance expertise: deconstructing the 'talent' account of individual differences in musical expressivity. In K. A. Ericsson (Ed.) *The Road to Excellence: the acquisition of expert performance in the arts and sciences, sports and games.* Mahwah, NJ: Lawrence Erlbaum Associates, pp. 107–126.

Sloboda, J. A. and Howe, M. J. A. (1991) Biographical precursors of musical excellence: an interview study. *Psychology of Music,* **19,** 3–21.

Sloboda, J. A. and Parker, D. H. H. (1985) Immediate recall of melodies. In Howell, P., Cross, I., and West R (eds) *Musical Structure and Cognition.* London: Academic Press.

Sloboda, J. A., Davidson, J. W., and Howe, M. J. A. (1994) Is everyone musical? *The Psychologist,* **7.7,** 349–354.

Sloboda, J. A., Hermelin, B., and O'Connor, N. (1985) An exceptional musical memory. *Music Perception,* **3,** 155–170.

Sloboda, J. A., Davidson, J. W., Howe, M. J. A., and Moore, D. G. (1996) The role of practice in the development of expert musical performance. *British Journal of Psychology.* **87,** 287–309.

Sosniak, L. A. (1985) Learning to be a concert pianist. In B. S. Bloom (Ed.) *Developing Talent in Young People.* New York: Ballantine.

Storfer, M. D. (1990) *Intelligence and Giftedness: the contributions of heredity and early environment.* San Francisco: Jossey Bass.

Terwogt, M. M. and Van Grinsven, F. (1991) Musical expression of moodstates. *Psychology of Music,* **19,** 99–109.

Vispoel, W. P. and Austin, J. R. (1993) Constructive response to failure in music: the role of attribution feedback and classroom goal structure. *British Journal of Educational Psychology,* **63,** 110–129.

Whitehurst, G. J., Falco, F. L., Lonigan, C. J., Fischel, J. E., DeBaryshe, B. D., Valdez-Menchaca, M. C., and Caulfield, M. (1988) Accelerating language development through picture book learning. *Developmental Psychology,* **24,** 552–559.

Winner, E. (1996) *Gifted Children: myths and realities.* New York: Basic Books.

Zenatti, A. (1969) Le developpement genetique de la perception musicale. *Monographs Français Psychologique,* **17.**

MUSIC IN THE REAL WORLD

CHAPTER 18

EVERYDAY USES OF MUSIC LISTENING: A PRELIMINARY STUDY

18.1 Introduction and research background

There exists a particular attitude to music listening which implicitly dominates much psychological theorizing and experimentation in the study of individual response to music. This is what the author has caricatured (Sloboda, 1989) as the *pharmaceutical* model. Listeners are construed as passive recipients of musical stimuli which have the psychological effect they do because of the way the human brain is constructed on the one hand, and the way the music is structured on the other. Although almost all psychologists would reject the crudest versions of this model (for instance, by stressing effects of experience and learning on listener response) dominant research practices nonetheless perpetuate key assumptions of this model. For instance, most studies of music listening present listeners with music which is not of their choosing in an environment (the laboratory) which is controlled and constructed by the experimenter.

The pharmaceutical approach may be one of the reasons for the particularly slow progress made in the scientific understanding of emotional and aesthetic response to music. Laboratory studies which show, for instance, that most listeners within a given culture will agree which adjectives, from a large checklist, best describe the emotional character (or their aesthetic evaluation) of a particular piece or performance, may have been used to draw over-strong inferences about how musical stimuli mediate affective and evaluative responses (Gabrielsson and Juslin, 1996; Hevner, 1936; Scherer and Oshinsky, 1977). It might be that, in some other listening context, quite different forms of consistency are obtained, or that consistency breaks down altogether.

This paper takes a diametrically opposite position to the pharmaceutical one, and emphasizes the role of the listener as an active agent, who makes choices about what music to listen to, where and when to listen to it, and what to listen for, according to needs, goals, and purposes. Music listening is, thus, intensely situational. One cannot begin to give a full account of the cognitive, affective, or aesthetic response of a listener, without paying detailed attention to the reasons why the person is listening to that particular music at that particular time (indeed, we also need a much fuller characterization of different *types* of listening that might be going on in different people in different contexts). Some recent psychological research has begun to acknowledge the importance of situation to musical response. For example, the work of North and Hargreaves (1996, 1997) shows how people's liking of and preference for different types of music is influenced by the activity which the music is accompanying (e.g. aerobics versus meditation). One could, however, go well beyond this, and surmise that the situation can determine, in a much more fundamental way, what it is that the listener hears in or extracts from the music.

Since the seminal work of Bourdieu (1984) it is generally accepted within the field of popular culture studies that consumers of cultural products appropriate these products to support their social identities, lifestyles, and personal purposes. These appropriations can be quite different from those predicted or planned for by producers and retailers (as is evident, for instance, in the account of the Sony Walkman's appropriation given by du Gay *et al.* 1997). In the light of this, it is somewhat surprising that theories of appropriation are typically supported by rather thin data-sets, relying on journalism or anecdote at worst, or a small number of in-depth case studies at best.

As far as we are aware, the 'functional terrain' of music listening situations has not yet been systematically mapped within contemporary Western culture. It is a curious paradox that we probably know (through the work of anthropologists and ethnomusicologists) more about the different purposes for which music is used within certain non-Western societies than we do about how it is used in western consumer societies (see, for example, Gregory, 1997). Only music performance seems to have attracted any significant and comprehensive work (Finnegan, 1989).

Nonetheless, some strands of psychological work provide some pointers regarding possible functions of music listening for particular people and situations. For instance, both Gabrielsson and Lindstrom (1996) and Sloboda (1992) have collected data on strong experiences to music, and have established a range of mood-altering functions that could be generally classified as therapeutic. Behne (1997) has shown that adolescents reporting high frequency of personal problems also report higher frequency of listening to music as some kind of escape (a classification described as 'sentimental'). Music is also used to reinforce social identities, a phenomenon particularly commented on in adolescence (Zillman and Gan, 1997).

The present study provides preliminary groundwork for a planned large-scale investigation into everyday uses of music.

18.2 Pilot tests

Some suggestive data has been obtained in two unpublished student projects supervised by the author (Neilly, 1995, De Las Heras, 1997). Neilly (1995) asked 20 undergraduate students to keep a diary of each time they exposed themselves to music by their own choice over a period of three days. She found that 60% of the sample used music to wake up/get up in the morning, 50% used music while they studied, 40% used music while they got ready to go out in the evening, and 30% used it at night to relax/go to sleep. Although it offers some suggestive pointers, this small sample of undergraduate students obviously cannot be taken to be representative of the population.

De Las Heras (1997) asked 82 music listeners to complete a comprehensive questionnaire about their use of records, tapes, CDs and radio in the home. The study included 45 Likert-scale items probing reasons and contexts for music use, which had been generated from a range of sources including intensive interviews. These items were factor analysed, and the six factors accounting for the greatest amount of the variance (50% in total) are listed in Table 18.1, with example items. The factor names are those suggested by De Las Heras on examination of the items contained within each factor, and should not be taken as definitive.

These factors and their associated items illustrate the way in which music listening behaviours are ranged along a particularly important dimension, that of control (related to choice and autonomy). For instance,

Table 18.1 Principal factors influencing music use (De Las Heras, 1997)

Factor name	% of variance	Example of item
Energy use	15	I use music to sing along to while I am tidying up the house
Transcendent	12	This music connects me with a higher self
Memory	7	I want to reminisce about times associated with earlier listening
Analytical	6	I like experiencing how the different parts of the music are put together
Radio	5	I like the radio because it is unpredictable: you don't know what will follow
Compensation	5	I play this type of music to get rid of negative moods

the sample item shown in Table 18.1 for the 'energy use' factor requires that the music being listened to is known by the listener (otherwise how can she sing along to it?), and has certain speed and rhythm characteristics that are compatible with the bodily movement of housework. This means that the listener must make very definite choices about the precise track to accompany such activity. Similar considerations come into play in the 'memory' factor, for obvious reasons. on the other hand the 'radio' factor suggests a desire to reduce control and choice. It is the surprise of someone else's choice which is valued, although even here the listener must exercise some choice (for instance, in choosing one station rather than another). It is also interesting to note that 'analytical' hearing, which corresponds most closely to the type of structure-based listening which is assumed to be necessary for serious 'high-art' appreciation, is only one of a wide range of listening modes employed by this group of self-defined music-lovers. Although this sample of listeners was more broadly based than Neilly's, they were still self-selected as regular music listeners with substantial CD collections. Their music-listening behaviours could arguably be both more specialized and more differentiated than an unselected sample of the population.

18.3 The Mass-Observation project

Since 1981, Sussex University has involved around 500 British people in an ongoing recording of their everyday lives (Sheridan, 1998). Participants are recruited through media advertisements, and agree to respond by post to a set of questions mailed about three times each year. Correspondents are encouraged to write in a free and open-ended fashion, answering those questions which most engage them. All the writers are volunteers and therefore self-selected. Women outnumber men by 3 to 1, and there is a preponderance of people over 40. Table 18.2 shows the list of general topics on which panel members were asked to write in 1995–1998. Respondents are encouraged to write to their Mass-Observation contact in personal letter, like a friend. All material is confidential, and cannot be removed from the archive. The archive has thus collected a uniquely broad picture of the views and experiences of individual citizens, offering many untapped opportunities for comparisons across different domains of activity.

The Autumn 1997 mailing focused on music. Although the overall style and presentation of questions was determined by Mass-Observation staff, the present author played a major role in determining the music questions and their areas of investigation. The overarching question was 'Please could

Table 18.2 Topics of Mass-Observation mailings in 1995–1998

1995	Daily meals
	The countryside
	TV soap operas
	Shopping
	Images of where you live
	Mothers and literacy
1996	The National Lottery
	Beef: BSE and the 'mad cow' debate
	The supernatural
	Using the telephone
	Unpaid work
	The next general election
1997	You and the National Health Service
	Doing a job
	Being overweight
	The death of Princess Diana
	Music
	Dancing
1998	The garden and gardening
	Having an affair

you tell us all about you and music'. All other questions were optional cues to focus correspondents on areas they might like to talk about. This paper looks in particular detail at two areas, which represent the extremes of the control/autonomy dimension identified by De Las Heras (1997): (1) personal use as chosen by the participant; and (1) non-chosen music experienced by the participant in public places. The key cues were (1) 'Do you use music in different ways? My mother used to play fast Greek music to get her going with the housework—do you have habits like this? Are they linked to particular times, places, activities or moods? For instance, you might use music in different ways at home, outdoors, or at work; in company or on your own; while you exercise, cook, study, make love, travel, or sleep; to cheer you up or calm you down'; and (2) 'Do you enjoy music in pubs? Restaurants and cafes? Supermarkets? Shops? Streets? Do you ever dislike music in public places?'. Other areas of questioning on music, not analysed in this paper, were: going to concerts; money spent on music; nature and location of collection and music playing devices in the home.

The archive holds data on the age, gender, occupation, marital status, and home address of all participants, which allowed selection of stratified sub-sets for analysis, and for the examination of possible effects of these variables on music listening. No attempt was made to examine effects of occupation, but possible effects of all other variables were tested for. There were no significant effects of marital status or geographical location (north, midlands, south) within the UK, so no further mention is made of these variables.

The Music Directive was mailed to 460 panel members (137 male, 323 female), and replies were received from 249 panel members. This represents a 54% response rate, which is typical for this panel. Of the respondents, 69 were male (50% of the men in the panel), and 181 were female (56% of the women in the panel). For detailed analysis, it was decided to select at random an equal number (15) of men and women in each of 3 age-bands, under 40, 40–60, and over 60. This proved possible for women, providing 45 female responses in total. Unfortunately there were only three male respondents under 40, and only 13 between 40 and 60, so the male sample for analysis was 31 in total (3+13+15).

18.4 Chosen personal uses of music

The selected sample of respondents' comments were analysed to discover recurrent functional and contextual themes in the responses. Table 18.3 shows the categories of response obtained. Explicit functions referred to by correspondents match quite closely the types of categories found in earlier studies. The use of music as a cue to reminiscence is the single most frequent use reported.

The activities which music accompanies are predominantly domestic and solitary. Indeed some respondents made a point of qualifying their use of music (e.g. 'the car is the only place where I can listen to it loud enough without annoying other people'). Several respondents made explicit links between activities/contexts and their psychological functions (e.g. on arrival home from work 'music lifts the stress of work: it has an immediate healing effect').

There are age and gender effects on the distribution of reported activities and functions. The mean number of reported activities in the home that are accompanied by self-chosen music decreases with age (2.4 for the youngest group, 0.6 for the oldest). However, it is not clear at this stage whether this result is artefactual (it may be that older people write less). For activities outside the home there is a similar age effect, but also a significant gender effect. Men report 0.7 activities on average, whereas women report only 0.3 activities.

In terms of functions, there are no significant age or gender effects associated with mention of the memory-association functions of music, but there is a significant tendency for women to mention mood altering or

Table 18.3 Percentage of Mass-Observation Respondents reporting various functions and activities chosen for music

Functions		
Reminder of valued past event	50	Memory
Spiritual experience	6	Transcendent
Evokes visual images	2	Sensorial
Tingles/goose pimples/shivers	10	
Source of pleasure/enjoyment	6	
To put in a good mood	16	Mood change
Moves to tears/catharsis/release	14	
Excites	2	
Motivates	2	
Source of comfort/healing	4	
Calms/soothes/relaxes/relieves stress	8	
Mood enhancement	8	Mood enhancement
To match current mood	6	
Activities		
To wake up to	6	
While having a bath	4	
While exercising	4	
To sing along to	6	
To work to (desk work)	14	
To work to (housework)	22	
On arrival home from work	2	
While having a meal	12	
Background while socializing	4	
To accompany sexual/romantic events	4	
Whilst reading	6	
In bed/to get to sleep	14	
While driving/running/cycling	22	
While on public transport (Walkman)	4	

enhancing functions more frequently than men (mean of 1.0 for women, as compared to 0.2 for men).

Women in general offer more articulate and detailed descriptions of their use of music for mood-related functions than do men (e.g. 'When I'm down I listen to this and go down as far as I can, then I cry, I cry deep from inside. I wallow in self-pity and purge all the gloom from my body. Then I dry my eyes, and wash my face, do my hair, put on fresh makeup, and rejoin the world.').

In sum, people tend to mention between one and four activities in which they use music of their own choice, and between one and two functions associated with that use. In this context of free verbal response, people are thus more able to retrieve activities than explain their functions. It is an aim of planned research to discover if more intensive and direct research methods will be able to uncover explicit or implicit functions associated with every deliberate act of music listening.

18.5 Music in public places

The main locations in which respondents reported experiencing unchosen music were pubs, shops (predominantly supermarkets), eating places, and streets (including covered shopping malls). There were a small number of mentions of other sources (such as on-hold telephone music, lifts, and music overheard from a neighbour's domestic premises).

Each mention of music in a public place was given a score of +1 if it indicated a liking for music in that context, and −1 if it indicated a dislike. Mean ratings for pubs and restaurants were both 0.0 (equal frequency of like and dislike). The mean rating for shops was −0.3 (more people dislike than like), and for streets was 0.1 (more people like than dislike). The mean rating of music for the separate categories of pubs, restaurants, shops, or the street did not differ according to age or gender, however if all instances of music in public places were combined, there was a significant age effect, such that the greatest dislike was expressed by the 40–60 year olds. There was also a significant gender effect, such that men were more likely than women to express dislike of music in public places.

The reasons people gave for liking or disliking music in public places were categorized into four major groups: (1) noise (e.g. intrudes, unable to hear, unable to concentrate); (2) the type of music or the quality of the performance; (3) whether the music was live or prerecorded; (4) whether the music matched or was appropriate for the atmosphere/context of its location. Again, a reason contributing to liking was given a score of +1 and a reason contributing to disliking was given a score of −1. There was no significant association of reason type to location, age, or gender, except in the case of noise, where there was an interaction of gender and age, such that around half of men at all ages cite noise-related reasons, whereas only women between 40 and 60 mention noise to the same extent. Older and younger women tend not to give this reason. Overall, noise was generally a contributory factor to disliking music in public places, whereas the other reasons were equally often positive as negative.

Table 18.4 provides representative quotes regarding each of the four main categories, giving in each case a predominantly positive, a mixed, and a predominantly negative comment.

Table 18.4 Selected quotations from Mass-Observation participants regarding music in public places

Pubs	'I love music in pubs restaurants and cafes but NOT TOO LOUD because that stops me being able to talk to people, unless I've gone to a pub to specifically hear a band. I like jazz in restaurants or piano music, in pubs I like folk or the rock music of my liking.' 'I do not enjoy music in pubs. It is such a shame that the days of going to the pub for a drink and conversation has gone. The noise racket is awful.'
Restaurants	'Music in pubs etc.—I like a bit of music and noise when I eat out. I hate silence in public places where you can hear every sound. It makes me feel very nervous.' 'I find music played in public places can often be intrusive. As a background, it can be beneficial, helping to break up the silence which can be inhibiting to conversation. All too often, though, the music is played at a level which prevents audible conversation and so has the effect of reducing conversation. And if you have the misfortune to be seated under the loudspeaker in a restaurant, it can put you off your food too.' 'I would not patronize a restaurant which piped music – not even "Egmont." Food and wine demand undivided attention.'
Shops	'Slow music in shops and supermarkets is soothing, fast music makes you buy more. In any case its a distraction, but quite enjoyable to hear chart hits I wouldn't otherwise hear (so THAT'S what Oasis sounds like!).' 'I have discovered Waterstones Bookshop in Newcastle plays good music: the last time I was there Beethoven's "Egmont" Overture was playing, and the trouble is that I pay more attention to the music than to finding the book I want.' 'Most shops have it much too loud and I hate it. In fact I've gone out of shops because the noise stops me thinking and have gone into shops without music playing purposely.'
Streets	'Both my husband and I have performed on the streets. My husband is still a regular busker. This to me is musical entertainment at its purest form. The joy of busking is its spontaneity. Your audience is free to come and go as it wishes, to pay or not pay, to listen or not listen. There is a beautiful freedom about busking that I love, and I hope we never lose street entertainment.' 'The music in the streets is acceptable. Quite often the musicians are quite good and anyway the noise is dispersed.' 'I also dislike the din that some cars make when they pass by, infesting the streets with their thumping noises from within. How they can drive properly with such a din in their cars, God knows. It concerns me too that they wouldn't be able to hear the sound of an ambulance

continued

Table 18.4, *cont'd* Selected quotations from Mass-Observation participants regarding music in public places

	or police car with such a noise going on inside their cars. It seems to me, rather like the fastest drivers, it is usually young men between the age of 17 and 25 who are the main culprits. They usually like to have their driving-seat window open, elbow leaning out of the car and looking macho.'
General	'I dislike music in public places like shops, pubs, etc. Much as I like listening to music, I like it to be the music I have chosen, and when I choose to listen.'
	'I positively dislike music in public places (pubs, restaurants, supermarkets, shops, streets), mainly because it's usually the sort of music that I wouldn't choose to listen to anyway, and I resent having it inflicted on me.'
	'Another thing I hate is music or radio in a car—I feel a real captive audience then and don't like it.'
	'I've got to listen to bad music as much as I have got to listen to good. As such I object to it. I didn't choose it, nor did anyone else—in the absence of getting immediate consensus from people of what they would like to hear—lets have none of it.'
	'But just as I don't want to intrude on others, I wish others wouldn't intrude on me.'
	'I heard that a mall in America solved the problem of rowdy teenagers hanging around all day by playing Mantovani all day long. This was such an assault on the teenagers' sense of 'cool' that they found other places to go. Must be powerful stuff.'

Much of the data suggests an ambivalence towards music in public places. Music in pubs and restaurants can be welcome if it is seen as enhancing the atmosphere, but it easily becomes disliked if the style is not to the respondent's taste, or it is too loud. Much music makes conversation difficult, and can distract people from their intentions. The area of most unequivocal liking appears to be live street-music provided by buskers. There is a strong hint that lack of control is at the root of much dislike of music in public. Where the music is pre-recorded, often emerging from hidden speakers, the sense of lack of control is heightened. Live music, with its possibility of interacting with the performer, offers a greater sense of control and participation. It would be consistent with the centrality of the control/autonomy dimension that groups most used to being able to exercise control and choice (men between 40 and 60, at the height of their earning power and associated social status) would have the most negative reactions to music in public, as these data show. The final section of Table 18.4 (General) highlights the overarching presence of control as a theme in respondents' comments.

A final concern of this paper was to explore possible relationships between chosen personal uses of music and attitudes to music in public places. Table 18.5 shows the outcomes of selected correlations on the quantitative indices reported above. Respondents who reported more self-chosen activities to music outside the home reported greater levels of liking of music in pubs.

Respondents who reported more mood enhancing or altering functions for self-chosen music reported greater levels of liking of street music, and were more likely to cite its live nature as a reason for liking it. These relationships, demonstrated in free-response data, offer a promising indication that patterns of music use in high-control contexts have implications for attitudes towards music in low-control contexts. One would expect more substantial relationships to emerge in research designs where such relationships were explicitly probed.

18.6 Discussion and conclusions

The data presented here confirm that listening to music (perhaps unlike performing it) is used by most people as a means of enhancing everyday activities that are mainly solitary and individualistic. The valued outcomes are mainly self-referring, internal, even solipsistic. Music seems to be a ready source of conflict between people as much as it is something which draws them together. This contrasts rather markedly with the participatory and social cohesion functions identified by ethnomusicologists as dominant forces in many non-western societies, where public music is the medium

Table 18.5 Correlations between chosen activities/functions and attitudes to music in public places

	Activities	Functions		
	Home	**Outside Home**	**Memory**	**Mood**
Dislike				
Pub	−0.13	−0.25*	−0.05	−0.21
Restaurant	0.01	0.03	−0.08	−0.14
Shop	−0.11	−0.03	−0.02	−0.08
Street	−0.04	−0.03	−0.15	−0.28*
Reason				
Noise	0.11	0.08	0.01	−0.08
Type	0.05	0.06	0.00	−0.06
Live	0.05	−0.03	−0.14	−0.23*
Atmosphere	0.01	−0.12	−0.12	−0.08

*p <0.05.

through which people share experience and relate to one another and the social group as a whole (e.g. Blacking, 1976). Indeed, one sees in the responses an explicit contrast between the private and personal work (often of considerable importance) which music allows an individual to accomplish, and the rest of their life which is enacted in the public arena (e.g. 'When I'm down I listen to this and go down as far as I can, then I cry, I cry deep from inside. I wallow in self-pity and purge all the gloom from my body. Then I dry my eyes, and wash my face, do my hair, put on fresh makeup, and rejoin the world.').

If music is a powerful source of reliving important memories then, unless such memories are shared, imposed music can alienate rather than unite. Maybe music can only perform the social cohesion functions noticed in smaller societies where the body of music doesn't change too much over generations and involves everyone (true folk music). Although music continues to play an important part in public life, the data from this study reinforce the caution that is needed in drawing strong inferences about emotional and other forms of significance of music from studies which present subjects with music not of their choosing in public or semi-public contexts.

Future research cannot, of course, rely on the free reports of a self-selected, and therefore unrepresentative sample of the population. A range of more focused methodologies, tracking the everyday use of music as it happens, and probing far more explicitly into its perceived functions and psychological outcomes, is the necessary next step in making progress in this area.

References

Behne, K. E. (1997) The development of 'Musikerleben' in adolescence: how and why young people listen to music. In I. Deliège and J. A. Sloboda (Eds.) *Perception and Cognition of Music*. Hove: Psychology Press.

Blacking, J. (1976) *How Musical is Man?* London: Faber.

Bourdieu, P. (1984) *Distinction* (tr. R. Nice). London: Routledge.

De Las Heras, V. (1997) What does music collecting add to our knowledge of the functions and uses of music? Unpublished MSc dissertation, Department of Psychology, Keele University.

du Gay, P., Hall, S., Janes, L., Mackay, H., and Negus, K. (1997) *Doing Cultural Studies: the Story of the Sony Walkman*. London: Sage.

Finnegan, R. (1989) *The hidden musicians: music-making in an English town*. Cambridge: Cambridge University Press.

Gabrielsson, A. and Juslin, P. (1996) Emotional expression in music performance: between the performer's intention and the listener's experience. *Psychology of Music*, **24**, 68–91.

Gabrielsson, A. and Lindstrom, S. (1996) Can strong experiences of music have therapeutic implications? In R. Steinberg (Ed.) *Music and the mind machine: the psychophysiology and psychopathology of the sense of music.* Berlin: Springer.

Gregory, A. H. (1997) The roles of music in society. In D. J. Hargreaves and A. C. North (Eds.) *The social psychology of music.* Oxford: Oxford University Press.

Hevner, K. (1936) Experimental studies of the elements of expression in music. *American Journal of Psychology,* **48**, 248–268.

Neilly, L. (1995) The uses of music in people's everyday lives. Unpublished undergraduate dissertation, Department of Psychology, Keele University.

North, A. C. and Hargreaves, D. J. (1996) Responses to music in aerobic exercise and yogic relaxation classes. *British Journal of Psychology,* **87**, 535–547.

North, A. C. and Hargreaves, D. J. (1997) Experimental aesthetics and everyday music listening. In D. J. Hargreaves and A. C. North (Eds.) *The social psychology of music.* Oxford: Oxford University Press.

Scherer, K. R. and Oshinsky, J. S. (1977) Cue utilisation in emotion attribution from auditory stimuli. *Motivation and Emotion,* **1.4**, 331–346.

Sheridan, D. (1998) Mass-Observation revived: the Thatcher years and after. In D. Sheridan, D. Bloome and B. Street (Eds.) *Writing ourselves: literacy practices and the Mass-Observation project.* Cresskill, NJ: Hampton Press.

Sloboda, J. A. (1989) Music psychology and the composer. In S. Nielzen and O. Olsson (Eds.) *Structure and perception of electroacoustic sound and music.* Amsterdam: Elsevier.

Sloboda, J. A. (1992) Empirical studies of emotional response to music. In M. Riess Jones and S. Holleran (Eds.) *Cognitive bases of musical communication.* Washington, DC: American Psychological Association.

Zillman, D. and Gan, S. (1997) Musical taste in adolescence. In D. J. Hargreaves and A. C. North (Eds.) *The social psychology of music.* Oxford: Oxford University Press.

CHAPTER 19

MUSIC: WHERE COGNITION AND EMOTION MEET

Music presents a puzzle. On the one hand, people love music and devote much time and effort to putting themselves in the way of it. On the other hand the levels of musical skill achieved by the vast majority of people in contemporary Western society are surprisingly low. On the face of it, music has all the characteristics which would lead one to predict that many people should be highly skilled at it. A long tradition of research into skill and its acquisition (cf. Ericsson and Smith, 1991; Ericsson, 1996) suggests that *structure* plus *motivation* plus *practice* leads to *skill*.

In reviewing these four aspects I will first provide evidence that most music has the kind of structure which is easily learned and understood by the human mind. Second, I will review evidence relating to motivation, and the very high value which many individuals place on their engagement with music. Third, I will review evidence of the intimate link between level and nature of practice activities and achievement in music. Fourth, and more speculatively, I will outline some potential inhibitors to musical achievement, in an attempt to formulate hypotheses about why, given such an apparently propitious set of circumstances, population outcomes in the area of music achievement are so dire. These inhibitors, whilst having individual psychological consequences, are rooted in wider social and cultural phenomena.

19.1 Naturally detected structures

The parallels between music and language are very great. Just as it has been shown that very young infants have already picked up certain structural regularities of spoken language, so similar research shows they know something about the structure of music. Sloboda (1985) has showed that children as young as 7 can consciously choose between well-formed and ill-formed musical sequences. Asked which of two teddies played the 'right' tune, and which 'made a mistake', children demonstrated knowledge of both simultaneous and sequential constraints that exist within Western tonal music.

Structural sensitivity has also been demonstrated by untrained adults in a wide variety of tasks. For instance, Sloboda and Parker (1985) asked psychology students to repeatedly listen to a short folk melody and attempt to reproduce it after each trial by singing it. Although almost no participant gave note-perfect recall, recalls showed structural sensitivity. For instance, recalls tended to preserve the metre and phrase structure of the original.

These and many other studies have established that music is represented in the mind in terms of the structures and regularities that it contains. When such structures cannot be detected, it is impossible for people to process and store the information efficiently. The music of a culture has a familiar syntax, and when this is missing, as for example in some forms of atonal music, processing is severely disrupted. Music is just like chess and the many other cognitive skills that psychology has studied. If a person cannot discover the structure, they cannot become an expert. The research literature on music shows that almost everyone in our culture has 'found the structure of music', through exposure to music irrespective of formal training. Therefore a prime condition for the acquisition of expertise has been fulfilled by the vast majority of our population.

19.2 How and why do people value music?

The proportion of people who can gain material advantage from being skilled at music must be small. Why is music attractive to people? Why are they motivated to listen to it, perform it, create it? Does it serve any useful purpose?

Many types of research have demonstrated that music can and does have important psychological benefits. Not only does music engagement seem inherently pleasurable, but it is often used for essentially therapeutic purposes. Strong and valued emotions seem to be at the core of music engagement (Sloboda, 1992).

There are a number of laboratory and clinical demonstrations of the mood altering powers of music, but more recently an interest has developed in real life uses of music, outside the laboratory or the clinic. For instance, Sloboda (1990) obtained 113 accounts of musical life events from 70 adults of varying musical background and experience. The question asked was 'do you have memories of any specific incident from the first 10 years of life which involved music in any way'. Many of the memories so elicited were deeply memorable, and often motivated lifelong enthusiasm for, and involvement with, music. The contexts in which these highly valued

Example 19.1 Excerpt from the response of a participant in the Sloboda (1990) study

---

'I was sitting in morning assembly at school. The music formed part of the assembly service. The music was a clarinet duet, probably by Mozart. I was astounded at the beauty of the sound. It was liquid, resonant, vibrant. It seemed to send tingles through me. I felt as if it was a significant moment. Listening to this music led me to learning to play first the recorder and then to achieve my ambition of playing the clarinet . . .'

---

experiences occurred were somewhat restricted, and this provides a very important clue for framing an answer to the puzzle with which this paper opened. Hardly any of these experiences occurred during music lessons or in the presence of a teacher. They occurred in time 'off task', alone or with friends, at home or at school (See Example 19.1)

Currently, a research team at Keele is gathering data on music use rather closer to the coal face (Sloboda *et al.*, 2001). Adults without musical training have been carrying pagers around with them for an entire week. The pager calls them at random intervals throughout the day. Every time they are paged they are asked to stop what they are doing as soon as they can safely do so, and complete a brief questionnaire in a booklet of identical sheets that they are also asked to keep with them at all times. They are asked to focus on any music that was occurring as the pager sounded, or, if no music was occurring, to recall the most recent occurrence of music since the previous paging.

What we have found so far is that music is experienced in an incredibly wide variety of circumstances. Hardly any of these have music as the main focus. The music is accompanying some other activity (such as washing up, socializing, exercising, working, travelling). Two sets of data are particularly pertinent to the current discussion.

First, participants were asked to estimate their mood on a number of bipolar scales both before and after the music. These scales factored into three major mood dimensions which we have labelled, in order of contribution to the variance, positivity, present-mindedness, and arousal (see Table 19.1). In general music increased emotional state towards greater positivity (e.g. more happy), greater arousal (e.g. more alert), and greater present-mindedness (e.g. less bored). But what seemed of particular significance to us is that mood change was greatest when participants exercised choice over the music they were hearing. Music maximally enhances well-being when participants exercise some degree of autonomy and self determination in the type of music they hear (see Table 19.2).

The second result of interest is the dissociation of emotional factors in some music-listening cases. While it is true overall that music makes people more positive, more aroused and more present-minded, a more

Table 19.1 Factor analysis of bipolar mood scales in pager study

Positivity (36%)	
Distressed	Comforted
Sad	Happy
Irritable	Generous
Insecure	Secure
Tense	Relaxed
Present-mindedness (14%)	
Bored	Interested
Detached	Involved
Lonely	Connected
Nostalgic	In-the-present
Arousal (12%)	
Drowsy	Alert
Tired	Energetic

differentiated pattern was evident in about 12% of the episodes. In some episodes, for example, positivity increased, while the other two dimensions decreased. In others, arousal increased, while nothing else did, and so on. Each of these patterns was associated with a particular set of circumstances and psychological purposes. People deliberately use music for different intended outcomes. Some examples of these episodes are given in Table 19.3.

From results such as these, a quite detailed picture is beginning to build up of *what* music does for people. But a much more intriguing scientific puzzle is to explain *how* music can 'mean so much' to people.

19.3 How are emotions mediated through music?

A range of research studies suggests that emotions are mediated through music in at least three quite distinct ways, *episodic associations, iconic associations*, and *structural expectancies*.

Table 19.2 Change in mood as a function of degree of musical choice in pager study

	Degree of choice		
	Low	**Medium**	**High**
Change in:			
Positivity	0.8	0.3	2.3
Present	0.6	3.0	3.2
Arousal	0.8	1.2	1.8
Average change	0.8	1.5	2.4

Table 19.3 Examples of mood change dissociation in pager study

Mood change pattern	Positivity up, present-mindedness down, arousal down
Everyday descriptor	'Chilling out'
Example	At home, relaxing with 6 friends and acquaintances. Wanted to do it. Ambient music on CD. Little choice over music. 'The music was very tranquil and relaxing. I was very, very tired.'
Mood change pattern	Positivity down, present-mindedness down, arousal up
Everyday descriptor	'nostalgic wallowing'
Example	At home, alone, washing up. Rock on radio. High choice over music. 'Favourite song I had not heard for some time. It brought back certain memories.'

Episodic associations are the type of effects which can be explained by what John Booth Davies (1978) has memorably described as the 'Darling They're Playing Our Tune' theory of emotion. Music can provide a powerful reminder of earlier events or periods in our lives, and the significant people or places that figured in them, particularly when these life events were strongly emotional. Strong and real as these associations are, they are not particularly interesting from a theoretical point of view, because they are entirely driven by idiosyncratic autobiographical contingencies.

Iconic associations are brought about by physical characteristics of the music that mimic or resemble the sound effects that could be created by non-musical events. Crude examples would be the mimicking of birdsong or of natural phenomena such as thunderstorms. More interesting are the ways in which music can suggest a particular kind of emotional character, by creating sounds typical of that emotion. Watt and Ash (1998), for instance, have recently developed the analogy, previously developed for visual materials by Michotte, of musical objects as 'virtual persons'.

Research at Keele has been more concerned with the third source of emotional engagement, that seems to come about by tracking the unfolding structures of a piece of music, and reacting to the confirmations and violations of expectancy that are created within those structures. Waterman (1996) showed that there are particular 'hot spots' in many pieces of music where people are prone to experience emotions particularly intensely. These can be tracked by asking people to report on 'thrills' (Sloboda, 1991). Thrills are reliable physical concomitants of emotional response, which include shivers down the spine, tears, or a lump in the throat.

It has been found that music hot spots usually involve particular structural events which tease structural expectancies, by repeatedly creating and resolving tensions, or by manipulating timing parameters that cause expected events to happen earlier or later than expected. Emotional response to music is thus an integral outcome of the intuitive structural analysis that goes on while listening. This is an important finding for a long-running debate in musicology. Some musicologists have tried to argue that 'pure' music listening means stripping away all mundane associations from music and hearing it as pure sound. Even if that were possible and desirable, our findings suggest that music would still be an intensely emotional experience. It is interesting and pertinent to note that in many traditional academic music contexts the official discourse is such that emotions don't get a look in. Everything is to do with form, content, history, and analysis. Perhaps this is the price that musicians felt they had to pay to have music accepted as a 'proper' discipline. This could be one more clue to the puzzle that motivates this lecture. You can't get fully inside music without becoming emotionally involved, yet such emotional involvement is exactly what many of the traditional institutions of music education have tended to inhibit and discount.

In sum, there is good evidence that people are strongly motivated to engage with music because of the valued psychological outcomes. These outcomes can be traced in part to the powerful emotions engendered when we listen to music, emotions which are enhanced by the structural expectations that we acquire within a musical genre or culture.

19.4 Acquiring musical expertise

Some recent research has been concerned with the processes by which a transition is made from the basic level of receptive competence, which is shared by all listeners within a culture, to the status of expert. There are, of course, many types of expertise, but much recent research has focused on a particular and relatively widespread form of expertise, the ability to perform notated music on a traditional acoustic instrument, such as piano or violin. This is a form of expertise which has been particularly widely promoted within the educational system. Almost every school has a recorder or wind band, or an orchestra, and most qualified music teachers, whether private or public, work within this tradition. Much of the research in this area is concerned to show the intimate link between achievement and focused deliberate cognitive engagement of the sort which is generally called practice.

Sloboda *et al.* (1985) made an extensive single-case study of an autistic musical savant, who was reported to be able to memorize long piano pieces just by hearing them over a few times. His quite phenomenal ability turned out not only to be specific to music (his verbal memory span was subnormal) but also specific to tonal music. Given a piece of mildly atonal music to memorize, his ability fell apart. We found biographical documentation which suggested that his ability to memorize grew gradually over 15 years of obsessive and repetitive work at this single task, to which he devoted almost all his waking hours.

Sloboda *et al.* (1996) probed systematically into the musical histories of 250 young people learning musical instruments. The data showed a strong relationship between objectively measured level of skill and the amount of practice undertaken, in any give year, and also cumulatively over the life span. The highest achieving group were undertaking on average 800% more daily practice than the lowest achieving group at the age of 12. Because differences in practice time were evident at considerably younger ages, we found similarly large disparities in total hours of accumulated practice time by early adolescence (see Table 19.4).

More recently, O'Neill (1997) tracked beginning instrumental learners over the first year of music lessons. This allowed her to administer a battery of measures before any exposure to the instrument at all. These included measures of IQ, standardized musical aptitude tests, and a motivational measure of resistance to failure (an adapted version of the Wisconsin Card Sorting Task). This is a particularly pertinent measure for early musical learning, where failure to be able to reproduce the fluent musical products they hear all around them is a constant experience of beginners. After 9 months all children were given the same piece to learn for two weeks, and their performance on this piece was video-recorded for evaluation by expert music examiners. There were large disparities between the children in the standard of these performances. Neither starting IQ nor musical aptitude predicted outcomes, but both the pre-instruction motivational variable and amount of practice on the piece were strong predictors.

There is a considerable amount yet to be discovered about what types of practice lead to better and faster learning outcomes. It is naive to suppose that an hour of one type of engagement is as good as any other, and some

Table 19.4 Key practice indicators from Sloboda *et al.* (1996)

Average minutes of daily music instrument practice at age 12 as a function of skill level				
Lowest achievement			Highest achievement	
1	2	3	4	5
15	30	60	60	120
Average hours of accumulated practice at age 13 as a function of skill level				
Lowest achievement			Highest achievement	
1	2	3	4	5
450	800	1400	1400	2500

preliminary evidence on efficiency of different practice strategies is now being collected. But none of this negates the main conclusion of this body of work, which is that in order to attain high levels of performance expertise within the classical performance tradition, large amounts of deliberate practice are required.

19.5 Where have all the musicians gone?

This more speculative section attempts to describe and explain some of the barriers to the achievement of musical expertise that appear to exist in our society.

The first barrier to achievement is a significant reduction (in comparison to many earlier periods) of the societal scaffolding which allowed people to progressively occupy intermediate rungs on a ladder of skill progression. There are decreasing numbers of widespread social institutions where moderate levels of performance skill are encouraged and celebrated. In an earlier age, one could expect to hear and join in music sung and played in the home. There would be sing-songs at the local pub, or at village festivals, where all and sundry could join it, at their own level. Playing along on a tin whistle or a violin would be tolerated, even encouraged. At a slightly more formal level, people might receive a structured learning environment within a church choir or a brass band. Here, there would be a level of discipline and correction of blatant errors, together with a regular cycle of rehearsals and concerts. These institutions could allow a gradual progression in skill and accomplishment, so that someone might move from the back desk to a soloist position. From this backdrop, the few might indeed move on to professional activity. But significant opportunities were there for many to reach some significant intermediate level of achievement. In times of mass conscription, even the armed forces provided significant opportunities for regular formal and informal music making.

The present society has seen the rungs in this ladder of progression gradually rot and fall out. The decline in church attendance and in the cohesion of local communities, has caused these institutions to wither, and they are not being replaced. Thus there is a widening gap between everyday contexts in which people operate as novices and those in which they can come to operate as experts. In general, what Simon Frith (1996) has called 'the academy' has come to appropriate the gateways which provide cultural scaffolding for moving up the ladder of achievement. The academy is constituted by 'the music departments, conservatories, and the whole panoply of formal arrangements and practices in which classical music in its various forms is taught and handed down the generations'.

It is significant that in our large-scale study of young people's musical achievement (Davidson *et al.*, 1996) the family environment of high achievers was quite unusual. Parents devoted great amounts of time and energy to the practical support of their children's learning. They often hired private tutors, they supervised practice sessions on a daily basis, they encouraged, cajoled, and sometimes even fought with their children when the children felt like watching TV rather than practicing. They have fought for their children's access to the academy.

I suggest that such unusual family environments are necessary these days to replace the scaffolding that local communities no longer provide. Most families are neither able to nor see the point in making these arrangements for their children. Arguably, the ubiquity of recorded music also inhibits practical music-making in the home and elsewhere.

The second barrier to achievement is the increasing framing of official discourse about music performance in terms of concepts of talent, achievement and success, rather than in terms of community, fulfilment, or transcendence. The National Curriculum for music is only the most recent manifestation of this, where attainment targets are more salient than any notion of why it might be interesting or personally relevant to achieve these targets. This reflects the very ambivalent attitude towards art that typifies many modern consumer societies. Art is often seen as of no value except as a commodity to be purchased by consumers for 'entertainment' in exchange for hard cash. Therefore musical expertise is only valued to the extent that it can earn money for the purveyors of entertainment, be they popular music recording companies or opera houses. What then matters most is to be better, more skilful, more innovative, more 'professional' than ones' peers. Hard work is taken for granted, but on top of that, only those with that special indefinable extra quality 'talent' are, at the end of the day, going to be able to command the attention which will earn their sponsors the kinds of profits that they seek. And so, the impossibly polished outputs of musical superstars are rubbed in the faces (or more precisely, the ears) of young people through constant media exposure. Young music learners are pitted against each other, in exams, competitions, festivals, with the aim of weeding out all but the 'really talented'. Even at the highest levels of training, in the conservatories and music colleges, where everyone is way above the average level of achievement, to come second in a competition is seen by many as having failed. In this context it is unsurprising that young people are discouraged from participation in an activity where there are so few winners and so many losers.

The notion that music could be engaged in purely for personal fulfilment, for the building up of community and friendship, for the sheer joy of making beautiful sounds together, is a strange, and almost reprehensible concept in many people's minds. Music is the poor relation in many schools—what has it got to do, after all, with the real business of equipping people to contribute to wealth creation? The message is projected that if you haven't got talent, you should stop wasting your time messing about with music, and concentrate on your maths or business studies.

The third and final barrier I want to postulate is the barrier of elitism or high art. The academy in most of its manifestations promotes the classical performance tradition as the paradigm and paragon of what music 'really' is, and what it is to be a musician. Limited nods in the direction of jazz and an assortment of exotica labelled as 'world musics' hardly modify the message that the academy sends to most people. The traditions and forms of the academy are, despite what some apologists claim, inaccessible to most people. Their inaccessibility is of two sorts. First, they do not reflect to most people the values and identities which they bring to music. Music of the academy is seen to be about class privilege and maintenance of a cultural *status quo* in which an elite minority dictate to the majority what constitutes good music. Second, the core exemplars of the forms of the academy (such as concertos and symphonies) demand such a level of individual and corporate proficiency and resource to execute that they have almost no points of contact with the levels of music-making that still survive in our culture (e.g. the karaoke bar). If elite music has neither resonances with one's own cultural identity, nor appears to be potentially learnable, then it hardly encourages mass participation.

It is, of course, encouraging when symphony orchestras go into schools, or when sympathetic school music teachers take an interest in students' love of pop. But if the academy, whether represented in schools or symphony orchestras, carries within its very structures and discourses the seeds of the problems I have identified, then the solution will not lie in minimal reforms within the academy but in the creation of new cultural and folk institutions. We need living and socially relevant forms to replace the church choir and the village brass band. Recent pleas by major figures in classical music for the government to reverse cuts in school instrumental provision may have come too late, if the social institutions which support music-making outside the academy are no longer there.

I have no idea what these social institutions might be, what they might build on, nor how they can be encouraged. Psychology cannot provide the answer to such questions. All it can do is indicate some of the conditions which must be met if these institutions are to enable the flourishing of individual development. The evidence reviewed above indicates to me that performance potential could be unlocked in millions of people if we could recreate social institutions which focused on musical enjoyment, and personal and communal fulfilment, rather than on the need to be best, or to meet the taxing performance requirements of a professional elite.

References

Davidson, J. W., Howe, M. J. A., Moore, D. G., and Sloboda, J. A. (1996) The role of parental influences in the development of musical ability. *British Journal of Developmental Psychology*, **14**, 399–412.

Davies, J. B. (1978) *The psychology of music*. London: Hutchinson.

Ericsson, K. A. (Ed.) (1996) *The road to excellence: the acquisition of expert performance in the arts and sciences, sports and games*. Mahwah, NJ, Lawrence Erlbaum Associates.

Ericsson, K. A. and Smith, J (Eds.) (1991) *Towards a general theory of expertise: prospects and limits*. New York: Cambridge University Press.

Frith, S. (1996) *Performing rites: on the value of popular music*. Oxford: Oxford University Press.

O'Neill, S. A. (1997) The role of practice in early musical performance achievement. In H. Jorgensen and A. C. Lehmann (Eds.) *Does practice make perfect? current theory and research on instrumental music practice*. Oslo: Norges Musikhogskole, pp. 53–70.

Sloboda, J. A. (1985) *The musical mind: the cognitive psychology of music*. Oxford: Oxford University Press.

Sloboda, J. A. (1990) Music as a language. In F. Wilson and F. Roehmann (Eds.) *Music and child development*. St Louis, Miss: MMB Inc.

Sloboda, J. A. (1991) Music structure and emotional response: some empirical findings. *Psychology of Music*, **19**, 110–120.

Sloboda, J. A. (1992) Empirical studies of emotional response to music. In M. Riess-Jones and S. Holleran (Eds.) *Cognitive bases of musical communication*. Washington, DC: American Psychological Association.

Sloboda, J. A. and Parker, D. H. H. (1985) Immediate recall of melodies. In P. Howell, I. Cross and R. West (Eds.) *Musical structure and cognition*. London: Academic Press.

Sloboda, J. A., Hermelin, B., and O'Connor, N. (1985) An exceptional musical memory. *Music Perception*, **3**, 155–170.

Sloboda, J. A., Davidson, J. W., Howe, M. J. A., and Moore, D. G. (1996) The role of practice in the development of expert musical performance. *British Journal of Psychology*, **87**, 287–309.

Sloboda, J. A., O'Neill, S. A., and Ivaldi, A. (2001) Functions of music in every-day life: an exploratory study using the Experience Sampling Methodology. *Musicae Scientiae,* **5**(1), 9–32.

Waterman, M. (1996) Emotional responses to music: implicit and explicit effects in listeners. *Psychology of Music,* **24**, 52–67.

Watt, R. and Ash, R. (1998) A psychological investigation of meaning in music. *Musicae Scientiae,* **2**, 33–54.

CHAPTER 20

MUSIC AND WORSHIP: A PSYCHOLOGIST'S PERSPECTIVE

20.1 Introduction

The role of music in worship is not a topic that has greatly exercised psychologists. Both the psychology of music and the psychology of religion are very much 'fringe' topics in contemporary psychology. The number of psychologists interested in both must be tiny. Accordingly, the most a paper like this can hope to do is ask some of the right questions, and speculate about possible directions in which answers may be sought.

It seems that the particular sequence of questions that a psychologist might hope to elucidate would be something like the following:

1 What goes on in people's minds when they are engaging with music? Or, more formally, what are the mental processes specific to the domain of music?

2 What goes on in people's minds when they are engaging in worship? What are the mental processes specific to the domain of worship?

3 In what way do the mental processes involved in music and in worship overlap? In other words, are there particular aspects of worshiping which are enhanced, reinforced, or afforded, by acts of 'musicking'.

4 How can we account for, or explain, these overlapping mental processes in terms of our broader understanding of human mental functioning?

These are, of course, weighty questions, requiring the input of musicians, theologians, liturgists, philosophers, as well as psychologists. This paper can hardly do more that make some preliminary comments in the direction of these questions.

In what follows I have tried to take a phenomenological approach to worship. That is to say, I concentrate on what I understand people to be doing or feeling in worship, and try to describe this in theologically neutral language.

Where it has seemed necessary, for ease of expression, to use terms like 'God', I am neither claiming to be theologically precise nor attempting to use any particular set of dogmatic assumptions, whether Christian or otherwise, to support the arguments.

20.2 The basis of human response to music: free or constrained?

Can we choose what mental processes to engage during some musical activity? If we cannot, then there is the possibility of a rather simple approach to the psychology of music. Each type of music will have a particular mental effect on a person, just as a particular drug will have a reliable effect on human physiology. In an earlier article I have called this model of musical response the *pharmaceutical* one (Sloboda, 1989).

It should not take too much reflection to reject the pharmaceutical model as hopelessly inadequate. When confronted with the same musical situation I have many options that I can exercise. Here are just a few:

1 I can pay no attention to the music at all, and pursue my own thoughts, memories, and fantasies.

2 I can derive personal associations to the music. When have I heard this music before? How was I feeling at the time I experienced this music? What personal events, feelings, reactions am I reminded of by this music?

3 I can exercise an analytic or critical faculty with respect to some aspect of the music. Is the soprano soloist singing in tune? What was that interesting harmony? Could this be Mozart? Is this a better performance of this piece than the one I heard last week?

4 I can engage with the music in a non-analytic, contemplative mode, in which, while being attentive to it, I am not focusing on any particular event, or making specific judgements. I am 'letting the music wash over me'.

5 I can engage with the music by attending to the relationship between myself and others also engaged in the music. Am I following the conductor? Does my voice blend with that of my neighbour? Is my neighbour experiencing what I am experiencing?

This list, which is not necessarily complete, shows that we have choices about the mental processes we engage in a musical context. Is there, in that case, anything we can usefully say about such processes that has any generality, or is it simply a case of 'you do your thing and I'll do mine'?

I believe we can go beyond total individualism by use of the notion of *affordances*. The term 'affordance' was introduced to psychology by the perceptual psychologist James J. Gibson (1996). In Gibson's eyes, human response can often be explained, not so much by reference to inner states, but by reference to characteristics of the environment which constrain and direct that response. So, for instance, a chair *affords* sitting. It has the necessary physical characteristics to allow someone to sit on it. If well designed it almost, by its very nature, *invites* you to sit on it. No one has to explain to you that it is for sitting. Even a very small child with no under-standing of the concept of a chair would still naturally end up sitting on it in the course of physical exploration. This is because the object fits to a set of human characteristics. Chairs have to be a particular way because humans are the way they are.

By affording some kinds of activities, environments discourage or even preclude others. It is rarely that the same object will afford both sitting and eating, for instance. On the other hand, most objects have multiple affor-dances. The same object that affords sitting can also afford throwing (you could pick up a light chair and throw it at an assailant).

Designers of everyday objects are beginning to understand how they can make life simpler by building in the right sorts of affordances (Norman, 1988). No one should ever have to struggle with a door, not sure whether to push or pull it, not sure whether the handle goes up or down. Appropriately designed handles will afford only a single movement, the correct one. A correctly designed concourse will naturally draw people in the intended direction.

When objects are used in social contexts, culture can shape the normative affordances of those objects, and these can change over time. Objects (e.g. Roman vessels) which were once used for cooking are now used as collectors' items, or objects of historical research. But there is a cultural inertia. Uses of objects change relatively slowly.

And so it is with music. We can choose what to do with music, but for most of us, the choices are limited by culture, background, social context, and the way the music itself has been designed (in Gibsonian terminology, the affordances it possesses). A key context for music has always been worship. It must be the case that (at least some) music affords worship. Our task is to demonstrate how.

Rather than attempt a formal definition of worship, I shall assume for the moment a shared intuitive understanding of the concept, and sweep back over the five 'ways of responding' to music that I outlined above.

20.3 Music as unattended background

It is tempting to say that if one is not attending to music then it cannot be said to be affording anything, let alone worship. But there are different ways of not attending to music. On the one hand, one can simply ignore the music and get on with what one was doing as if it wasn't there. This tends to be my response to subdued canned music in supermarkets, restaurants, and other public places. I can also be at work, deeply involved with a piece of writing, and be almost totally unaware of concurrent recorded music. On the other hand, in some contexts the mere presence of the music may limit my responses and direct them in certain ways. For instance, music in a worship setting may define a period of time in which participants neither speak nor move about. So, although I may not be listening to the anthem, I am, perforce, sitting still, in the presence of others, with the memories of particular acts or words that have preceded the music. Worship may certainly happen in such contexts. But if I am truly ignoring the music, then the most that the music can be contributing to my worship is to signal a beginning and end to the time period within which particular sorts of mental activity may take place. Such signals can be provided in many ways, and are not in any sense special to music.

20.4 Music as a source of personal associations

There has now accumulated a significant body of data which confirms that music is a particularly powerful evoker of other times and other places. It is no accident that almost every single guest who has ever appeared on *Desert Island Discs* has been able to use music to appropriately illustrate his or her life story. The majority of Western adults seem to remember particularly well the popular tunes of their adolescent years, and retain a strong emotional response to them. In one of the earliest contemporary texts on the psychology of music (Davies, 1978), this aspect of music psychology was wittily characterized as the 'Darling, They're Playing Our Tune' theory of musical response.

There is considerable psychological evidence to show that we remember highly emotionally charged events in a unique way. Brown and Kulik (1977) coined the term 'flashbulb memory' to characterize this type of memory, which seems to be characterized by a vivid literal memory of all the incidental details surrounding the emotion-provoking incident. In the earliest study on flashbulb memories individuals were asked whether they could remember exactly what they were doing when they first heard the news that President J. F. Kennedy had been assassinated. Most people recalled exactly where they were, what time it was, who they were with, what was said. If music was playing at the time, then the music would also be remembered.

The situation is complicated for music, however, in that the past musical event may, in itself, have been a source of strong emotion. I will discuss the nature of such strong emotion and the evidence for it in a later section. Sufficient for now to say that the association of a present musical experience may be self-referring; the present experience retrieves the thoughts and feelings of an earlier experience of that music, rather than of the other events which accompanied the music. Such experiences are often positive, sometimes profoundly so.

The associationistic function of music may be tight or loose. A tight association is the association generated by a specific piece of music (e.g. Bach's *Prelude and Fugue in G* for organ). A loose association is to a type or genre of music (e.g. baroque organ music). Many people operate with loose associations which determine their willingness to engage with music in certain circumstances. Individuals whose strong personal associations with popular music are to situations of alienation and degeneracy are unlikely to be spurred to worship by such music. Such associations can be self-reinforcing. Because many people in our culture associate organ music with worship settings (as a result of experiencing many previous worship settings involving organ music) but do not so associate pop music, organ music can in itself appear 'sacred' and pop music 'profane', leading to cultural practices which reinforce the role of some types of music in worship, and exclude others. Appearances generated through such associations alone are, however, arbitrary and culturally contingent. The issue of whether some kinds of music have intrinsic features which better afford worship than others is a separate question, and one to which we will return.

The consequences of musical associations for worship are, I think, rather clear. Music has a particular power to remind us of important past events in our life, and the profound feelings which accompanied them. This can lead to celebration, joyful remembrance, or the revisiting of pain and suffering. It can lift us out of our current preoccupations and re-focus our attention on the wider landscape of our lives. By bringing together in our consciousness events which may be distant in time, it can help us to get a better sense of the cradle-to-grave continuity and unity of ourselves as persons.

Music is by no means the only source of powerful reminders of times past. But because of its inherent capacity to evoke strong emotion, it is likely to be a particularly powerful route to personal associations.

20.5 Music as a vehicle for the exercise of judgement

The preceding section glossed over a crucial problem, the problem of representation and equivalence. How does a person recognize a piece of music experienced in the present as an instance of something they have heard before in the past? It can rarely be the case that the physical stimulus is identical in all respects. Only repeated hearings of the same recording in exactly the same acoustic conditions would guarantee that. What is it, then, that we use to make judgements of equivalence?

This is not a problem unique to music. It relates to any experience that we classify and categorize. How do we identify different instances of the handwritten letter 'a' as such, given that they may be written in different handwritings, orientations, sizes, etc.? Simplifying 30 years of intense scientific work in a few sentences is not easy, but the essence of mainstream theorizing about the matter is that humans make progress by forming representations of objects which are less like 'photographs' and more like 'lists'. In other words, a letter 'a' might be represented as

- a bounded circular space
- a vertically oriented line attached to the right edge of that space.

In the process of representing objects in this way, some detailed information from the original is lost, but a more useful level of underlying structure is gained, because the representation is more abstract than the stimulus from which it is derived. Several physically different objects can be captured under the same description in a way that identifies their common function.

Psychologists are not claiming that individuals always have conscious verbal access to the nature of their representations. In many cases, the existence of the representations can only be inferred on the basis of how people actually classify objects, i.e. which objects are perceived by people as similar or identical to one another.

In music, for instance, we know that, by and large, people do not represent music in terms of its absolute pitches or frequencies. Unless a person has an acutely developed sense of absolute pitch, he or she will judge as 'identical' the sequences C–D–E–F–G and D–E–F#–G–A, so long as they are not played consecutively. This judgement will be made by anyone with sufficient exposure to tonal music. It does not require formal training. Formal training will simply allow someone to verbalize what it is about these two sequences that make them sound the same. They are both ascending major scales starting on their respective tonics and ending on the fifth degree.

To summarize a very large amount of research, it appears that in listening to music, humans are normally representing what they hear, at least in part, as a (non-verbal, intuitive) structural description of that music (in terms of pitch classes, tonality, metre, tension and resolution, continuities and discontinuities, repetitions and transformations etc). What it means to recognize a piece of music is to discover a match between the structural description of the current experience and a previously stored structural description.

In a very important sense then, the mere fact of being able to recognize a piece of music means that (intuitive and subconscious) judgements were exercised on both previous and current hearing. These were the judgements that assigned *this* event to *this* pitch class rather than the neighbouring one, and so on. Of course, there are different levels of judgement. It does not require detailed note-by-note judgement to identify two pieces of music as 'organ music' or 'pop music'. It requires much detailed judgement to recognize two events as performances of the same piece, and even more judgement to reliably differentiate the two performances.

20.6 Ineffability and judgement

What the preceding discussion highlights for us is the fact that there is an great deal of 'knowing' of one sort or another going on in engagement in music, which is not necessarily translated into 'saying'. I have a sense that this gap between knowing and saying is one that offers particular affordances for worship. At the heart of much worship is the sense of being in the presence of that which is beyond capture by human concepts. In approaching the object of worship we are approaching that which is at the limits of our apprehension. And yet, neither the object of worship nor the activity of worship is alien to us. In worship, there is fulfilment. We discover in the object of our worship intimate knowledge and understanding but cannot adequately say what it is we know or understand. The adjective which describes those things which we can know but not say is 'ineffable'. Human experience of God has always possessed an ineffable core.

One recent project in the philosophy of music which seems to have crucial implications for our understanding of the role of music in worship is the attempt to clarify in what ways, if at all, musical knowledge is ineffable. This project has been undertaken by Diana Raffman in her recent book *Language, Music, and Mind* (1993), and what I have to say here draws very deeply on her thinking.

Raffman identifies three distinct ways in which individuals may know more than they can say about a musical experience. She has a particular concern to determine whether any of these types of ineffability are logically necessary for all listeners at all times, but this concern need not be ours. If ineffability can be experienced at all, then it may be relevant to worship.

20.6.1 Structural ineffability

The first type of ineffability identified by Raffman is *structural ineffability*, and it relates to limitations in the ability to verbalize high-level structural features which affect the way that music is represented. She provides some examples of experiences falling into this category which will be recognizable to many experienced musicians:

> Having easily reported the pitches, rhythms and times-signature of a heard piece, along perhaps with some of its local grouping, time-span, and prolongational structures, a listener (perhaps even a highly expert one) finds himself at a loss: 'I am feeling that E-natural in a certain distinctive way, but I can't say just how. I know it's the leading tone, and that it's preparing the return to the tonic, and I know it's a weak prolongation of the E-natural in the previous bar . . . but somehow I feel there is more going on'. Or a performer feels himself compelled to play a certain passage in a certain way (e.g. to slow down, or to get louder, or to increase the vibrato speed)—consciously feels, knows, that it must be played thus, and yet cannot say why . . . What I want to suggest is that unconscious structural representations— in particular, relatively global levels of representation—are 'making themselves felt' in our conscious experience, yet their contents elude our verbal grasp. (pp. 31–32)

Another way of experiencing this kind of ineffability is the sense of 'rightness' about a particular musical event. We feel that 'it had to be like that', even though we have no conscious access to explicit reasons for the judgement. It seems to me that this maps rather straightforwardly onto an aspect of worship which concerns our apprehension of 'the larger design of things'. We can marvel or wonder at the rightness and beauty of aspects of creation at the same time as being unable to do more than catch hints of the underlying nature of the phenomenon. There is a kind of inexhaustibility to this level of ineffability, which spurs scientific and other intellectual endeavours. Our efforts to understand can be likened to peeling an infinitely large onion from the inside. There is always another higher level of explanation beyond the one that has been discovered. The permanent gap between intuitive contemplation and intellectual understanding is a central feature of the worshipping experience.

20.6.2 Feeling ineffability

The second type of musical ineffability is characterized by Raffman as *feeling ineffability*. This comes about because of the essential sensory-perceptual or experiential nature of music. Knowing a piece of music involves, along with other things, *knowing what it sounds like*. 'A person deaf from birth cannot know a piece of music' (p. 40). This does not mean that a trained musician has to hear a particular new piece of music to know it. It is possible to compute what it sounds like (at least to some degree of specification) by examining a score, provided that one has a rich enough base of prior musical experience to fall back on. But without this sensory underpinning there is no possibility of full knowledge.

This type of ineffability is by no means unique to music. All sensory experiences, from sunsets to 'the taste of last night's chicken curry' have the same ineffability. They require 'actual occurrent sense-perception of the relevant stimuli at some point' (p. 4). Yet, according to Raffman, there seems to be a special quality to the feeling ineffability of musical knowledge that commands our particular attention in the way that last night's curry does not. Her thought is that it is the grammatical structure of music that (mis)leads us to expect something effable as an end result of 'following' a piece of music. 'Music's grammatical structure may mislead us into semantic temptation' (p. 41) in a unique way not brought about when we observe a sunset, or even a painting. This comes about because of music's formal similarity to language.

I'll try and put this another way. Music's formal structure and its similarities to speech (sequential, unfolding over time) suggests to us that it is saying something to us, or pointing our attention to something. What it is pointing to, among other things, is the actual sensual experience itself, which by definition cannot be fully described in words. Unlike a sunset, therefore, music *announces itself to us*. This power of music to draw our attention to our own sensations and encourage us to consider them as significant seems also to me to have an obvious purpose in worship. Many traditions of worship encourage the development of an attentiveness and a readiness to be 'spoken to'. Yet, few traditions encourage worshippers to expect that the 'word of God' will always come directly through language, spoken or imagined. Rather, the message may come through images, experiences, sensations, memories. And so worshippers are encouraged to be still and pay attention to everything. Music may smooth our path towards such attentiveness by in some way simulating a situation in which we sense we are being spoken to, thus sharpening our attentiveness accordingly. Since the music is not literally saying anything (in the strict linguistic sense), our attentiveness is available for other purposes. We are made ready to 'hear God's voice'.

20.6.3 Nuance ineffability

Raffman proposes that the third and final type of musical ineffability is *nuance ineffability*. This type of ineffability comes about because we do not have verbal categorizations or schemas as fine-grained as the stimuli we can discriminate. For instance, we may be able to characterize a pitch as 'middle C'. If we are particularly acute, we may be able to label it as 'a slightly sharp middle C', but none of us would be able to operate at the level of cycles per second. Although most of us could detect that there was some difference between two pitches of 250 Hz and 255 Hz respectively, we would not be able to name the difference at that level.

The reasons for nuance ineffability are inherently psychological. Raffman cites a number of such reasons, of which I think two are compelling. First, as Raffman argues, 'it is hard to see what point there would be to a schema whose 'grain' was as fine as perception'. The fact that we describe musical stimuli in broad categories (such as C, D, etc.) is arguably a result of our need reduce the intolerable information load that would be placed on our cognitive system by representing every nuance. In other words, human processing limitations make total effability nuances a psychological impossibility. Second she argues that the just-noticeable-difference (JND) for perceptual properties varies with stimulus and observer characteristics (including alertness, health, etc.).

If these arguments are correct, there will always be a residual ineffable component in any conceivable representation of music. As Raffman poetically describes it, musical experience will always be characterized by 'an evanescent corona shimmering around the structural frame of the piece' (p. 96).

This ineffability is a kind of opposite to structural ineffability. Structural ineffability occurs because, however powerful our mental telescopes. We can never quite get a fix on the biggest picture. Nuance ineffability occurs because our mental microscopes can never reach the smallest level of magnification. I forget who said that there is a complete universe in a drop of water, but such sentiments describe exactly the inexhaustible detail within a musical performance. Such detail is, of course, present in any sensory experience, but again, as was the case with feeling ineffability, we can suppose that the quasi-linguistic nature of music points us towards the 'shimmering corona' and encourages us to endow it with significance. In worship there are contemplative states in which tiny, usually ignored, details of experience are perceived in great clarity, as if for the first time. Musical experience may encourage such states.

To conclude this rather lengthy analysis of musical ineffability, we can see that there are strong arguments for supposing that much musical experience challenges us to go to the limits of our ability to pass easy judgements. We are constantly getting tripped up over one or another form of ineffability. It doesn't seem to me that the act of making well-practiced verbal judgements (about music or anything else) has any particularly special relevance for worship. Where worship seems to be afforded a particularly strong foothold is precisely at the boundaries of what can be said. Music brings us particularly effectively into an awareness of the ineffable, and thus into a core attribute of worship.

20.7 Music as a vehicle for non-judgemental contemplation

The preceding section has suggested what I now need to say explicitly. There may be a sense in which, while listening to music, we cannot help but make judgements about it. These are not so much verbal judgements, as those subconscious and automatic acts of assigning notes to the basic categories of representation. There is much research literature that shows that when we are very familiar with particular structures and codes, our cognitive system performs these routine analyses whether we like it or not. Therefore, when I refer to non-judgemental contemplation, I really mean an attitude of mind in which a listener does not engage in specific verbally based activities leading to verbal judgements (e.g. 'what key is this in?', 'is the trumpet playing in tune?', etc.).

In a restricted sense, therefore, the pharmaceutical model rejected earlier may have some merit. Within a given musical culture, and among individuals who have had comparable prior musical experience, there may be some automatic and subconscious mental processes which are indeed determined primarily by the nature of the particular piece of music being heard. However, if these processes are predominantly inaccessible to consciousness, what is it that a listener may be aware of that derive directly from these processes but are neither associations, nor verbal judgements? One major category of such objects of awareness is the category of affective experiences: feelings, moods, and emotions. It seems clear that there are at least some musically generated affective states which are not simply triggered through association to previously experienced instances of the same or similar music. Music has some inherent characteristics which promote affective responses.

Two lines of evidence (more extensively reported elsewhere, Sloboda 1991) support this assertion. First, music is reported by a wide range of individuals as evoking, often on first hearing, emotions and feelings of an unprecedented intensity and unique character. If someone has feelings she never had before to music she never heard before, then specific associations cannot be playing a major role in the generation of that state. Second, the nature of the affective response to music is sometimes determined by very precise structural characteristics of the music, such as a particular harmonic structure, and seems to be shared by members of a culture. In general these structures are rather abstract, and can be realized in a wide range of specific sequences. It is not the case that there is any simple one-to-one mapping between a key, melody, interval, or chord, and a specific emotion.

There are two main structural determinants of affective response to music. The first, which we could call 'global', relates to overall characteristics of a piece or a section. For instance, smooth, quiet, slow music tends to evoke moods of repose or resignation. Fast, jagged, load music tends to evoke agitated moods, whether of happiness or anger. There seems often to be some rather straightforward analogy being drawn to the characteristics of a human being's behaviour when in such moods. So, for instance, a sad person tends to behave slowly and quietly.

The second determinant, which we could call 'local' relates to the moment to moment changes in affect which are experienced as the music unfolds. So, although we may experience a whole piece as 'sad', we find that sadness reaches a peak of intensity at a particular moment. It appears that many of these moments are determined by the precise confirmations and violations of expectations that are built up in the course of listening. Of course, two people listening to the same piece of music may not always experience the same emotion to such an event, any more than the same person may do so on different hearings. But what the available data do strongly suggest is that if these moment-specific emotions are felt at all, then they are felt at the same points in the music by all listeners. Variations in emotional experience are not caused so much by idiosyncratic ways of representing the music, as by contextual factors (e.g. the prevailing degree of emotional arousal in the individual, the importance of the event of which the music forms a part, etc.) and by the individuals own construal of the emotional response (e.g. one individual may find it wholly therapeutic to be moved to tears by a musical passage, another individual might find it excruciatingly embarrassing).

An example of a musical feature that appears to provoke emotional responses associated with crying (e.g. tears, lump in the throat) is the repeated suspension or appogiatura. Many composers and commentators have explicitly recognized this characteristic as indicative of pathos, and this does not seem to be an arbitrary feature to serve the same effect. The emotional response has something to do with the repeated harmonic tension and relaxation that such structures produce within a tonal context.

It is particularly relevant to the discussion of the role of genre in worship to note that these structural features are not the province of narrow genres.

One can find exactly the same use of appogiaturas in baroque orchestral music as in 1980s pop ballads, yielding exactly the same kind of emotional effect. What can differ, but not in a simple way that is mapped onto genres, is the complexity, subtlety or 'disguisedness', of the way in which a basic structure is deployed by the composer. It is such subtlety which distracts us from noticing too readily that the same underlying structure is present in two pieces of music that affect us in similar ways, and adds a sense of wonder or newness to what might otherwise seem manipulative and overly sentimental.

History has a refining effect. By and large, what survives from ages past is the interesting and unusual rather than the trite. Contemporary music, on the other hand, contains much which is of little value, precisely because history has not yet been able to weed out that which people do not value. I am convinced that many of the value judgements about genres suitable for worship are based on average 'triteness' ratings on the pieces of each genre known to an individual. On these grounds, the average pop track is bound to be triter than the average sixteenth-century anthem. So, also, I have to say, is the average piece of music especially written for church use in the twentieth century.

Here, then, is where individual differences will 'get in the way' of the contemplative response. Many people will resist the emotional effect of some music, simply because the effect is too blatant or obvious. Such resistance is not unique to music. I have heard people complain that they find themselves resisting being moved to tears by the crude manipulative dramas of soap operas. Several musicians I know complain that they find tears coming to their eyes during the performance of 'Land of Hope and Glory' at the Last Night of the Proms, even though they claim to loath the music, and the shallow sentimentality of the occasion. They almost feel ashamed of their response and try to suppress it.

For true contemplation, it is necessary to mentally instruct oneself to forget where the music comes from, to forget one's associations to it, to forget whether one likes it or not, and simply let it work its effect. There is a strong element in worship of quieting one's own inner voices to 'let God speak'. This is often expressed as a subjugation of one's own will and inclinations to God's. Precisely because music does have such strong personal associations, but also *of its own nature* evokes emotional responses which may be quite at variance with one's personal predispositions towards it, there is a clear sense in which the contemplation of music embodies the particular challenge to 'self' that marks out contemplative worship.

20.8 Music as a vehicle for experiencing personal relationships

Engaging with music can bring the participant into particular kinds of relationship with others. I have already alluded in the previous section to the fact that music has a tendency to coordinate at least the shape of the rise and fall of emotional response to music in a body of people. We are all likely to feel most strongly at the same point, even if the precise colour of our feelings differ from one to another.

Such coordination becomes even more focused when we are engaged together in making music. In music-making we are contributing to a larger whole, so that our small individual contribution becomes more significant. This happens in two ways. First, and more simply, our effort is amplified (as when a large body of people are all singing the same tune). Secondly, and more profoundly, new things are achieved through coordination of different activities. New aspects of a melody emerge when it is put in counterpoint with another one, because added to the individual characteristics of each melody on is now the harmonic and rhythmic structure that is created by the relationship of the two melodies.

Music is thus a very good analogy for certain key aspects of worship. In almost every religious tradition there is the notion of a worshipping community, that in some way the coordinated worshipping of a body of people united by common activity is somehow more powerful and effective than individual prayer. Worship reflects human solidarity. And secondly, worship is expressive of relationships between one individual and another. Any relationship is more than the sum of the two individuals. Something new and valuable is realized in the meeting of persons; and in many traditions, including the Christian one, some of the profoundest theological concepts are attempts to grasp just what the newness consists in.

There is, of course, a major problem about communality. A sense of solidarity is not, in and of itself, a guarantee of goodness. Music, and other forms of communal activity can inspire people to unite for evil as well as good ends. Sometimes, the 'godly' act is to refuse to be caught up in communality, and stand alone. It seems to me, therefore, that music can only be used for effective communal worship where there is already an existing community, bound by common understandings and commitments, where trust and 'good works' underpin relationships. In this context music in worship deepens and strengthens mutual commitments. Music cannot, in and of itself, create community.

20.9 Conclusions

I hope that this paper has demonstrated that there are several characteristics of human response to music which are particularly effective affordances for worship. Many of the mental processes encouraged by music are also present in worship. What I have not done is to show, in any very systematic way, that activities other than music do not have the same auspicious set of affordances, thus demonstrating music's unique role. We really need a comprehensive psychological analysis of all human activities that might impinge on worship, comparing and contrasting the affordances of each. But that is a task for a different time and place.

References

Brown, R. and Kulik, J. (1977) Flashbulb memories' *Cognition*, **5**, 73–99.

Gibson, J. J. (1966) *The senses considered as perceptual systems*. Boston: Houghton Mifflin.

Norman, D. A. (1988) *The psychology of everyday things*. New York: Basic Books.

Raffman, D. (1993) *Language, music, and mind*. Cambridge, MA: MIT Press.

Sloboda, J. A. (1989) Music psychology and the composer. In S. Nielzen and O. Olsson (Eds.) *Structure and perception of electroacoustic sound and music*. Amsterdam: Elsevier.

Sloboda, J. A. (1991) Empirical studies of emotional response to music. In M. Riess-Jones (Ed.) *Cognitive bases of musical communication*. Washington, DC: American Psychological Association, pp. 33–46.

CHAPTER 21

EMOTION, FUNCTIONALITY, AND THE EVERYDAY EXPERIENCE OF MUSIC: WHERE DOES MUSIC EDUCATION FIT?

21.1 Introduction

This paper is intended to raise broad issues about the nature and purpose of general music education. Although it is grounded in an empirically observable phenomenon (the decline of engagement of young people in traditional forms of music activity), it goes far beyond scientifically validated data in an attempt to locate the phenomenon we observe within a broad historical and cultural context. I am, however, not a social historian, and I am painfully aware that I may be doing badly what others unknown to me have done much better. I hope readers will take this as an opening contribution to a debate which not enough people in music education research appear to be participating in, rather than a polished and finalized set of positions.

21.2 Why do children drop out of instrumental music?

A phenomenon which has been reported with concern by observers of UK music education is the decline of engagement by young people with those forms of musical activity which have been traditionally encouraged and supported within the school system (particularly the playing of traditional acoustic musical instruments). This decline may be mirrored in other countries, but the focus of this paper is on data from the UK, and its implications for music education in the UK.

The transition from primary to secondary education appears to be a point of particular vulnerability. Many children appear to 'leave instrumental music behind' as they make this transition. This has recently been confirmed by data from a large-scale study of young people's participation in music (cf. Ryan *et al.*, 2000). In this longitudinal study we have been able to collect data from 684 school-aged children (aged 11–12) at three points in time: (a) in the last half of the final year at primary school; (b) in the first half of the first year at secondary school; and (c) in the second half of the first year at secondary school.

Children were asked the same question at each point: 'do you play a musical instrument?'. Among these 684 children, 420 answered 'yes' at point (a). By point (c) only 229 of these were still playing; 191 children (45% of the players) had given up playing.

Although detailed quantitative analysis of the correlates of this massive drop-out is still under way, I'd like to present here two illustrative vignettes, drawn from intensive interviews with two of the children concerned. A sample of 76 children were interviewed at point (a) and again at point (c). The vignettes presented here are from two children who showed a very high degree of instrumental engagement at point (a) but who had given up playing by point (c), one year later. Their names have been changed.

Mary was receiving weekly group violin lessons at school when we first interviewed her. She had learned the violin for two years, but had not taken any Grade exams. She reported playing the violin for upwards of 21 hours per week (3 hours per day).

Lucy was receiving weekly individual piano lessons at her teacher's home when we first interviewed her. She had been learning the piano for 3 years, and had passed Grade 3. She reported playing the piano for between 11 and 15 hours per week (2 hours per day).

Mary and Lucy's weekly investment in their playing puts them both in the top 5% in terms of instrumental time investment within the playing cohort. These levels of investment equal or exceed the age-average (2 hours per day) for the highest achieving players in the study of practising time carried out by Sloboda *et al.* (1996). Mary and Lucy could, therefore, have been expected to be on a trajectory similar to those reported for those children in Sloboda *et al.*'s study who succeeded in competitive entry to a nationally recruiting specialist music school.

Three significant features characterize the accounts given by Mary and Lucy at point (a) while identifying as players.

1 *'Fun' is a key motivating concept, both for individual playing and participation in lessons.* When asked 'What does being involved in music mean to you?', Mary responded: 'It gives me a chance to practice because I like playing my violin, and most children in my class play instruments, so I just thought it would be fun.'. In response to the question: 'What do

you like about playing the violin?' she said, 'I just like practising it, and I like playing it.' To a similar question, Lucy answered, 'Well its just fun really. I just enjoy doing it. It's a hobby, something to do.'

2 *While playing, achievement is valued (e.g. grade success, being able to play a difficult piece, playing in front of people).* Mary expanded her liking of playing the violin by saying 'sometimes the music we have to play is quite hard but it seems easy after a while'. When asked, 'What do you like about playing in front of people?' Lucy replied 'Um, its just that you can show off your talent because you only do that to like your family and music teacher really'. Later she explained: 'I enjoy playing the piano. You can get different grades for it and things, so like all your hard work to pay off when you get to pass an exam or something.'

3 *Parents and instrumental teachers are key players in the discourse concerning support.* In response to the question: 'What did your parents think when you first started playing the violin?' Mary said: 'Me dad was quite interested and happy for me, me mum, she doesn't like the violin because its screechy, she says I'm happy for you, and she's glad that I've got an instrument because I've been on about it all like for a long time, she says I'm happy that you've got the instrument the violin because you've always wanted it . . . '. In response to the same question, Lucy said 'they were really pleased and they said that I was making good progress as well.'

Of her violin teacher, Mary said; 'She's really kind. I did have one teacher and I didn't like her much because if we forgot our violins she used to go tell secretary and then we were in real trouble. But that wasn't all the reason. She didn't give us the chance to pick what music we wanted to play.' Lucy described her piano teacher thus: 'He's always like cheery, and he doesn't shout at you or anything if you get it wrong, he buys books for you to play out of and he just helps you work out notes and things.'

When asked if they thought they would still be playing their instruments in secondary school they both said yes.

Five new features characterize the discourse of these two interviewees at point (c):

1 *Playing an instrument is seen as 'boring'.* When asked 'Can you tell me why you decided to give up the violin?' Mary said 'Cos I didn't like it.' 'What didn't you like about it? 'I don't know. When I first started

playing it, I used to really like instruments but then I just went off it. I just found it boring . . . '. In response to the question, 'Why did you give up the piano?, Lucy said 'Well I'd been playing since year 2, and I'd got up to grade 3, and I just got bored with doing exams and that.'

2 *Previously valued achievements are discounted.* Mary, who at point (a) had enjoyed practising, now 'hated' it. When asked how her teacher reacted to her giving up she said: 'I think she was a bit upset really cos I had been doing quite well just before I quit, and she was like a bit upset that I was, she said I was making good progress, and if I'd carried on a bit longer I would have got some more grades.' 'And how do you feel about having given up now?' I feel quite glad actually. When Lucy was asked 'Do you ever regret having given up?' she replied: 'No . . . . It was.. the exams and practising all the different ones I didn't like doing.'

3 *Other activities are valued more highly than music (e.g. academic lessons, homework, seeing friends).* Mary said 'I hated practising, and I had other things to do, like homework and going outside and playing with my friends, and its just like that took over.' In response to a question about whether she might take up an instrument the following year, Lucy said no, because 'the first year at high school, when you do instruments you miss your lessons, and the you have to catch up, so you worry about having to catch up on your lessons.'

4 *Dropping out of music is associated with discourses of autonomy and self-determination.* When asked whether she missed playing, Mary said no 'because I always used to play at five o'clock till six o'clock, an hour every night. My mum used to push me about doing my practice. I just missed it for a bit, but then I got used to it, doing things I really wanted to do.' Lucy got explicit support from her mother for autonomous choice to stop—'I told my mum first, and she said she wouldn't make me do anything I didn't want to do. So she told my (private) teacher for me.'

5 *Future engagement in music is not ruled out but is conceptualized in terms of instruments and social networks that were marginal to (and possibly conflicting with) previous involvement.* When asked 'If you were to take up an instrument again, is there anyone who you think would be particularly helpful or supportive to you?' Mary nominated her grandmother. In the earlier interview Mary had told us that she used to play the piano, which she actually preferred to the violin (although found it more difficult). Her grandmother played the piano, and Mary sometimes went to her grandmother's house to play the piano there, which used to be in Mary's house. When Lucy was asked whether there was

any instrument she might consider taking up in the future she nominated the saxophone because 'my friend plays cornet, and I go to their jazz concerts, and I like the sound of the saxophone.'

21.3 The sociocultural environment for young people

In gaining a clearer understanding of how a well-embedded daily activity can collapse like a house of cards within a 12-month period, I'd like to propose four conjectures which link these vignettes to wider social and cultural trends.

Conjecture 1. Instrumental playing is a 'hobby'. It is in the nature of hobbies to 'grow out of them'. Therefore an understanding of the 'take' that a lot of children have on musical activities requires a broader understanding of the psychology and sociology of hobbies.

Conjecture 2. Instrumental playing 'comes from' the culture of the primary school, where musical activity is just 'part of the furniture'. It's underpinnings are undermined through the transition to secondary school because:

- instruments are 'less important' than 'academic' subjects
- the peer groups through which instrumental activities are reinforced have been disrupted
- secondary music teachers are (for structural and cultural reasons) in a less good position than their primary colleagues to maintain a shared set of values and expectations within which positive engagement can proceed.

Conjecture 3. Instrumental playing is associated with parental control and a focus of everyday life on the home. The desired focus of the preadolescent life shifts in the direction of increasing assertions of autonomy, identification with peer groups, and life outside the home.

Conjecture 4. For many young people instrumental playing has no inherent 'purpose' which relates to their activities and goals, even those which might involve music in other ways.

For these conjectures to be validated, evidence from a number of sources will be relevant. Some of this evidence exists already. One of the most important sources of evidence comes from detailed studies on the musical lives of individuals in different subcultures within UK society. This shows how people appropriate music for their specific personal and social uses in ways which are often unique, and which have little to do with the forms and activities of music which are found within educational establishments. Two major examples of this approach are provided by Green (2001) in relation to the lives of popular musicians, and De Nora (2000) in relation to the personal lives of adult non-musician women. Another example is given by Sloboda *et al.* (2001) who obtained a one-week 'diary' of musical engagement from adult non-musicians using an 'experience sampling methodology' (originated by Czikszentmihalyi and Lefevre, 1989). Participants carried pagers with them at all times for a week, and made a structured entry into a 'diary' every time the pager sounded. They were required to report on concurrent activity and the nature, purpose, and effect any music happening in the context of that activity. The study showed that the vast majority of music takes place in the context of (and subsidiary to) non-musical activity. The most common types of activity are what we call 'maintenance' activities, those essential routines of everyday life which everyone has to perform many times each day (e.g. washing, cleaning, cooking, travelling, etc.). Usually these activities are enacted alone, and music seems to be a resource through which the individual addresses issues of personal autonomy and identity. Because of this, the accounts of participants from a range of studies suggest that music is often a source of conflict where different individuals occupying the same space have different relationships to, and needs from, the music. The same music that affirms and reinforces one person's psychological agendas can simultaneously threaten another's.

Sloboda *et al.* (2001) also investigated change in emotional state as a result of the music experienced. In general, participants experienced greater and more positive change when the music was chosen by them.

Unfortunately, all the studies of this sort known to us have been undertaken with adult participants. The details of the intimate hour-by-hour musical lives of children in contemporary society are almost unknown to us. We really need to know much more about what children autonomously use music for in their everyday lives. In particular, we need to know what are the 'natural' varieties of performance that are given meaning within their solitary, family, and social settings. Then we can begin to understand better how formal instrumental playing maps (or fails to map) onto these natural categories.

21.4 The goals and attitudes of classroom music teachers

A second source of evidence relevant to an understanding of why children drop out of formal music relates to the nature of what it is they are running from. An important new source of information on this matter comes from a recent survey of 750 heads of music in UK secondary schools catering for ages 12–16 (York, 2001). Seventy-eight per cent of respondents had degrees based in classical music, with 50% being either classical pianists, organists, or singers. The most commonly used public sources of support and resources for their teaching were BBC Radio 3, Classic FM, and *BBC Music Magazine*. The most commonly used specialist sources of information were the Qualifications and Curriculum Authority (55%) and the local music service (50%). Use of agencies such as British Phonographic Institute, the Musicians Union, or the Performing Rights Society was almost nonexistent.

Respondents were asked if they knew 20 pieces of music from various genres and periods , and could name the most associated composer or performer. Although over 95% could correctly answer for classical titles such as *The Four Seasons* (Vivaldi) or the 'Ode to Joy' (Beethoven), only half answered correctly for 'Wannabe' (Spice Girls), and only tiny numbers were correct for 'Kind of Blue' (Miles Davies—15%), and 'Rockafeller Skank' (Fatboy Slim—9%).

York concludes from these and other data that:

> School music culture tends to be introverted and avoids looking for models of current practice from the art of music rather than relying on the received knowledge of music education. . . . Many teachers seem to be engaged in using pop and rock to extend pupils' musical interests into other styles. . . . but the vast majority of teachers are doing this with little or no training or professional experience in pop or rock.

Although York's analysis focuses on the genres used by music teachers, there is implicit in his data the assumption that this is about more than genres. It is about different approaches to music, including ways of thinking about it and responding to it. One cannot just insert a popular genre into the set of classroom practices that have been developed to deal with classical music.

Musical subcultures are defined by much more than the style of music they use (it is also how used, in what contexts, for what purposes, assuming what type of inter-personal relationships, accruing what meanings). Labels such as 'pop' and 'rock' are coarse-grained and uninformative. Take, for instance, the case of 'techno'.

Techno is neither 'performed', 'composed', or 'appraised' within parameters that fit neatly with UK National Curriculum formulations. The music is 'constructed' in real time out of computer-manipulated elements at the disposal of a 'DJ'. Its primary function is to support communal (but individualistic) dancing designed to induce certain altered states of awareness.

Dancers may only experience the intended effects after several continuous hours of engagement. A short extract experienced in a classroom setting provides an incomplete, even misleading, basis for appraisal. The basis for valid appraisal exists only for someone attending a techno club and dancing to the music. No classroom teacher could hope to adequately address issues relating to techno with their students without specific understanding of, and exposure to, that sub-genre and its role for its habitual users. The same point can be made for almost any other sub-genre.

21.5 Determining the place of music in education

Music education in schools cannot function effectively without an implicit agreement between stakeholders (e.g. teachers, student, parents, government, etc.) about what it is for. The 'meaning of music' is a constantly shifting function of the discourses of these diverse groups, which may coalesce around a 'dominant ideology' which gains enough inter-group consensus to generate a stable educational agenda. I would argue that such a stable agenda existed in mid twentieth-century music education, but its underpinning consensus collapsed as a result of major cultural shifts, most evident from the 1960s onwards.

At risk of caricature, but emboldened by the analyses of writers such as Cook (1998) and Small (1998), the dominant paradigm of the early to mid twentieth century might be described as follows.

Classical artworks (as epitomized by Bach or Beethoven) represent the pinnacle of musical value. Deeper appreciation and understanding of such artworks is the most important (and universally applicable) aim of music education. Such appreciation and understanding is most accessible to those who have the technical and theoretical skills to perform these works. All performance-based education is oriented towards enabling a significant minority (or even a majority) to acquire the necessary skills to be able to perform at least some works from the canon. The most profound end result of a musical education trajectory is the development of the ability to add to the canon of masterworks through compositional activity. This is necessarily confined to the few. Music is necessarily best taught by people trained in the understanding and performance of the classical canon.

A revised version of this characterization emerged in the 1960s–1980s, primarily articulated through the liberal educational establishment, justifying some broadening of the syllabus but still very much framed by the pre-existing dominant paradigm. It ran something like the following.

Lesser forms of musical activity (e.g. world music, pop, jazz, etc.) have their legitimate place within the syllabus, and may be necessary 'stopping points' for many people. A wide range of musical activities and genres permit the development of valuable skills, including technical skills relating to the perception and production of organized sound, the ability to subordinate the personal to the goals of a group, self-discipline, etc. Music can be a useful vehicle for interdisciplinary education, relating it to its cultural, historical, and scientific context. *But*, whatever broadening of the syllabus is contemplated, music education must remain controlled by those who have been through a full classical training themselves, since this remains the pinnacle of the musical pyramid, to which all, in the end, aspires.

Our present dilemmas may be an indication of the unsustainability of even this liberalized view of music education. It may be no longer possible to muster stakeholder consensus around any version of the educational enterprise which prioritizes the classical canon. Strong cultural forces have been at work which account for the collapse of this consensus. I identify seven such forces. There may, of course, be more.

21.6 Key cultural trends

21.6.1 Multiculturalism

An important consequence of the multiculturalism that increasingly has characterized the United Kingdom since the Second World War is the fact that European history and culture no longer defines British history and culture. The classical canon is the product of European history and culture, and its defence therefore increasingly becomes identified with a xenophobic 'fortress' mentality which places it on the margins of the cultural spectrum.

21.6.2 Youth culture

In developed countries, prosperity gives young people unprecedented freedoms and spending power. This allows them to set cultural agendas rather than accept agendas laid down by others. The effects of this are being felt throughout secondary education, not just in music, but it is arguable that stakeholder consensus is still holding together (just) in disciplines where the educational agendas relate more directly to occupationally relevant skills. Parents and children will ally themselves with school management where the earning potential of their child is at stake. They are less likely to do this when neither school management nor government is able to articulate a shared vision of the value of music which is stronger that the child's own lived experience.

21.6.3 Electronic communication

Unprecedented choice, and miniaturization of delivery technology, gives much greater individual autonomy in musical experience than has been possible hitherto. Young people can easily and cheaply create their own musical 'worlds'. Institutions such as schools no longer comprise a privileged route of access.

21.6.4 Feminism

This movement has had many profound effects on culture. One important effect is the progressive replacement of the hierarchic by the democratic as the paradigm of cultural organization. In the context of music, this has rendered the paradigm forms of the classical canon increasingly problematic. The symphony concert represents the pinnacle of such forms. Everything from the nature of the building to the social organization of symphony orchestras points to the subjugation of the entire cultural project to the will of the (overwhelmingly predominantly male) 'maestro' who is himself subjugated to the will of the (male) composer. Feminism foregrounds alternative modes of organization where leadership is more shared and fluid, and where the musicians are as likely to have generated their own music as they are to be reproducing music of others. Although the pop group is not without major contradictions as an expression of feminism (not least because the membership of such groups is still overwhelmingly male, and because the music industry attempts to be far more controlling of pop musicians than classical patrons ever had the power to be) it is hard to imagine major industrial nations according symphony orchestras the explicit or implicit role as 'cultural ambassador' that is now accorded to a country's major popular artists. When the London Symphony Orchestra visits the USA no one notices or cares. When the Spice Girls visit, this is front page news.

21.6.5 Secularism

Christianity (along with all forms of organized religion) has suffered a massive decline as a social force in the last 40 years (Brown, 2001). People look within themselves and their personal networks rather than outside for sources of personal meaning and fulfilment. Personal emotional work, rather than confirmation of the social/divine order, becomes a key focus of musical activity. Key musical organizations to which almost all children used to be exposed (the church choir) are no longer experienced by most children. I have argued elsewhere that churches have probably been responsible for keeping alive a 'ladder of opportunity' for classical music performers in every town and village for the last century. This ladder now has many missing rungs (Sloboda, 1999, Chapter 19, this volume), and schools have neither the resources nor the social influence to bridge the gaps.

21.6.6 Niche cultures

In the age of easy electronic communications affiliations between individuals are increasingly based on 'special interests' rather than shared social or civic obligations (and the geographical proximity which this presupposes). Young people can be swapping information (and music clips) with people on the other side of the world. Schools, which could easily relate to the civic (e.g. village brass bands, the church, the Town Hall) are cut out of the loop of shifting grass-roots affiliations. The decline of the 'civic' has been most prominently documented by Putnam (2000).

21.6.7 Postmodernism

All the above are sometimes considered as key manifestations of a postmodern society, characterized by a free, even anarchic cultural 'market', in which the conditions for one segment to acquire cultural dominance do not exist. There are significant national differences in all these factors. For instance, the cultural homogeneity of small-town America, with the far stronger grip of religion, and relatively weak incursions of feminism, can probably still sustain a music education system which meets more dominant cultural needs.

The consequence of cultural fragmentation is that we music educators no longer occupy a privileged vantage point. We represent a small (and increasingly marginal) subset of these subcultures that coexist in the population. Furthermore it is an assumption of postmodernism that the conditions for the re-establishment of a new 'dominant cultural ideology' do not exist. We cannot hope for any easy return to the stability we once enjoyed. A national curriculum for music was probably introduced at the very moment in history when its sustainability had never been less certain. The classical conservatoire culture is vibrant and valuable. It just won't do for the majority of our children. In this context it is important to defend teachers, who are not to blame for the 'failure' of music education. The present rapid rate of cultural change is leaving many public institutions 'high and dry' in one way or another.

21.7 What should viable and engaging UK music education look like?

On the basis of the above it is at least conceivable to hypothesize that classroom music, as currently conceptualized and organized, is an inappropriate vehicles for mass music education in twenty-first century Britain. Hints of the parameters of a more effective music education environment may well be found within the somewhat anarchic mixed economy of out-of-school music provision in this country. Such anarchy may be crucial breeding-ground for the celebration of personal autonomy and cultural differentiation that is a prerequisite for focused and goal-directed musical engagement in a postmodern society. This is not simply an anarchy of musical styles and genres, or even of technologies, but an anarchy of social relationships, where boundaries between the teacher and student role are creatively redrawn.

Variety may well be the key concept. I indicate eight areas where it may be possible to significantly increase the variety available to our young people:

1. *Varied providers.* There should be no monopolies of provision but a healthy alliance of national, regional, and local interest groups.

2. *Varied funding.* There should be a mixture of state, voluntary, and commercial funding, reflecting the different interests that have a legitimate stake in music education.

3. *Varied locations.* Music education should be delivered throughout the community, in schools, music centres, community centres, shops, homes, cultural centres (e.g. libraries, museums).

4. *Varied roles for educators.* To support a wider range of musical cultures and activities, those supporting young people need to adopt a wider range of roles than has traditionally been conceived. These include teacher, animateur, coach, mentor, impresario, fundraiser, programmer, composer, arranger, and studio manager.

5. *Varied trajectories.* Young people need a wide range of 'entry and exit' points from musical engagement. These should vary from long-term syllabi for some, but should include a far wider variety of short-term projects for others, who may dip in and out according to the needs and parameters of the project, rather than be subject to the tyranny of the school term or year.

6. *Varied activities.* The range of activities available to young people should mirror more closely the types of musical activities available in the subcultures they value. This will involve a wider menu of visits, workshops, concerts, talks, programme planning, and assistance in activities such as DJing. It is probable that the DJ is the most common 'deliverer' of music within the community. How many young people get meaningful help in developing the role of DJ?

7. *Varied accreditation of achievement.* A range of certificates of participation/ competence is needed to accredit and document participation. Existing agencies need to broaden the range of qualifications on offer, and new agencies should develop them. There is nothing wrong with graded music exams or GCSEs. We just need more choices for young people who value accreditation.

8. *Varied routes to training competence (beyond GRSM, BMus, PGCE).* If people are to be suitably trained to support young people's music-making, then a far wider range of training and continuing professional development opportunities must be on offer than then traditional 'teacher education' model. Indeed, until this happens, it is hard to see how major change will occur.

It is quite difficult to predict what the final role of schools might be in a wider more inclusive view of music education. However, school music is the one aspect of the provision which we can guarantee all children to receive. Perhaps its most useful role is to provide a core anchor point where diverse experiences may be reflected upon, integrated, and coordinated.

References

Brown, C. (2001) *The death of Christian Britain.* London: Routledge.

Cook, N. (1998) *Music: a very short introduction.* Oxford: Oxford University Press.

Czikszentmihalyi, M. and Lefevre, J. (1989) Optimal experience in work and leisure. *Journal of Personality and Social Psychology,* **56**, 815–822.

De Nora, T. (2000) *Music in everyday life.* Cambridge: Cambridge University Press.

Green, L. (2001) *How popular musicians learn: a way ahead for music education.* London: Ashgate.

Putnam, R. (2001) *Bowling alone: the collapse and revival of American community.* New York: Simon and Schuster.

Ryan, K., Boulton, M., O'Neill, S. A., and Sloboda, J. A. (2000) Perceived social support and children's participation in music. In C. Woods, G. Luck, R. Brochard, F. Seddon, and J. Sloboda (Eds.) *Science, music, and society: Proceedings of the 6th International Conference on Music Perception and Cognition.* Newcastle, Staffordshire: Keele University.

Sloboda, J. A. (1999) Music: where cognition and emotion meet. *The Psychologist,* **12.4**, 450–455.

Sloboda, J. A., Davidson, J. W., Howe, M. J. A., and Moore, D. G. (1996) The role of practice in the development of performing musicians. *British Journal of Psychology,* **87**, 287–309.

Sloboda, J. A., O'Neill, S. A., and Ivaldi, A. (2001) Functions of music in everyday life: an exploratory study using the Experience Sampling Methodology. *Musicae Scientiae,* **5**(1), 9–32.

Small, C. (1998) *Musicking: the meanings of performance and listening.* Hanover NH: Wesleyan University Press.

York, N. (2001) *Valuing school music: A report on school music.* London: University of Westminster and Rockschool Ltd.

CHAPTER 22

THE 'SOUND OF MUSIC' VERSUS THE 'ESSENCE OF MUSIC': DILEMMAS FOR MUSIC–EMOTION RESEARCHERS

COMMENTARY ON *CURRENT TRENDS IN THE STUDY OF MUSIC AND EMOTION*, A SPECIAL ISSUE *OF MUSICAE SCIENTIAE* (2001–2) *EDITED BY PATRIK N. JUSLIN AND MARCEL R. ZENTNER*

22.1 Introduction

I was a musician long before I was a psychologist. Specific performances of individual compositions spoke to me as no human being I knew had spoken, certainly by the age of 5. These, mainly recorded, performances became friends, comforters, inspirers, pointers to possibilities beyond the norms of my life. I knew these pieces as a lover knows a beloved. I knew every crevice, every corner, every quirk which made this piece individual, even odd, but identifiable as distinct and itself, different from every other piece, even though sharing so much in common. Within many pieces, I had favourite parts, and parts that I got bored with, or struggled to understand. And after a while my infatuation with a particular piece waned, and I sought new experiences with different pieces. Were emotions involved? Obviously! But specific emotions were embedded within something much more complex and multifaceted. Being 'into' these pieces of music was about learning who I was, what I might hope for, and something about what love and commitment could be for me. In other words, my involvement with these pieces of music was about the deepest and most ultimate aspects of being: self-knowledge, spirituality, transcendence, and growth. They were not only my friends, they were my guides.

Because I heard some of these pieces on the radio (used for example as interludes between spoken items), without any textual or background information, I did not always know their names. But I could often conjure up a complete auditory 'image', just as a lover might visualize the behaviour and personality of someone watched from afar, but to whom one had never been introduced. Name and genre knowledge came much later: sometimes many years later.

I was astonished and surprised to make the discovery, probably some seven or eight years after my first exposure, that a number of short pieces, which I had heard separately at different times, actually were part of a single entity – the Tchaikovsky *Nutcracker Suite*. It was a similar surprise to finding out that several quite different people one knew in different contexts all turned out to be brothers and sisters. How could these characters, all so different, so individual in such distinct and quirky ways, known and loved in such different times and places, have come from the same source?

Why have I made this small excursion into the autobiographical? It is because reading some of the contributions to this special issue raised in me an echo of this childish surprise. For instance the *Nutcracker Suite* appears as one of the items in Table 2 of Vastfjall's masterly analysis of the music mood induction literature. As I surveyed this list, I wondered how it was that this kaleidoscopic collection of deeply loved friends could be 'reduced' by Parrott (1982) to one of several dozen other named items that induced 'positively valenced affect' when used in a mood induction experiment, with the implication that it didn't much matter which of these several pieces were being heard at the time, or who was hearing them, or how well they knew the pieces, which bits of them were liked more or less, or indeed that there might be subtle differences between the induced feelings which were far richer than any psychometric scale could ever detect. I felt the same jolt as I might if overhearing a local bigot write off individual members of a family that I knew well as 'all the same' because they were members of a particular ethnic minority.

Is it not understandable that many people (particularly those most intimately involved with music) feel a sense of uneasiness, possibly verging on outrage in the most extreme cases, that psychological research may be failing to address the most fundamental and essential aspects of what it is to be humanly involved in music? Loved pieces of music are being reduced to a set of 'effects' such as might similarly be realized by the colour of paint on a wall, or the administration of caffeine.

For many years I held this unease at arm's length. To do this I had two main defences: the scientific reification of the variable, and a rejection of elitism (or at least, my own simplistic takes on these hugely complex issues).

Reification of the variable is an intellectual viewpoint which asserts that the only things one can really understand are the things one can control and measure (in the instrumental ways available within experimental or quasi-experimental settings). While control over variables is completely necessary for very many aspects of scientific activity, including hypothesis testing, it is in fact an error to believe that one can do good science if one limits one's thinking and observations to that which can be expressed in terms of those variables. On the contrary, without experiencing the fullest complexity of a phenomenon, one cannot know what it is that the variables within one's theory are supposed to be explaining. The danger for scientists is that we 'filter out' those aspects of the experience that are not encompassed within the dimensions that we use to describe and talk about them, and so what we work on becomes an almost unrecognizable parody of the phenomenon we are supposedly investigating. In the case of 'musical mood induction procedures' it is hard to recognize much that would be considered music listening by a person such as the child I once was. Such activity might indeed be taking place in some of the people being studied, but the level of description and measurement is often such as to completely exclude that experience from the discourse.

I am not here talking principally about ecological validity, although this is a linked concept. Situations are ecologically valid if they resemble actual life experiences in significant ways. People listen to recorded tracks that they may not have heard before in everyday life whilst performing a range of cognitive tasks, so there is *prima facie* ecological validity when people are asked to listen to such tracks in a laboratory setting. My concern is more about which aspects of that listening situation are being measured, and whether they can lead to real knowledge unless they are continually being held up against the known fullness of human musical experience.

My second defence was based on a rejection of elitism. For many years, it appeared to me (and others) that the experimental psychology of music could be seen as contributing to the liberation of the music-listening public from the grip of notions promoted by the academic music establishment that derived from a nineteenth-century bourgeois conception of art-music as a small set of masterworks that formed the canon, and whose greatness transcended culture and history. Some of our work, and parallel work undertaken by ethnomusicologists, and the increasing number of proponents of the 'new musicology', was engaged in a process of 'depriveleging' these masterworks and their cultural niches (i.e. the classical concert-hall *habitus*, to use the term coined by Bourdieu, 1977, whose sad death was announced as I write this in January 2002; see also Small, 1998). This process had, and continues to have, worthy aims (excellently outlined and critiqued by Cook, 1998). It is a part of a programme of democratization of taste whereby any type of music experienced in any kind of context is as worthy of interest and study as any other. Thus, chart music experienced through a Walkman in the subway is no more or less worthy of study than Beethoven experienced in the concert hall. Indeed, one might even argue that chart music in the subway deserves more study, since this is a predominant cultural experience, whereas concert-hall music is a specialized niche. Science has therefore allied itself with grassroots sensibilities and present-day realities over and against the outmoded cultural imperialism rooted in a yearning for an idealized past.

It may not be coincidental that the intellectual and cultural home of this grand democratization project is, and has always been, North America. In popular culture it is hard to argue that any figures have been of greater global significance in this project than Elvis Presley and Andy Warhol. In academia, the pivotal figures have also been American (e.g. Susan McClary, 1991). Music sciences (particularly psychological sciences) have been profoundly influenced by the democratizing principles of behaviourism, of whom the most profound twentieth-century icon remains the American psychologist B. F. Skinner (who was at his apogee just as Presley and Warhol were emerging to an unsuspecting world). Behaviourism allowed a major escape from 'reputation and pedigree' in describing and accounting for human behaviour. It told us to ignore a person's heritage, rank, wealth, or status, and just concentrate on what he or she actually did (described in language which was similarly 'value free' and which could equally well be—and was—applied to non-human animals). The 'cognitive revolution' of the 1960s never abandoned the fundamental tenets of behaviourism, it just showed how behaviourist ideals could be applied to the measurement of the mental (including emotions and subjective reports) as well as the physical.

North American journals retain the highest scientific prestige within most areas of psychology, and most of the English-speaking research community adopts the conventions and research agendas that such prestigious outlets set. The contributions to this volume predominantly reflect 'Anglo-Saxon' intellectual values derived from the behaviourist programme (I say 'Anglo-Saxon' rather than North American, since these values have a second historic axis in Great Britain, and neighbouring countries of north-west Europe).

What first gave me cause to explicitly question the Anglo-Saxon programme as applied to music was my exposure to the ideas of the British sociologist of music, Simon Frith (1996). Frith made the observation that the rejection of elitism did not necessarily involve (as many had assumed) the rejection of connoisseurship. People who listened extensively to the products of popular rather than 'high-art' musical culture could have a knowledge of that music which was just as articulated, subtle, and differentiated as the commentaries of classical music theorists. In other words, just because the materials and contexts of much popular music were mundane and everyday, it did not follow that the mental contents of such listening must be similarly 'stripped down' and mundane. What was true of my relationship to the *Nutcracker Suite* at age 5 could be true of any person's relationship to any music of any genre.

If this is the case, then the unease of those who question the Anglo-Saxon scientific agenda cannot be written off as an elitist backlash. Rather it suggests that 'cultural democratization' contains within it elements of a new cultural imperialism, an imperialism which seeks to downplay those elements of the musical experience which are individual, personal, complex, subtle, unreplicable; in favour of those elements which are communal, public, simple, plain, and replicable.

Although such imperialism may mesh well with strands of Anglo-Saxon science, it surely cannot relate in any simple way to the needs of science. Far more likely are economic motivations, deriving from the commodification of musical goods and services, and the need to predict and control musical consumption in the interests of profit. If significant psychological effects of music can be linked to a few key variables, along which musical products can be measured and classified, then the possibilities for mass marketing and mass consumption are hugely increased. If people can be encouraged, in subtle ways, to believe that these key variables are the 'main story' about music, then they will be much more susceptible to indiscriminate consumption of musical products which fit these descriptors.

The most clear, and bizarre, example of this process in recent years is the commercialization of the 'Mozart effect' (Rauscher *et al.*, 1995), whereby a small series of exploratory and rather inconclusive experiments was seized on by commercial interests bent on persuading anxious parents that they could improve their child's chance of economic success (through higher school grades) if they played Mozart to their child. Forget that Mozart wrote several hundred distinct works, which have received several thousand different recorded interpretations. The consequence of the way that music has been commodified is that a smart profiteer may take any set of Mozart performances (one guesses those for which the copyright and reproduction rights costs are the least), put them together on a compilation CD, and then reach thousands of eager purchasers. Whether families may benefit from the use of such recordings is not the issue here. The issue is that experiential horizons may be insidiously narrowed. When a piece of Mozart is appropriated instrumentally as a kind of auditory vitamin pill, it becomes less likely to be encountered as a unique and highly personal cultural communication which has the power to speak at many levels, teach, inspire, become deeply known.

I would claim that the Mozart effect is one (although probably among the oddest) of a set of commercially inspired projects whose outcomes are gradually but inexorably 'thinning out' the musical habitus of the industrialized consumer, in the interests of production efficiency and profit. Instead of drawing on a multifaceted cultural discourse where Mozart's music is understood as a highly differentiated collection with a rich history of usage and assimilation, an entire repertoire can be 'reinvented' as 'the music that makes you smart', thus cutting it away from 250 years of cherishing, and re-presenting it as the vapid and culturally monochrome product of a advertising copywriter's pen.

22.2 Orientation and purpose

My reasons for opening this commentary with remarks which might seem overly speculative and culturally barbed are twofold. First, scientific activity can never escape from the cultural and economic forces which surround its practitioners. It befits us to examine our own practices and the degree to which our assumptions of objectivity are in fact deeply conditioned by our cultural outlook. Second, this commentary is being written at a unique juncture in history, following a series of events (11 September 2001) which many (including myself) believe will change the world more profoundly than any other set of events in living memory. These events have revealed that an ever deepening understanding of, and rational reaction to, the cultural and economic programme of the world's richest nations, is the most important task facing all intellectuals, whatever their discipline. That programme must neither be hailed as self-evidently good, nor self-evidently evil, but like all other cultures that have existed in the world, a complex mixture of the functional and the dysfunctional. The way we do our science can reinforce either of these trends, and, for many people at this moment in history, it is just not an option to 'carry on as normal' without evaluating the effect of the programmes we participate in.

My main question, therefore, to the contributions in this special issue, is to what extent the research reported points to, explicates, and encourages the understanding of diversity and complexity in musical experience. For diversity to be authentic, rather than stochastic, such diversity requires relating to the autonomous experience of the individual listener as agent, meeting the musician as autonomous agent, and generating an interaction through the music which reflects and draws upon the motives, beliefs, aspirations, and goals of the players.

In posing this specific question of these contributions I am using them as an 'opportunity sample' of cutting-edge research in music and emotion which is somewhat representative of the field as a whole. My comments are thus intended to be interpreted in relation to 'the state of the discipline', rather than as specific critiques of these contributions which, having been through vigorous and rigorous peer review, should be assumed to represent a sample of the best quality work that is going on within the discipline. My question is more, what values do these contributions promote or undermine (whether explicitly or implicitly).

In doing this I am not for a moment suggesting that individual studies which explicitly address the issues I have raised are more scientifically worthwhile than those which don't, or that all scientific studies should be of a particular nature.

The papers fall into three main groups. The first group contains the contributions of Gabrielsson (2002), London (2002), and Vastfjall (2002). These are summative reviews which highlight in different ways the continuing attempt of the research community to achieve greater clarity on whether and how real emotions and moods may be induced by exposure to music, and how this relates to other ways of 'knowing' emotion-based aspects of music (e.g. through judgements of emotional 'character' or association). A key question I address through the contributions of this group as 'Does music really make us feel things; and if so, how?'

The second group contains the contributions of Scherer *et al.* (2002), and Schubert (2002). These present new data on listeners' emotional experiences, and are indicative of the ways in which music-emotion research has gone beyond the summative Likert-type rating scale as a means of tapping listener response. A key question for the papers in this group is 'How do we gain the most accurate picture of what is going on emotionally when people listen to music?'

The third and final group contains the contributions of Juslin *et al.* (2002), and Trehub and Nakata (2002). These also present new data, but explore the link between performer-controlled variations and listener response. Although the performer–audience situation is very different in these two papers (expert instrumental performers to adult listeners in Juslin *et al*; parents to babies in Trehub and Nakata) they share a concern with mapping communicative options available to performers. This group allows us to address the question 'How can performers affect the emotional experience of listeners?'

I will deal with these issues in turn, and then conclude with some summative remarks.

22.3 Does music really make us feel things, and why?

The celebrated English conductor Sir Thomas Beecham (a noted wit) is reported to have once said: 'The English don't like music: but they do love the sound it makes'. London expresses this quite profound distinction when he says:

> The acoustic qualities (of music) have expressive correlates and may trigger emotional responses, and of course one cannot have music without sound. However, musical expression is more than this: it requires the attention to the music *qua* music, rather than as mere sounds.

This distinction has encouraged several scholars (among whom London identifies Kivy) to see to what extent 'garden variety' emotion induction can be loaded onto music as sound, leaving music *qua* music free to engender feelings by a different route. Kivy (1999), for instance, wishes to claim that it is the aesthetic qualities of music which engage music-specific emotion—'Sad music emotionally moves me, qua *sad* music, by its musically beautiful sadness'.

My reading of this is that *recognition* of emotion (e.g. sadness) is a function of identifying characteristics of the sound that could equally well be instantiated in non-musical sounds (e.g. speech), or by picking up specific cultural associations of the sound (e.g. organ music is 'churchy'). In some contexts, this may lead to the listener *feeling* that emotion (or some other emotion). However, that entire process may proceed without any music-specific processes being invoked. I may cry when I hear sad music for exactly the same reason as I cry when I hear a person expressing grief through their vocalizations. Therapeutic and other behavioural effects of music may be mediated at this level alone; in which case it is more appropriate to say that the effects rely on the shadow cast by music on to the soundscape, but that they are not effects of the music *qua* music.

Musically relevant emotion requires, according to my reading of Kivy and others, an aesthetic response to the individuality of that work, not what it has in common with other musical works, far less with non-musical stimuli. Kivy identifies one possible perceived quality that can drive this process, 'beauty'. I am sure this is the right kind of quality to support his arguments, but wonder if we need (1) to unpack this rather imprecise concept, and (2) characterize a wider range of ways in which music can be experienced and individuated. Beauty can, for instance, be related to both biologically and culturally induced factors, as well as nature and degree of prior exposure to related stimuli. Familiarity may be another key determinant of aesthetic judgement (as developed in the Berlynean approach, for instance). However, more work is probably needed to explain precisely what specific kinds of familiarity and unfamiliarity yield strong aesthetic attraction. If one uses analogies from human relationships (e.g. falling in love), they suggest a complex interplay between familiarity (the tendency of many people to fall in love with someone that resembles a parent) and novelty (we tend not to fall in love with people we know well unless we discover ways of seeing them in a 'new light'). The notion of 'revelation' seems pertinent—which may be characterized as the joint and simultaneous experience of something as wholly new and unexpected together with the experience of its absolute 'rightness and inevitablity' (see Sloboda 1989, 1999, 2000, for further exploration of these issues).

In order to engage these kinds of conceptual domains, it seems that a decision of some sort (whether conscious or subconscious, whether influenced by learned or innate factors) is required of the listener. This is the decision to treat the musical stimulus as intentional and personal (i.e. emanting from, or representing, an autonomous agent with communicative intentions). It doesn't much matter whether the stimulus actually so emanates (for instance many people experience natural phenomena, flowers, mountains and sunsets, in similar ways, and ascribe these to the intention of a creator). It is that decision that allows us to respond to music in the way that Kivy and others are pointing to.

The elaboration and development of these kinds of concepts seem not to be a priority of the mainstream experimental literature on musical emotion. The mere fact that music is presented to a listener is very often taken as a grounds to assume that music-*qua*-music listening is going on, and so the emotional effects are ascribed to 'music'. This is a gross oversimplification.

It was therefore a great relief to read, in Vastjfall's review of the music mood induction literature, that many researchers recognize that 'the music by itself will not automatically induce the desired mood state, and that (listeners) should try really hard to get into the mood, using whatever means they find most effective'. Furthermore 'within the same experiment, some participants report to be highly affected by the manipulation, whereas others remain unaffected'. Allowing participants choice over the music used in mood induction appears to increase the reliability and intensity of the outcome. All of these findings suggest that the apparent 'power' of music rests on the full engagement of the listener, and is not a 'pharmaceutical' property of the sound stimulus. Commonalities of response between listeners arise only when their intentions, beliefs, cultural background, and experience can also be commonalized. Cultural homogenization may be the prerequisite for 'induction laws' to be derived by science. Vastjfall's review suggests that, despite the strong cultural pressures for homogenization of taste, individuals resist, and continue to respond to music in ways which individuate and differentiate them. They will not accept *Swan of Tuonela* in place of 'Nothing compares to you', whatever similarities at the level of 'sound characteristics' these two items may have.

The data reviewed by Gabrielsson (2002) shows how difficult it is to show commonality of response to music, either at the level of basic physiology or at the level of aesthetic response. Studies which correlate physiological responses to basic emotion categories (e.g. Nyklicek *et al.* 1997) rarely yield a straightforward outcome. The clearest outcome of this study was a correlation between respiratory variables and arousal level of the music. When musical sound parameters are arousing, people tend, on the whole, to breathe faster and deeper. What is missing from many of these studies is an appropriate non-music control (e.g. the sound of machinery or traffic). If the arousing properties of the musical stimulus are the same as those of non-musical stimuli, then we learn nothing much from these studies about the specific ways in which music-*qua*-music engages the emotions and the corresponding physiology.

One of Gabrielsson's most important contributions to the research literature is his series of studies on 'strong experiences to music'. These studies show that musical experiences sometimes allow people to enter into what Maslow (1976) has described as 'peak experiences'. Although these experiences have an emotional component, they are hugely more complex than the 'garden variety' basic emotions of happiness, sadness, etc. in ways that are not fully explored. There is little evidence that these experiences are 'determined' by musical parameters in any clear way. There is no 'set' of musical works which are guaranteed to provide these experiences. The accounts given by Gabrielsson's respondents show that strong experiences arise in situations which often contain complex biographical and non-musical factors which interact with the musical experience in unique ways. According to Maslow (1976), music and sex are the most reliable ways of engendering peak experiences. Understanding why this is requires a great deal more systematic and painstaking collection of idiographic data than has been undertaken up till now, both with musical and non-musical experiences. There is also a need for imaginative theorizing if the work is to progress beyond the stage of anecdote and natural history.

I am aware that any attempts to separate varieties of listening to music-*qua*-music from other modes of engagement with it are open to the very claims of elitism (and prescriptiveness) that I have been at pains to distance myself from. One might argue that if some people listen to music without those mental processes which are being proposed 'special to music-*qua*-music' then they legitimize these modes of listening as 'real music listening' by the mere fact that they exist. I admit that the issues here are sensitive. What need re-emphasizing is that there is much evidence to suggest that individuated and personally engaging involvement with music appears to be a primary human impulse, which is demonstrated in young children (further discussion of this point may be found in Section 22.5 below), in people with no formal musical training at all, and in many of the world's musical cultures. 'Taking music personally' seems to be a fundamental human response. It is at least possible that depersonalizing and deindividualizing music in the particular ways noted in commercially oriented cultures requires various types of psychological narrowing or 'reining in'. It is precisely such 'narrowing' tactics that cultural elites have traditionally employed. When the narrowing I have focused on is apparently presented as part of 'popular' culture, then those who resist it can be branded as elitist. This, however, I would argue, is a misreading of the situation. The resistance to the narrowing of the musical habitus is not driven by middle-aged white male Beethoven lovers. It is as likely to come from rock lovers, techno lovers, jazz or folk lovers; and as likely to be felt by someone with no musical training at all as someone with a conservatoire diploma. All these forms of music engagement are coming to have common cause as marginal cultural forms, under threat because their economic yield is insufficient. If cherishing relatively powerless minority values under threat from powerful global interests is elitism, then I gladly sign up to being an elitist!

22.4 What is going on emotionally when people listen to music

Gabrielsson's 'strong experience' studies are limited by the fact that they are retrospective, and allow participants to select one experience from a lifetime's experiences. Such experiences must, however, be grounded in (and perhaps experienced as special in contrast to) everyday musical experience. Various studies (e.g. Sloboda and O'Neill, 2001) suggest that the average person experiences music perhaps 3–4 times every day. People are, thus, very experienced and accomplished 'handlers' of musical experience, and emotions are bound to be shaped by and responsive to these experiences.

The two papers in this section represent two different responses to the need to get closer to the actual musical experience. Scherer *et al.* undertook a retrospective study, but within a narrowed time frame ('the last time when listening to.. music produced a strong emotional state in you'), whereas Schubert gathered 'on-line' continuous responses during the music experience itself. Scherer *et al.* were unable to find features of the music or of the situation which strongly predicted emotional response. Out of a list of proposed determinants, a catch-all category of 'other factors' was the most frequently cited determinant. Scherer *et al.* conclude that 'since these determinants vary enormously over participants one can assume that whether an emotional reaction occurs or not may be determined, to a very large extent, by factors that are very specific for each individual'. Furthermore, Scherer *et al.* found that, in a free response situation, where participants wrote down whatever words they chose to describe their musical experience, the basic emotions, such as happy, sad, angry, etc., occurred rather rarely. Most often participants described their experience in more complex ways, in which 'being moved' was the most frequent component. From these findings they conclude that 'it is all the more surprising that a large portion of current research on the emotional effects of music seems to focus on such a small number of such "basic" emotions'.

Schubert's studies have brought 'continuous response' methodologies to new levels of methodological sophistication. These methodologies attempt to reflect the fact that emotional and other evaluative responses are not constant over the entire duration of a piece of music, but change dynamically in some kind of relation to what is going on in the music at the time. Although some studies (e.g. Krumhansl, 1997) have attempted to measure continuous response physiologically, most studies have used the manual response of the listener, who continuously adjusts a scale cursor according to the relative level of some experienced quality (such as tension, intensity, and specific emotions).

Schubert's contribution to this volume is a critical analysis of the significance that we can place on the reported fact that inter-rater correlations (between different people listening to the same piece of music) are high. Such reports are often used to support claims that different people have similar emotional reactions to the same piece of music. Schubert shows that a significant amount of this covariance can, in fact, be artefactual, due to serial correlation effects. He proposes statistical techniques for minimizing these artefacts in future studies, and concludes that we should treat inter-rater correlations of less than 0.8 with suspicion, even if statistically significant.

The implication of Schubert's work is that listeners are probably more different from one another in their response curves than a statistically naive approach to curve similarity would suggest. One possible reason for this is that the 'cognitive' load on a listener who is continuously responding is just too high. It may be that the respondent cannot meaningfully bring the cursor to bear on musical experience at every moment, and so there are 'dead patches' where the cursor simply remains at the last deliberately chosen location, or is placed at a 'resting-point' until the next event where a deliberate linkage can be made. Both these strategies could produce spurious inter-rater correlations.

A possible alternative to the continuous response methodology is a discrete sampling methodology where the listener makes a discrete response every time a particular experience occurs, or when the intensity of the experience moves over some threshold. This is the approach adopted by Waterman (1996) who asked respondents to press a button every time they 'felt something'. A typical respondent might press 3–4 times per minute, and Waterman found clear positive statistical relationships between different listeners in the places they chose to press, and structural commonalities between the musical locations of these presses. However, retrospective accounts of the reasons for these choices yielded wide individual differences. It may be concluded from data like this that there may be aspects of musical response (such as surprise or arousal) which can be predicted from measurable aspects of the musical stimulus, but that the experiences generated by those effects will be a complex function of the way in which the person concerned is engaging with the task.

22.5 How can performers affect the emotional effects of listeners?

Trehub and Nakata summarize intriguing evidence to suggest that infants have very clear preferences for particular types of adult vocalizations, and that these characteristics are shared by infant-directed speech and song.

In general, these characteristics (including high pitch and slow rhythm) are recognized (by adult listeners) as communicating positive emotional engagement (high pitch = joy, slow speed = tenderness). These preferences are accompanied by behavioural and physiological outcomes, which suggest that these vocalizations have an arousal-regulating function. Infants are actually comforted, engaged, and calmed by such vocalizations.

Caregivers' infant-directed vocalization patterns are also characterized by the repetitive use of rather few rhythmic and melodic contours. Trehub and

Nakata hypothesize that this repetition assists the infant in both recognition (of the caregiver) and learning (of speech and communication). However, they suggest that each caregiver's repertoire of vocal patterns is somewhat individualistic at the level of individual melodic and rhythmic elements. There is no such thing as a universal caregiver's song. This means that, from the very earliest times, infants are encouraged to identify specific musical patterns or elements which characterize and individuate the various 'significant others' in their lives.

In this context it may not be surprising that music listeners of all ages are prone to attempt to relate to music as if a significant other was present in the music and attempting to communicate something. In doing so, we are simply extending and enriching our earliest memories of the context in which we first heard and emotionally responded to communication from caregivers.

The data summarized by Trehub and Nakata suggest that adults (and older children) provide distinctive vocalizations to infants not because they are infants *per se*, but because infants elicit in most of us warm, caring, and affectionate responses. It is the affective nature of our response which determines the expressive content of our speech and song, rather than the age of the person we are speaking or singing to. This is confirmed by the fact that infants are equally happy listening to adult-directed speech and song if that speech or song is expressive of love or comfort. Both types of communication share similar acoustic qualities.

In sum, it appears that humans in the role of infant caregivers (and this can extend as young as preschool siblings) have an intuitive grasp of the ways in which their infant-directed vocalizations may be productive in the lives and development of infants. Shared characteristics of the signal (relating to overall pitch, speed, repetition, etc.) underpin potentially universal arousal and mood outcomes, whilst individually idiosyncratic characteristics assist with person recognition and differentiation.

Juslin *et al.* are also concerned with a decomposition of musical performance parameters into different sources with different potential outcomes on listeners. Their concern is with trained adult performers delivering short but complete musical compositions for adult listeners to hear. Their computational approach assumes (and formally characterizes) separate sources of variability between performers, makes predictions concerning differential effects of these sources on listener judgements, and then tests these by selectively manipulating presence or absence of the different sources in synthesized performances.

Their data demonstrate that the presence or absence of different sources of variation do, indeed, have systematic (if rather complex) effects on listener judgements of the peformance as 'clear', 'gestural', 'human', 'musical', 'sad', and 'expressive'. The specific emotion of sadness was best communicated by the presence of performance parameters (labelled by the authors as 'emotional expression') relating to overall characteristics of tempo, sound level, articulation, tone attacks, etc. These are exactly the 'statistical' characteristics which Juslin and others (Juslin, 2001; Juslin and Laukka, 2003) have demonstrated link emotionally communicative music and speech (and which therefore are, in one sense, not special to music). This can be taken as a rather elegant demonstration that the communication of emotion does not require the processing (by either performer or listener) as 'music *qua* music'. For that to happen (as indicated by, for instance, a listener judgement that the performance is 'musical') further sources of variation must be inserted (those that Juslin *et al.* characterize as 'generative' and 'motional'). Note that emotional expression remains important. Taking this out reduces perceived musicality; but to influence judgements of musicality it must act through and with other sources of variability, including those generative sources which are intimately bound up with the structural (e.g. syntactic and segmental) characteristics of the music.

This study demonstrates important listener effects by computationally manipulating the presence or absence of formally defined sources of variance. This does not in itself demonstrate that human performers manipulate these parameters independently, let alone under intentional control. Evidence does exist from a variety of sources that musicians can significantly alter their performances according to emotional and musical intentions (e.g. Davidson, 1993). The most convincing analyses of what this achieves (for listeners) has been provided by Juslin and colleagues in respect of the 'emotional expression' component of the GERM model. Substantial further work will be required to tie down the communicative parameters of other components (either of this model or yet to be formally characterized).

However, even this preliminary work allows a very clear conclusion. Performance effects of music on listener experience are multicomponential, with some components directly addressing basic or 'garden' emotional parameters, and other components (in combination or separately) affecting a broader range of judgements and reactions that listeners may legitimately make to music. Indeed, given the huge diversity between individual performers and performances that Juslin and others have documented, it would be somewhat strange if listener responses were not characterizable by an equivalent diversity.

22.6 Concluding remarks

My question, 'to what extent the research reported in this issue points to, explicates, and encourages an understanding of diversity and complexity in musical experience' has a clear answer. Although based on 'behaviourist/ cognitivist' foundations, the present studies actually do point to, and explicate, this diversity in a range of ways.

What goes on when a listener engages with music is above all a function of how that listener construes the musical event. In particular, it matters if and how the listener believes that there is an intentional agent behind the music. From earliest infancy, we are set up to 'read' music-like stimuli as emanating from a human agent who has intentions and feelings towards us. In the earliest times, our concerns are probably limited. Is this a person I recognize and know, and do they mean well towards me? As we grow and develop our conceptual apparatus for construing music as indicative of agency grows and becomes more complex in ways which empirical science has perhaps not addressed as fully as it might.

As we grow, we come to realize that particular communications are called music, and others, with some shared characteristics, are not. Within the domain of music we come to make finer distinctions (distinctions of genre, function, quality, culture). We come to appreciate that much music is crafted (often with much sweat, pain, and commitment) by specific individuals to whom this matters more than almost anything else they do. We learn that certain pieces of music have been preserved lovingly by many generations, and that entire and costly cultural institutions have been set up to ensure that these works are available to all citizens and remain alive in the minds, hearts, and fingers of performers. We learn that some pieces of music are loved fanatically by some groups of individuals, and loathed passionately by others. We learn that some pieces of music make their progenitors rich and famous. We learn that some societies ascribe to music such power for potential harm that they strictly regulate it, or even ban it. All of this frames and potentiates our reactions, before we even switch on the radio, select a track, or walk into a church, concert hall, or disco. Our knowledge about music and its cultural position reaches down to the most mundane act of reception (e.g. half-hearing piped music in a shopping mall) and transforms it (see for instance, De Nora (2000).

We also come to know that, within the cultural market place, there are competing ideologies that use music as a battleground. Disputes rage about what is proper music, music of value, music worth teaching in schools, music worth subsiding with taxpayers' money. The role of academia in general, and science in particular, is to be aware of all this, to document, and explain. Science, however, is also a cultural product, and its adherents are no more immune to their social and cultural background than anyone else. The science of music, with its particular origins, can be presumed to be under constant pressure to align with values of the dominant cultures which support and fund it. These cultures have predominantly economic imperatives which underpin science's aims to classify and de-individuate in favour if isolating broad trends and key marker variables.

These imperatives can lead to the deconstruction of the richness of a cultural object like a piece of music into a set of 'effects' whose impact on health, economic success, consumer behaviour, etc. can be measured, predicted, and controlled.

Fortunately or unfortunately (depending on one's perspective) the papers in this volume have demonstrated that the process of deconstruction is a hugely difficult task, and that any apparently firm statement regarding the emotional effects of music have to be hedged with so many caveats and qualifications as to significantly hinder the prospects for large-scale commercial exploitation of these findings. Individual variations, both between different pieces of supposedly 'similar' music, and between supposedly 'similar' people remain large, and mainly unexplained. Even mood induction often seems to require those submitting to the induction to 'try hard' to get into the required mood!

What we can say, with increasing scientific certainty, is that there are certain characteristics of the 'sound of music', which are shared by several non-musical stimuli (particularly speech, and gesture) which allow simple emotional messages to be 'read off' the sound surface, and which allow certain basic effects of arousal modulation to occur. That being so, much music may be used by some agents as something else than (and something less than) music. They throw away the kernel and market the husk.

There are moral and scientific reasons to adopt a critical stance to this programme. The moral reasons relate to the purposes and intentions of those producing the music. It is a signal disrespect to those who conceived of their music as addressing ultimate issues of life, death, love, identity, war and peace, to appropriate it purely for analgesia or profit. If music is to be used for such stripped-down purposes, let people who have these purposes make their own stripped-down products rather than diminish the work of others by recycling it. The scientific reasons relate to our duties to represent, not ignore, the huge variety of musical objects, activities, and contexts, which this world actually contains. Underlying laws and patterns may exist, but we are very far from having adequately sampled the universe of these aspects. Even within those that we have sampled, the sheer richness individuality of each music experience must be among the most salient facts that we have to come to terms with. In doing music science we may indeed be pushing at the limits of what science can tackle or achieve.

I could be accused of coming dangerously close to implying that the present authors are catering to commercial interests simply because they attempt to deconstruct music and emotion into more manageable parts. This is certainly not my belief. As scientists we should, of course, be wary of letting others misuse musical emotion findings, but there is nothing inherently wrong with attempts to simplify a phenomenon to make it manageable to study empirically. The only people who can afford to take in everything at once may be those that rely entirely on armchair speculation. Any attempt to delineate various subcomponents represents a laudable step towards a more theoretically informed approach that can help to organize disparate findings. It is a basic principle of any theorizing and modelling that one must simplify or 'deconstruct' the essentials. In science there is no serious alternative. My comments should not, therefore, be seen as favouring a romantic notion of art as an inscrutable mystery, too complex to be ever dealt with properly by science. Rather, our attempts to deconstruct need to be constantly held up against the richness of everyday (and peak) musical experience to ensure that it is the full experience we are attempting to explain, and not some conveniently simplified portion of it.

References

Bourdieu, P. (1977) *Outline of a theory of practice* (Trans R. Nice). Cambridge, UK: Cambridge University Press.

Cook, N. (1998) *Music: a very short introduction*. Oxford: Oxford University Press.

Davidson, J. W. (1993) Visual perception of performance manner in the movements of solo musicians. *Psychology of Music*, **21.2**, 103–113.

De Nora, T. (2000) *Music in everyday life*. Cambridge: Cambridge University Press.

Frith, S. (1996) *Performing rites: on the value of popular music*. Oxford: Oxford University Press.

Gabrielsson, A. (2002) Perceived emotions and felt emotions: same or different? *Musicae Scientiae, Special Issue 2001–2*, 123–148.

Kivy, P. (1999) Feeling the musical emotions. *British Journal of Aesthetics*, **39**, 1–13.

Juslin, P. N. (2001) Communicating emotion in music performance: a review and empirical framework. In P. N. Juslin and J. A. Sloboda (Eds.) *Music and emotion: theory and research*. Oxford: Oxford University Press. pp: 309–337.

Juslin, P. N. and Laukka, P. (2003) Communication of emotion in vocal expression and musical performance. Different channels, same code? *Psychological Bulletin*, **129.5**, 770–814.

Juslin, P. N., Friberg, A., and Bresin, R. (2002) Toward a computational model of expression in music performfnace: the GERM model. *Musicae Scientiae, Special Issue 2001–2*, 63–122.

Krumhansl, C. L. (1997) An exploratory study of musical emotions and physiology. *Canadian Journal of Experimental Psychology*, **51**, 336–352.

London, J. (2002) Some theories of emotion in music and their implications for research in music psychology. *Musicae Scientiae, Special Issue 2001–2*, 23–36.

Maslow, A. H. (1976) *The farther reaches of human nature*. New York: Penguin Books.

McClary, S. (1991) *Feminine endings: music, gender and sexuality*. Minnesota, MN: University of Minnesota Press.

Nyklicek, I., Thayer, J. F., and Van Doornen, L. J. P. (1997) Cardiorespiratory differentiation of musically-induced emotions. *Journal of Psychophysiology*, **11**, 304–321.

Parrott, A. C. (1982) Effect of paintings and music, both alone and in combination, on emotional judgements. *Perceptual and Motor Skills*, **54**, 635–641.

Rauscher, F. H., Shaw, G. L., and Ky, K. N. (1995) Listening to Mozart enhances spatial-temporal reasoning: towards a neurpsychological basis. *Neuroscience Letters*, **185**, 44–47.

Schubert, E. (2002) Correlation analysis of continuous emotional response to music: correcting for the effects of serial correlation. *Musicae Scientiae, Special Issue 2001–2*, 213–236.

Scherer, K. R., Zentner, M. R., and Schact, A. (2002) Emotional states generated by music: an exploratory study. *Musicae Scientiae, Special Issue 2001–2*, 149–172.

Sloboda, J. A. (1989) Music psychology and the composer. In S. Nielzen and O. Olsson (Eds.) *Structure and perception of electroacoustic sound and music*. Amsterdam: Elsevier. pp. 3–12.

Sloboda, J. A. (1999) Music performance and emotion: issues and developments. In S. W. Yi (Ed.) *Music, mind, and science*. Seoul: Seoul National University Press, pp. 220–238.

Sloboda, J. A. (2000) Music and worship: a psychologist's perspective. In T. Hone, M. Savage, and J. Astley (Eds.) *Creative chords: studies in music, theology and Christian formation*. Leominster: Gracewing, pp. 110–125.

Sloboda, J. A., and O'Neill, S. A. (2001) Emotions in everyday listening to music. In P. N. Juslin and J. A. Sloboda (Eds.) *Music and emotion: theory and research*. Oxford: Oxford University Press.

Small, C. (1998) *Musicking: The meanings of performance and listening*. Hanover, NH: Wesleyan University Press.

Trehub, S. E., and Nakata, T. (2002) Emotion and music in infancy. *Musicae Scientiae, Special Issue 2001–2*, 37–62.

Vastfjall, D. (2002) A review of the musical mood induction procedure. *Musicae Scientiae, Special Issue 2001–2*, 173–212.

Waterman, M. (1996) Emotional responses: implicit and explicit effects in listeners and performers. *Psychology of Music*, **24**, 53–67.

CHAPTER 23

ASSESSING MUSIC PSYCHOLOGY RESEARCH: VALUES, PRIORITIES, AND OUTCOMES

23.1 Introduction

What criteria can we use to evaluate research in music psychology? Do these criteria provide any guide for researchers, or prospective researchers, wishing to decide what to research, or whether to do research at all?

These are the questions which motivate this chapter, and, in exploring them it will be necessary to address broader questions, to do with the social responsibilities of scientists, academics, and educated citizens. How do we decide where to devote our energies? Can we make such decisions in rational ways, which optimize both our own personal fulfilment, and our need to earn a living, but also address the needs of society? These questions are hard to answer, but I believe we all have a responsibility to think about them to the best of our abilities.

I write this chapter in the main because these issues have been facing me personally and relentlessly in recent years. Although I am concerned to offer a systematic and informed treatment of these issues, I will, at some points, need to be more personal than is customary in academic discourse. It seems to me that in this particular area of debate the personal is appropriate, and maybe even necessary. Attitudes towards values and priorities are so intimately connected to a person's social context and background that removing them from the discourse can hide key assumptions that motivate the argument, and thus obscure the basis of the argument as rooted in the realities of lived experience.

Many intellectual and moral issues which 'come to a head' at a particular point of time do so because they have been 'building up steam' for a long time. Although dilemmas about the value of research came to dominate my concerns in the last half decade, they have been there in a less urgent form for considerably longer.

A question which I have posed repeatedly to anyone who will listen is: suppose all the music psychology in the world had never been written, and was expunged from the collective memory of the world, as if it had never existed, how would music and musicians be disadvantaged? Would composers compose less good music, would performers cease to perform so well, would those who enjoy listening to it enjoy it any less richly?

In all my years of asking this question, I have to admit to never having received a fully convincing answer that was truly specific and substantial. Some respondents have pointed to the intrinsic interest of music psychology research, and the fact that many musicians and music-lovers seem to find it interesting to learn something about music psychology. However, interest or curiosity is not a very substantial outcome. I can be interested in the personal lives of media celebrities. This does not of itself make their lives useful, to them or to me.

What is even more alarming than the absence of convincing answers is the sense that to many who have been posed it, this just doesn't seem an important enough question to have any sort of ready or worked-out answer. This appears to be, in part, because there appears to be little or no well-developed literature where such questions are framed and answers attempted, certainly not in music psychology. Social benefit is not a consideration in the training of many psychology researchers (perhaps even most). Ethical considerations tend to be confined narrowly to the treatment of experimental volunteers (for instance, British Psychological Society, 1993).

The lack of attention to social benefit may also be a consequence of employment culture. Schmidt (2000) has suggested that professional employment, such as that offered to most academic researchers, can often subvert and distort the idealism and social responsibility of professionals, subordinating their work to the narrow political and economic goals of their employing organizations. Organizational culture (including a tendency to burden professionals with cripplingly high workloads) can inhibit professionals from seeking to make the meaningful difference to society that may have first inspired them to join their chosen profession. Few university researchers are explicitly encouraged to put social benefit at the top of their work agendas.

23.2 The social and personal benefits of music

One area in which there has now been substantial research investment is that of the effects or benefits of music engagement on non-musical aspects of health, well-being, and psychological functioning.

The main aim of much of this research is to document the nature of the benefits that are experienced through music engagement. In the most notorious case (the 'Mozart effect'; see for example Hetland, 2002; Rauscher, 2002) it has been discovered that exposing people to certain kinds of background music improves their performance on some cognitive tasks, even though they many not be paying focal attention to the music. Other more complex studies have demonstrated that involvement in music education programmes improves intellectual and social outcomes for children across a range of measures.

Some of the evaluated uses of music are genuinely new, as for instance the use of recorded music in the pre-operative stage of surgical procedures, as a means of enhancing anaesthetic effects (see, for instance, Nilsson *et al.*, 2003). Other research focuses on pre-existing types of musical interventions, and examines effects in a systematic way. For instance there are now a number of studies (Costa-Giomi, 1999; Schellenberg, 2004) which show clear effects of traditional instrumental instruction on intelligence.

It is of considerable significance that this research is being undertaken against a backdrop of cutbacks and retrenchment in school music provision in a number of countries. The research is therefore part of a wider 'advocacy' movement (Hallam, 2000; ISME, 2003) to save music education from further cuts in public spending and to argue for a restoration, or even an increase, in the availability of music education within populations.

However, there are a number of issues to address before we can unambiguously propose that such research has demonstrable social benefit.

23.2.1 Demonstrating benefits versus producing benefits

The first issue relates to a potential confusion between 'research which demonstrates benefits' and 'research which produces benefits'. A very clear example of research which demonstrates benefits is given by Schellenberg (2004). He tracked 144 schoolchildren who were randomly assigned to four different year-long educational enrichment programmes, keyboard lessons, voice lessons, drama lessons, and no lessons. By comparing WISC-R IQ measures before and after the intervention, he demonstrated improvements in IQ for the two music groups which were significantly greater than for the other two groups.

In this research, Schellenberg did not devise or employ innovative or unusual music education programmes. These were 'off the peg' programmes, within well-established pedagogic traditions, that have already benefited thousands of children. His contribution was to undertake research in the tradition of the 'random controlled trial' model perfected within medical research, to prove a causal relationship between existing well-used musical interventions and a socially beneficial and possibly non-obvious outcome (increased IQ).

Schellenberg's research is good and original science. That is not in doubt. However, the research itself has not, at this point, yielded any new social benefits. It has simply documented existing benefits. For the research itself to have benefits, it would, for instance, have to be influential on the decisions and resource-allocation activities of providers and consumers of music education programmes, so that the number of children participating in them significantly increased over a period of time.

23.2.2 Research as documentation versus research as advocacy

This observation moves the argument to a second set of issues. These are concerned with the process of turning research findings into socially beneficial outcomes, and the role of the researcher in such processes. Let us examine some of the potential difficulties that arise. Paramount among these is the unpredictability of the relationship between the publication of a research finding and the realization of its social benefits. It could be plausibly argued that the primary responsibility of a scientist is to publish findings at the earliest opportunity. However, changes in policy and other social arrangements which might enshrine the results of research in new outcomes might take years, or even decades, to bring about. They might never be realized. For instance, research which has showed the viability and environmental benefits of motor traction engines that do not use fossil fuel has not led to the large-scale development of such engines. This in, in part, because the development costs of the necessary infrastructure are so substantial. For instance, the BMW corporation has developed a prototype 'Hydrogen Car', but there are only currently a handful of filling stations in the world where such cars could be refuelled (Dunlop, 2001). There is always a development cost to the implementation of any new research finding. Resources (of time, money, advocacy) must be committed up front before the predicted benefits will start to flow. Researchers, as researchers, can document these processes, but in order to play a role in the social implementation of their research, they must step out of the researcher role into the advocacy role, to assist in mobilizing the necessary resources.

The question which these considerations lead to is this. How can a scientist plan, conduct, and report research in a fashion which does not compromise principles of objectivity, but which maximizes the likelihood of mobilizing the necessary advocacy to realize whatever potential social benefits accrue to the research?

One model, which is increasingly available to researchers in the more technological sciences, is the business model. Such a model is, indeed, at the heart of policy in many corporations and institutions that employ researchers. Agencies exist to assist researchers to protect their intellectual property and to exploit it in conjunction with entrepreneurs, manufacturers, and those in the business of selling and advertising. Researchers are increasingly advised by those who employ them that if they suspect that a line of work on which they are engaged might have commercial spin-offs, these potential spin-offs are identified at the earliest opportunity, so that the research can be 'shadowed' and 'championed' by those more expert than the researcher in advocacy and development. This model is generally most appropriate when the outcome of the research is a tangible product, such as a new technology, a new invention, or, in psychology, a new psychometric test. It is generally pursued with most vigour when institutional managers detect that there is a high potential for short-term or medium-term financial rewards.

Although such a model may be relevant to some music researchers, operating at the more technological and 'product-oriented' end of our discipline (for instance in research which has direct implications for sound-engineering or sound-reproduction) it appears largely irrelevant for the greater bulk of research in music psychology.

A search of two major research databases (CAIRSS and PSYCINFO) using the search terms social+benefits+music, and conducted on 25 November 2003, yielded 14 articles in total for the period 1983–2003. These papers are listed in Table 23.1.

Although this is not necessarily a comprehensive list of all research on social benefits (see for instance Hallam, 2000), it can be seen as a representative sample of the extent and topic spread of research studies in which the social benefits of music are directly and explicitly addressed by the researcher. The absolute number of studies is low: as would be expected from informal observations about the low explicit priority given to social benefits within the research community. The articles all fall within four clearly defined topic areas:

- care of the elderly (5 items)
- child development (3 items)
- music in education (2 items)
- therapy (4 items).

Most of the studies describe complex behavioural applications involving music. They examine 'ways of behaving' with challenging, disabled, or needy subgroups, that are suggested as having subtle 'quality of life' benefits. Few of these subgroups are likely to form powerful self-advocacy organizations, and few are clearly defined consumer groups that would attract the obvious interest of the business community. The tools offered within these research studies are largely addressed to 'carers' whether professional or voluntary. Several of the carer groups identified are small or relatively low-status groups (e.g. music therapists, elderly-care nurses). There is unlikely to be

Table 23.1 Research on social benefits of music

Title	Author(s)	Citation details	Topic
Music and quality of life in older adults	D. D. Coffmann	*Psychomusicology*, **18.1**, 2002, 76–88	Care of the elderly
Neuroscience applications in marital and family therapy	E. A. Tootle and L. Sperry	*Family Journal: Counselling and Therapy for Couples and Families*, **11.2**, 2003, 185–190	Therapy
The magic within the music: exploring the use of music in psychotherapy with adolescents	C. D. Diraimondo	*Dissertation Abstracts International: Section B: the Science and Engineering*, **63(5-B)**, 2002, 2578	Therapy
The contribution of music to positive aging: a review	T. Hays, R. Bright, and V. Minchello	*Journal of Aging and Identity*, **7**(3), 2002, 165–175	Care of the elderly
First-time mothers' use of music and movement with their young infants: the impact of a teaching program	W. Vlismas and J. Bowes	*Early Child Development and Care*, **159**, 1999, 43–51	Child development
Talent Development IV: Proceedings from the 1998 Henry B and Jocelyn Wallace National Research Symposium on Talent Development	N. Colangelo and S. G. Assouline (Eds.)	2001 (publisher not given)	Music in education
Popular music styles in Nordoff–Robbins clinical improvisation	K. S. Aigen	*Music Therapy Perspectives*, **19**(1), 2001, 31–44	Therapy

Title	Author	Source	Category
The use of music therapy to address the suffering in advanced cancer pain	L. Magill	*Journal of Palliative Care*, **17(3)**, 2001, 167–172	Therapy
Music therapy: enhancing communication between family caregivers and their loved ones with dementia	C. I. Gardner	*Dissertation Abstracts International*, **60(60-A)**, 1999, 1953.	Care of the elderly
Long-term benefits of music intervention in the newborn intensive care unit: a pilot study	J. M. Standley	*Journal of the International Association of Music for the Handicapped*, **6.1**, 1990–1, 12–22	Child development
Play as improvisation: the benefits of music for developmentally delayed young children's social play	A. S. Gunsberg	*Early Child Development and Care*, **66**, 1991, 85–91	Child development
The unique power of music therapy benefits Alzheimer's patients	S. Smith	*Activities, Adaptation and Ageing*, **14.4**, 1990, 59–63	Care of the elderly
It's cool because we like to sing: junior high school boys' experience of choral music as an elective	M. A. Kennedy	*Research Studies in Music Education*, **18**, 2002, 24–34	Music in education
Music and movement for the elderly	M. Morris	*Nursing Times*, **82.8**, 1986, 44–45	Care of the elderly

any potential for 'patenting' or 'commercial exploitation' of the research findings reported. Therefore, the 'business model' for advocacy is likely to be inappropriate, without considerable modification.

The constituencies ready to undertake advocacy in such areas would seem to those whose principal motivations are humanitarian, ethical, and compassionate rather than commercial.

23.2.3 Commissioned policy-relevant research

A research model which is increasingly used by government and larger corporations in the commissioning or supporting of research which aims directly to address key policy questions. Quite small organizations can also commission developmental or evaluative research on their activities. Two projects I have been recently involved in illustrate different applications of this model.

Between 1998 and 2001 a research project on Young People's Participation in Music took place, with funding and support from a major grant awarding agency (the Economic and Social Research Council of Great Britain (ESRC), and *an Advisory Committee drawn from* key agencies and organizations concerned with music participation in young people (see *http://www.keele.ac.uk/depts/ps/ESRC/esrcmenu.htm*). Some results from this project are outlined in Sloboda (2001—reprinted as Chapter 21 of this volume) and Ryan *et al.* (2000).The social issue which drew this constituency together was the experienced decline or dropout of participation in active music-making (particularly the playing of musical instruments) by British young people in their early adolescence. A better understanding was sought of the factors which influence long-term commitment to instrumental performance, in order to develop policy and practice in the area of music education. The advisory board worked with the researchers to develop and improve the research protocol (involving questionnaires and interviews to young people, their parents, and their teachers). Following the completion of the preliminary data analysis, the research team worked with members of the advisory board to produce and publish a set of 'Practitioner and Policy Implications' which were agreed to emerge from the research findings and which could be addressed to teachers and educational policy-makers (reproduced in the Appendix to this chapter). These have been widely distributed, and have fed forward into other discussions at national level about music education policy.

This level of engagement with policy-makers is, to our best knowledge, unusual within the music psychology confraternity. It has ensured that some of the ideas contained within the research have influenced subsequent policy debates, at least within the UK. The project team have also taken as much trouble to disseminate these findings to groups of practition-ers around the world as to more traditional academic audiences, underta-king what could be described as direct advocacy work alongside the more traditional 'objective' reporting of research results.

However, even with such an explicit focus on policy and practice it is not easy to prove that the research has contributed (or will contribute) to tangible social benefits. Such benefits would only accrue some time after significant increases in the number of agencies and individuals operating in accordance with these implications, and would probably only be meas-urable in relevant outcomes some years later. Even if such increases could be quantified, attributing them directly to this research project would be highly problematic. Many practitioners and policymakers may have operated on the basis of such principles without any knowledge of our specific research findings or recommendations. In general, we would have to fall back on a general faith that spreading sound ideas into relevant communities is likely to have more positive social benefits than not doing so.

The second project that illustrates a 'commissioning' approach, was a focused piece of evaluative research within a single educational establish-ment (Sloboda *et al.*, 2003). This research was designed to address a com-monly observed problem among high-level performers, which is the unreliability of achieving optimal levels of expressive performance in repeated performances of the same piece of music. Even highly rehearsed performances can fail to 'come alive' for reasons which are often unclear to the performers themselves. A pedagogic approach to this problem, entitled 'Feeling Sound' had been developed by one of the authors (Gayford), and piloted in workshops with both amateur and professional musicians. This involved teaching participants a set of attentional tools for focusing more effectively and consistently on expressive (in addition to technical) param-eters of the performance.

The researchers worked with institutional managers of a tertiary-level college of music to raise funds for the research, and recruit participants from among its students. Key pedagogic leaders within the institution assisted in student recruitment. The study itself was based on the random allocation clinical trial method, where volunteers, matched for gender and year on the course, were randomly assigned to either an experimental or a control group, Students in the experimental group received the 'Feeling Sound' training, students in the control group were placed on a waiting list for potential enrolment in a future course. Level of expressive performance of a test piece was assessed twice for all participants, once before the inter-vention, and once after it. A significant advantage was found for the experimental group as compared to the control group. In some cases, the intervention led to radical changes both in the way that participants reported thinking and feeling about music, and also in the quality of their playing as observed by their instrumental teachers.

The measured effects of the course on performance-quality ratings were modest, and several participants observed that, even though the course had lasted for an entire academic year (9 months), they felt they were only at the beginning of incorporating the implications of what they had learned into their playing. Several participants predicted that the substantial gains of participating in the programme were still to be realized, some way into the future.

From a 'social benefits' perspective, the danger of this study (which is, in some ways quite typical of many intervention studies within the behavioural sciences) is that its benefits may not spread beyond the small group of individuals participating in the study. Funding problems have meant that the intended repetition of the course for a second cohort of students within the college has not taken place. Also, only one person (the progenitor of the method) is really qualified to teach such a course. For a method like this to achieve its full benefit, more teachers need to be trained and more institutions need to hire teachers to work with their performers. Creating the conditions in which such outcomes are made more possible takes one well beyond the realm of research *per se*, and into the arena of advocacy, organizational development, and fundraising. Few researchers and practitioners have the necessary skills to bring this about. As a result, many such initiatives fade away when the specific trial is completed and specific personnel move on, leaving little trace in the community as a whole.

The approach to these problems currently being developed within the 'Feeling Sound' team, is the creation and dissemination of a set of resources which can be used and modified by practitioners within their own contexts without the need for the direct involvement of the method's progenitor. Time will tell whether this is a productive approach.

23.2.4 Contextualizing benefits: ensuring that one person's benefit is not another person's loss

There is an ambiguity to much research carried out in a 'first world nations' context. This ambiguity has been noted in respect of other conditions which have sometimes been labelled 'diseases of affluence'. For instance, a great deal of medical research is aimed at problems caused by the over-consumption of the high-fat foodstuffs cheaply available in affluent nations (and increasingly in developing countries; see, for instance, James, 1998). Obesity is an outcome of the huge disparities in distribution of the world's resources. Medical research into obesity, and programmes for the obese, have been criticized by some as addressing the symptoms of a social problem rather than its underlying cause. Obesity would cease to be a major social problem if there was a more just distribution of the world's resources, so that overconsumption was a financial impossibility for most people. Medical research on obesity may be seen as accepting and bolstering the social *status quo* by putting more resources in the way of people who already have too much.

Several influential organizations and foundations have publicly argued that the priority for health researchers (and those bodies which fund healthcare) should now be an exploration of the ways in which the cheap and effective advances in healthcare of the last century (now taken for granted in every developed country) can be extended to be available to every person in the world. A few low-cost and high-outcome remedies available to every person on this planet would be far more cost-effective over a shorter timescale, in terms of lives saved, than further development of high-cost procedures for low-frequency conditions (as was argued, for instance, by Bill Gates at the 2002 World Economic Forum).

A similar argument could be proposed for music. The availability of music education within the developed nations (including North American, Europe, and Australasia) is far greater than elsewhere in the world. Even within the developed nations, the level and extent of provision within the countries where most research is undertaken (the USA, Canada, the UK) exceeds that of others (such as Greece or Portugal). When put alongside the music education opportunities available to a Rwandan child, or an Indian child, what is available in the West is truly munificent. These facts would incline some to argue that any advocacy might be better deployed at providing proper schooling for children in these developing and war-torn countries, worrying further about advanced nations only when the rest of the world had caught up.

It could be further argued that the apparent shortcomings of music education in the West are also a result of the peculiarities of the affluent consumer society. Opportunities for music may have to be created in schools within advanced nations because such activity has almost ceased to exist within the home and everyday society. The fragmentation of sociability brought about by an individualistic and media-dominated lifestyle, where families and individuals conduct their personal lives 'behind closed doors' and 'in front of the TV' rather than in the street and in the fields, means that the natural social contexts in which group music-making has flourished for tens of thousands of years, without the intervention of educators or psychologists, have withered away (see Sloboda, 1998 (this volume Chapter 19); Sloboda, 2001 (this volume Chapter 21).

It might be argued that more of the full benefits of musical engagement are still felt by those societies where day-to-day sociability and the pooling of physical labour is still a necessity. These societies tend to be among the less affluent of the planet. One could argue that if the societies in which music psychologists flourished became less over-affluent, music would naturally take root again in people's lives. Increasing school music is trying to patch the symptoms without addressing the real problem, which is the dysfunctionality of the society in which citizens of developed countries live.

From this kind of perspective, it is no longer enough to identify potential benefits of research. One also needs to ask whether the benefits outweigh the costs. The training of a researcher is an expensive business—it takes many years and involves the resources of many institutions. Specific research projects can also easily cost thousands, or hundreds of thousands of pounds or dollars, much of which is often devoted to salary payment. Developing and implementing research findings can require considerably more resource.

Even more problematical is identifying the 'what if' costs. What if the money and resource that had been devoted to training and supporting music psychology research had instead been put into research on a cure for cancer, or had been invested in a regional development programme? How can we assess potential benefits of hypotheticals?

At a personal level I have constantly been struggling with the issue of justifying what I do for a living, in a world where there appear to be so many more pressing issues requiring the resources of collective human intelligence. In the context of the state of the world, the question that poses itself to me, repeatedly, and in increasingly stark form is:

> How can I allow myself the luxury of researching music psychol-
> ogy, when half the world's population lives below the poverty
> line, when millions of children die of malnutrition and avoidable
> disease every year, when the activities and consumption patterns
> of the rich world are destroying the ability of the planet to sustain
> human life into the long term future, and when violence between
> people grows increasingly dangerous as the means to inflict
> violence become every more lethal and large-scale.

These interlinked problems are recognized, at least in part, by almost all leaders on the world stage. Xavier Solana, EU High Representative for Commmon Foreign and Security Policy, recently wrote:

> Almost 3 billion people, half the world's population, live on less
> than 2 Euros a day. 45 million continue to die every year out of
> hunger and malnutrition. Sub-Sahara Africa is poorer now than

it was 10 years ago. In many cases, the failure of economic growth has been linked to political problems and violent conflict. In some parts of the world, notably Sub-Saharan Africa, a cycle of insecurity has come into being. Since 1990, almost 4 million people have died in wars, 90% of them civilians. Over 18 million people worldwide have left their homes or their countries as a result of conflict. (Solana, 2003)

A secondary question is:

If I can allow myself the privilege of conducting music psychology research, how is that privilege best and most responsibly exercised so as to be more than 'harmless' (which I believe almost all music psychology research to be), but actually contributing in a direct way to the greater human good?

23.3 The personal and the political in music psychology research

Most human decisions can be accounted for, in large part, by an analysis of social and historical context in which people live, and the ways in which events and social forces shape them as individuals. Researchers are no different. The choices made by researchers reflect their social contexts. There are no context-free tools for making completely rational decisions about how to expend one's energies. It would be dishonest, and incomplete, to present the ideas of this chapter as flowing from a disinterested and leisurely rational analysis. These considerations repeatedly and disruptively forced themselves upon me during a period of my life when societal events were generating enormous emotional charge, in my immediate circles and also in society at large. I was forced to rethink my priorities as a result of the huge waves of anger, sorrow, despair, guilt, compassion, mingled with hope and determination, that have swept through the air around me these past 5 years. To understand these processes an excursion into politics and biography is required.

23.3.1 Responding to world events—a personal account

In the 1980s I was active in the anti-nuclear movement. This was an international movement to encourage the two major nuclear powers of the world, the USA and the USSR, to make real and lasting mutual steps to dismantle their nuclear arsenals, whose use could signal the end of human civilization. We believed (and I still believe) that the only way this would happen would be for one side to make a unilateral step, in the hope of encouraging the other side to do likewise. This would lead to further steps yielding a progressive mutual reduction in tension and danger. The reality we faced was that each side refused to move until the other side made the first move. This created a stalemate which meant that, far from disarming, both the USA and the USSR continued building up their arsenals until the point at which the USSR suddenly and catastrophically broke apart.

There was a peculiar kind of security in the cold-war world. The balance of power seemed to provide a crazy stability, based on the maintenance of a very low likelihood of a very terrible nuclear cataclysm. Within this global system, the anti-nuclear movement rarely caught the imagination of large swathes of the population, certainly not in the West, and it was perceived as marginal, ineffective, and 'communist', at least in the UK where I have always lived and worked. It never occurred to me for a moment that involvement in this movement could or should be central to my life. It was something I did weekends and evenings when other people played golf or did their garden. It had little or no direct impact on my research work or my career. It was part of my 'charitable work'.

The break-up of the Soviet Union, far from ushering in world peace, led to a world which was awash with weaponry of all sorts, and where social fragmentation along ethnic and other lines was leading to greater instability within regions and within states. It was almost as if the USSR–USA stalemate of the 1950s to the 1990s had kept the lid on a whole set of simmering social and political problems which began to boil over as soon as the lid was lifted. The certainties of the post-war period were swept aside, and although there were some hugely exciting and positive developments, such as the liberation of the South African people from Apartheid, and the re-democratization of Eastern Europe, they were soon overshadowed by new lethal threats.

The new threats were ones which in the main did not emanate in any simple way from the actions of nation states, nor were they confined to specific countries or regions of the world. 'Globalization' became an increasing reality, spreading both its benefits and its dangers into every corner of the world. The AIDS epidemic was perhaps one of the first phenomena to make it real to people that globalization was real, and potentially death-dealing. Increasingly the threat to the world's environment brought about by human consumption and pollution, spurred and moulded by the increasingly powerful multinational corporations, came to be recognized as real. The end of human life as we know it became something which was not a low probability outcome of nuclear cataclysm, but a certain consequence of continuing doing exactly what we were doing (for example, through global warming and the depletion of the ozone layer). Many of the environmental challenges the world faces come about through the increasing disparity in wealth between the few percent of the world's richest people, and the majority of the world's poor. The profligate consumption of oil and other commodities by the people of the advanced nations, particularly the USA, destabilizes not only the environment, but the very means to life of those in the poorest parts of the world. Deprivation fuels anger and violence, and the 1990s saw a significant increase in the number of regions of the world where ethnic and tribal violence flared up in conflict of one variety or another.

Although Western leaders and opinion formers liked in general to characterize these new civil wars as evidence of 'ancient ethnic hatreds' which were bound to resurface, and proof of the 'uncivilized' nature of these peoples, and their needs to be brought 'democracy' and 'control', a more critical (and I believe accurate) reading recognizes that whenever people with little power and resource are deprived or oppressed by a greater power, it is tragically easy for the oppressed to turn against each other, rather than uniting with one another to challenge the oppressor. People fight one another for control of those small resources allowed to them by the higher powers, and in doing so, leave those powers freedom to extend their power even further.

My growing acceptance of this perspective on the world's problems was helped along by exposure to systems and people who were able to clearly articulate a world view which has been labelled as radical (although it is seeming much more mainstream these days). I have been particularly influenced by the writings of Noam Chomsky (2003) and George Monbiot (2003). I also gained much from 15 years of involvement with a radical self-help movement called Re-Evaluation Counselling, founded by the American activist Harvey Jackins (1963). A friendship network containing many strong radical feminists also assisted my convictions to mature. For most of the 1990s these perspectives trickled into my research work in rather unobtrusive ways. They were partly responsible for my increasing interest in social and motivational factors underlying the acquisition of musical skills, and the search for wider cultural explanations for the unequal distribution of 'talent', analogous to the explanations being developed in radical politics to explain the unequal distribution of wealth within societies. Still, however, I was able to see a very clear distinction between my career, as a music psychologist, and the rest of my life in which critical social perspectives took other forms.

The events that began to unravel my carefully constructed compartmentalization of my life began on 24 March 1999, when, without the authority of either Parliament or the United Nations, my country, along with 18 other members of NATO, formed an alliance to start the first European air war since 1945. During this 78-day war, they dropped 23 000 bombs on Serbia and Kosovo, more than were dropped in Britain during the entire Second World War. Over 500 civilians were killed in the air-raids, thousands more were injured. Depleted uranium and cluster bombs were used in large numbers. These proscribed weapons will continue to maim and irradiate for generations. This was no feared hypothetical nuclear exchange. This was actual, unprovoked, old-fashioned, conventional invasion of one sovereign state by others, the kind of war which nuclear weapons were supposed to have rendered obsolete, particularly in Europe, the presumed 'theatre' for nuclear war.

The immediate and total outrage I felt towards my government was, luckily, shared by many. We disbelieved the claims of Tony Blair and Bill Clinton that there was no alternative. We remain convinced that events were manipulated from the White House to ensure that no matter what concessions Milosevic made, war would happen. We were appalled that war could be so readily accepted as an answer to an admittedly real problem by so many intelligent people, when the entire Soviet empire had crumbled only a few years earlier without a single bomb being dropped or army mobilized. We were shocked that people could so easily be convinced that replacing one ethnic cleansing (of Albanians by Serbs) with another (of Serbs, Jews, Roma and all other non-Albanians by Albanians) could be accepted as any kind of 'victory' for the people of the region. We were horrified that after the end of the war, a punitive sanctions regime was imposed on Serbia by NATO and the EU, which denied hospitals the most basic medicines and supplies, harming the very people that this war was supposed to help. My own sense of outrage and injustice was so complete that I joined a delegation to Serbia to help document at first hand the ruinous effect that the war and sanctions had had on the civilian population of Serbia, particularly the children. I found myself unable to sleep at nights, and often unable to concentrate on my work, which seemed trivial, irrelevant, and self-indulgent. I was able to focus some of my energies by researching and writing about the worst failings of the West in the Kosovo crisis (Sloboda, 2001).

For the first time in my life I realized, fully and on every emotional level, that the direction that the leaders of the West were taking the world, with money taken from my taxes, was diametrically opposite to the direction in which I wished them to go. These were not people who shared my world view, with a few wrinkles separating us. These were people whose notion of the world, and where it should be going, had diminishingly few points of contact at all with mine, or with those of the people I considered to be my 'reference group'.

I became convinced that the 'new interventionism' foisted on the world by the USA and Britain, was part of an immensely dangerous wedge, which would augur instability and tribulation on a massive scale. I was in absolute accord with the words of the British journalist Marc Almond (1999) who said: 'Even those who wholeheartedly endorse the humanitarian justification for the Nato action must be aware that, when the first cruise missile smashed through the thin skin of international law, the world's door was opened on to a void.'

This void was, I feared, to be filled by those whose argued that if the world's most powerful and most heavily armed states were not going to play by international rules from now on, then anything was fair game for those with less power but growing hatred and frustration at the privations and humiliations imposed on them by the 'global world order'. A self-destructive cycle of local instability, terrorism, reprisals, more terrorism, and even greater reprisals seemed to me inevitable. The victims of all of this would be the ordinary people, particularly the world's poor, in whose name this violence would be enacted, while actually making life worse for them.

My worst fears were realized on 11 September 2001. If March 1999 lit a fuse within me, 9/11 was detonation. Within hours of the fateful event, my reading of the words coming from the White House convinced me that the US administration was pulling out of its back pocket its long-harboured plan to engineer total military, economic, and cultural control over the Middle East and Asia, in order to bring about the 'Project for the New American Century'. Within days of 9/11 I knew that the main focus of my life had to change from music psychologist to activist for global peace and justice, and I soon shared that commitment with some of my closest friends. If I could not achieve such a change, I felt I would fall apart, morally, mentally and spiritually.

At that time I made the personal commitment that I would undertake no significant writing project in music psychology, or on any other topic, without conscious and deliberate linkage to issues of global justice, through which exploration, articulation and promotion of alternatives to prevailing societal norms could be addressed. My first, tentative, enactment of that commitment is to be found in Sloboda (2002, Chapter 22 of this volume). A second piece entitled 'The War, What War? Psychology in Denial' (Sloboda, 2003), offers a more trenchant and forthright critique of psychology's general failure to respond in any substantive way to the main historical trends outlined above.

At the time that I first made my life commitment to peace and justice, I had no idea how or when I would manage to combine this with the need to earn a living and support my family. However, I made the assumption that I might have to abandon music psychology completely, and so began putting my academic house in order. The book of which this chapter is part was conceived as one part of that tidying up, a coda to a 30-year phase of my life which was about to come to an end.

More than two years on from 9/11, a lot of bad things have happened in the world, and my responses to those bad things have developed in a range of directions that I certainly could not have predicted. A few good things have happened too, one of which is the phenomenal resurgence of a global anti-war movement on a scale which no one could have predicted before the Iraq crisis. This is part of a wider grass-roots mobilization which includes environmental campaigners and 'anti-globalization' social activists who challenge the damage done to peoples by the policies of the World Bank and other instruments of neo-liberal capitalism. This movement brought together a wealth of creative energies and initiatives which I became swept up in. Out of all this a potential solution to my personal dilemmas has been found in the form of a part-time job with a peace and disarmament non-governmental organization, which will ensure that, taken together with my evenings and weekends, the majority of my time will, indeed, be directly devoted to the causes to which I am committed. This leaves a proportion of each week still available to devote to academic pursuits, if I so choose. Where music psychology fits within this is something I shall no doubt be exercising myself about for some years to come.

23.3.2 A typology of levels of social engagement

It is only in the context of my personal journey that I am able to attempt some characterization of what different levels of socially responsible academic engagement might look like. It arises from the issues and dilemmas I have had to face in my own career. However, in making this characterization I am hoping to provide some kind of template against which other researchers could assess their own position, and become more explicit about the role of considerations about social benefit in their own work, rather than leaving such considerations implicit or unaddressed. I am sure that the template offered is crude and insufficiently nuanced, but its simplicity will perhaps be more productive in allowing a variety of elaborations and modifications which might make more sense within the very diverse set of personal and cultural experiences that characterize a research community.

The template postulates four successive levels of social engagement, which involve increasingly prominent roles for considerations impacting on academic activity 'from the outside'.

Level 1—Sensitivity to historic academic norms

Within academia there are generally accepted norms which, if adopted and followed in both letter and spirit, are usually held to contribute to the general social good. These include the belief that all knowledge is public knowledge, and the consequent imperative on academic researchers to communicate their knowledge through public channels. Academic freedom includes the freedom to promote and support unpopular conclusions, regardless of social or political pressures to do otherwise. Academics are enjoined to be truthful, and to provide evidential support to their communications, by, for instance the full citation of sources, and the availability of their raw data. They are enjoined to subject their work to informed critique through peer review prior to publication. Scientific researchers are required to consider the ethical impact of their research, specifically in terms of avoiding potential harm to those upon whom they experiment. Researchers who conduct themselves in an exemplary fashion within their chosen area of research can be said to be exercising *Level 1 social engagement*.

Researchers who depart from these norms, whether through carelessness and unprofessionalism, or for personal political or financial gain, cannot easily claim to be contributing to the social good in any way.

Level 2—Sensitivity to applicability

Researchers may choose to follow their intellectual interests in a range of directions, but retain a sensitivity to the possibility that some research might turn out to have practical or policy implications that could yield specific social benefits. If a researcher, on realizing potential applicability, takes actions designed to explore or promote that applicability, then they can be said to have moved to *Level 2 of social engagement*.

The range of appropriate actions is considerable. They may, for instance, undertake additional research to develop the applicability of their findings. They may seek to present the results of their research to practitioners, or discuss their findings with policy makers. On this model applicability is an occasional spin-off of a programme whose motivations are varied, but should include Level 1 social engagement.

Level 3—Focus on applicability

At this level, researchers make choices about what to research which are influenced by the prior assessment of potential applicability. If the applicability assessment is not favourable, the research does not get done.

This model is often the enforced model for researchers working for companies or government agencies. They are hired to research a particular problem, and their continued employment depends on the outcomes of their research being applicable. However some researchers in universities, who are free to choose the topics they research, may still choose a focus on applicability. This choice has, in many Western academic circles, at least until recently, been seen as likely to produce second-rate science. Pure 'blue-skies' research, has, it is often argued, more often encouraged the intellectual creativity which has led to theoretical breakthroughs, which then, often considerably later, begin to have practical applications. It can also be argued, in a similar vein, that it is not always possible to make an accurate assessment of the applicability of research in advance of conducting the research. Finally, it is often argued that applicable research is often that which is subservient to the less than admirable motives of funders and commissioners, which may often be flawed from an ethical point of view.

Level 4—Focus on values

Applicable research can be, and often is, socially unbeneficial. Research could be conducted, for instance, on how to use music to encourage people to buy and consume more alcohol. The research is clearly applicable, but hardly beneficial (other than to breweries and wine shops). In some contexts, researchers may well find that most research which they are being asked to carry out conflicts with their core values. In other contexts, resources which are being devoted to research may, while not directly conflicting with core values, be considered by the researcher, be more properly devoted to more urgent, or larger, social needs. In such cases the researcher may be drawn to seek other activities which express their values more directly. It cannot always be assumed that such considerations may be expressed within the specialist sub-discipline in which a researcher has gained experience. They may require changing research fields, or they may require stopping doing research altogether.

Perhaps the most frequent rebalancing of life priorities experienced by Western researchers is the 'career break' normally taken to raise a family. Considerable numbers of people, mainly but not exclusively women, possess value systems which put the needs of their children above the needs of their profession. Not only is this accepted in many societies, but the right to do this without detriment to later career is enshrined in employment law. But the issues facing parents actually face everyone all the time. What are my priorities at this moment? Why am I doing what I do? How much of my life's resources (of time and energy) should I devote to any one activity, and why? What should I do for pay, and what should I do without pay—in what proportion? Of course there are constraints. Not everyone is free to decide these things afresh at every life juncture, but it can be argued that the maintenance of personal integrity and fulfilment requires that people assess the fit between their values and their actual activities on a reasonably regular basis, and make adjustments to the nature and balance of their activities accordingly. In these adjustments, very little can be accepted as an unchanging given. Expertise and experience in a given field is only one of a number of considerations that must be taken into account.

23.4 Concluding remarks

In relation to my own trajectory through music psychology, as depicted in the four roughly chronological sections in this book, I would want to claim that Part A (cognitive processes) describes work which is primarily operating at Level 1 (driven by sensitivity to academic norms). Part B (Emotion and motivation) is focused at Level 2 (sensitivity to applicability), Part C (Talent and skill development) shifts to Level 3 (focus on applicability), and Part D (music in the real world) increasingly represents Level 4 (focus on values). I am well aware that a typology that fits so relatively neatly onto my own intellectual trajectory might lack generality, and I am only too ready to have these ideas modified, or even swept aside, by robust contact with other models.

What I do hope, however, is that the debate about values will continue within the music psychology community, and become more central to our published work than it has been hitherto, at least within the concerns of those parts of the community with which I have had most contact.

References

Almond, M. (1999) What have we started? The Independent, 6 June. *http://www.independent.co.uk/sindy/stories/C0606907.html*

British Psychological Society (1993) *Code of Conduct, Ethical Principles and Guidelines*. Leicester. *http://www.bps.org.uk/documents/Code.pdf*

Chomsky, N. (2003) *Hegemony or survival: America's quest for global dominance.* London: Hamish Hamilton.

Costa-Giomi, E. (1999) The effects of three years of piano instruction on children's cognitive development. *Journal of Research in Music Education*, **47**, 198–212.

Dunlop, N. (2001) BMW's paradigm shift: the Hydrogen Car. *http:// www.edmunds.com/news/innovations/articles/46906/article.html* 20 July.

Hallam, S. (2000) *The power of music*. Performing Rights Society, London. *http://www.thepowerofmusic.co.uk/*

Hetland, L. (2002) Listening to music enhances spatial-temporal reasoning: evidence for the 'Mozart effect'. *Journal of Aesthetic Education*, **34**(3/4), 105–148.

ISME (2003) Advocacy web pages. International Society for Music Education. *http://www.isme.org/article/archive/25*

Jackins, H. (1963) *The human side of human beings. Seattle:* Rational Island Publishers.

James, P. Y. (1998) Diet-related diseases shift global burden. *Global Health and Environment Monitor*, **6.2**, 1–2. *www.ceche.org/monitor*

Monbiot, G. (2003) *The age of consent*. London: Flamingo.

Nilsson, U., Rawal, N., and Unosson, M. (2003) A comparison of intra-operative or postoperative exposure to music—a controlled trial of the effects on postoperative *Anaesthesia*, **58.7**, 699.

Rauscher, F. (2002) Mozart and the mind: factual and fictional effects of musical enrichment. In J. Aronson (Ed.) *Improving academic achievement: Impact of psychological factors on education.* (pp. 267–278). San Diego: Academic Press.

Ryan, K. J., O'Neill, S. A., Boulton, M.J. and Sloboda, J. A. (2000) Perceived social support and children's participation in music. In: *Proceedings of the Sixth International Conference on Music Perception and Cognition.* Staffordshire: Keele University.

Schellenberg, G. (2004) Music lessons enhance IQ. *Psychological Science*, **15.8**, 511–514.

Solana, J. (2003) *A secure Europe in a better world.* European Council, June 2003. *http://ue.eu.int/pressdata/EN/reports/76255.pdf*

Schmidt, J. (2000) *Disciplined minds: a critical look at salaried professionals and the soul-battering system that shapes their lives.* Lanham, Maryland: Rowman and Littlefield.

Sloboda, J. A. (1998) Music: where cognition and emotion meet. *The Psychologist*, **12.4**, 450–455.

Sloboda, J. A. (2001) So much expended for so little good. In: K. Dreszov, R. Waller and B. Gokay (Eds.) *Kosovo: the politics of delusion.* London: Frank Cass.

Sloboda, J. A. (2002) The 'sound of music' versus the 'essence of music': dilemmas for music-emotion researchers (commentary). *Special issue on Music and Emotion, Musicae Scientiae*, **6.3**, 235–253.

Sloboda, J. A. (2003) The war, what war? Psychology in denial. *DECP Debate.* British Psychological Society, Issue 107, 6–11.

Sloboda, J. A., Gayford. C. and Minnassian, C. (2003) Assisting advanced musicians to enhance their expressivity—an intervention study. In: *Proceedings of the 5th triennial conference of the European Society for the Cognitive Sciences of Music (ESCOM)*. Hannover University of Music and Drama.

APPENDIX: YOUNG PEOPLE AND MUSIC PARTICIPATION PROJECT*

S. A. O'NEILL, M. BOULTON, K. RYAN, AND J. A. SLOBODA

Practitioner and policy implications

1 *Provide structured opportunities for young people which give them increasing choice, control and responsibility for organizing and developing their own musical involvement.* Findings from numerous parts of the study point to the importance young people place on choosing their own musical instruments, music, and musical activities. This is particularly important following the transition to secondary school where many young people feel that compared to primary school, they are given less opportunity to take responsibility for various aspects of musical involvement and decision-making. One can sense the frustration that this might cause as young people reach a point in their development where they seek to establish a greater sense of independence and control over the choices they make. Young people who continue to play instruments following the transition to secondary school are more self-directed and autonomous in the musical activities they are involved in compared to those who give up. They are also more likely to report having a classroom music teacher or instrumental music teacher who communicates a belief in their potential to do well and enables them to choose music they like and want to learn to play.

2 *Provide young people with instruments that they associate with valued role models.* There is a mismatch between the instruments children want to

*Funded by the Economic and Social Research Council, February 2002. See *http://www.keele.ac.uk/ depts/ps/ESRC/Practitionerimp.doc*

learn to play and the instruments they actually play, particularly at school. This mismatch is especially prominent among boys. The majority of children in both Year 6 and Year 7 reported playing the recorder. This certainly affords opportunities since it is a small, light, inexpensive and relatively durable instrument that most children can learn to play and therefore gain experience of active music-making. However, children do not associate playing the recorder with their musical role models in the adult world. As such, they view the recorder as 'not a real instrument' or a 'child's instrument' which is limited in its ability to express the music young people are most interested in playing. Those who are most likely to continue learning to play an instrument report valuing the instrument they play and identifying positively with adult role models who play a similar instrument.

3 *Start learning to play an instrument younger, and at least one year before making the transition to secondary school.* The findings indicate that those children who are more likely to continue playing after making the transition to secondary school had already been playing an instrument for at least a year while they were at primary school. Starting an instrument younger, and having played an instrument for longer, appears to act as a protective factor in terms of continued interest and commitment toward the instrument at secondary school.

4 *Provide opportunities and encourage young people to play in musical groups outside of school hours.* Young people who have more close associates who play instruments in terms of family members and friends, and who engage in group musical activities outside school hours, are more likely to continue playing instruments following the transition to secondary school.

5 *Help to establish within young people positive beliefs and values about musical involvement.* Young people who continue playing instruments following the transition to secondary school have greater confidence in their own ability, and find playing more important and enjoyable than those who give up. They also don't mind a challenge and believe hard work will lead to improvements compared to those who give up.

6 *Provide young people with structured goals and appropriate challenges.* Children who have been involved in performance groups and have taken a music examination are more likely to continue playing instruments after making the transition to secondary school. However, there was no difference between those who continue and those who give up in terms of the highest grade achieved or the mark awarded

on exams. What appears to be important is not so much that children attain the highest levels on music exams, but rather that they gain a sense of having a structured goal to work towards that is viewed as a challenge or opportunity to improve their skills and not just as an opportunity to display their competence. In other words, many teachers involve their students in music examinations, but what appears to be important is that these examinations are not viewed as merely opportunities to display competence (i.e. achieve high grades). Rather, it appears more important for music examinations to be viewed by children as a challenge that will motivate them to learn more and make more progress.

7 *Young people are helped if they believe their parents are supportive of their involvement in musical activities.* The most important differential source of support comes from parents. Children who stay involved in learning to play an instrument believe that their parents are supportive of this activity far more than children who give up. Siblings' and friends' direct support is far less important, although it helps if friends believe in music as an activity for all. The support offered by teachers appears to make less of an impact, although it helps if the child feels that music is valued at the school, that the music teacher and instrumental music teacher are able to communicate a belief in the child's potential to do well at music and teach music the child values and wants to learn to play.

BIBLIOGRAPHY OF JOHN A. SLOBODA 1974–2003

This is not a complete bibliography of the period, but contains all psychology publications that have appeared in normal academic outlets (e.g. peer-reviewed journals and books) as well as a representative sample of items concerning music that have appeared in outlets used by music professionals (e.g. educational and practitioner journals, and some serious general-circulation periodicals, such as the *BBC Music Magazine*). Submitted conference proceedings and abstracts are excluded.

The list is ordered chronologically by date of publication, and, within each year, by alphabetical order of co-author surname, where appropriate. Items are numbered in sequence for convenience of reference.

Items that are reprinted in this collection are indicated by an asterisk. Permissions to reproduce are listed at the beginning of this book (pp. xxvii–xxix).

1 Sloboda, J. A. (1974) The eye-hand span: an approach to the study of sight-reading. *Psychology of Music*, **2**, 4–10.

2 Sloboda, J. A. (1976) The effect of item position on the likelihood of identification by inference in prose and music reading. *Canadian Journal of Psychology*, **30**, 228–238.

3 Sloboda, J. A. (1976) Visual perception of musical notation: registering pitch symbols in memory. *Quarterly Journal of Experimental Psychology*, **28**, 1–16.

4 Sloboda, J. A. (1976) Decision times for word and letter search: a holistic word identification model examined. *Journal of Verbal Learning and Verbal Behaviour*, **15**, 93–101.

5 Sloboda, J. A. (1977) Phrase units as determinants of visual processing in music reading. *British Journal of Psychology*, **68**, 117–124.

6 Sloboda, J. A. (1978) Perception of contour in music reading. *Perception*, **7**, 323–331.

7 Sloboda, J. A. (1978) The locus of the word-priority effect in a target detection task. *Memory and Cognition*, **5**, 371–376.

8*Sloboda, J. A. (1978) The psychology of music reading. *Psychology of Music*, **6**, 3–20.

9*Sloboda, J. A. The uses of space in music notation. (1980) *Visible Language*, **15**, 86–110.

10 Sloboda, J. A. (1980) Visual imagery and individual differences in spelling. In: U. Frith (Ed.) *Cognitive Processes in Spelling*. London: Academic Press.

11 Sloboda, J. A. and Gregory, A. H. (1980) The psychological reality of musical segments. *Canadian Journal of Psychology*, **34**, 274–280.

12 Sloboda, J. A. and Edworthy, J. (1981) Attending to two melodies at once: the effect of key relatedness. *Psychology of Music*, **9**, 39–43.

13 Sloboda, J. A. (1982) Music performance. In: D. Deutsch (Ed.) *Psychology of Music*. New York: Academic Press.

14 Rogers D. R. and Sloboda, J. A. (Eds.) (1983) *Acquisition of Symbolic Skills* (Proceedings of a NATO Human Factors Programme Conference, Keele, July 1982). New York: Plenum Press.

15 Sloboda, J. A. (1983) Neil O'Connor and the MRC Developmental Psychology Unit. *British Journal of Developmental Psychology*, **1**, 405–408.

16 Sloboda, J. A. (1983) The communication of musical metre in piano performance. *Quarterly Journal of Experimental Psychology*, **37A**, 377–396.

17 Sloboda, J. A. (1984) Critical review of J.R. Anderson, *Cognitive Psychology* (1981) *Quarterly Journal of Experimental Psychology*, **33**, 317–322.

18 Sloboda, J. A. (1984) Critical review of Wing and Seashore tests of musical ability. In: H. Goldstein and P. Levy (Eds.) *Tests in Education: a book of critical reviews*. London: Academic Press.

19*Sloboda, J. A. (1984) Experimental studies of music reading: a review. *Music Perception*, **2.2**, 222–236.

20 Sloboda, J. A., Hermelin, B., and O'Connor, N. (1985) An exceptional musical memory. *Music Perception*, **3.2**, 155–170.

21 Sloboda, J. A. (1985) Expressive skill in two pianists: style and effectiveness in music performance. *Canadian Journal of Psychology*, **39**, 273–293.

22 Sloboda, J. A. (1985) Infant Perception. In: A. Branthwaite and D. Rogers (Eds.) *Children Growing Up*. Milton Keynes: Open University Press, pp. 61–81.

23 Sloboda, J. A. (1985) Perception and knowledge. In A. Branthwaite and D. Rogers (Eds) *Children Growing Up*. Milton Keynes: Open University Press.

24 Sloboda, J. A. (1985) *The Musical Mind: the cognitive psychology of music*. Oxford: Oxford University Press (reprinted with a new preface in 1999).

25 Sloboda, J. A. and Parker, D. H. H. (1985) Immediate recall of melodies. In: P. Howell, I. Cross, and R. West (Eds.) *Musical Structure and Cognition*. London: Academic Press.

26 Sloboda, J. A. (1986) Achieving our aims in music education research. *Psychology of Music*, **14.2**, 144–145.

27 Sloboda, J. A. (1986) Acquiring skill. In: A. Gellatly (Ed) *The Skillful Mind*. Milton Keynes: Open University Press.

28*Sloboda, J. A. (1986) Cognitive psychology and real music: the psychology of music comes of age. *Psychologica Belgica,* **26.2**, 199–219.

29 Sloboda, J. A. (1986) Computers and cognition. In: A. Gellatly (Ed) *The Skillful Mind.* Milton Keynes: Open University Press.

30 Sloboda, J. A. (1986) Reading: a case study of cognitive skill. In: A. Gellatly (Ed) *The Skillful Mind.* Milton Keynes: Open University Press.

31 Sloboda, J. A. (1986) What is skill? In A. Gellatly (Ed) *The Skillful Mind.* Milton Keynes: Open University Press.

32 Sloboda J. A. and Rogers D. R. (Eds). (1987) *Cognitive Processes in Mathematics.* (Selected and edited papers from the first International Keele Cognition Seminar, March 1985). Oxford: Oxford University Press.

33 Sloboda, J. A. (Ed.) (1988) *Generative Processes in Music: the psychology of composition, performance, and improvisation.* London: Oxford University Press.

34 Sloboda, J. A. (1988) *L'esprit musicien: la psychologie cognitive de la musique.* Brussels: Pierre Mardaga. (French Language Translation of The Musical Mind).

35 Sloboda, J. A. (1988) *La mente musicale: psicologia cognitivista della musica.* Bologna: Il Mulino, 1988. (Italian translation of *The Musical Mind*).

36 Sloboda, J. A. (1988) Musique et memoire: le point de vue du psychologie. (Music and memory: the psychologist's view). *Inharmoniques,* **4**, 106–119.

37 Gellatly, A., Rogers, D. R., and Sloboda, J. A. (Eds) (1989) *Cognition and Social Worlds.* (selected and edited papers from the second International Keele Cognition Seminar, March 1987). London: Oxford University Press.

38*Sloboda, J. A. (1989) Music as a language. In: F. Wilson and F. Roehmann (Eds.) *Music and Child Development: Proceedings of the 1987 Biology of Music Making Conference.* St. Louis, Missouri: MMB.

39 Sloboda, J. A. (1989) Music as a skill. In: S. Nielzen and O. Olsson (Eds.). *Structure and Perception of Electroacoustic Sound and Music.* Amsterdam: Elsevier.

40 Sloboda, J. A. (1989) Music, composers and scientists: a relationship of equals. In: S. Nielzen and O. Olsson(Eds.) *Structure and Perception of Electroacoustic Sound and Music.* Amsterdam: Elsevier.

41*Sloboda, J. A. (1989) Music psychology and the composer. In: S. Nielzen and O. Olsson (Eds.) *Structure and Perception of Electroacoustic Sound and Music.* Amsterdam: Elsevier.

42 Sloboda, J. A. (1989) What do psychologists have to say about nuclear war? In. J. Hartley and A. Branthwaite (Eds.) *The Applied Psychologist.* Milton Keynes: Open University Press.

43 Sloboda, J. A. (1990) Combating examination stress among university students: an institutional survey. *British Journal of Guidance and Counselling,* **18**, 124–136.

44 Sloboda, J. A. (1990) Musical excellence: how does it develop? In M. J. A. Howe (Ed.) *Encouraging the Development of Exceptional Abilities and Talents.* London: Wiley.

45 Sloboda, J. A. (1990) Ongakuteki na Yushusa wa Dono Yoni Hattatsu Suruka? (How does musical excellence develop?) Translated by Fumiko Fujita. *Journal of Research in Music Education (Japan)*, **64**, 163–168.

46 Sloboda, J. A. (1990) Que puede ensenar la psicologia de la musica an los musicos? *Musica Y Educacion (Spain)*, **3.2**, 335–355. (translated by Ubaldo Perez).

47 Sloboda, J. A. and Howe, M. J. A. (1990) Reasons for choosing specialist music schooling: an interview study. *Journal of the Music Masters and Mistresses Association*, No 25, November, 17–20.

48 Howe, M. J. A. and Sloboda, J. A. (1991) Early signs of talents and special interests in the lives of young musicians. *European Journal of High Ability*, **2**, 102–111.

49 Howe, M. J. A. and Sloboda, J. A. (1991) Helping children to become highly competent adults: what can parents do? In: J. Radford (Ed), *Talent, Teaching and Achievement*. London: Jessica Kingsley.

50 Howe, M. J. A. and Sloboda, J. A. (1991) Young musicians' accounts of significant influences in their early lives: 1. The family and the musical background. *British Journal of Music Education*, **8**, 39–52.

51 Howe, M. J. A. and Sloboda, J. A. (1991) Young musicians' accounts of significant influences in their early lives: 2. Teachers, practising and performance. *British Journal of Music Education*, **8**, 53–63.

52*Sloboda, J. A. (1991) Empirical studies of emotional response to music. In: M. Riess-Jones (Ed) *Cognitive Bases of Musical Communication*. Washington, DC: American Psychological Association, pp. 33–46.

53 Sloboda, J. A. (1991) Music structure and emotional response: some empirical findings. *Psychology of Music*, **19**, 110–120.

54*Sloboda, J. A. Musical Expertise. (1991) In K. A. Ericsson and J. Smith (Eds) *The Study of Expertise: prospects and limits*. Cambridge: Cambridge University Press.

55 Sloboda, J. A. and Howe, M. J. A. (1991) Biographical precursors of musical excellence: an interview study. *Psychology of Music*, **19**, 3–21.

56 Howe, M. J. A. and Sloboda, J. A. (1992) Problems experienced by talented young musicians as a result of the failure of other children to value musical accomplishments. *Gifted Education*, **8.1**, 16–18.

57 Sloboda, J. A. (1992) Etudes empiriques de la reponse emotionnelle a la musique. *Analyse Musicale*, **26**, 14–21.

58*Sloboda, J. A. (1992) Psychological structures in music: core research 1980–1990. In: Paynter, R. Orton, T. Seymour, and T. Howell (Eds.) *A Compendium of Contemporary Musical Thought*. London: Routledge, pp. 803–839.

59 Sloboda, J. A. and Hopkins, J. (1992) Promoting mental health in the workplace: the Staff Care concept. In: D. R. Trent (Ed) *Promotion of Mental Health*, Vol. I. Aldershot: Avebury, pp. 297–304.

60 Sloboda, J. A. and Howe, M. J. A. (1992) Transitions in the early musical careers of able young musicians: choosing instruments and teachers. *Journal of Research in Music Education*, **40**, 283–294.

61 Sloboda, J. A. (1993) Begabung und Hochbegabung. In: H. Bruhn, R. Oerter and H. Rosing (eds) *Musikpsychologie: ein Handbuch*. Reinbek: Rowholt, pp. 565–578.

62*Sloboda, J. A. (1993) Musical ability. In: K. Ackrill and G. Bock (Eds). *The Origins and Development of High Ability* (Ciba Symposium 178). Chichester: Wiley, pp. 106–118.

63 Sloboda, J. A. (1993) Weighing of the talents. *Nature*, **362**, 115–116.

64 Sloboda, J. A., Hopkins, J. S., Turner, A., Rogers, D.R., and McLeod, J. (1993) An evaluated staff counselling programme in a public sector organisation. *Employee Counselling Today*, **5.5**, 4–12.

65 Aiello, R. with Sloboda, J. A. (1994) *Musical Perceptions*. New York: Oxford University Press.

66 Brodsky, W., Sloboda, J. A., and Waterman, M. (1994) An exploratory investigation into auditory style as a correlate and predictor of music performance anxiety. *Medical Problems of Performing Artists*, **9.4**, 101–112.

67*Sloboda, J. A. (1994) Book review of *Language, Music, and Mind* by Diana Raffman. *Mind and Language*, **9.3**, 377–385.

68 Sloboda, J. A. (1994) Book review of *Music and the Mind*, by Anthony Storr. *Music and Letters*, **75**, 122–124.

69 Sloboda, J. A., Davidson, J., and Howe, M. J. A. (1994) Is everyone musical? *The Psychologist*, **7.7**, 349–354.

70 Sloboda, J. A. (1994) Music performance: expression and the development of excellence. In: R. Aiello with J. Sloboda (eds) *Musical Perceptions*. New York: Oxford University Press, pp. 152–172.

71 Sloboda, J. A., Davidson, J., and Howe, M. J. A. (1994) Musicians: experts not geniuses. *The Psychologist*, **7.7**, 363–365.

72 Sloboda, J. A. (1994) What makes a musician? *European String Teachers Association Review*, **2**, 31–34.

73 Deliège, I. and Sloboda, J. A. (Eds) (1995) *Naissance et developpement du sens musical*. Paris: Presses Universitaires de France.

74 Deliège, I., and Sloboda, J. A. (Eds.) (1995) *The Origins and Development of Musical Competence*. London: Oxford University Press/Paris: Presses Universitaires de France.

75 Howe, M. J. A., Davidson, J. W., Moore, D. G., and Sloboda, J. A. (1995) Are there early childhood signs of musical ability? *Psychology of Music*, **23**, 162–176.

76 Rogers, D. R., McLeod, J, and Sloboda, J. A. (1995) Counsellor and client perceptions of the effectiveness of time-limited counselling in an occupational scheme. *Counselling Psychology Quarterly*, **8.3**, 221–231.

77 Sloboda, J. A. (1995) Are we all musicians? Evidence from the biographies of young instrumentalists. *The Physiological Society Magazine,* **19**, 32–33.

78 Sloboda, J. A. (1995) Psychology of music today: the need for applicable psychology. In: M. Manturszewska, K. Miklaszewski, and A. Bialkowski (eds.) *Psychology of Music Today.* Warsaw: Frederick Chopin Academy of Music, pp. 19–24.

79 Sloboda, J. A. (1995) Talent, motivatie, oefening en succces (Talent, achievement, motivation and success). In: F. Evers, M. Jansma, P. Mak and B. Devries (Eds.) *Musiekpsychology [Psychology of Music].* Assen: Van Gorcum, pp. 27–40.

80 Sloboda, J. A. and Davidson, J. W. (1995) L'interprete en herbe. In: I. Deliège and J. A. Sloboda (eds.), *Naissance et developpement du sens musical.* Paris: Presses Universitaires de France, pp. 199–222.

81 Sloboda, J. A. and Davidson, J. W. (1995) The young performing musician. In: I. Deliège and J. A. Sloboda (Eds.) *The Origins and Development of Musical Competence.* London: Oxford University Press/Paris: Presses Universitaires de France.

82 Sloboda, J. A., and Howe, M. J. A. (1995) Biographical precursors of musical excellence: an interview study. In: M. Manturszewska, K. Miklaszewski, and A. Bialkowski (eds.) *Psychology of Music Today.* Warsaw: Frederick Chopin Academy of Music. pp. 338–357.

83 Davidson, J. W., Howe, M. J. A., Moore, D. G., and Sloboda, J. A. (1996) The role of parental influences in the development of musical ability. *British Journal of Developmental Psychology,* **14**, 399–412.

84 Howe, M. J. A. and Sloboda, J. A. (1996) Early signs of talents and special interests in the lives of young musicians. In: A. J. Cropley and D. Dehn (Eds.) *Fostering the Growth of High Ability: European perspectives.* Norwood, NJ: Ablex Publishing Corporation, pp. 233–246.

85*Sloboda, J. A. (1996) Emotional responses to music: a review. Invited keynote paper. In: K. Riederer and T. Lahti (Eds.). *Proceedings of the Nordic Acoustical Meeting (NAM96).* Helsinki: The Acoustical Society of Finland, pp. 385–392.

86*Sloboda, J. A. (1996) The acquisition of musical performance expertise: deconstructing the 'talent' account of individual differences in musical expressivity. In: K. A. Ericsson (Ed.) *The Road to Excellence: the acquisition of expert performance in the arts and sciences, sport and games.* Mahwal, NJ: Lawrence Erlbaum Associates, pp. 107–126.

87 Sloboda, J. A., Davidson, J. W., Howe, M. J. A., and Moore, D. G. (1996) The role of practice in the development of expert musical performance. *British Journal of Psychology.* **87**, 287–309.

88 Brodsky, W. and Sloboda, J. A. (1997) Clinical trial of a music generated vibrotactile therapeutic environment for musicians: main effects and

outcome differences between therapy subgroups. *Journal of Music Therapy*, **24**, 2–33.

89 Clarke, E. F., Parncutt, R., Raekallio, M., and Sloboda, J. A. (1997) Talking fingers: an interview study of pianists' views on fingering. *Musicae Scientiae*, **1.1**, 87–108.

90 Davidson, J. W., Howe, M. J. A., and Sloboda, J. A. (1997) Environmental factors in the development of musical performance over the lifespan. In: Hargreaves, D. J. and North, A. C. (Eds.) *The Social Psychology of Music*. Oxford: Oxford University Press, pp. 188–206.

91 Deliège, I. and Sloboda, J. A. (Eds.) (1997) *Perception and Cognition of Music*. Hove: Psychology Press.

92 O'Neill, S. A. and Sloboda, J. A. (1997) The effects of failure on children's ability to perform a musical test. *Psychology of Music*, **35.1**, 18–34.

93 Parncutt, R.P., Desain, P., Clarke, E. F., Raekallio, M., and Sloboda, J. A. (1997) An ergonomic model of keyboard fingering for melodic fragments. *Music Perception*, **14.4**, 341–382.

94 Sloboda, J. A. and Newstead, S. E. (1997) Guidelines for PhD examiners: an evaluation of impact. *The Psychologist*, **10.9**, 407–410.

95 Davidson, J. W., Sloboda, J. A., Moore, D. G., and Howe, M. J. A. (1998) Characteristics of music teachers and the progress of young instrumentalists. *Journal of Research in Music Education*, **46.1**, 141–160.

96 Howe, M. J. A., Davidson, J. W., and Sloboda, J. A. (1998) Innate talent: reality or myth? *Behavioural and Brain Sciences*, **21.3**, 399–442.

97 Sloboda, J. A. (1998) Brain waves to the heart. *BBC Music Magazine*, November, pp. 31–33.

98*Sloboda, J. A. (1998) Does music mean anything? *Musicae Scientiae*, **2.1**, 21–32.

99 Sloboda, J. A. (1998) Peer counselling as a resource in the teaching of psychology. In: Radford, J., Van Laar, D., and Rose, D. (Eds.) *Innovations in Teaching Psychology*. Edgbaston: SEDA, pp. 110–120.

100 Sloboda, J. A., Clarke, E. F., Parncutt, R., and Raekallio, M. (1998) Determinants of finger choice in piano sight-reading. *Journal of Experimental Psychology: Human Perception and Performance*, **24.1**, 185–203.

101 Parncutt, R., Sloboda, J. A., and Clarke, E. F. (1999) Interdependence of right and left hands in sight-read, written, and rehearsed fingerings of parallel melodic piano music. *Australian Journal of Psychology*, Special Issue on 'Music as a Brain and Behavioural System', **51**(3), 204–210.

102 Sloboda, J. A. (1999) *Cognition, Emotion, and Performance: three lectures on the psychology of music*. Warsaw: Chopin Academy of Music.

103*Sloboda, J. A. (1999) Everyday uses of music: a preliminary study. In: S. W. Yi (Ed.) *Music, Mind, and Science*. Seoul: Seoul National University Press, pp. 354–369.

104 Sloboda, J.A. (1999) (contributions to) Music and the mind. In: M. Oliver (Ed.) *Settling the Score: a journey through the music of the 20th century.* London: Faber and Faber, pp. 211–235.

105*Sloboda, J. A. (1999) Music performance and emotion: issues and developments. In: S. W. Yi (Ed.) *Music, Mind, and Science.* Seoul: Seoul National University Press, pp. 220–238.

106*Sloboda, J.A. (1999) Music: where cognition and emotion meet. *The Psychologist,* **12.4**, 450–455.

107 Sloboda, J. A. (1999) Preface to the 1999 reprinting of *The Musical Mind: the cognitive psychology of music.* Oxford: Oxford University Press, pp. ix–xx.

108 Sloboda, J. A. and Howe, M. J. A. (1999) Musical talent and individual differences: a reply to Gagne. *Psychology of Music,* **27.1**, 52–54.

109 Sloboda, J. A. (2000) Individual differences in music performance. *Trends in Cognitive Science,* **4.10**, 397–403.

110*Sloboda, J. A. (2000) Music and worship: a psychologist's perspective. In: T. Hone, M. Savage, and J. Astley (Eds.) *Creative Chords: studies in music, theology and Christian formation.* Leominster: Gracewing, pp. 110–125.

111 Sloboda, J. A. (2000) Why are musical enjoyment and musical achievement at such different levels in contemporary society? In W. Jankowski (Ed.) *Czlowiek – Muzyka – Psychologia: ksiazka dedykowana Professor Marii Manturzewskiej [Education – Music – Psychology: in honour of Professor Maria Manturszewska].* Warsaw: Frederik Chopin Academy of Music.

112 Juslin, P. N. and Sloboda, J. A. (Eds.) (2001) *Music and Emotion: theory and research.* Oxford: Oxford University Press, pp. 487.

113*Sloboda, J. A. (2001) Emotion, functionality, and the everyday experience of music: where does music education fit? *Music Education Research,* **3**(2), 243–253.

114 Sloboda, J. A. (2001) Entries on 'Affect', 'Memory'. In: S. Sadie (Ed.) *The New Grove Dictionary of Music and Musicians.* London: Macmillan.

115 Sloboda, J. A. and Juslin, P. N. (2001) Psychological perspectives on music and emotion. In: Juslin, P. N, and Sloboda, J. A. (Eds.) *Music and Emotion: theory and research.* Oxford: Oxford University Press, pp. 71–104.

116 Sloboda, J. A. and Lehmann, A.C. (2001) Performance correlates of perceived emotionality in different interpretations of a Chopin piano prelude. *Music Perception,* **19.1**, 87–120.

117 Sloboda, J. A. and O'Neill, S. A. (2001) Emotions in everyday listening to music. In: Juslin, P. N. and Sloboda, J. A. (Eds.) *Music and Emotion: theory and research.* Oxford: Oxford University Press, pp. 415–430.

118 Sloboda, J. A., O'Neill, S. A., and Ivaldi, A. (2001) Functions of music in everyday life: an exploratory study using the Experience Sampling Methodology. *Musicae Scientiae,* **5**(1), 9–32.

119*Sloboda, J. A. (2002) Dotu musicali e innatismo. In: J. J. Nattiez (Ed.) *Enciclopedia della Musica: Vol II Il sapere musicale*. Torina: Giulio Einaudi Editore, pp. 509–529.

120*Sloboda, J. A. (2002) The 'sound of music' versus the 'essence of music': dilemmas for music-emotion researchers (commentary). Special issue on Music and Emotion. *Musicae Scientiae*, **6.3**, 235–253.

INDEX

11 September 2001 attacks 380, 411
ability see musical ability
academic norms 413
acquisition
  of musical ability 266-7, 303-4
  of skill 246-8
aesthetic attraction to music 382-3
affordances 195, 347
age, individual differences 324-5
algorithms for key identification 134-5
ambiguity 8
applicability of research 413-14
  see also benefits of music
appogiaturas 210, 221, 260, 356-7
appropriation theories 320
architecture, music as 194-5
Armstrong, Louis 251-5
art, attitude towards 341
associationistic function *see* memory
asynchrony 98
'audiation' 302
autistic subject (NP) 108-11, 166,
    249-51, 254
autobiographical memory study
    181-8, 257-8

background, music as unattended 348
bar lines 57-60
beaming notes 21-2
behaviourism 378
beliefs, teacher's 300-1
benefits of music
  aims of research 396-7
  and the 'business model' 399
  commissioned policy-relevant research
    402-4
  demonstrating benefits vs. producing
    benefits 397-8
  documenting vs. advocacy 398-402
  IQ measures 397-8
  justifying research 406
  'Mozart effect' 379-80, 396-7
  musical interventions 397

boys, gender stereotyping of 271,
    288, 310
business model 398-9
busking 328

categorization of sounds 177-8
change
  mood-altering effect of music 335, 384
  music as agent of 204
  see also cognitive re-appraisal
children
  autobiographical memory study
    181-8, 257-8
  development of emotional response to
    music 205-6
  development of skill by 247-8, 256-9
  development to able adult 311-12
  dropping instrumental tuition
    362-5, 402
  expressive performance by 291-2
  importance of non-threatening
    environment for 258-9, 308-11
  individual differences in ability 277-9,
    297-301, 303
  infant musicality 277, 291, 298-9,
    387-8
  relationships with significant adults
    269-71, 363-4, 388
  sibling differences 299
  see also music education
chord relationships 125-7
church *see* worship
clef signs 51
closure, tonal 144
cognitive re-appraisal 199-201
commercialization of music 379-80,
    391-2
commissioned policy-relevant research
    402-4
commodification of music 379-80,
    391-2
commonalities of response 384, 386-7
competitions, music 186, 341

composers
  as architects 194-5
  credibility of music psychology to 191-2
  dialogue with psychologists 192-4
  intentions of 231-2
computer music 168
conflict, over choice of music 366
connectionist models 127, 248, 266, 267, 304
consonance, overtone 122-4
contemplative response to music 357
continuous response methodology 386
contour
  melodic contour analysis 78-81
  visual 18
control
  and mood change 335, 384
  and music listening 328-9
cross-cultural research
  individual differences 217
  non-Western music 304
  pitch relationships 124
cue-impoverishment of music 226-7
cultural democratization 378-80
cultural position of music 390-1
cultural trends 369-72

'Darling, They're Playing Our Tune' theory 348
democratization, cultural 378-80
demonstration, teaching as 160
Deutsch, Diana 117
discrete sampling 387

ecological validity 101-2, 129, 131, 377
education *see* music education
electronic communication 370
elitism 341-2, 377-9, 385
emotion
  aesthetic attraction to music 382-3
  between-person variation 217
  children's development 205-6
  cognitive content of 204-8
  commonalities of response 384, 386-7
  cue-impoverishment of music 226-7
  definitional problems 216-17
  dynamic intensity of 225
  episodic associations 336-7
  expectancy violations 211-12, 229-31, 232-3, 337
  experimental control problems 231
  expertise and 254-6
  external factors 208-9, 228

feelings vs. judgment 227-8
  forced verbal response 206-8
  free verbal response 204-6, 386
  function of music and 199-201
  heart reactions 212, 221, 260
  iconic associations 337
  intensification of 204-5
  intensity over content 226-7
  intrinsic musical factors 209-13, 228
  link to musical events 220-2
  and meaning (Raffman's view) 158
  measuring 218-19
  'peak experiences' 258, 309, 384-5
  performance-response relationship 236-9
  performer's 216, 225-6
  performer's intentions and 238-9
  performer's interpretation and 233-4
  physical manifestations of 168-70
  release of 204
  self-ascription of positive 228
  'shivers' response 210-12, 221, 260
  and structures 259-60
  'tears' response 210, 221, 260, 356-7
  violation of expectations 211-12, 229-31, 232-3, 337
  virtuosity as source of 234-6
  within-person variation 218
  see also autobiographical memory study; mood
enjoyment, importance of in learning 258-9, 308-11, 341-2, 363
ensemble playing, reading ability and 20
episodic associations 336-7
examinations, music 280-1, 341, 373
expectation
  misreading and 14-15, 37-8
  of teacher 300-1
  violation of 211-12, 229-31, 232-3, 337
expertise
  acquisition in noninstructional settings 248-55
  acquisition of skill 246-8, 258-9
  children's development of 247-8, 256-9
  definition of 243-6
  and emotion 254-6
  jazz musicians 251-5
  practice patterns and 269, 270, 279-83, 306-7, 339, 365
  prodigies 249-51
  savants 108, 249-51
  tacit 248
  see also musical ability
expressive performance
  by children 291-2
  devices used 284-5, 388-90
  'Feeling Sound' training 403-4
  generative 290-2
  imitative 286-90

individual differences in 217
individuality of 233-4
intuitive 267-8, 305
slowing 142-3
technical skills and 268-71, 283-6
understanding and 305-6
unreliability of achieving 403
when sight-reading 38-40
see also emotion
extreme performances 234
extrinsic motivation 270-1, 307-11
'eye-hand' span (EHS) 35-7

failure, resistance to 300, 339
family environment 270, 340-1, 363
feeling ineffability 157-9, 352-3
feelings
    dynamism of 166-8, 225
    vs. judgment 227-8
    see also emotion
feminism 370
'fixation' by poor readers 6-11
'flashbulb memory 348-9
folk tunes *see* melody recall research
Frith, Simon 379
functions of music 197-9

gender
    individual differences 324-5, 328
    stereotypes 271, 288, 310
generative expression 290-2
generative theory of tonal music
    (GTTM) 139-43
Generative Theory of Tonal Music
    (Lerdahl and Jackendoff) 102-4
genetics 276-9, 297-8
giftedness *see* talent
Goldovsky experiment 13-14, 37-8
'good ear', a 176
grammar *see* language; structures
grouping hierarchies 136-9
    see also generative theory of tonal
        music
GTTM (generative theory of tonal music)
    139-43

heart reactions 212, 221, 260
'helpless orientation' 300
heritability of musical ability 276-9,
    297-8

hierarchical representation 111, 135-46,
    164-5
hierarchical tree theory 89-90
'hobby', instrument playing as 365

iconic associations 337
idiots savants 108, 249-51
imitative expression 286-90
improvisation 291-2
individual differences
    age 324-5
    in children's ability 277-9, 297-301, 303
    in contemplative response 357
    cross-cultural 217
    in expressive performance 288-90
    gender 324-5, 328
    siblings 299
individuality, expression of 233-4
ineffability of music 153-4, 156-61, 351-5
infant musicality 277, 291, 298-9, 387-8
inheritance of musical ability 276-9,
    297-8
intentions
    composer's 231-2
    performer's 238-9
    'reading' into music 388, 390
interventions, musical 397
intrinsic
    motivation 270, 307
    musical factors 209-13, 228
intuitive performance 267-8, 305
IQ measures 397-8

jazz musicians 251-5
judgment, versus feelings 227-8

key, establishing 129-35
key-distance effect 126-7
Klavarscribo system 46-7, 67
Kosovo crisis 410
Krumhansl, Carol (work of) 121-9

language, music as a
    autobiographical memory study 181-8,
        257-8
    cultural 'grammar' of music 302
    phonology 177-8

language, music as a *(Continued)*
  semantics 179-81
  syntax 178-9
Language, Music and Mind (Raffman)
  (book review) 153-62, 351
learning
  of pitch relationships 124-5
  see also music education
ledger lines 51-2
Leverhulme Project 277-9, 280, 282
listening
  age differences 324-5, 326
  control and 328-9
  gender differences 324-5, 326, 328
  listener as active agent 319-20
  Mass-Observation project 322-9
  personal uses of music 324-6
  'pharmaceutical' approach to 319,
    346, 384
  pilot studies into 321-2
  in public places 326-9
  uses of music 324-9
literacy, musical 10-11
Longuet-Higgins, seminal work of 99

Mass-Observation project 322-9
'mastery orientation' 300
meaning of music
  emotion and (Raffman's view) 158
  emotive properties mistaken for
    content 158-9
  and music education 368-9
  see also language
'melodic process' 144
melody recall research
  breath analysis 83-4, 106-7
  data analysis 74, 105-6
  harmonic analysis 85-7, 106
  hierarchical tree theory 89-90
  intersong contamination 76
  melodic contour analysis 78-81
  method 76-8, 104-5
  metrical analysis 81-2, 106
  musicians vs. nonmusicians 87-8
  phrase structure analysis 84-5, 106-7
  recall vs. recognition 74-6
  rhythmic analysis 83
  transcription problems 71-4
  untrained subjects in 75
memory
  autobiographical memory study 181-8,
    257-8
  for carols 186
  exceptional recall ability (NP) 107-11,
    166, 249-51, 254
  expressive performance and 287-90

'flashbulb' 348-9
  for hymns 186
  mnemonic functions of music 197-8,
    217, 348-9
  nature of musical 18-19
  negative musical 184-5, 186, 271,
    308-11
  for nursery rhymes 186
  reading span 16-18, 29
  see also melody recall research
men's listening 324-5
'mentor' 311-12
methodology
  agreed methods in psychology of music
    99-100
  continuous response 386
  discrete sampling 387
  forced verbal response 206-8
  free verbal response 204-6, 386
metre
  recall of 81-2
  sight-reading of 38-40
metrical structure (in GTTM) 140
misreading 14-15, 37-8
modular processing 218
monitoring own performance 15-16
mood
  -altering effects of music 334-8
  see also emotion
motivation
  autistic player's (NP) 253-4
  extrinsic 270-1, 307-11
  and 'helpless orientation' 300
  intrinsic 270, 307
  Louis Armstrong's 253-4
  and 'mastery orientation' 300
  resistance to failure 300, 339
'Mozart effect' 379-80, 396-7
multiculturism 369
musical ability
  acquisition of 266-7, 303-4
  definition 265-6
  individual differences in children's
    277-9, 297-301, 303
  inheritance of 276-9, 297-8
  nature of 301-3
  teacher's belief about student's 300-1
  'technical' 304-6
  see also expertise
musical subcultures 367-8
music education
  accreditation of achievement 280-1,
    341, 373
  cultural trends and 369-72
  cutbacks in 397
  dropping instrumental tuition 362-5, 402
  funding for 372
  and meaning of music 368-9
  parental support and 270, 340-1, 363

practitioner and policy implications
417-19
providers of 372
purpose of 368-9
sociocultural environment and 365-7
'teacher education' 373
transition from primary to secondary
362, 365
variety as key concept in 372-3
see also music teachers
music notation
bar lines 57-60
clef signs 51
clustering in 64, 66-7
improving 21-3
information conveyed by 5-6
Klavarscribo system 46-7, 67
layout compared with text 43-4
ledger lines 51-2
legibility of 65-6
level of detail in 46-8
need for 67
orthochronic *see* orthochronic
notational system
psychological effectiveness of 65-8
size of 52-3
specificity of information 61-2
symbolic structure of 63-5
tablatures 45-6
time notation 54-61
time signatures 57
transcriptions and 72-4
type of information 62
vertical alignment of notes 57-60
see also orthochronic notational system
Music Perception journal 117-19
music reading
cognitive load of 7
compared to prose reading 3-4
conscious awareness during 11
copying paradigm 31-4
early studies of 29-31
and ensemble playing 20
experimental research into 5
eye movement studies 29-30
'fixation' by poor readers 6-11
goals of 27-8
improving learning of 19-20
'interference problem' 32-3
lack of insight 11-12
and musical memory 5
musical text and 21-3
musicians vs. nonmusicians 31-4
neglected area of study 3-5
silent reading 28-9
span 16-18, 29
visual task hypothesis 28-9
see also sight-reading
music teachers

beliefs about student's ability 300-1
expectations from psychology of music
246, 247
knowledge of musical subcultures
367-8
not blamed for 'failure' of music
education 372
training of 373
see also music education; teaching

National Curriculum for music 341, 371
negative musical memories 184-5, 186,
271, 308-11
neumes 48-50
niche cultures 371
nonmusicians
implicit knowledge of 247
melody recall by 87-8
and music reading 31-4
notation *see* music notation; orthochronic
notational system
notational systems, new 22-3
nuance ineffability 159-61, 353-4
nursery rhymes 186

orchestral parts, set quality 22
orthochronic notational system
2-D function of 63
abstract nature of 44-5
clustering in 64, 66-7
multiple staves 53-4
spacing of 66
specificity of 62
staff in 48-54
time notation 54-61
universality of 67
overtone consonance 122-4

page-turning 11
paradigmatic status *see* 'psychology of
music'
'peak experiences' 258, 309, 384-5
performance
technical ability 304-6
see also expressive performance
performers
children 186
emotion of 216, 225-6
expression of individuality of 233-4
extreme performances by 234

performers *(Continued)*
  faithful to composer's intentions 231-2
  virtuosity 234-6
personal associations 197-8, 217, 348-9
personal relationships, music as vehicle
    for 358
personal uses of music 324-6, 366
  see also benefits of music
'pharmaceutical' approach to listening
    319, 346, 384
phonology 177-8
physiological responses 100, 384
pitch
  predominance of 121
  rare intervals 130
  relationships 122-5
plainchant melodies 49
policy-relevant research 402-4
political issues 407-15
polyphonic music 53
pop music 357, 367
postmodernism 371-2
practice 269, 270, 279-83, 306-7, 339, 365
prodigies 249-51
prolongational reduction (in GTTM) 140
'proof-readers' error' 12-13, 37-8
psychology of music
  agreed methods 99-100
  agreed problem 97-9
  agreed theoretical frameworks 100
  appropriate research 101-2
  author's current position and 412
  comes of age 102-4
  composers and 191-2
  and 'democratization of taste' 378
  empirical measurement and 119-21
  engagement with policy-makers 402-3
  and musical experience 97-9
  personal and political in 407-15
  questions asked by 195-7
  'reduction' of music in 376
  reification of the variable 376-7
  researcher's personal values 395-6,
      414-15
  and uniqueness of music 101
  'value' of 395-6, 406-7
  Western tonal music dominates 121
public places, music in 326-9

reading *see* music reading; sight-reading
re-appraisal *see* cognitive re-appraisal
recall *see* melody recall research;
    memory
reductional hierarchies 135-6, 137-9
Re-Evaluation Counselling 409
reification of the variable 376-7

relationships
  children's with significant adults
      269-71, 363-4, 388
  chords 125-7
  with 'mentor' 311-12
  performance-responses 236-9
  personal 358
  pitch 122-5
religion *see* secularism; worship
representation
  hierarchical 111, 135-46, 164-5
  nature of musical 164-6, 350-1
  Raffman's levels of 154-6
research
  academic norms 413
  applicability of 413-14
  evaluation criteria 395-6
  'Feeling Sound' training 403-4
  focus on values 414-15
  Krumhansl's 121-9
  limitations of 127-9
  personal values of researcher 395-6,
      414-15
  sensitivity to applicability 413
  social engagement levels 412-15
  see also benefits of music; melody recall
      research
resistance
  to emotional effects of music 357
  to failure 300, 339
rhythm, recall of 83
rhythmic notation 54-61
rise times 98

savants 108, 249-51
school
  cutbacks in provision in 397
  negative musical memories of 184-5,
      186, 271, 308-11
  see also music education; music
      teachers; teaching
scientific analysis of music
  aversion to 175
  benefit to musicians 175-6
  and dominant cultural values 391
  see also psychology of music
score *see* music notation
secularism 371
self-administered therapy, music as
    216
semantics 179-81
'shivers' response 210-12, 221, 260
sibling differences 299
sight-reading
  expressive variation in 38-40
  'eye-hand' span (EHS) 35-7

good readers compared to poor
   readers 35-7
master readers compared to good
   readers 38-40
metrical reading 38-40
misreading 12-16, 37-8
notational convention and 67-8
see also music reading
sight-singing 20
skill *see* expertise
slowing, expressive 142-3
social factors
   the academy 342
   cultural trends 369-72
   elitism 341-2, 377-9, 385
   family environment 270, 340-1, 363
   knowledge about cultural position of
      music 390-1
   music education and 365-7
   purpose of music in society 341
   reduction in social opportunities for
      music 340-1, 405
   social engagement in research 412-15
   see also benefits of music
span
   'eye-hand' (EHS) 35-7
   reading 16-18, 29
staff-lines 48-54
stereotypes, gender 271, 288, 310
structural ineffability 156-7, 352
structures
   conventional 232
   dialectical 232-3
   and emotion 259-60
   hierarchical representation 111,
      135-46, 164-5
   internal musical characteristics and
      emotion 220-1, 356
   naturally detected 333
   see also representation
subcultures, musical 367-8
synchrony 98
syntax 178-9

tablatures 45-6
talent 275-6, 286, 297-301
teachers *see* music teachers
teaching
   demonstration as 160
   see also children; music education;
      music teachers; school

'tears' response 210, 221, 260, 356-7
technical skills
   and expressive performance 268-71,
      283-6
   and performance ability 304-6
   see also practice
'thrills' response 210-12, 221, 260,
   356-7
time signatures 57
time-span structure (in GTTM) 140
tonal centre, establishing 129-35
tonal closure 144
tone-deafness 289
top-down processing 13-14

uniqueness of music 101

violations of expectancy 211-12, 229-31,
   232-3, 337
virtuosity 234-6
visual contour 18

Western tonal music dominance 121
women's listening 324-5
worship
   associations and 349
   communality of 358
   contemplative response to music 357
   music's ineffability and 352, 353, 354-5
   music as a source of personal
      associations 348-9
   music as unattended background 348
   psychology of music and 345-6

Young People's Participation in Music
   project 402
youth culture 370

Zimmerman, Krystian 234-5